P9-AGQ-833

The Free-Market Innovation Machine

The Free-Market Innovation Machine

Analyzing the Growth Miracle of Capitalism

WILLIAM J. BAUMOL

PRINCETON UNIVERSITY PRESS
Princeton and Oxford

Published by Princeton University Press, 41 William Street, Princeton, New Jersey 08540

In the United Kingdom: Princeton University Press, 3 Market Place, Woodstock, Oxfordshire OX20 1SY

LIBRARY OF CONGRESS CATALOGING-IN-PUBLICATION DATA

Baumol, William J.
The free-market innovation machine : analyzing the growth miracle of capitalism / William J. Baumol.
p. cm.
Includes bibliographical references (p.) and index.
ISBN 0-691-09615-5
1. Capitalism. 2. Economic development. 3. Technological innovations—Economic aspects. I. Title.
HB501 .B38 2002
330.12'2—dc21 2001056044
CIP

British Library Cataloging-in-Publication Data are available

This book has been composed in Stone Serif by Princeton Editorial Associates, Inc., Scottsdale, Arizona

Printed on acid-free paper.

www.pup.princeton.edu

Printed in the United States of America

10 9 8 7 6 5 4 3 2 1

CONTENTS

PREFACE

If the past century of economic policymaking has taught us anything, it is that achieving strong long-term growth often has less to do with macroeconomic policies than with good microeconomics, including fostering competitive markets that reward innovation and restricting government to only a limited role.

—*The Economist* magazine,
7 October 2000, p. 21

The unifying framework is the characteristic of knowledge as a semi-public good, with non easily enforceable property rights. Its diffusion, in principle, is good for social well being, but bad for private returns: No one wants to invest in the creation of new knowledge, if the rents generated are not, at least partly, appropriable. Institutions that govern the creation and the diffusion of knowledge have invariably been molded by this tradeoff.

—Navaretti, Dasgupta, Mäler,
and Siniscalco, 1998, p. 1

Much like the professor who never changed the questions on his examinations—only the answers—some of the content of this book is a repetition of material in an earlier volume,[1] but the focus is quite different. In that book, which was also related to growth issues, I was concerned primarily with the entrepreneur, and the apparently mysterious propensity of the supply of that factor of production suddenly to dry up, braking the economy's growth, or to expand unexpectedly, by some unspecified process of spontaneous generation, leading the economy to take off. I concluded that much of the expla-

1. Baumol (1993).

nation for such swings is to be found in the way in which the market mechanism—together with institutional arrangements—influences, not the creation, but the *allocation* of entrepreneurship between productive and unproductive (rent-seeking) pursuits. It was my contention that entrepreneurs as a group do not just appear or disappear in some primordial ooze. Rather, they can be and are reallocated by economic conditions and circumstances into (or out of) activities that appear not to be entrepreneurial because of the preconception that enterprising activity is necessarily productive. But entrepreneurs, like many others, are motivated primarily by prospects of wealth, power, and prestige, and, like people in any other occupation, entrepreneurs range widely in the degree to which morality and concern over the public welfare constrain their activities. Consequently, when institutional arrangements happen to offer greater rewards to enterprising rent-seeking or to destructive activities such as warfare or organized crime than they offer to productive entrepreneurial activity, we can expect an economy's entrepreneurial effort to be allocated away from the more productive undertakings. In the earlier book, I concluded that the most promising way for a society to stimulate productive entrepreneurial activity is to reduce the rewards to unproductive or destructive rent-seeking. I also went beyond this generalization and provided some concrete illustrations of such policy measures.

The orientation of this book is very different. Here, my purpose is to begin to analyze what may well be the most critical attribute of the free-market economy (the type of economy in which we live): its ability to produce a stream of applied innovations and a rate of growth in living standards far beyond anything that any other type of economy has ever been able to achieve for any protracted period. My central contention here is that what differentiates the prototype capitalist economy most sharply from all other economic systems is free-market pressures that force firms into a continuing process of innovation, *because it becomes a matter of life and death for many of them.* The static efficiency properties that are stressed by standard welfare economics are emphatically *not* the most important qualities of capitalist economies. Rather, what is clear to historians and laypersons alike is that capitalism is unique in the extraordinary growth record it has been able to achieve; in its recurring industrial revolutions that have produced an outpouring of material wealth unlike anything previously seen in human history.

Moreover, it seems indisputable that innovation accounts for much of this enviable growth record. But what attributes of capitalism are responsible for this dramatic superiority in its record of innovation? The answer I propose here is that in key parts of the economy the prime weapon of competition is not price but innovation. As a result, firms cannot afford to leave innovation to chance. Rather, managements are forced by market pressures to support innovative activity systematically and substantially, and success of the efforts of any one business firm forces its rivals to step up their own efforts. The result is a ferocious arms race among the firms in the most rapidly evolving sectors of the economy, with innovation as the prime weapon. At the same time, there is profit to be earned by an innovating firm by licensing others, at a suitable price, to use its proprietary technology. The result is widespread cooperation among firms in the dissemination of up-to-date technology, and that, in turn, hastens widespread replacement of obsolete products and processes. These developments, I suggest, are a crucial part of the explanation of capitalism's growth accomplishments.

This does not mean that entrepreneurs have been deprived of any important role. On the contrary, they continue to contribute critical technical breakthroughs and other vital forms of stimulus to growth. The point, rather, is that their role has become only part of the story. Alongside their own activity, which itself is not unprecedented historically, a new, systematized, bureaucratized, and highly efficient set of parallel activities is being carried out within the innovative oligopolistic corporations, as a means to make the process of technical change as riskless as possible. And it is this that transforms innovation and growth from a process beset by fortuitous elements into a powerful mechanism—a machine whose products are innovation and growth.

A striking example will suggest how this has changed the processes of discovery and innovation. In the early days of petroleum exploration, those who carried it out were quite suggestively described as "wildcatters." Many of them relied on little more than intuition, superstition, and recourse to magic in selecting the sites where their drilling would take place. I understand that, nowadays, this process continues to be referred to as "wildcatting," but the decisions on drilling location are often made in faraway laboratories and offices. Which of the locations under consideration offers the most promising prospects is determined with the aid of computers systematically conducting complex analyses of the known geological attributes of those locations. It is this sort of systematized approach to discovery and invention that lies at the heart of the innovation assembly-line of the free-enterprise economy. The goal of this book is to investigate the economic forces that have not only led to this sort of change, but that also impose and can be expected to continue to impose such change upon the economy.

ON RELEVANT LITERATURE

There is a great deal of writing, much of it of very high quality, that is pertinent to this book and from which I have profited enormously. Yet, curiously, with the exception of very brief discussions by Marx, Engels, and Schumpeter, whom I will cite and quote from repeatedly, I have been unable to find anything that deals *directly* with my subject, despite what seems clearly to be the fundamental importance of the issue—explanation of the incredible growth record of the free-market economies. I must emphasize that this is not intended as a criticism of any of the literature to which I am about to refer. Clearly, it is no deficiency of other writers if they choose to explore topics other than mine. Still, this huge gap in the literature seems rather remarkable.

The reader may well ask whether this judgment is unfair to the very qualified economic historians who have written so illuminatingly about related subjects—David Landes, Nathan Rosenberg, Moses Abramovitz, Fernand Braudel, Paul David, Joel Mokyr, Douglass North, and others. They have, indeed, made enormous and very pertinent contributions, but a little consideration shows that they are dealing with a different, if closely related, subject. As historians, their topic, in Landes' words, is "How did we get here?" or, as Rosenberg and Birdzell put it, "How the West Grew Rich." That is, what forces in the past led to the construction of the growth-machine economy? Although in this book I will offer the observations, or perhaps rather the conjectures, of a very amateur historian on the subject, my topic is not how the growth machine happens to have been born (and why in the West and not elsewhere). Rather, my concern is, having gotten here, to document that the economy of the "here" is indeed dominated by what I characterize as a growth machine, and to explain how that machine works. Thus, phenomena such as oligopolistic competition that uses innovation as a weapon, or the nature of the profit incentives for technology licensing and trading, seem clearly to be important components of the mechanism, but quite appropriately play little role in the historical accounts. Still, despite the difference in orientation, I owe the historians a very great debt for the thoughts they stimulated and the realities they described. Here, I must single out Nathan Rosenberg for his careful review of some of my material, and David Landes, not least for his very encouraging conclusion that we had reached similar explanations of the medieval Cistercians' industrial revolution and the circumstances that prevented medieval China from achieving any substantial record of applied innovation, despite its remarkable profusion of early inventions.

Of course, I was also stimulated by the very valuable macroeconomic literature on growth, including, obviously, the pathbreaking work of Robert Solow, Kenneth Arrow, Paul Romer, and Robert Lucas. Later in the book I do point out that their models are ahistorical and that their endogenous innovation processes are largely concealed in black boxes. But that, too, must not be taken as criticism of work I unreservedly admire; rather, it means only that they employed constructs entirely appropriate for their objectives but that the territory that they chose to explore was different from mine.

There is also an informal literature close to the issue that is the focus of this book, in particular the work of Richard Nelson and of F. M. Scherer (1999), with their many valuable insights, some of which will be cited in what follows. Finally, the more formal microeconomic and general equilibrium literature is very powerful. Karl Shell was one of its earliest contributors, followed by the recent Helpman–Grossman and Aghion–Howitt works, and significant pieces by William Nordhaus and Paul Krugman. Important contributions have also appeared under the sponsorship of the Fondazione Eni Enrico Mattei (FEEM) and the Schumpeter Society. To all of these the same remark applies. I, among the many other economists interested in growth, owe them much but, so far as I am aware, their central concerns have been different from mine.

A PERSONAL WORD

As usual, I want to end the preface with deeply felt thanks to those who have contributed to the book's ideas and its preparation. The list I provide is unusually short, not because few have contributed but because the sources of the contributions are so many and so diffuse. I have studied a great number of books and articles on the subject. Writings on the theory include the work of Kenneth Arrow, Karl Shell, Paul Romer, and *many* others. Then there is the very helpful work of economic historians, notably David Landes, Nathan Rosenberg, Paul David, and Joel Mokyr. Among those who helped me more directly are Richard Nelson, F. M. Scherer, and Boyan Jovanovic. To all of them, as well as to two anonymous reviewers, I am indeed deeply grateful. Others who have contributed ideas, directly or indirectly, can be inferred from the many items cited in the Bibliography.

I must also single out Michael Weinstein, with special thanks for his very generous 1999 *New York Times* article about my work-in-progress on the book. It was exceedingly perceptive, and seemed to elicit interest in the work throughout the world. (I first saw the article at a party in Jerusalem, where two guests came with copies they had downloaded from the Internet that afternoon, the day of its appearance.)

However, two other people have played a more continuing role in the completion of this book. Peter Dougherty, economics editor at Princeton University Press, read carefully through the manuscript, made invaluable suggestions on exposition, and has helped to lead me through the process of its completion. It is indeed a pleasure to work with him.

And then there is Sue Anne Batey Blackman, with whom I have worked, hand in glove, lo these many years. She unerringly supplies me with ideas, data, literature, and relevant facts. She virtually rewrote the manuscript (as she has with at least one other) to strip it of obscurities, redundancies, and barbarities. The confidence I have in her work was illustrated strikingly some years ago at a small meeting called at his office by a noted U.S. Senator. A senior official connected with the White House made an assertion that I knew to be in conflict with some of Sue Anne's figures. Without hesitation, I simply said, "Sir, your statement does not fit the facts." In sum, I can only acknowledge appreciation, dependence, and continuing deep affection.

The Free-Market Innovation Machine

CHAPTER 1

Introduction: On the Engine of Free-Market Growth

The Bourgeoisie [i.e., capitalism] cannot exist without constantly revolutionizing the instruments of production. . . . Conservation of the old modes of production in unaltered form was, on the contrary, the first condition of existence for all earlier industrial classes. . . . The bourgeoisie, during its rule of scarce one hundred years has created more massive and more colossal productive forces than have all preceding generations together.

—Karl Marx and Friedrich Engels, 1847

As soon as quality competition and sales effort are admitted into the sacred precincts of theory, the price variable is ousted from its dominant position. . . . But in capitalist reality as distinguished from its textbook picture, it is not that kind of competition which counts but the competition from the new commodity, the new technology . . . —competition which commands a decisive cost or quality advantage and which strikes not at the margins of the profits and the outputs of the existing firms but at their foundations and their very lives. This kind of competition is as much more effective than the other as a bombardment is in comparison with forcing a door.

—Joseph A. Schumpeter, 1947, p. 84

Under capitalism, innovative activity—which in other types of economy is fortuitous and optional—becomes mandatory, a life-and-death matter for the firm. And the spread of new technology, which in other economies has proceeded at a stately pace, often requiring decades or even centuries, under capitalism is speeded up remarkably because, quite simply, time is money. That, in short, is the tale told in this book—an explanation of the incredible growth of the free-market economies. The capitalist economy can usefully be viewed as a machine whose primary product is economic growth. Indeed, its effectiveness in this role is unparalleled. The primary purpose of this book is to attempt an explanation of how this machine works. Note the underlying observation: that its extraordinary record of innovation and growth is hardly fortuitous. Nor is it the result of unrelated external developments analogous to the end of the "Little Ice Age" that occurred just after the inception of the Industrial Revolution and that probably contributed substantially to agricultural output. The point is that, once capitalism was in place and fully operational, a flow of innovation and the consequent rise in productivity and per capita gross domestic product were to be expected. Whatever the deficiencies of the free market, it is certainly very good at one thing: the manufacture of economic growth.

And, as is true of the other accomplishments of the market economy, none of this was the result of deliberate decisions or planning. The free market, once the institutional impediments to its development had been reduced sufficiently, just grew by itself and by itself became the machine that generates innovation and growth in dramatic profusion. For, as will be shown here, the market economy's makeup is such as automatically to ensure that result. This suggests that the analysis provided in this book, if it proves valid, promises to be of substantial value in practice, particularly to those nations that have not yet shared in the growth benefits proffered by the market, and whose relative poverty seems actually to be increasing.

How large a share of the economy is constituted by the growth machine? If we focus on the machine's central component alone—its research and development (R&D) activity—the numbers are not impressive. In 1998, total U.S. expenditure on R&D from all sources amounted to about $227 billion, or some 2.6 percent of gross domestic product (GDP). This share of GDP was growing, but only slowly: an average of about 1.4 percent per year over the forty-five years, 1953–98.[1]

This is, however, too narrow a view of the growth apparatus. The available estimates indicate that more than 60 percent of the labor force in the United States is engaged in activities in the "information sector" of the economy (though it is difficult to define and measure unambiguously)—far more than in manufacturing and agriculture, which, combined, constitute less than 20 percent of the total. This sector includes the processing, recording, analysis, and dissemination of information. It also encompasses the training of those who will carry out the nation's R&D in the future. Of course, much of the activity of the information sector has little connection with growth, but it is implausible that its growth-supporting work constitutes a negligible

1. National Science Board (2000).

share of the total. The evident conclusion is that, whereas the core activity in the growth machine is hardly enormous in size, a very substantial part of the U.S. population that is economically active outside the household is at least peripherally engaged in running the machine.

CENTRAL TOPICS OF THE BOOK

It is the spectacular and historically unprecedented growth rates of the industrialized market economies—the growth rates of their productivity and their per capita incomes—that, above all, set them apart from all alternative economic systems. Average growth rates for about one and a half *millennia* before the Industrial Revolution are estimated to have been approximately *zero,* and, although there was undoubtedly some growth starting around the tenth century, it proceeded at a snail's pace by modern standards. Even the most well-off consumers in pre–Industrial Revolution society had virtually no goods at their disposal that had not been available in ancient Rome. In fact, many consumption choices available at least to more-affluent Roman citizens had long since disappeared by the time of the Industrial Revolution. In contrast, in the past 150 years, per capita incomes in a typical free-market economy have risen by amounts ranging from several hundred to several thousand percent![2] So, when public indignation contributed to the collapse in the late 1980s and early 1990s of many of the world's communist regimes, and when even the masters of China turned toward capitalist enterprise, what they wanted, surely, was to participate in the growth miracle that Karl Marx and Friedrich Engels were able to discern so early in the experience of capitalism.

This book seeks to explain the unprecedented and unparalleled growth performance of the capitalist economies and provides a theory of the imperfect but, nevertheless, creditable efficiency of the capitalist growth process. The analysis attributes this performance primarily to competitive pressures, not present in other types of economy, that force firms in the relevant sectors of the economy to unrelenting investment in innovation and that, contrary to widespread belief, provide incentives for the rapid dissemination and exchange of improved technology throughout the economy. Finally, the book moves toward the integration of growth theory into the central body of mainstream economic analysis. It is clear that innovation plays a far larger role in

2. See Baumol, Blackman, and Wolff (1989). Nordhaus (1997) used the history of lighting to study long-term growth rates of real wages; he found that the quantity of illumination that could have been bought with just one hour of labor in 1992 would have required the wages of more than 1,800 hours in 1900.

the activities of many key firms and industries than the current theoretical literature takes into account. My goal here is to indicate ways in which the analysis of business decisions can be reoriented to eliminate this significant gap. Let me indicate what I hope to achieve here in each of these areas.

Explaining the Growth Miracle of Free Enterprise

The virtual absence of any explicit attempt to explain the fabulous growth record of the free-enterprise economies in general, with their transformation of living standards and creation of technological innovations undreamed of in any previous era, is perhaps the most glaring omission of recent economic growth theory, despite all of its substantial contributions. I have been unable to find any systematic theoretical work seeking to account for this incredible record, or any investigation of why this economic system is so different in its productivity accomplishments from all other economic systems that have ever been tried.[3]

I will concentrate on a number of explanatory influences, including some necessary preconditions for the existence of a workable free-market economy, some likely consequences of the existence of such an economy, and some items that are both. Among the most important of these conditions are:

- **Oligopolistic competition** among large, high-tech business firms, with *innovation as a prime competitive weapon,* ensuring continued innovative activities and, very plausibly, their growth. In this market form, in which a few giant firms dominate a particular market, *innovation has replaced price* as the name of the game in a number of important industries. The computer industry is only the most obvious example, whose new and improved models appear constantly, each manufacturer battling to stay ahead of its rivals.
- **Routinization** of these innovative activities, making them a regular and even ordinary component of the activities of the firm, and thereby minimizing the uncertainty of the process. It is estimated that some 70 per-

3. So far as I have been able to find, the issue is addressed directly only in some four pages of Marx and Engels' *Communist Manifesto* (1848) and in six pages of Schumpeter's *Capitalism, Socialism, and Democracy* (1947), examples of which appear in this chapter's opening quotations. These comments are meant to distinguish my subject matter from the mass of historical and theoretical work, much of it profound, dealing with such subjects as the special history of the advent of capitalism in Western Europe, the role of innovation in growth, etc. The contributions of David Landes, Nathan Rosenberg, Joel Mokyr, Richard Nelson, and F. M. Scherer come at once to mind, and there are many others. But my special focus here is on capitalism as an enormously powerful growth machine. My task is to investigate how the machine works and why it is so effective.

cent of U.S. research and development spending is now done by private industry, much of it incorporated into firms' day-to-day activities.

- **Productive entrepreneurship** encouraged by incentives for entrepreneurs to devote themselves to *productive* innovation rather than to innovative rent-seeking (the nonproductive pursuit of economic profit such as occurs in inter-business lawsuits), or even to destructive occupations, such as criminal activities
- **The rule of law,** including enforceability of contracts and immunity of property from arbitrary expropriation.
- **Technology selling and trading,** in other words, firms' voluntary pursuit of opportunities for profitable dissemination of innovations and rental of the right to use them, via licensing, even to direct competitors.

All of these are features of a capitalist, or free-market, economy; in other types of economy they are either absent or exist in far weaker form. I will argue that these features are crucial for the explanation of the extraordinary growth accomplishments of the free market. Moreover, neither their consequences nor their origins are mere accidents, but contain elements that economic analysis can help to explain.

Imperfect but Substantial Economic Efficiency and Growth under Capitalism

My second central topic is the rough economic efficiency of the growth process of the free-market economies. Textbook accounts suggest that free-enterprise economies are characterized by a tendency toward *static efficiency.* That is, firms are driven by market forces to use the most economical of the available methods of production and to supply the product mix best suited to consumer demands. But, according to these accounts, these economies are also distinguished by extreme violation of the requirements of efficiency *in the growth process.* Most notably, the very substantial *spillovers* that derive from innovation—the fact that a considerable proportion of the benefits of innovation is enjoyed by persons who have not contributed to the innovation—are said to lead to a magnitude of innovative activity far below the optimum level.[4] If inventors could retain more of the gains for themselves, the argu-

4. A dramatic example is the transistor, invented at Bell Laboratories, then owned by AT&T. For a variety of reasons, AT&T, whether voluntarily or involuntarily, allowed others free use of this invention, which then became one of the key contributors to the information age. But surely no major invention has provided benefits only to its inventor. Indeed, it is the general public that has gained the most from inventions ranging from timekeepers to electricity to telephony.

ment goes, there would surely be more inventions, and current inventors would surely put more effort into the process. Yet this conclusion seems to fly in the face of the observation that the main achievement of the capitalist economy is in fact its spectacular and unrivaled growth performance, and not its rather questionable static efficiency.

One need not be an economic historian to conclude that disparities in *static* efficiency do not constitute the really dramatic difference between the capitalist economies and the economic systems that preceded it, as well as those that were until recently designed to displace it. Undoubtedly, the rules of static efficiency were violated in both medieval China and the defunct Soviet Union where, for example, input prices must frequently not have been those that induced the most efficient use of labor and raw materials. But such efficient pricing is probably also widely missing today in the United States, Japan, and Germany. And even if these three countries came closer to satisfying that criterion, one may well doubt that the resulting contribution to living standards would be profound.

These observations underlie one of the main heterodox conclusions of this book: although the capitalist *growth* process certainly does not quite meet the requirements of perfect economic efficiency, there is reason to believe that it comes far closer than standard economic theory might lead us to conclude. Spillovers do, indeed, tend to impede the introduction of innovations whose social benefits (unlike their private returns) exceed their costs. Yet I will argue that, once the beneficial *distributive* consequences of the spillovers of innovation are taken into account, the result is likely to approximate something like optimality, in a sense to be defined. Finally, the profitability of the rental of proprietary technology enhances the rapidity with which the economy moves toward the current technological frontier, that is, toward adoption by most or all producers of the latest and most appropriate technology and product specifications. These forces together lead to a degree of efficiency in growth that, though far from perfect, is nevertheless impressive.

Incorporating Growth Analysis into Mainstream Microeconomic Theory

Innovation and growth surely originate from the activities of individuals and business firms—the entities studied in microeconomic analysis. Growth therefore cannot be fully understood without incorporating it into microeconomic theory. Yet the *core* of that body of analysis contains little on the subject. It will be argued in this book and, I trust, demonstrated that innovation can fortunately be integrated into the standard structure of microeconomic analysis more directly and more easily than might be expected. This is made possible by the competitive market pressures that force firms to integrate innovation into their *routine* decision processes and activities, thereby subjecting it to standardization and to the calculus of profit maximization. In addition, its place in the structure of microeconomic theory is facilitated by the recognition that, to a profit-seeking firm, investment in research and development is just another investment option, and that the products of this R&D are just intermediate inputs to the production of other outputs by the proprietor of the innovation and other business firms.

As a longtime practitioner of microeconomics, I certainly do not want to denigrate its very substantial accomplishments. On the contrary, this book is built with the very effective analytic tools that the microeconomic literature has provided. However, it is apparent that the standard microeconomic analysis, in giving secondary place to innovation and failing to treat it as a primary weapon of competition, has not gone far enough in a direction vital for comprehension of the accomplishments of the free-market economic system. Innovation has been relegated to a peripheral place in the microeconomic literature, outside the central structure of the analysis. There has been a profusion of very illuminating microeconomic writings on innovation, but these have generally dealt with relatively narrow (though important) issues, rather than addressing the place of this activity in the theoretical structure as a whole. This new literature continues to lie well outside the main structure of microeconomic analysis, the body of material that at least used to be called "value theory." Prices and directly related variables still are at the heart of microeconomics, while the theory of innovation remains in the outskirts. Certainly, perusal of any economics principles textbook for first-year students will show a substantial number of chapters devoted to the price mechanism, and sometimes, but not always, there will be a single chapter in which innovation has a central role. Thus, it is no exaggeration to say that in economic analysis innovation is only a sideshow and is certainly excluded from the central ring of the main performance.

In drawing attention to this omission, I am not repeating the banal observation that the "realism" of economic theory is far from perfect, a criticism that has been leveled repeatedly at the most creative writings of economics for well over a century. Rather, the argument of this book is in the opposite spirit. It suggests that, once outlays on innovative activity are recognized as just one of the investment options open to the firm, then the theory of capital and investment already provides the logic and the instruments with which one can quickly close much of the gap. Once this is done, innovation can and should become a centerpiece of the microanalytic literature, as it is in the economy of reality. It will thereby contribute both to the understanding of the actual economy and to its utility in application.

An integrated theory of innovation that brings its position in microtheory closer to that of price should help us to deal with a number of issues. The analysis of innovation should provide an explanation of the amount spent on innovation, and should show how it fits in with the determination of the other variables of the pertinent market model. It should be capable of dealing with the role of innovation in the theory of resource allocation, income distribution, and welfare analysis, and in dynamic as well as static models. In each of these areas this book will seek to provide a beginning, though it will not pretend to explore its subject definitively. What I do hope to end up with is a preliminary mapping of the subject as a whole, showing that the way is now open for exploration and deeper analysis by others, some of whom may find it convenient to take off from the approaches that will be illustrated here.

One of the reasons innovation is absent from the core of microtheory is failure to take account of the routinization of much of inventive and innovative activity, a subject to which we will return. For this transformation of the process makes it far easier to incorporate rivalry in innovation into the core of the microeconomic theory of the firm. We can far more easily subject such a customary, regular, and predictable activity to systematic analysis than the erratic, unpredictable "Eureka! I have found it!" kind of discovery, to which romantic histories attribute the bulk of invention. Routine innovation changes all that, because the decision process and its competitive consequences become nearly indistinguishable from those characterizing any other form of investment. A firm's management is faced with an ordinary budget-allocation decision in which investment outlays are apportioned among competing uses such as plant and equipment, advertising, and R&D. In a sense, all of these are abstracted into many anonymous money-earning opportunities for the firm. Their common feature is that they all entail outlays now whose (risky) payoffs can be expected only in the future. The decision on which new variant of some major type of equipment will be purchased by the firm is based per se not on considerations such as the ingenuity of its design or its economical use of fuel, but, ultimately, only on the payoff it promises. The same is true of the decision about whether additional investment funds should be devoted to marketing or to research.[5] Thus, the range of applica-

5. Of course, the results of investment in R&D are less clearly foreseeable than those of investment in expanded plant, for example. But, for analysis of the two investment decisions, the difference is only a matter of risk, and a difference only in degree.

tion of the standard and well-developed theory of investment can at once be extended to include the routinized innovation process.

In short, the analysis of routine innovation can get substantially further and can yield more clear-cut microeconomic conclusions than can analysis of an innovation process that is largely fortuitous and unpredictable. Indeed, it can put us well on the road to "an integrated theory of innovation" that will promote our understanding of the workings of the economy and help us to extend the range of useful applications of the analysis.

THE GROWTH-PROMOTING ATTRIBUTES OF CAPITALISM: HAMLET'S REAPPEARANCE

It is tempting to argue that the avoidance by recent growth theory of any systematic study of the capitalist growth miracle is like a performance of Shakespeare's *Hamlet* without its central character, the Prince of Denmark. Ophelia, Polonius, and Hamlet's mother and uncle all play their roles, but Hamlet himself is missing from the stage.[6] So, too, the growth literature is full of invaluable analyses. But much of it is unsuited to deal directly with the distinction between the growth accomplishments of capitalism and those of other economic systems, because these analyses are preponderantly ahistorical, and all explicit references to the special features of free-market economies have been expunged.[7]

This book attempts to break away from this orientation, taking at least a preliminary step toward the historical orientation of Marx and Schumpeter, by coming to grips with the uniqueness of capitalist growth. In brief, the following features of innovation in the free-market economies indicate more fully the logic of my analysis, which has already been suggested.

---

6. The phrase "a performance of Hamlet without the prince of Denmark" was widely used in Great Britain some decades ago, and was also employed by Joseph Schumpeter.

7. Clearly, Paul Romer (1990) and Robert Lucas (1988) and, soon after them, Gene Grossman and Elhanan Helpman (1991a and b), building upon Robert Solow's fundamental work (1956), among others, have made a major breakthrough by inaugurating a formal theory of endogenous innovation. There is no conflict between anything that will be said here and what they have written. Indeed, I trust they will agree with me in regarding their research and mine as complementary, with the two together providing the basis for an analysis of innovation that is, as it should be, integrated into the central corpus of economics. However, their work is not designed to deal with the difference between the growth record of capitalism and that of other economic forms. Their analysis is ahistorical and macroeconomic and does not emphasize routine innovation as distinguished from endogenous innovation activity of just any variety. None of this can be considered a shortcoming of their models, given their very different purposes.

Capitalism Is Unique Not in Invention but in Innovation

Although a number of other economies have produced an astonishing profusion of inventions, virtually none of them possessed a mechanism that induced, let alone rendered mandatory, the cascade of innovation that has characterized free enterprise. Here I use the term "innovation," distinguished from invention, in the Schumpeterian sense: as the recognition of opportunities for profitable change and the pursuit of those opportunities all the way through to their adoption in practice; in particular, as the activity of recognizing economically viable inventions and doing whatever is necessary to bring them to market or to ensure their effective end-use by some other means.[8] Medieval China and ancient Rome had their spectacular profusion of inventions, but most of them proved to be dead-ends in the absence of a systematic innovation mechanism capable of ensuring that they would not languish.

Beyond Mere Incentive: Invention as a Life-and-Death Matter for Capitalist Firms in Sectors Ripe for Invention

The market mechanism achieves much of its efficiency and its adaptation to consumer desires through financial incentives, by providing higher payoffs to those firms that are more efficient and whose products are most closely adapted to the wishes of consumers. The same mechanism obviously drives innovation in an even more powerful way. For oligopoly firms in the high-tech sectors of the economy, it is in fact a matter of survival. The firm that lets its rivals outperform it substantially in innovative products and processes is faced with the prospect of imminent demise. The firm must innovate or die. To paraphrase Dr. Johnson, the prospect of hanging is a powerful stimulus to the imagination.

Irresistible Pressure for Routinized Corporate Innovation as a Supplement to Independent Innovative Activity

To protect themselves from the risks just described, business enterprises have incorporated innovative activity into their routine operations. Such innova-

8. Innovators, who prepare inventions for the needs of the market and promote their sales, are often not primarily inventors themselves. Thus, James Watt's partner, Matthew Boulton, was clearly the market planner and salesman for the Boulton–Watt steam engines, and, arguably, Edison was more innovating entrepreneur than inventor. "Although popular American legend elevates Edison above his peers, he did not in fact make any quantum leaps in [electric] technology [when he discovered his carbon-filament lamp in 1882]. The first lighting by electricity took place with the electric-arc lamp as early as 1845 . . . Edison combined technical inspiration with commercial perspiration when he also generated electricity and distributed it from the Pearl Street substation in New York in 1882" (Nordhaus, 1997, p. 37).

tion activity is no longer a largely unpredictable process, in which changes in social psychology control the fortuitous appearance of individuals who possess the determination and inspiration needed for innovation. Particularly in the high-tech sectors of the economy, the pressures of the competitive market force firms to systematize the innovation process and to seek so far as possible (in the immortal words of the great comedian W. C. Fields) "to remove all elements of chance" from the undertaking.[9]

As Schumpeter and others have already noted, innovation is, as a result, increasingly becoming an accustomed and predictable procedure. Business firms systematically determine the amounts they will invest in the R&D process, systematically decide on the ways in which they will interact with their rivals in this area, and even systematically determine what it is that the company's laboratories should invent.

In substantial portions of the oligopolistic sectors of the economy, where huge firms dominate markets, innovation has become the preferred competitive weapon. Indeed, the contest for better new products and processes becomes an arms race, with failure to keep up constituting a threat to the firm's survival. This is a force that contributes substantially to capitalist growth.

Competition makes it too risky for firms to depend primarily for their new products and processes on the unpredictable efforts of independent inventors. Instead they have changed much of the economy's R&D into an internal, bureaucratically controlled process, as, for example, in pharmaceuticals, computers, and even photography. They have *routinized* it.

FEEDBACK: INNOVATION STIMULATES FURTHER INNOVATION

Once innovation takes off, including in this not only the inventions themselves but also their successful marketing and profitable utilization, this facilitates and stimulates further innovative effort. The obvious connection is that the demonstrated profit opportunity is sure to attract other inventors, other investors, and other entrepreneurs whose task it is to ensure that invention is put to effective and remunerative use.

But successful innovation encourages more of this activity in other ways, as well as helping to ensure the success of this further effort. As is well recog-

9. This phrase is uttered when a novice (whom Fields is seeking to lure into a card game) questions the morality of "games of chance," Fields hastens to reassure his victim: "Young man, when you play with me, all elements of chance have been removed!"

nized, new products have often given others the idea for related new products that either serve as superior substitutes (for example, the jet airplane as substitute for propeller planes) or serve as supplements to the preceding new products or service (for example, the electric refrigerator as something that followed the creation of the electricity network). The one invention may also indicate ways to make it easier and less costly to manufacture other new products. Finally, the innovation process itself leads to improvements in the way R&D is carried out, thereby providing another stimulus to further innovation. In sum, innovative activity can be considered a cumulative process, in which there is feedback from one innovation to the next; once the free market has launched its innovation machine, the inherent structure of the mechanism leads the machine to grow more powerful and productive with the passage of time.

MARKET INCENTIVES FOR RAPID DISSEMINATION

Depending on prices, it is often most profitable for the monopoly owner of an innovation to specialize in the business of renting the input to others rather than using it itself as an input to its own final product. Sometimes the highest profits are obtained by the owner of the rights to an invention if it simultaneously uses the invention as an input in its own production *and* rents its use to others. As a result, there is widespread technology trading and marketing of licenses for a firm's proprietary technology in the United States and, apparently, in other countries with technologically advanced economies. Many firms do not fight to keep the technology to themselves, and some actively promote it as a profitable business. Such dissemination of technology as a profit-seeking business practice helps to spread the use of the latest techniques and production of the latest goods and services. It speeds the elimination of obsolete economic activities, and the financial rewards of technology dissemination help to internalize the externalities of the innovation process.

DOES THIS EXAGGERATE THE ROLE OF INNOVATION?

Innovation is, of course, a primary source of the capitalist growth miracle, starting off with the "wave of gadgets"[10]—the surge of innovation that prob-

10. This, according to T. S. Ashton in his classic little book (1948) on the Industrial Revolution, is the way in which one schoolboy (quite appropriately) defined that revolution.

ably began to gather force as early as the fourteenth century and perhaps first reached a substantial pace early in the nineteenth century. It can be argued that virtually all of the economic growth that has occurred since the eighteenth century is ultimately attributable to innovation.

Yet, one may well maintain quite reasonably that this is an exaggeration. For example, as economic growth literature emphasizes, much has undoubtedly been contributed by investment in the capacities of the individual—in "human capital"—notably through expansion of education, through learning-by-doing, and through the spillovers from accumulated learning. Similarly, crucial contributions to growth have been made by enormous investments in plant and equipment. But with the very limited resources available to the extremely impoverished societies of earlier centuries, there was little possibility of diversion of any substantial quantity of resources to either of these types of investment.[11] For the bulk of the population of earlier periods of history, bare survival was the critical problem, and it left only minimal resources for investment in education and productive capacity. Only the productive surpluses that innovation began to make possible, first in agriculture and mining and then in manufacturing, made feasible the enormous increases in investment in inanimate and in human capital that are widely judged to have contributed greatly to economic growth. So it is reasonable to say not only that innovation has contributed to the growth process, both directly and at second remove, but that without it the process would have been reduced to insignificance.

REMARK ON THE ROLE OF GREED

I have often heard it said by intelligent observers (who were not economists) that the prosperity and growth achieved in the free-market economies are wonderful things, but that the process was seriously sullied by the exercise of greed that it stimulated. This is not a new issue; indeed, it is related to a Renaissance debate involving some of its leading thinkers, which they raised on religious grounds: How could a beneficent and all-powerful deity allow human conduct to be governed by such unsavory motivations? One of Adam Smith's most brilliant contributions was a viable resolution of this dilemma that remains illuminating today.

11. It is also noteworthy that neither investment in human capital nor investment in physical capital is a distinguishing feature of free-market economies. Both were, for example, very substantial in the economy of the Soviet Union. Thus, emphasis of these two sources of growth contributes to the ahistorical character of many growth models.

In effect, Smith demonstrated that competition is capable of dealing with the problem and that it does deal with it effectively. That is what the famous (but much misunderstood) "invisible hand" passage in *The Wealth of Nations* is really about. This passage tells us that competition obviously provides the minimally acceptable solution, by preventing the greedy "merchants and manufacturers" from deriving any excessive profits from their ill-motivated activities. Thus, it denies them the fruit that their greed-driven efforts were designed to attain.

But that is only the beginning of the miracle of competition according to Smith. For, rather than only eliminating any excess reward to the exercise of greed, it turns the tables and harnesses that greed to serve the general welfare. Under competition, greedy producers must strive to provide a better product on better terms than their rivals are offering. They must find out what consumers want, and they must match their output to those wants. They must supply as much of their product as they can induce consumers to accept at the low prices enforced by the competitive market.

As Smith explains:

> As every individual . . . endeavours as much as he can . . . so to direct [his] industry as its produce may be of the greatest value; every individual necessarily labours to render the annual revenue of the society [its GDP] as great as he can. He generally, indeed, neither intends to promote the public interest, nor knows how much he is promoting it. . . . [B]y directing [his] industry in such a manner as its produce may be of the greatest value, he intends only his own gain. . . . [H]e is in this, as in many other cases, led by an invisible hand to promote an end which was no part of his intention. . . . By pursuing his own interest he frequently promotes that of the society more effectually than when he intends to promote it. ([1776] 1904, p. 481)[12]

It is to be noted that the issue relevant for Smith and for the discussion of this book is not whether the motivation force in question is to be viewed approvingly as "responsible pursuit of the profit motive" or is more appropriately classed among the seven deadly sins. Rather, the analysis starts from the position that the profit motive is very much alive and very widely present. It exists and cannot be wished away. Then the pertinent question is not only whether there exist arrangements that can prevent its most objectionable consequences but whether, more than that, they can redirect the forces engendered by this motive so as to benefit society and not just fail to harm

12. It will be noted that the passage contains no explicit reference to competition, but its role is surely clear from the context.

it. Smith's answer is that there is such an institution—competition—though he warns us that it is an institution that needs to be defended from the predictable (and widely observable) attempts by those who are affected by its constraints to evade it or undermine it altogether.

This story is particularly applicable to free-market innovation and growth. Without the profit-driven competition of the innovating firms seeking to be the first to learn how to make the better mousetrap or the better computer, and to bring these products rapidly to market, more quickly and cheaply than their rivals, and without the opportunities for profitable dissemination that allows technical progress to pervade the economy rapidly, how much more modest would the growth record of the market economies have been? All this is patently driven by what some call the "profit motive" although others, less affectionately, just call it "greed." But it is greed harnessed to work as efficiently and effectively as it can to serve the public interest in prosperity and growth.[13]

CONCLUSION: THE FREE-MARKET ECONOMY AS INNOVATION MACHINE

As already asserted, it seems clear that it is innovation, not price-setting, to which management gives priority in important sectors of the economy. It is persistently forced to do so by the market. But the central body of microeconomic analysis gives its attention primarily to price determination, and by doing so may, arguably, be omitting a critical feature of the competitive process in more recent periods. Further, the omission removes the bridge that can connect the static and the dynamic analysis.

Of course, price legitimately plays an important role in the central economic models: as a conduit of information to the market it is an indispensable variable of general equilibrium theory. However, I will argue that innovation plays a role of at least comparable importance for the theory of the firm and competition. And, although recent macromodels of growth have turned their attention to endogenous technical change,[14] they have not sought to explore the heart of the free-market growth process, which is the competitive pressure that forces firms to create, seek out, and promote inno-

13. Of course, it arguably is not a very good promoter of other public interests in terms of objectives such as preservation of the environment, prevention of unemployment, and many others. I have no intention of minimizing the importance of these considerations, but merely want to point out that they are not the subject under discussion here.

14. See footnote 7 above.

vations. It is essential for a credible theory of endogenous technical change to treat explicitly the role of market forces as major determinants of innovative activity itself along with price and other pertinent variables.

Free-market economies *are* fundamentally different from all other economies that the world has known. The most spectacular and, arguably, the most important manifestation of that difference is the extraordinarily superior growth performance of free-market economies. This book explores the mechanism that accounts for that performance. Using a blend of theory, history, and bits of more recent data, I seek to provide an analytic approach that not only deals with capitalist growth per se, but also indicates how the analysis can be brought from the isolated suburbs of the theory of the firm and industry and moved into its center, where it surely belongs.

PART I

The Capitalist Growth Mechanism

CHAPTER 2

The "Somewhat Optimal" Attributes of Capitalist Growth: Oligopolistic Competition and Routinization of Innovation

innovations are rarely the dramatic breakthroughs that Schumpeter may have had in mind but rather small improvements in a new process or product in which genuine novelty and imitation-with-a-difference shade imperceptibly into one another.

—Blaug, 1999, p. 110

It is something of a puzzle, therefore, why the capitalist innovation system has performed so well. There certainly is nothing like the twin theorems of welfare economics around to support an argument that capitalism "can't be beat."

—Nelson, 1996, pp. 54–55

The phrase "somewhat optimal" appears to be an oxymoron, but actually describes the growth processes of capitalism effectively. Indeed, there is no foundation for a claim that free-enterprise economies automatically tend to satisfy the requirements of ideal economic efficiency in the growth process. Yet there are substantial reasons to conclude that the patently extraordinary growth record of the free-enterprise form of economic organization is hardly accidental, and that it is in large part attributable to the pressures of the free market upon the business firm, which force it to spend liberally and continually on the innovation process and to make its innovations available to others if those others are willing to pay an attractive price. Moreover, I will argue that the capitalist growth mechanism has welfare properties far more desirable than the literature of economics seems hitherto to have suggested.

CHAPTER 2

INNOVATION AND THE GROWTH PERFORMANCE OF CAPITALISM

Per capita income in the leading capitalist economies is growing at a rate that apparently permits something like an eightfold multiplication in a century (as John Maynard Keynes predicted in 1932).[1] I suggest this number is so large that it defies comprehension. What would our lives be like if we were recipients of an average family income today, and then seven-eighths of that amount were suddenly removed? In contrast, it is estimated (very crudely, of course) that in wealthy eighteenth-century England real per capita income had just about reattained the level it had reached in third-century Rome, some fifteen centuries earlier. Words do, indeed, fail to convey the incredible growth record of the industrialized free-market economies. Undoubtedly, it is these spectacular and unmatched growth rates that distinguish them most from *all* other economic systems. In no other system, current or in the past, has the average income of the general public risen anywhere nearly as much or as quickly as it has in North America, Western Europe, and Japan. Though the Soviet Union planned its economy and forced its population to invest heavily in factories and hydroelectric dams, it failed to produce enough materially to raise the standard of living of its population, as the free-market economies have been able to do.

What is the secret of their extraordinary success? That is the economic puzzle that undoubtedly is critical to the degree of prosperity achievable in the future. Its answer is what the world's poorer countries are anxious to learn. The central purpose of Part One of this book is to provide some of the missing explanations—to describe the features of the free-market economy that make it into a fantastically effective machine for the production of innovations and for the consequent growth in its output. This book will emphasize three components of that explanation: the fierce competition among many of the economy's enterprises, seeking to come up with the better new mousetrap or the better way to produce the old mousetrap; the resulting routinization of the innovation process that reduces the firm's dependence upon fortunate happenstance in the form of an appropriate invention that just happens to appear; and the competitive pressures to disseminate proprietary technology voluntarily—to make it available, for a suitable return of course, even to direct competitors.

1. Keynes (1932, pp. 364–65). I must thank Senator Daniel Patrick Moynihan for calling this passage to my attention.

In particular, I will contend here that routine innovation processes—those guided by standard business-decision principles—are a key part of the story. They are, indeed, of great and probably growing importance, with more than two-thirds of U.S. R&D expenditure channeled through business firms. That is one of the key components of the free market's innovation mechanism, and one that will be emphasized in this book. It thereby focuses on a source of the economy's stream of new products and processes that is more dependable than the lone inventors who are so widely regarded as the prime creators of technical change.

THE CONTINUING IMPORTANCE OF UNROUTINIZED ENDOGENOUS INNOVATION

However, the critical and growing role of routine innovative activity does not mean that independent innovation no longer plays a significant role.[2] F. M. Scherer (1980, p. 438) provides a long list of major technical inventions introduced by newly created firms, whose personnel were presumably not subject to the pressures for routinization that one expects in large, established enterprises. His examples include the incandescent lamp, alternating electric current, radio telegraph and telephony, the dial telephone, the synchronous orbit communications satellite, the turbojet engine, the sound motion picture, self-developing photography, and the electronic calculator, among many others. One can even offer the plausible conjecture that *most* revolutionary new ideas have been, and are likely to continue to be, provided preponderantly by independent innovators.[3]

But once their initial undertaking proves successful, the inventors or the associated entrepreneurs often establish new firms that in many cases grow large and themselves routinize their innovation. Henry Ford and his automobiles provide only one of many examples. Such subsequent innovation,

2. Though I obviously do not agree fully, Richard Nelson (1996) even concludes that "Schumpeter's prognostication that as science grew stronger technical innovation would become more predictable and routine has turned out to be a bad call" (p. 81). However, Nelson does not seem to be disputing that a good deal of R&D has become a routine corporate activity.

3. There is also a good deal of R&D activity in universities and government laboratories. Clearly, this is not research conducted by business, but much of it is different from the work of the independent innovator under discussion. For example, much of the activity of the independent innovator is conducted in pursuit of wealth, and it consists primarily of applied rather than basic research.

like most innovations produced by routine processes, is primarily devoted to product improvement, increased reliability, enhanced user-friendliness of products, and the search for new uses for those products. Though the routine innovations tend to be less dramatic, both the independent and the routinized innovation activities undoubtedly contribute significantly to economic growth, as Nathan Rosenberg has emphasized (see, e.g., 1976, p. 66).

The main point here is that there is no reason to expect the independent inventor or innovator to become obsolete any time in the foreseeable future. Indeed, there is a serendipitous relationship between the routine and the independent economic activities, whose results are arguably superadditive, with the whole greater than the sum of the parts.

PROBLEMS BESETTING INNOVATION AND GROWTH UNDER FREE ENTERPRISE

For all its achievements, it cannot be claimed that the capitalist economy has no shortcomings as an engine of growth. There are good reasons to suspect that innovation under free enterprise will be far from optimal, including the following.

Benefit Spillovers. The first and most widely recognized source of imperfection is the existence of substantial spillovers of the benefits generated by innovation. Generally, a considerable share of the benefits of a particular innovation goes, without compensation of the innovators, to individuals or groups who have made no contribution to the discovery and development of that invention. Often, these non-paying beneficiaries even include competitors of those who hold the rights to the innovation. Thus, it is generally inferred that investors are unlikely to devote the socially optimal quantity of resources to the innovation process.

Other Externalities. Recently, the economics literature has begun to emphasize other sources of differences between the private and social costs of innovation. For example, Philippe Aghion and Peter Howitt (1998) have drawn attention to this side of Schumpeter's "creative destruction" concept. New products and processes can destroy the marketability of their predecessors, even though these would otherwise have retained considerable value. If the proprietors of the older assets are individuals or groups different from the innovators, the latter will have no incentive to take these losses in value into account in deciding on the magnitude of their innovative activities. For example, the creators of Microsoft Excel were not deterred by the prospect that they would drive the suppliers of other spreadsheet software out of business, even though the now dominant product is arguably only marginally better than the others. An innovation with an expected market value of $10 million will be an attractive proposition to the innovator if its expected private cost is $7 million. But it will be a net loss to society if the process also makes $8 million in older assets obsolete.

Proprietors' Withholding of Technological Information. A third and less commonly discussed source of inefficiency in the growth process is the incentive for the proprietors of an invention to deny its use to others, notably to competitors, by means of secrecy, patents, and recourse to litigation to enforce those patents. It would obviously be inefficient for a superior process or product feature to be restricted to only one of the firms in an industry, because the others might prove to be the more efficient producers if the innovation became available to them.[4] Even if the innovation were not to become available to other firms, they might manage to survive but they would then be supplying products of inferior quality, produced by obsolete processes. If the products of that industry are varied, many suppliers of close-substitute goods may be able to remain in the market, despite the resulting inefficiency in their operations, if each possesses proprietary technology or product features that it can prevent the others from using. In other words, deliberately erected obstacles to dissemination need not prevent simultaneous survival of a number of firms, but the result can be highly inefficient. In addition, mitigation of this problem for growth entails an offsetting danger: weakening of this third obstacle to optimality in the free-enterprise growth process can exacerbate the first. That is, anything that facilitates the easy and rapid dissemination of technology appears to enhance the spillovers of innovation by making it easier for non-innovators to derive a share of the benefits.

Inappropriate License-Fee Levels. A fourth difficulty relevant for the efficiency of the free-enterprise growth process also has not been discussed as widely as the spillover problem. This relates to the pricing of technology licenses. An obvious way simultaneously to reduce the severity of both the first (spillovers of benefits) and third (technology withholding) of the problems that have just been discussed is for firms with proprietary technology to

4. Thus, Litton sued Honeywell for patent infringement in the latter's use of a superior mirror coating in the ring laser gyroscope now used to guide and steer most commercial aircraft. As this book was being written, Litton's initial court victory was still under appeal. There is much evidence indicating that Honeywell was indeed the superior producer in the period to which the dispute pertains. Litton, of course, denies Honeywell's superiority, and recently improved technology may be changing the competitive balance.

find it profitable to license its use. This clearly ameliorates the dissemination problem and simultaneously reduces spillovers by offering direct compensation to investors in innovation. But profitability depends on the license fee that the owners of the technology are able to obtain. If it is too low they will have no incentive to license. And if they do license, will they not have an incentive to extract a license fee that is far too high from the viewpoint of economic efficiency?

Rent-Seeking and Destructive Entrepreneurial Activity. Entrepreneurs are widely credited with a key role in economic growth. But business persons and innovators can be expected to direct their efforts to where the money is. Many will be tempted to choose activities that promise to be lucrative regardless of the benefits these activities offer or do not offer to society, as in the many cases when firms institute lawsuits against rivals, seeking to curb the vigor of the rivals' competitive activities and hoping, in addition, for some monetary payoff in the form of damage payments imposed by the courts.[5] Entrepreneurs will sometimes devote innovative ideas as well as their energies to the creation of monopolies, and even to criminal activities. That is hardly the most effective avenue to growth.

"Winner Take All" Patent Races. A sixth problem that can handicap the efficiency of the innovation process is the "winner take all" property of some patent races. Partha Dasgupta and Joseph Stiglitz (1980) have demonstrated that R&D expenditure can be excessive in terms of social welfare when competing firms, in an attempt to win an innovation race, duplicate efforts and rush to get ahead of one another's innovation programs. In addition, if the winner takes all, the efforts of those who have sought the desired innovation, but failed to obtain the patent, are wasted. Although such duplicative effort does reduce the risk that a sought-after invention will not be discovered, there seems to be no assurance that this decrease in risk will be worth the expenditure of resources that goes into the race. Moreover, the absence of any reward to the runners-up may exacerbate the risks of the innovation process and it may mean that somewhat inferior, but nevertheless valuable, substitutes for the winning invention are denied to potential purchasers whose special needs they may meet satisfactorily.

5. A number of concrete illustrations are provided in chapter 4 of my 1993 book on the theory of entrepreneurship. For example, the Sewell Plastics company sued a group of Coca-Cola bottlers in the U.S. Southeast for starting a rival bottle-producing cooperative that supplied bottles at less than half Sewell's earlier price. Sewell sued, openly demanding that the bottlers agree to purchase *only* from Sewell. The court threw the case out.

HOW THE MARKET DEALS WITH THE IMPEDIMENTS TO EFFICIENCY IN INNOVATION

The market economy does have attributes that mitigate these problems, though it can hardly be claimed that it deals with them optimally. This is a second central theme of Part I of this book. With the exception of the problems associated with "winner take all" patent races, on which only a few comments will be offered (in the appendix to this chapter), all of the efficiency impediments just listed will be dealt with in the chapters that follow. And it will be shown that for each of these difficulties the market mechanism has features that make them less serious than they might otherwise have been.

For example, contrary to what may at first be thought, it will be shown that firms emphatically do have strong reasons to disseminate their technology, reasons not commonly noted in the literature. Thus, firms other than the owner of the proprietary technology are not driven to reliance on obsolete products and processes.

One reason for voluntary dissemination is that proprietary technology is like any other asset in this respect—it is profitable to rent it out *if the price is right.* After all, if the price is sufficiently high, employment of its technology by others will be the most profitable option to the owner. And it will pay the prospective renter to offer such an attractive price whenever it is in a position to put the technology to better use than the proprietor. As a result, it is not surprising that substantial markets in technology licenses have emerged.

A second reason for voluntary dissemination arises, paradoxically, from the pressures of competition. Exchange of technology need not undermine the competitive position of the enterprise. Indeed, it may well strengthen that position. If a firm supplies its technology to a rival and the favor is reciprocated, both firms, having the use of their combined inventions, will end up strengthened relative to a third competitor that has only its own resources to rely upon for new products and processes. Because of this, market forces provide a strong incentive for the formation of what amount to informal technology consortia, with extensive or even complete sharing of the information. I will also show that such technology consortia provide an incentive for enhancement of investment in innovation, rather than discouraging such outlays. I will provide evidence that these consortia are not theoretical fictions, but that they exist and are widespread in reality. In sum, it will be shown that market forces provide strong incentives for the rapid dissemination of innovation, and do not generally encourage the hoarding of such proprietary property that could significantly impede economic growth.

Each of the other main impediments to optimality in the growth process will also be analyzed, and in each case it will be shown that there is reason to conclude that the handicap is at least far less serious than seems often to be believed. On the contrary, reasons will be given to expect a fairly impressive performance by the free market in at least some of these areas.

This may all sound as if I am hinting that, from the point of view of innovation and growth, the market mechanism almost is all for the best in this best of all possible worlds. But this is far from my purpose. As in the case of the efficiency analysis that deals with the performance of the economy in matters other than growth, application to the real world is characterized by a multitude of warts and blemishes. Monopoly power, ill-considered government intervention, private miscalculation, and ignorance all can and do degrade the performance of the economy. Moreover, nothing that will be said in Part One of this book is meant to argue that even a theoretical market equilibrium is necessarily characterized by optimality properties. Rather, my much more limited claim is that market forces tend to yield an economic performance far closer to the requirements of economic efficiency than at least a superficial reading of the standard analyses might lead one to believe.

SUMMARY

We are left with the following account of the production and distribution of technology in the capitalist growth process. First, continued investment in innovation is ensured by the arms-race character of competition in the high-tech oligopoly industries that will be explored in the following chapter. Such competition also forces firms to routinize the innovation process as a means to reduce their risks. These incentives are enhanced, not undermined, by technology trading and licensing—primarily because those processes serve, via the access (license) fees, partially to internalize the externalities of innovative activity. Second, innovative activity by the firm is stimulated by the requirement for success in technology-exchange negotiations that a negotiating party have something of value to offer to the firm whose technology it hopes to acquire. Because of licensing and technology trading, innovations are now disseminated with historically unprecedented rapidity. Rather than benefiting just a severely limited subsector of the industry and the economy, leaving other producers to fend with obsolete techniques and products, the advantages of technical advances are quickly made available to all. This, too, can be expected to make a significant contribution to economic growth.

These conclusions suggest that the innovation process may be characterized by some efficiency properties that do not seem to be widely recognized in the literature. Although it cannot be denied that the activity is beset by a number of significant imperfections, that still leaves the free-market economies with a flow of innovations of unprecedented magnitude. And even the efficiency-handicapping spillovers of innovation offer a valuable tradeoff between naked productive efficiency and acceptable division of its benefits. By distributing the benefits of technical progress widely among the population, spillovers enhance the economic health of society and surely add social value to the growth accomplishments of the free-market economy.

The role of innovation, investment, and education in the growth of the industrialized economies is, of course, widely recognized. But usually these are, at least by implication, treated as exogenous products of happenstance, not as a predictable product of the free-market growth machine. Thus, consider the following passage by Angus Maddison (2001, p. 21), plainly an astute and well-informed student of growth on whose data many growth analysts quite appropriately rely:

> Between 1820 and 1913, British per capita income grew faster than at any time in the past—three times as fast as in 1700–1820. The basic reason for improved performance was the acceleration of technical progress, accompanied by rapid growth of the physical capital stock and improvement in the education and skills of the labour force, but changes in commercial policy also made a substantial contribution. In 1846 protective duties on agricultural imports were removed and in 1849 the Navigation Acts were terminated. By 1860, all trade and tariff restrictions had been removed unilaterally. In 1860 there were reciprocal treaties for freer trade with France and other European countries. These had most-favoured nation clauses which meant that bilateral liberalisation applied equally to all countries.

It is clear that this passage does not connect the innovation and other immediate stimuli of economic growth to what I maintain is their fundamental source—the capitalist economy. Yet without this connection, without recognition of the market economy as an innovation- and growth-producing machine of unparalleled effectiveness, one cannot hope to offer a systematic explanation of the outpouring in the industrialized economies in the past two centuries. Without that, the story appears as one great set of coincidences with little internal coherence, one that could just as easily have happened elsewhere, in radically different circumstances, and that could end as abruptly, as it may appear to have begun. But it will be shown in this book that there is every reason not to accept such a view.

APPENDIX

REMARKS ON HETEROGENEOUS-PRODUCT RACES

Since it is not a central concern of this book, only a few comments will be offered on the patent race issue. Much of the literature on competition among innovators interprets the process as one in which there is a single prize—the winner takes all. The inventor who reaches the patent office first, as when Alexander Graham Bell beat his rival in the invention of the telephone by several hours, becomes the sole possessor of the legal right to profit from the invention. There are, of course, inventions of this sort, particularly when the new products or processes that the rival inventors have tried to create are homogeneous—essentially identical. It is apt to be true of technical advances whose sole purpose is to reduce the cost of a homogeneous final product, because the innovation that provides the greatest cost saving can clearly outcompete any rival, leaving no place in the market for an inferior cost-cutting substitute.

Inventions, however, are generally not so homogeneous. The research and development laboratories of two competing firms often turn out innovations that are imperfect substitutes for one another. One may be superior to the other in some features but inferior in others. Or one may be only marginally inferior and therefore salable at a price that is a bit lower than the other's. In such cases, as already suggested, the race offers many prizes; the winner receives the highest payoff, but those who come in close behind obtain compensation commensurate with the value of their performances.[6]

In a highly competitive market the relationship among the payoffs to the different innovators in the race is readily analyzed with the help of the standard rent model associated with David Ricardo. In such markets, competition forces the imperfect substitute innovations to be priced so as to offer purchasers of their services exactly the same net benefits. Thus, if purchasers are homogeneous, the difference between the rent payments to the suppliers of

---

6. In his Ph.D. dissertation, Chung Yi Tse (1996) introduced innovation races very close to what has just been described and analyzed their welfare properties systematically and far more deeply than is done in the brief discussion here. His results also indicate that the races need not conflict with economic efficiency.

any two (imperfect) substitute innovations must be equal to the difference in the benefits they provide to buyers.

This result follows not only from the behavior of product buyers but also from that of profit-seeking investors in innovation. Investment in the innovation process will be increased only if it is expected to raise the probability of winning a more valuable prize, if, for example, it increases the likelihood of winning the second profit prize rather than the third. If freedom of entry into the innovation process reduces expected profits to zero, however, higher expected payoff prizes will be offset precisely by the higher cost of obtaining a superior invention. So the expected gross earnings from the second prize should exceed those of the third by precisely the incremental cost necessary to advance the firm from being the expected winner of the third prize to winner of the second.

Ricardian rent theory teaches us that such a differential rent arrangement should be consistent with efficiency in allocation of resources among activities that are expected to produce heterogeneous but substitute innovations. Indeed, that is what the writings of Chung Yi Tse (1996) indicate more formally for a rather more restricted set of circumstances. Clearly, these arguments are fully valid if entry into the innovation race faces no barriers. We will see later that the need to sink costs in an innovation process does constitute an entry barrier that may sometimes be substantial. In that case, however, the problem for economic efficiency is attributable to the entry barriers, not to the innovation races that occur in free-market economies.

CHAPTER 3

Oligopolistic Rivalry and Routinization to Reduce Uncertainty

[The entrepreneur's innovative] function is already losing importance and is bound to lose it at an accelerating rate. . . . For . . . innovation itself is being reduced to routine. Technological progress is increasingly becoming the work of trained specialists who turn out what is required to make it work in predictable ways.

—Schumpeter, 1942, p. 132

Invention was once . . . simply a nonroutine economic activity, though an economic activity nonetheless. Increasingly, it has become a full-time, continuing activity of business enterprise, with a routine of its own.

—Schmookler, 1966, p. 208

This chapter discusses the transformation of the innovation process in response to competitive pressures, a transformation that has changed a major portion of the activity from an entrepreneurial to a managerial affair.[1] It offers some evidence that firms have increasingly taken over the process of technical change, transforming it from a fitful and uncertain discovery process into something closer to a routine internal matter governed by the bureaucratic and managerial procedures that also control many of the other activities of the large corporation. This is yet another consequence of the role of innovation as one of the primary weapons of competition among the oligopolistic rivals in modern high-tech industries.

1. As noted in chapter 1, in this book the term "innovation" will be used to mean the recognition of an economically promising opportunity for change and the carrying out of whatever steps are necessary to implement that change. Thus, the term is used in an inclusive sense, to encompass all the pertinent activities—the processes of invention and of successive improvement before introduction, as well as the act of introduction itself.

PRESSURES OF OLIGOPOLISTIC COMPETITION, PROFITS, AND THE ROUTINIZATION OF INNOVATION

One of the consequences, as well as a cause, of routinization of the innovation process is a change in the character of its expected profits. This is a two-way relationship: the profit-earning mechanism drives firms toward routinization of the innovation process, and routinization, in turn, tends to limit the resulting profits.

The engine of growth in Schumpeter's earlier model is the extraordinary profit that innovation promises to the lone entrepreneur. But in the many industries that are composed of a multiplicity of rival and actively innovating firms, a stream of viable innovations may not bring positive economic profits to an enterprise. Rather, as I will argue in this chapter, the firm will tend to expect to earn no more on its innovation outlays than it does on its investment in plant and equipment, for example. If entry into innovative activity is absolutely free, then, ex ante, the representative firm must expect no more than the rate of profit currently earned in other competitive industries from its routine inventive/innovative activity, no matter how rapid the rate of technological progress it is able to achieve. In a world in which markets with innovating oligopolies are effectively competitive, in seeking to ensure survival every enterprise will be forced to spend the profit-maximizing amount on innovation. But the competition of other innovating oligopolists means that, absent some extraordinary talent or other superior inputs, it cannot expect any positive economic profit. Routinized innovation, in such circumstances, promises no more profit than similarly routinized outlays on machinery or marketing. Even the expected returns to any unusual and continued innovative success must normally be attributable to superior personnel or other superior inputs, and it must be anticipated that these rewards will go to the suppliers of those inputs as rents, rather than yielding economic profits to the firm.[2]

I will suggest later that the nature of the innovation process may require some modification of this conclusion because the process itself can impede entry and exit to some degree. Nevertheless, reality offers significant examples (see below) consistent with the expectation that expenditures on inno-

2. This observation that under competitive conditions the expected profits of routine innovation can be expected to be zero has been made by several of the writers who deal with endogenous innovation. Thus, see Romer (1990, p. 873) and Grossman and Helpman (1994, p. 36).

vation will yield no more than normal profits, a picture clearly different from that painted by the Schumpeterian model.

Of course, zero *expectable* profit does not mean that every firm will end up with zero economic profit ex post. Obviously, some firms will be more successful than the average in their innovations, and others less successful, with corresponding effects on their profits. So the enterprise will sometimes turn out, ex post, to have earned considerably more than zero profit, if luck or skill have made its innovative performance superior to that of its competitors. But it also cannot rule out the possibility that those rivals will prove to be the more successful innovators, with serious and perhaps even disastrous consequences for itself.

This variance in outcomes is an important part of the story—it is a significant component of the mechanism that drives the modern corporation. The securities market often is highly responsive to the firm's performance in the introduction of novel processes and products. The price of the firm's stock is likely to suffer if anticipations are disappointed because a new product either does not match expectations or fails to appear on schedule. The financial pages of newspapers are full of such stories, particularly reports on expected new models of computer hardware and software. All of this indicates the sort of market pressures that force firms to systematize and routinize their expenditures on innovation.

Consequently, in a number of industries in which rapid innovation is widespread and significant, many managements are driven to conclude that they cannot afford to leave their innovations to chance. They simply cannot risk reliance on the fortuitous appearance of new ideas, often contributed unpredictably by outside sources, and as likely to be offered to other enterprises as to themselves. These firms feel forced to incorporate the generation of new techniques and new or improved products as a critical part of their day-to-day, routine operations. It is built into the company's organization and budgeted like any other activity. Specialized personnel are assigned to this task and are provided with costly facilities. Although this may not remove the uncertainty from any one of the innovation-development projects, it increases the likelihood that *some* successful innovations will emerge at reasonably regular intervals. For example, each large pharmaceutical manufacturer is constantly testing a multiplicity of new medicines, knowing that most of them will be failures but fairly confident that a few will succeed.

Thus, routinization is one major means by which these firms reduce the risks they face in their innovation rivalry. There are (at least) two other ways that these oligopolies keep these risks within bounds. First, as was argued in chapter 1 (and will be explored more fully in chapter 4), through the process of oligopolistic competition, in which investment in innovation takes on the character of an arms race, firms often settle down to an equilibrium that can endure for some time. In such an equilibrium the competing enterprises hold the line on their innovation expenditure, in the expectation that their rivals will do the same. So the overall research budgets in pharmaceuticals, computers, consumer electronics, and many other fields are usually fairly profitable, at least in the short run. This equilibrium is reinforced by the threat that, if one of the competitors "raises the ante" by a substantial increase in R&D outlays, the others will make that move unprofitable by matching the spending rise. Nevertheless, from time to time such an equilibrium tends to break down, as one of the rival firms encounters an irresistible innovation opportunity that requires significant enhancement of its spending, or the entry of a new rival—perhaps a small firm with a big idea—upsets the equilibrium balance. Second, as we will see in chapters 6 and 7, the rival innovator firms frequently seek to reduce risk by coordinating their innovative activity through means such as research joint ventures, or engage in technical cooperation through innovation trading or by licensing of proprietary technology even to direct competitors. These steps can clearly reduce the risk of outperformance by rivals and also cut the cost of improvement of technology. It will be argued also that these forms of cooperation among horizontal competitors are generally benign in terms of the public interest. Moreover, these steps help considerably to explain the unprecedented growth record of the free-enterprise economies—thus moving us toward one of the objectives of this book.

However, we should pause here to observe that the innovation that constitutes a quantum leap will probably never become the predictable product of routine R&D, but may typically have to come from the offbeat efforts of the unpredictable, imaginative entrepreneur, independent and unorthodox—in short, the entrepreneur of legend. Yet if it is true, as knowledgeable observers have concluded (see, e.g., Rosenberg, 1982, pp. 52–70), that the social benefits contributed by the initial innovations are typically smaller than those provided by the accumulation of subsequent incremental improvements,[3] many of them not particularly exciting individually, then it may fol-

3. The case of the computer is suggestive. We need only compare the cost and the capacity of the earliest computers with those of today, which are, arguably, attributable to incremental improvements. For example, the share of current number of calculations per second contributed by the incremental improvements must surely exceed 99 percent of the total.

low that the public's greatest debt in this domain is to the dogged manager of R&D activities, rather than to the inspired entrepreneur.

EVIDENCE ON THE MAGNITUDE OF ROUTINIZED INNOVATION EFFORT

The data appear to confirm that much of the economy's innovation activity has become yet another humdrum activity of the firm. A number of observers, following Schumpeter's recognition of the phenomenon in 1942 (1947, chapter XII), have drawn attention to the growing share of the economy's innovations that flow in a routine manner from ongoing operations of the corporation. Even as early as 1953, according to Jacob Schmookler (1957), some 60 percent of the patents granted in the United States derived from business firms, with the remaining approximately 40 percent contributed by independent inventors. Of the business-derived patents, some two-thirds were contributed by firms' R&D personnel, and the bulk of the remaining third by supervisors, engineers, and scientists in the operating end of industry (for more recent evidence, see Griliches, 1989, pp. 291–330).

Thus, corporate R&D has taken over a substantial portion of the field and has transformed it into a bureaucratized activity. Of course, it has not altogether preempted the work of the independent inventor, which still accounts for many of the most spectacular and revolutionary recent innovations (this will be discussed in the following chapter). But leading economic historians have concluded from their evidence that much of the U.S. economy's productivity growth is attributable not only to those dramatic breakthroughs, but perhaps even more to the accumulation of small improvements and minor technical modifications of preexisting products and processes (see, e.g., Rosenberg, 1982, pp. 62–70). This sort of improvement is most typically provided by corporate R&D activities. It follows that an economy's routine R&D investment probably contributes very materially to its economic welfare. Certainly, the resources devoted to this activity are substantial and have risen considerably. Industry funding of R&D in the United States (in constant 1992 dollars) nearly quadrupled between 1970 and 1998 (increasing from about $34 billion to nearly $133 billion). This entailed a remarkable average real rate of increase of 4.8 percent per year over this period of more than a quarter century. Nearly 70 percent of the United States' R&D was paid for by private firms in 1998, and industry accounted for an even larger share of R&D performance—close to 75 percent in 1998 (National Science Board, 2000).

Whereas, in the past, price may have been a primary instrument in the rivalry of business firms, casual observation suggests that, in major sectors of U.S. industry, innovation has increasingly grown in relative importance as an instrument used by firms to battle their competitors. In all of the economy's "high-tech" industries this appears to be true, and the relationship probably spills over to many others. It is reported that in 1997 firms in the computer and data-processing services sector spent over 13 percent of their total revenues on R&D, while for drugs and medicines the figure was 10.5 percent, and for office, computing, and accounting machines over 9 percent was devoted to this purpose. Substantial shares of revenues were also devoted to this purpose in firms that manufactured optical and photographic equipment, communications equipment, electronic components, and several others (National Science Board, 2000, p. 2–28).

Yet one must not exaggerate the pervasiveness of dependence upon innovation as a primary tool of competition. There is strong evidence that the bulk of innovation is contributed by a few industries—the economy's "high-tech" industries—and in a very small number of countries: "Of the $500 billion [at purchasing power parity exchange rates] in estimated 1997 R&D expenditures for the 27 OECD countries, 85 percent is expended in just 7 countries. . . . The United States accounts for roughly 43 percent of the OECD members' combined investments. . . . Not only did the United States spend more money on R&D activities in 1997 than any other country, it also spent as much by itself as the rest of the G-7 countries—Canada, France, Germany, Italy, Japan, and the United Kingdom—combined" (National Science Board, 2000, pp. 2-40–2-41). It must, however, not be concluded that the significance of our analysis is reduced by the limited number of industries and countries to which the scenario described in this chapter applies fully. For it is precisely in these arenas that one finds the main engine of growth of the entire economy.

CORPORATE PROCEDURES IN ROUTINIZED INNOVATION

A considerable degree of routinization is now standard in a wide variety of firms, most notably in telecommunications, computer manufacturing, and pharmaceuticals. But it is also true in many other industries, all of which devote a substantial staff and facilities largely or exclusively to the creation of new products and processes. The control of such facilities is normally in the hands of managers rather than entrepreneurs, and many of these undertakings are subjected to complex bureaucratic controls that discourage free-swinging and heterodox approaches to the task. This is not the realm of the unexpected, of the unrestricted exercise of imagination and boldness that is the essence of entrepreneurship. It is, rather, the domain of memorandums, rigid cost controls, and standardized procedures, which are the hallmark of trained management.

Management typically controls the firm's R&D activities with the help of the budgeting process. The R&D division of the company must compete with the other branches of the firm for its funding. Recognizing that an increase in expenditure on research can reduce the funding available for marketing or plant and equipment, the people who conduct these vital activities of the firms must regularly make their case for financing to those in control of the budget process. Thus, as one report characterizes the procedure, "In the typical company the purpose of [new product] planning is for the business manager to get financial approval from the company's senior management team. The business manager presents his case to the senior management and if approved, he is then on the spot to achieve the plan."[4]

But not only does management control the magnitude of the firm's R&D activity, it often gets involved in its details. After receiving reports on the innovations currently to be expected from the R&D division of the firm, management may decide, in the normal course of its operations, which of these ideas are sufficiently promising to merit further development outlays and, ultimately, which should be introduced to the market, as well as when and how this should be done (see, e.g., Scherer, 1980, pp. 408–10).

Frequently, the research division is even told what the firm needs most urgently to have invented; that is, a menu of prospective inventions is preassigned to the R&D division. This is not a new development. The story of James Watt and the steam engine provides a good illustration. Until 1781 the engine had been used, virtually exclusively, to pump water out of mines. However, on one of his marketing trips, Watt's entrepreneur partner, Matthew Boulton, became convinced that the mine-pumping market was approaching saturation. He then decided that milling and other such activities constituted a limitless opportunity for sales of the engine: "I think that mills . . . present a field that is boundless and that will be more permanent than these transient mines" (Boulton to Watts, 7 December 1782). The difficulty was that up until then the engine had been used only to provide the

4. Gary Reiner, "It Takes Planning to Put Plans into Action," *New York Times*, 12 March 1989, section 3, p. 3.

up and down motion needed for a pump, whereas the contemplated new applications required rotary operation. One method for translation of vertical into rotary motion, the crank, had been known for centuries, but two years earlier (!) one James Pickard had taken out a patent that barred its use. Consequently, Boulton urged Watt to invent a substitute for the crank. Watt succeeded in producing and patenting a number of such devices. One of them, the sun and planet gear, was employed thereafter in the bulk of the Boulton and Watt engines, presumably including those that powered Fulton's steamboat and the early rail locomotives (see Dickinson, 1937, pp. 112–16).

Managerial assignment of invention goals is now not uncommon. Firms regularly indicate to their R&D branches what inventions are needed most urgently. And this decision, too, has sometimes been routinized to a remarkable degree. At Eastman Kodak, for example, the research task for the firm's film research laboratory has been directed by a standardized process. Each year the company collects a sample of photographs taken by both professional and amateur photographers (with permission of the owners of the photos). Computers are used to simulate systematic qualitative variations in prints of these photographs (producing ranges of contrast, relative sharpness of foreground and background, brightness and balance of colors, and so on). The computer turns out these "pseudo-photographs," which the naked eye cannot distinguish from real camera products, and which embody the contemplated ranges in picture quality—ranges that at that time no one knows how to attain by photographic means. Consumer and professional photographer panels are then used to decide which of the computer-generated pseudo-photographs promise to be most salable, and the company laboratories are then assigned the task of inventing a film that will automatically yield the desired modifications of reality.

Apparently, engineers are trained systematically to seek the innovation assignments that most urgently need to be carried out. In an illuminating book by Henry Petroski (1996), a member of the faculty at Duke University, this is demonstrated by a series of striking examples, including the evolution of common items such as the paper clip, the zipper, and the beverage can. The title of the book, *Invention by Design,* indicates the nature of the story. It describes, for example, how problems of weight and transport costs, the risk of cuts during opening of cans, the need to strengthen containers of liquid under pressure, and the disposal problems caused by "pop-top" openers successively provided agenda for research in the beverage container industry. In short, this critical step in routinized innovation, the process of determining what innovative research is next to be carried out, has itself become a topic for illuminating academic research and for engineers.

THE RELEVANCE OF SUNK COSTS FOR THE FIRM'S DECISIONS UNDER ROUTINIZATION

It has already been argued in this chapter that when innovation becomes routine the conclusion that it is usually a source of economic profits must be revised. But it does not follow that in the oligopolistic markets with which we are concerned the profits from routinized innovation can always be expected to tend to zero. A major reason is the role of sunk innovation cost, and the way in which it differs under routine and nonroutine innovation.

When innovation is an irregular process with inventions apparently (though probably not really) becoming available by happenstance at random intervals, so far as the invention's proprietor is concerned much of the cost of any particular innovation is a sunk outlay of the past, a cost that therefore should be ignored in rational current decision-making. This is particularly clear when a firm's activities are based largely on a single invention, or where an entrepreneur devotes a lifetime of effort to one innovation. The investment in such a project is clearly a sunk outlay, a piece of ancient history, whose magnitude should, in a rational decision process, affect neither prices nor marketing decisions on the day the innovation is brought to market.

Matters are radically different when the firm, routinely and at regular intervals, adopts an R&D budget. In this case, the magnitudes of the apparently sunk costs should and do affect the outcome of the decision process. The standard conclusion in the economics literature that rational decision makers should ignore sunk costs because "bygones are bygones," and are not subject to retrospective modification by current acts, is quite right if interpreted with care. But prospectively sunk costs do matter before they are incurred; indeed, they obviously can make an enormous difference.

Somewhat more relevant to the current discussion is the important role of costs sunk in the past if they give decision makers information about costs they will consider sinking in the future. For example, a government that expropriates foreign investments on the assumption that it is no longer possible for their proprietors to withdraw them, is very likely to find those foreigners much more reluctant to sink capital in that country thereafter. The experience of those who have undertaken sunk investments in the past is particularly important for a continuing activity that requires such outlays at regular intervals. There, sunk costs and the returns they have yielded clearly do matter for current and future decisions, and cannot be left out of account in a rational decision process.

For our discussion, the crucial difference between sunk costs that are irrelevant and those that are not corresponds, roughly, to the distinction between inventions more or less fortuitously produced and the inventions yielded by a routine and continuing process. Where an act of invention is a unique event, the past outlays of effort and capital it required become irrelevant bits of past history once the product reaches the market. All that matters for current decisions in a financially viable firm that supplies such an innovation is the revenues that it can generate on the market, whether or not previous expenditures are covered by them.[5]

The situation is clearly very different if the innovation process and the cost-sinking it entails are continuous. Here, tomorrow's sunk costs are still entirely variable today, and the fate of sunk outlays of the past is likely to affect any rational decision on the resources to be devoted to innovation in the future. This, in turn, will presumably affect the number of the innovations that can be expected to emerge from the firm's R&D activities as well as the significance of the typical innovation. And the continuing need for resources to flow into sunk R&D investment means that success, either private or social, of what we may think of as the innovation assembly-line must be judged by a comparison of *all* the costs, including the sunk costs, to the yields of the activity. It will certainly not always be true that the most revolutionary innovations must be deemed the most successful. Indeed, because the sometimes heavy costs of the ongoing innovation process may well offset much, if not all, of the resulting gain, the most innovative firm will not necessarily be the one that is most profitable.

5. If the returns are insufficient to cover the debts incurred through the sunk outlays of the past, it will, of course, matter to the proprietors of the innovating firm, who may face bankruptcy. However, this still may not matter to society, since the firm's failure may merely transfer the assets to other hands. The histories of independent inventors and the entrepreneurs who tried to bring the products of their ideas to market are full of such cases—of firms that suffered insolvency and of successor entrepreneurs who took over the rights to the innovations at distress-sale prices. But the irrelevance of the sunk costs means that matters can, and often do, turn out the other way, and those involved may reap returns far exceeding the funds they have laid out on the enterprise. The point is that the magnitude of the initial outlay is largely irrelevant for the future success of such an undertaking.

CHAPTER 3

SUNK COSTS AND THE POSSIBILITY OF NONZERO EXPECTED PROFITS UNDER ROUTINE INNOVATION

Routinization makes a difference for the profitability of outlays on technical change, as we have just seen. There is some tendency under the regime of routinization for economic profits to be driven toward zero. However, where the sunk costs of the innovation process are significant, these constitute a barrier to entry that restores the possibility of positive profits for the affected industry as a whole, and not just for its most successful innovators.

As already noted, when the firm's research and development activities become as routine as its warehousing or its marketing, one expects from standard analysis that anything close to absolute freedom of entry (perfect contestability) will drive the firm's *expected* economic profits toward zero. There seems to be nothing special about the use of innovation as an instrument of competition that endows it with a capacity greater than that of any other routine activity of the firm to generate economic profits. Market pressures should force every firm to select something close to the profit-maximizing level of investment in innovation, but entry should reduce prices or raise input costs sufficiently to squeeze out any profits. This is certainly the impression of members of top managements in high-tech firms with whom I have discussed these issues over the years. They recognize that there are noted examples of innovations that were spectacularly successful and profitable. Nevertheless, they report that their R&D investments are usually expected to yield little or nothing more than what economists would call "normal competitive profits," of course after allowance for a suitable risk premium.[6]

We will see next why this story may not be quite right, as we delve further into the issue of sunk costs. Some industries may earn positive economic profits from their investment in innovation because of a second attribute of

6. There is anecdotal evidence, and more, supporting the contention that, contrary to widespread impression, innovative industries overall often earn no extraordinary profits. From the Federal Reserve Bank of Boston's Regional Review (1996, p. 14): "'The computer industry hasn't made a dime. . . Intel and Microsoft make money, but look at all the people who are losing money all the world over. It is doubtful the industry has yet broken even,' said Peter Drucker in a recent interview . . . but is it true? Paul Gompers of the Harvard Business School and Alon Brav of the University of Chicago . . . looked at companies that went public from 1975 to 1992, most of which were high-tech firms, and found their rate of return to be about average [i.e., zero economic profit], once they adjusted for risk and company size." Bronwyn Hall's (1993) study has also produced supporting results. She reports that "the effect of R&D investment on the rate [of return] used by the stock market to discount the firm's dividends was roughly the same as that of ordinary investment" (p. 292).

sunk costs—their role as barriers to entry that can limit competition. Here it is important to distinguish between the degree of competition in the final product market and that in innovative activity. In many oligopoly industries, entry into production may be extremely difficult because the sunk investments that are required may be very substantial. Yet, at the same time, it may require very little capital to embark on the process of seeking a better mousetrap, intended for production by that industry. The computer industry provides clear examples of how much easier it can be to enter a field engaged in (risky) innovative activity per se than to enter the oligopolistic manufacturing arenas that make use of the innovations. In the following discussion, it is ease of entry into innovation activity rather than production that will be our focus.

Profitability of an industry is substantially affected by the magnitude of its sunk costs because, as has been argued in the literature on contestable markets, the need to sink costs constitutes the purest form of barrier to exit and entry. Sunk costs are all but synonymous with costliness of exit, for they mean that the firm that incurs them cannot simply walk away with its financial investment intact. And costliness of exit is, in turn, tantamount to riskiness of entry. Where exit is difficult, entry must incur a commensurate risk cost, and entrants will not be attracted unless expected profits are sufficient to cover that additional cost. More than that, the need to incur sunk costs makes the entrant vulnerable to strategic countermeasures by the incumbents, in the manner described by game-theoretic models, and that possibility must clearly exacerbate the risks of entry, with little corresponding risk of strategic retaliation borne by the incumbent.

Where costs sunk in the innovation process are fairly minor, entry (actual or threatened) will indeed force the average return to innovation in the industry to approximately zero. A firm that lags behind its rivals in innovation in its products or processes can be expected to suffer losses from the innovation race. Even a firm that is in the vanguard may find that its supercompetitive profits are very transitory because they attract ambitious entrants.

But if entry is not quite so free because the sunk costs of the innovation process are substantial, the most successful firm can hold out against either drastic price cuts or any increased spending on product quality that would erode its profits. The prices and costs that yield a substantial surplus to the most successful innovator can, however, permit at least the closest of the runners-up to operate profitably, though their profits will normally be more modest. These profits and their difference from one firm to another will then be explainable by the Ricardian rent model, with rewards to the different supermarginal innovations corresponding to differences in the market values of their degree of superiority over the marginal innovation. Any economic profits that accrue to the incumbents in the industry will, then, be protected from entry so long as they do not exceed the minimum amount needed to attract new firms into the field, given the risks entailed in any required sunk investment. For this reason, the zero expected profit conclusion is considerably weakened.

Still, casual observation suggests that there is a good deal of truth to that story, as we have seen. The most extreme cases of routine and predictable innovation—the annual introduction of new automobile models or new spring clothing fashions—do not seem to promise vast economic profits to the participants as a group. This seems even more so for the continuing innovation wars that characterize the computer industry. At the very least, such impressionistic evidence serves as a warning against easy acceptance of the earlier Schumpeterian view that investment in innovation is a reliable source of economic profits.

CHAPTER 4

Oligopolistic Rivalry and Routine Innovation Spending: Theory of the Engine of Unprecedented Capitalist Growth

competition of the kind we now have in mind acts not only when in being but also when it is merely an ever-present threat. It disciplines before it attacks.

—Schumpeter, 1947, p. 85

In this chapter we come to what, in my view, is the main influence explaining why the growth performance of the capitalist economy continues to be so different from that of all other economic forms. Using tools not much beyond the elementary textbook level, I will focus on a feature of free competitive markets to which I ascribe much of the extraordinary growth of the market economies. That feature is the process by which oligopolistic competition determines the level of innovation expenditure and its trajectory over time. That is, we turn now to the free-market economy's *production* of innovation. I argue that this process is basically analogous to an arms race among mutually suspicious nations, in which each feels it necessary to be second to none in the weapons it has at its disposal. In more traditional terms, the appropriate model involves a kinked profit curve in profit–R&D spending space that keeps the individual firm's R&D spending up to industry norms. The kink point here is constrained by the equivalent of a ratchet mechanism, which permits the spending norm to increase occasionally, but makes it difficult for firms to cut back their R&D outlays. This competitive arms race in innovation spending can also be described by what has been called (after Lewis Carroll) a "Red Queen game" (see Khalil, 1997), in which it is necessary to run as rapidly as possible in order just to stand still.

A second purpose of this chapter is to begin to show how easily routine production of innovation can be incorporated into the basic theory of microeconomics, even at the elementary-textbook level, which is the subject of part II of this book. We will see that elementary and standard treatment using only partial equilibrium methods yields substantive conclusions about the determination of the amount that a firm will invest in the innovation process.

The discussion uses a model of an oligopolistic industry, in which, as already suggested, most routinized innovation takes place. The model here takes no account of risk and uncertainty. Of course, the R&D devoted to any particular project—to the creation of any special new product or process—involves great uncertainties about cost, the time that will be required, or even whether anything useful at all will emerge. But here I will assume that the R&D activity of any firm with which we are concerned is on a scale sufficiently large to include a considerable number of such projects. Then, to simplify the discussion, one can assume that something like a law of large numbers applies, and that the overall value of the innovations that will emerge from the firm's R&D is moderately predictable, even if that of any individual R&D undertaking is not.[1]

The heart of the story is the key role of oligopolistic competition in the process of free-market growth. Thus, it is my contention that one of the primary reasons for the failure of any other economic arrangement even to approximate the capitalist growth record for any considerable period is the absence of oligopolistic rivalry in those other economies. I need only add a word of explanation for the emphasis on oligopoly, with its small number of large competing firms, rather than any other market form. The answer, whether or not it is fully convincing, is straightforward. Monopoly will not do because, by definition, it is immune, or largely immune, from competition, and that can materially weaken its incentive to invest in innovation.[2] At the other extreme, the small firms that inhabit a world of near-perfect

1. The applicability of the law of large numbers here must not be exaggerated. The law would apply fully only if the chance of success of one R&D project does not depend on the success of others. Where they are interdependent, failure in one may sink many others, making innovations something nearer to a "house of cards" activity.

2. However, one should note that only monopolies, notably the old AT&T with its Bell Laboratories, seem to be in a position to carry out substantial basic research, particularly if they are regulated and regulation permits them to recoup their research outlays. Another part of the explanation lies in the heavier spillovers that basic research generates, discouraging such activity by competitive firms, which fear that too much of the benefit will go to competitors. I also recognize that innovations are often contributed by small firms (see the next chapter) but, except when it is carried out by trade associations, it is rarely routinized. Here, Schumpeter's views on the role of large firms in innovation should also be recognized.

competition or even monopolistic competition tend to lack the resources, they do not have the stimulation of observed interdependence with their rivals (there is no observable "race" among them), and the spillover problem may well prove particularly severe in such an environment. Almost by definition, it is only in oligopoly, where a few large (often giant) firms dominate a particular market, that competitive races among established firms can occur, and only in oligopoly that rivals observe and keep track of one another's behavior.[3] Those are the reasons, supported by extensive consulting experience with such firms, for my focus on this particular market form. Thus, almost all of the innovative rivalry we will be discussing occurs in the economy's oligopoly industries. So, paradoxically, it is an economy's oligopolies, which are often particularly suspect as a threat to the public interest, that may well prove to be the main industrial contributors to growth and standards of living.

TEMPORARY EQUILIBRIUM IN AN (INNOVATION) ARMS RACE

If it is true that in a number of high-tech industries innovation is the prime weapon of competition, a simple story emerges. The profit-maximizing firm will adopt the quantity of R&D expenditure at which expected marginal profit yield is zero. But this magnitude will depend on the behavior of the other firms in the industry. A firm that falls behind in its innovations for a substantial period of time can expect considerable erosion of its market either because its product is considered inferior by customers or because its costs, and therefore its prices, are higher than those offered by rivals for products of comparable quality. Consequently, no firm will in the long run dare to underspend its competitors systematically.[4] Thus, one can expect an industry norm to emerge, with firms that engage in substantial R&D outlays generally mak-

3. And oligopolistic industries are important for the economy not only because of their role in innovation. In addition, they probably constitute the largest share of U.S. output, and the revenues of the largest oligopoly firms outstrip the gross domestic products of entire economies such as Denmark and Norway.

4. Witnesses in patent litigation lawsuits or antitrust cases involving competing technology repeatedly testify (and internal firm documents confirm) that the firms try avidly to keep track of the innovative activities of their rivals in making their own plans. The market-leader firm's management is often concerned about the catch-up plans of its nearest rival, and that rival measures its performance and its reputation in terms of quality of technology against that of the market leader. I offer no specific citations because of court-imposed confidentiality rules.

ing sure that their R&D expenditures are up to that norm.[5] That norm will constitute an equilibrium in the arms race, but one that is only temporary—a truce, not a full end to hostilities.[6]

Still, firms will be tempted to exceed the equilibrium norm, and such enhanced spending would very likely be profitable if rivals could be counted upon to ignore the challenge and keep to their previous levels of expenditure. For that would enable our spoiler firm—the firm that upsets the tacit arrangement under which no player previously violated the industry spending norm—to outperform its rivals in terms of price and/or product quality and take customers away from them. However, each firm is aware that such passive reaction cannot be expected from competitors. Rather, the rivals are likely to respond by matching any spoiler's increased rate of investment. The likely consequence of the spoiler's initiative, then, is that the industry will end up with a new and higher R&D investment norm, but with none of the firms having gained any (relative) advantage over its competitors.

Total profits cannot be expected to be the same as they were before, once the spoiler firm has caused a general increase in R&D investment in the industry. Very plausibly, as in the case of rivalrous inflation of an industry's advertising, the industry's firms, including the spoiler, may well end up with less profit than before. This does not mean that increases in R&D expenditure will never occur. Rather, it implies that they will take place when the R&D effort of some firm has provided a highly promising breakthrough, calling for an increase in investment outlay whose profit prospects are unusually bright.

The net result of this scenario is a time trajectory characterized by long periods of fairly steady R&D spending, with each firm in temporary equilibrium, keeping up with the industry norm. Then, when breakthroughs occur, the norm will shift to the right and industry expenditure will remain at this higher level until the next stochastic shock stimulates further movement. So

5. Recall Schumpeter's characterization of the role of competition: "in capitalist reality as distinguished from its textbook picture . . . [the] kind of competition which counts [is] the competition from the new commodity, the new technology . . . competition which strikes not at the margins of the profits and the outputs of the existing firms but at their foundations and their very lives" (1947, p. 84). Or, as Nelson puts it, "given that its rivals are induced . . . to invest in R&D a firm may have no choice but to do likewise" (1996, p. 52).

6. The nature of this "norm" is deliberately kept vague here, because in practice firms follow one another's spending practices only roughly and approximately. This is partly because no two firms are perfectly alike, nor are the attitudes of their managements. Partly it is so because firms may be imperfectly informed about the R&D spending of their rivals. The norms may be vaguely based on sales, assets, market shares, or other criteria, or on a combination of these.

the arms-race model of R&D spending leads to a kink—a sharp change in pattern—in its profit relationship and a ratchet in its innovation spending levels. This may well be a key feature of the free-market economy that helps substantially to account for its growth record.

GRAPHICS OF THE ARMS-RACE MODEL OF INNOVATION PRODUCTION

We can make the technological scenario more explicit with the help of a microeconomic model explicitly based on Paul Sweezy's kinked demand curve. That model is used to explain why prices apparently tend to "stick" in oligopoly markets. The underlying mechanism is an asymmetry in the firm's expectations about its competitors. The firm hesitates to lower its price for fear that its rivals will match the price cut, so that the firm will end up with a few new customers but dramatically reduced revenues. On the other hand, it fears that, if it increases its price, its rivals will *not* follow suit, so that it will be left all by itself with an overpriced product. Thus, such a firm normally will set its price at the industry level, no more and no less, and leave it there unless the competitive situation changes drastically.

The innovation story is similar. Consider an industry with, say, five firms of roughly equal size. Company X sees that each of the other firms spends about $20 million a year on R&D. Company X will not dare to spend much less than $20 million on its own R&D for fear of falling behind in salability of its product. On the other hand, Company X sees little point in raising the ante to, say, $30 million because it knows that if it does so the others can be expected to follow suit.

The story is described graphically in figure 4.1, which shows a marginal cost (MC) curve and two marginal revenue (MR) curves, *MRJ* and *HMR,* all as functions of the amount of R&D spending by Company X. For simplicity, the curves are drawn as straight lines. The MR curves reflect the two possible competitor responses. If each time Company X expands its spending its rivals do the same, the MR resulting from X's enhanced R&D will be quite low (line *HMR*), because Company X will fail to pull ahead of its rivals. On the other hand, if competitors let X increase its R&D spending *without increasing their own,* then X can expect its increased product quality to put it well ahead of the others, and so its MR from R&D spending will be relatively high (line *MRJ*).

In figure 4.1, Company X expects mixed reactions from its competitors. They will follow its lead when it increases its R&D, but they will not follow any decreases. The result will be the Z-shaped piecewise-linear locus, *SCAMR,*

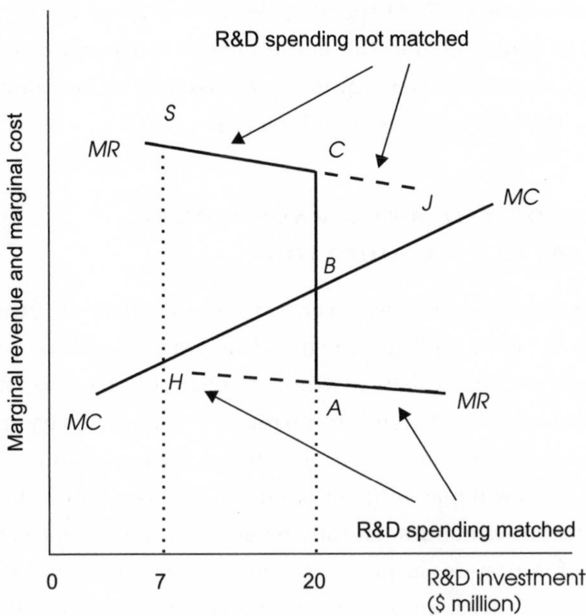

FIGURE 4.1
Sticky R&D Investment at the Industry Norm

with a vertical break between points *A* and *C* at the current level of R&D investment ($20 million in the example). The explanation is straightforward. If each firm in the industry spends $20 million a year and Company X were suddenly to decrease R&D spending—say, to $7 million per year—it has good reason to fear that competitors would not match that cut. With competitors still spending $20 million, Company X can expect to lose a good deal of revenue, and find itself moving backward along the "not matched" MR curve *MRJ* to point *S*. However, if Company X decides to increase its R&D spending *above* $20 million, it will move along the low "matched" MR curve (*HMR*). For its rivals will feel threatened and will match the increase.

But that is not the end of the story. All five firms in the industry will continue to invest the same amount until one of them enjoys a research breakthrough leading to a very promising new product (as happens from time to time, particularly in high-tech industries). That fortunate firm will then expand its investment in the breakthrough product, because doing so will pay off even if the other firms in the industry match the increase. The piecewise-linear MR curve for the breakthrough firm will shift upward and rightward (figure 4.2) from *MRBMR* to *MR′B′MR′*, and its *MC* = *MR* point, *B′*, will move

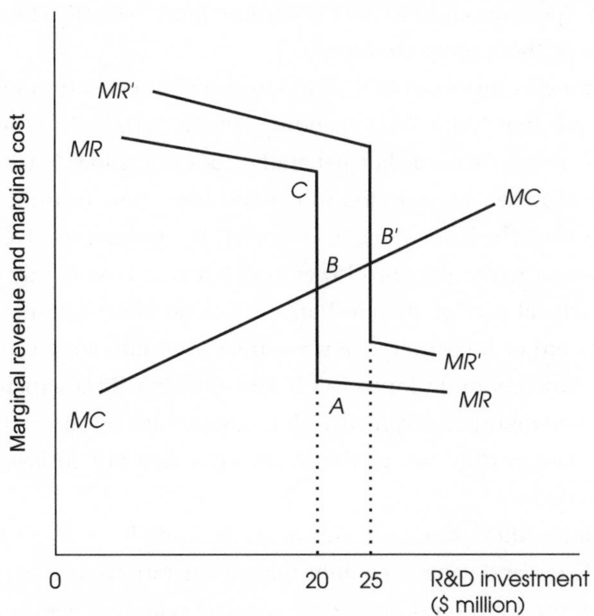

FIGURE 4.2
Shift in the Industry's R&D Investment Norm

to the right, to an amount larger than $20 million ($25 million in the graph). Other companies in the industry will feel forced to follow. So now the industry norm will no longer be a $20 million investment per year, but will instead be $25 million per firm. No firm will dare to drop back to the old level, fearing that no other company will follow such a retrenchment move. Again, the common story of armaments races among countries parallels the story of innovation battles among firms.

In game-theoretic terms, the arms race that has just been described can be interpreted either as a prisoners' dilemma game, or as a Red Queen paradox. The payoff matrix is obvious. It entails the highest payoff to both (all) parties if they can conclude an effective disarmament treaty, a collusive arrangement in which both agree to keep expenditure on R&D to a minimum. However, as in the story of so many cartels, we can expect little trust among the parties because each knows that if one of them can successfully conceal a massive investment in R&D it will perhaps steal a march at their expense, earning huge profits while the others' returns are low or even negative. Moreover, the antitrust institutions make direct communication difficult. Consequently, the firms all end up spending heavily on the innovation process, with a moderate profit—perhaps close to zero economic profit—to all. The payoff matrix is, of course, thoroughly familiar.

The process just described is, in effect, equipped with a ratchet. It is an arrangement that holds R&D spending steady, permits it in certain circumstances to move forward, but generally does not allow it to retreat.[7] R&D spending can then be expected to expand from time to time, but once the new level is reached, the ratchet—enforced by the competitive market—prevents a retreat to the previous lower level.[8] It is at least highly plausible that this is a critical part of the mechanism that accounts for the extraordinary growth record of free-enterprise economies and differentiates them from all other known economic forms, with ever-growing R&D expenditure norms leading to ever more rapid growth.[9] It is competitive pressures that force firms to run as fast as they can in the innovation race just to keep up with the others.

The main shortcoming of this analysis, aside from its omission of both strategic issues and general equilibrium considerations, is that it does not explain how the initial industry norm of R&D spending is selected. It merely tells us that, once selected, it will tend to persist, and that, when things change, the moves will generally be toward the right of the previous norm. But this indeterminacy may be a feature of reality rather than a deficiency of the model. It is a consequence of the nature of the issue we are studying, in which there exists a continuum of potential equilibrium levels of expenditure. Any R&D expenditure norm for an industry can become an equilibrium

7. In chapter 14, it will be assumed that these outlays are fixed in nominal terms. This does not affect the argument here, but it does play an important role in the macro growth model in which the cost of R&D can change cyclically.

8. This statement somewhat exaggerates the effectiveness of the ratchets in preventing the economy from ever sliding backward in its expenditure on R&D. After all, even in machinery, ratchets sometimes slip. In R&D investment, firms may, for example, be forced to cut back their R&D expenditure if business is extremely bad; or they can simply make mistakes in planning how much to spend on investment; or they may be discouraged by repeated failures of their research division to come up with salable products. The economy's ratchets are indeed imperfect, but they are there. They cannot completely prevent backsliding in R&D expenditure, but they can be a powerful influence that is effective in resisting such retreats.

9. Jones (1995) has argued that there are sharply diminishing returns to R&D effort, on the basis of data for research employment in the period 1950 to 1988. These apparently expanded more than fivefold while total factor productivity growth was "relatively constant or even declining." However, McGrattan (1998) has disputed this conclusion. She provides longer-term data suggesting that returns to R&D effort do not decline nearly as sharply as Jones implies, if they decline at all. In any event, the argument on R&D spending here does not depend on the outcome of that discussion, but does assume that the marginal return to R&D activity is positive. For studies showing this, see Griliches (1992, p. 45) and Nadiri (1993, p. 11).

if history and its fortuitous circumstances make it so. Oligopoly equilibria and the character of breakthrough innovations that influence their intertemporal trajectory are inherently unpredictable. One cannot expect a theoretical model to be able to determine what in reality is inherently indeterminable.

THREE GROWTH-CREATING PROPERTIES OF INNOVATION

We have just discussed reasons to expect that the market mechanism will force firms to devote at least a steady stream of expenditure to innovative activities. With luck, the resulting R&D effort will be level and will yield a fairly steady flow of innovations. But a steady flow of innovation does not mean that GDP remains constant. Rather, a level flow of innovation can result in steady *growth* of the economy's output.[10] Here we must take note of three critical features of innovation that can, so to speak, magnify the contribution of technical change to the economy's GDP:

1. *The cumulative character of many innovations.* Many innovations do not merely replace older technology and make that technology obsolete; rather, they add to what was previously available, thus constituting a net increase in the economy's store of technical knowledge. Such innovations can be said to entail creative knowledge accumulation rather than creative destruction.
2. *The well-known public-good property of information in general, and of innovation in particular.* Improved technology, once created, need not contribute to the output only of the firm that made the breakthrough. At relatively little additional cost, it can also add to the outputs of other enterprises. Thus, although this public-good property can impede attainment of the optimal amount of innovation expenditure, it also has a beneficial side, constituting an economy of scope in the generation of technological improvements for a multiplicity of firms.
3. *An" accelerator" feature of innovation.* A level stream of innovation usually means that output will be not level but growing. An economy whose R&D produces a level output of one innovation per month, with a given productivity contribution, will obtain a GDP that is higher each month than it was in the previous month. The economy's ability to produce out-

10. Here the word "steady" means "continuing" and is not meant to deny the possibility of diminishing returns.

put will grow constantly even though the flow of innovations that fuels that output growth remains level at one invention per month.[11] This acceleration relationship applies to innovation generally, so that, if the competitive market mechanism described in the previous graphs leads firms to devote a constant level of resources to R&D, we would expect continued growth of GDP to result.

Of course, as noted, the ratchet principle tends to *increase* the expenditure of resources on innovation, not just to leave them level. Our acceleration principle tells us about the effects of this, too, if there are no diminishing returns to R&D innovation productivity (but note the Jones argument described in footnote 9 above). The acceleration relationship indicates that, if the level of R&D spending were to increase just once, for example, and then stay at that new higher level forever, the growth rate of GDP would also move upward. GDP would then grow at a faster rate forever.

All of this reinforces the role of the competitive market mechanism and its stimulation of innovation as a contributor to the extraordinary growth that characterizes the world's free-enterprise economies. But at this point one may well pause to ask whether the analysis does not exaggerate the facts. It tells us that R&D investment norms can be expected to increase from time to time, and that the ratchet serves to resist retreat to the previous lower investment levels. This then implies that the GDP growth rate can be expected to keep rising, and the natural question is whether history is consistent with such a picture. The answer is, in fact, yes, but before we show this, let us be clear that the analysis never asserts that this must continue forever. For example, R&D personnel may find it increasingly difficult to come up with good new ideas, so that, even if more and more is spent on R&D, it is conceivable that, some day, its results will be worth less and less.

But what about the facts? Of course there have been decades during which catastrophes such as wars and depressions have kept GDP from rising or have even reduced it. But ten-year periods are too short for the evaluation of the long-run performance of market economies. We can say that there have now been about six half-centuries since the modern free-market economy made its debut. The first half of the eighteenth century is generally taken to have preceded the birth of the British Industrial Revolution, with GDP per

11. This does not, of course, mean that there is a fixed relationship between R&D spending and rate of growth of the economy's output. All that is assumed here is that a rise in R&D will generally increase growth to some degree relative to what it would have been otherwise, other things being equal.

capita consequently rising more slowly than in the second half. And, during the century as a whole, GDP per capita in Western Europe surely rose a substantial amount, but one that was less than 50 percent.[12] In the nineteenth century we observe a similar pattern, with relatively modest growth even in England until after 1830, and in France, Germany, and the United States until well after that. Thus, growth in the second half of the century was presumably higher than in the first, and in the century as a whole per capita GDP in Western Europe did something between doubling and trebling—far better than the previous century. The twentieth century's growth, too, sped up during its second half and, remarkably, per capita GDP ended up seven or eight times as large as it began.[13]

CONCLUDING COMMENT

This chapter has provided a concrete model that can help us to understand the role of competition among high-tech oligopoly firms in the remarkable growth record of the free-enterprise economies. It is an arms-race model with the addition of the ratchet attribute of innovation investment. The first of these features—the arms-race analogue—can explain the presence of powerful norms for R&D investment in leading oligopoly industries. The ratchet, in turn, implies a propensity of such an industry not to retreat from the current standard for R&D spending, and occasionally to move to a new and higher standard that all major firms in the industry are apt to feel they must match.

Let me emphasize here that the scenario described in this chapter does not stop at the invention portion of the story. The competing oligopolies are obviously not usually content to let promising inventions languish in the companies' research facilities. Indeed, the firms normally have built into their structure the organization and the personnel whose task it is to prepare process inventions for adoption into the company's production processes, to prepare new products for market, and to carry out their introduction. In short, the oligopoly firms routinize not only inventive activity but the entire

12. Indeed, according to Maddison's calculations (2001), this is all per capita GDP rose between 1500 and 1820.

13. There are noted analysts who argue that the true figure was far greater than this. See, for example, the work of William Nordhaus (1997). DeLong (2001) adds: "William Nordhaus brackets the growth of real wages over the past century as somewhere between a 20-fold and a 100-fold increase. Alan Greenspan—Chairman of the Federal Reserve—has [suggested adjustments of the statistics that lead] to an estimate of a thirty-fold increase in material wealth over the past century."

innovation process, thereby ensuring its long-run continuation. As this book maintains, it is the presence of the full innovation process, and not just its invention component, that most directly differentiates the capitalist growth mechanism from that of all other economic arrangements. All this, then, is at least a worthy candidate for the role of the Prince of Denmark in our performance of Hamlet.

CHAPTER 5

Independent Innovation in History: Productive Entrepreneurship and the Rule of Law

he was . . . the entrepreneur extraordinaire, *with all the requisite traits for the role: nerve, persistence, dynamic energy, a talent for propaganda, a capacity for deception, imagination.*

—A description of Ferdinand de Lesseps in McCullough, 1977, p. 53

Interviewer: *"Why do you rob banks, Mr. Sutton [notorious thief of the mid-twentieth century]?"*
Sutton: *"Because that's where the money is."*

It is, as a business proposition, a matter of indifference to the man of large affairs whether the disturbances which his transactions set up in the industrial system help or hinder the system at large, except in so far as he has ulterior strategic ends to serve.

—Veblen, 1904, pp. 29–30

Innovation is a heterogeneous product.

—Baumol's third tautology

So far, we have stressed two features of the capitalist economy that, arguably, contribute to its unequaled growth record. First and, perhaps, most fundamental is the role of innovation as a primary competitive weapon, and the resulting innovation arms race. Second is the routinization of innovation that transforms it from a sequence of fortuitous occurrences into a businesslike activity that can be relied upon and is reasonably predictable. We have yet to deal with two other very relevant attributes of the free-market economy. One of these, to be studied in the next two chapters, is the profit offered by voluntary dissemination of proprietary technology and its licensing as a normal business activity. The other feature, which is the subject of this chapter, is the contribution of the independent innovator—Schumpeter's entrepreneur. In particular, this chapter will discuss the incentive that capitalism provides to entrepreneurs to channel their activities in productive directions, rather than, as in many other forms of economic organization, in directions that contribute little to output growth or even impede it.

Because entrepreneurship is hard even to define and therefore impossible to measure statistically, much of this chapter is based on historical anecdote. Yet a good deal of this historical evidence seems to me to be compelling.[1]

THE REVOLUTIONARY CONTRIBUTIONS OF INNOVATORS OUTSIDE THE ESTABLISHED FIRM

This book's focus on routinized innovation (which is guided by standard business-decision principles) is not meant to imply that nonroutine innovation (which does not emerge from established firms as part of their regular planning of competitive strategy) has become unimportant. The routine character of many innovation processes is helpful to us because it facilitates their incorporation into standard economic models of investment and other parts of microeconomic analysis. More to the point, it is an activity that was, for all practical purposes, never undertaken in any pre-capitalist economy and that patently contributes considerably to growth in the free-market economies. Routinized innovation is, indeed, of great and probably growing significance, as was suggested earlier by the fact that the bulk of U.S. R&D is now channeled through business firms. But innovation stemming from other sources has also been important and certainly continues to be so. Independent innovators continue to play a crucial role. I have already cited Scherer's long list of major technical inventions introduced by entrant firms, which were consequently not subject to the pressures for routinization that one expects in large, established enterprises.

One can even offer the plausible conjecture that most of the really revolutionary new ideas have been, and are likely to continue to be, provided preponderantly by independent innovators. But, as already noted, that is usually only the beginning of the tale. Once a new invention proves successful, the inventors or the associated entrepreneurs often provide the product through new firms that in many cases grow large and themselves specialize in routine

1. As that noted economic historian David Landes once remarked, "One good anecdote is worth more than a number of questionable statistical tables." (This statement was made orally at a conference, and is reproduced here from memory, but with permission.)

innovation. Such subsequent innovation, like most innovations produced by routine processes, is primarily devoted to product improvement, increased reliability, enhanced user-friendliness of products, and the search for new uses for those products. Though these routine innovations tend to be less dramatic than the original and strikingly revolutionary idea, both independent and routinized innovation activities undoubtedly contribute significantly to economic growth, as Rosenberg has emphasized (see, e.g., 1976, p. 66). In this process there is no reason to expect independent inventors or innovators to become obsolete any time in the foreseeable future. It is more plausible that this division of the work of technical progress will continue, with the independent entrepreneur providing many if not most of the more revolutionary and heterodox contributions, while the routine innovation activities of the oligopoly corporations take those contributions and improve and extend them, often well beyond what their capabilities could have been imagined to be.

ON THE SIGNIFICANCE OF THE ENTREPRENEUR

The place of entrepreneurs in the process of growth is well recognized and widely accepted, though their general absence from the theoretical literature is noteworthy. Here, I use the word "entrepreneur" in the Schumpeterian sense to mean the bold and imaginative deviator from established business patterns and practices, who constantly seeks the opportunity to introduce new products and new procedures, to invade new markets, and to create new organizational forms.[2] In short, the entrepreneur is the *independent innovator,* in the broadest sense, meaning that the activities of this individual include, but go considerably beyond, technical inventions and their utilization.

For it is important to recognize that the innovating entrepreneur often makes no productive contribution at all, and in some cases even plays a destructive role, engaging in what Thorstein Veblen described as "systematic

2. Thus, I do not use the term to refer to anyone who creates a new firm, however conventional and insignificant. This more common usage, incidentally, is probably closer to the original interpretation of the term when it was introduced into English in the nineteenth century. For an example of the insight that can be brought by rigorous analysis to the entrepreneur as firm creator, see Sharon Gifford (1998). Professor Gifford takes off from Israel Kirzner's observation that alertness and attention to opportunities are crucial attributes of the entrepreneur. Gifford then points out that limits upon entrepreneurs' available time raise the issue of the allocation of their attention between the management of their established enterprises and the formation of newer enterprises. On this basis, Gifford derives a variety of illuminating results.

sabotage" of production (for example, coming up with a new way to enforce output restrictions upon the members of a cartel in order to keep prices high). This does not happen fortuitously, but occurs when the structure of payoffs in an economy is such as to make unproductive activities such as rent-seeking (and worse) more profitable than activities that are productive.

The entrepreneur is at once one of the most intriguing and one of the most elusive in the cast of characters that constitutes the subject of economic analysis. In the writings of the classical economists the appearance of this important figure was frequent, but shadowy, without clearly defined form and function. In the literature of formal theory, at least until very recently, only Schumpeter and, to some degree, Frank Knight (1921) succeeded in infusing this character with life and in assigning to entrepreneurs a specific area of activity to any extent commensurate with their acknowledged importance.[3] But, to do so, these writers were forced to sacrifice analytic tractability and substantive mathematical representation. In more recent years, although economic events continue to underscore the significance of their role, entrepreneurs have nonetheless virtually disappeared from the mainstream theoretical literature. There is a good reason why entrepreneurship should elude the theorist, because by its very nature we cannot describe exactly what entrepreneurs do. An innovation, by definition, is something that has never been carried out before, or at least never in exactly the same way. It is a heterogeneous product *par excellence.* Anything done a second time is no longer an innovation. How, then, can generalized statements be made about it? This chapter will nevertheless suggest what I consider a promising direction for further work on the theory of entrepreneurship. But the discussion will have to be based more on history than upon mathematics.

There are important reasons why we cannot simply give up and ignore the behavior of entrepreneurs. If we are interested in explaining what Trygve Haavelmo has described as the "really big dissimilarities in economic life," and in accounting for the extraordinary growth performance of the capitalist economies in particular, we cannot overlook the role of the entrepreneur. Recent empirical evidence as well as experience indicate that the entrepreneurial function is a vital component in the process of growth of output and productivity. For example, most empirical studies on the nature of the production function have concluded that sheer capital accumulation and expansion of the labor force leave unexplained a substantial proportion of the

3. For more on the entrepreneur in the history of economic ideas, see Mark Blaug (1999).

historical growth of the nation's output. This is suggested, for example, in one of Robert Solow's seminal papers (1957, p. 320). He observes, on the basis of American data for the period 1909–49, that "[g]ross output per man-hour doubled over the interval, with 87½ percent of the increase attributable to technical change and the remaining 12½ percent to increase in the use of capital."[4] But much of technical change, that is, innovation, presumably required entrepreneurial initiative. Thus, if we ignore the entrepreneur we cannot fully explain a very substantial proportion of the historic growth of the West.

The literature of development policy has also emphasized the importance of the entrepreneur, both in the Schumpeterian sense and as the creator of new enterprises of any sort. Discussions seeking to explain the success of some economies and the failure of others emphasize differences in the availability of entrepreneurial talent and in their motivational mechanisms. Plans to stimulate development include provisions for the training of entrepreneurs and for the encouragement of their activities. The absence of entrepreneurs is sometimes cited as a significant obstacle to growth. Whether or not they are assigned the starring role, they are clearly not considered minor characters.

THE ENTREPRENEUR AS ALLOCATED RESOURCE

In line with these views, it is sometimes asserted, as an explanation for the slowdown of growth of an economy, that, for some mysterious reason, the spirit of entrepreneurship and with it the entrepreneurs themselves have disappeared. Or when an economy takes off, the (unexplained) emergence of a

4. Solow's article has, understandably, led to an enormous literature, some of it critical. For example, Solow's quantitative estimate was challenged in an article by Jorgenson and Griliches (1967). However, none of the revisions proposed there and elsewhere seems to have denigrated the role of the entrepreneur. Jorgenson and Griliches (1967) reevaluated the magnitude of the role of technical change as a residual, estimating the remaining contributions to labor productivity directly in terms of expansion in the quantities of inputs measurable by conventional methods. It is undoubtedly true that growth in output contributed by entrepreneurship and innovation often requires corresponding increases in input quantities, but that does not mean that the entrepreneur has played little or no role in the generation of such output increases. It merely means that, since the amount of entrepreneurial activity is difficult to quantify, the correlation between that activity and the quantities of conventional outputs makes the role of the enterpreneur even more difficult to measure.

Moreover, more recent work by Jorgenson, Gollop, and Fraumeni (1987), which, on the basis of highly sophisticated econometric analysis, assigns a primary role to the capital stock in the remarkable postwar rise in U.S. labor productivity, nevertheless attributes more than one-third of the annual growth rate in labor productivity to innovation (pp. 1–2).

cadre of entrepreneurs is given at least part of the credit. My position, in contrast, is that this is implausible. Entrepreneurs are not suddenly created in profusion by spontaneous generation and their ranks are not suddenly decimated by some undescribed plague. Rather, it is my belief that the explanation for this rise and fall of entrepreneurial activity is grounded in simple dollars and cents—in the changes in the economy's structure of payoffs. Baldly put, the activities that promise the greatest monetary (or other) returns lead to a reallocation of entrepreneurs from one sector of the economy to another, and this reallocation can take forms that give the appearance of the vanishing or emergence of entrepreneurs as a group.

As an input, entrepreneurship, like any other input, can be reallocated from one task to another by a change in the relative profit prospects offered by the available alternative uses to which entrepreneurship can be put. The efforts of entrepreneurs are reallocated by shifts in the sectors of the economy and the lines of activity where profit seems most easily to be earned. Perhaps not for all entrepreneurs, but surely for many of them, the identity of the line of endeavor that offers the most promising prospect of profits is a matter of great moment. Toward the beginning of his *Capital,* Marx suggests that, in the profit-making production process, chairs and tables lose their distinctive attributes as usable items of furniture. Rather, both are transformed into abstract embodiments of value, into prospective sources of financial gain, and are in that sense homogenized. The same is true of the alternative occupations available for the efforts of the entrepreneur. All become homogenized into abstract opportunities for the acquisition of wealth, power, or prestige, and the pricing arrangements that determine prospective profitability therefore can have a profound influence on the pattern of allocation of the economy's entrepreneurial resources. When an industry reaches a stage at which the opportunities for further innovation seem, perhaps temporarily, to be exhausted, it is not surprising to find entrepreneurial effort flowing out of that field and into others where the opportunities for the profitable introduction of change seem brighter. The propensity of entrepreneurs to redirect their efforts in this way has long been recognized and its contribution to the dynamism of the economy accepted.

However, sometimes the productivity consequences of such a reallocation are more questionable. For example, a change in the laws in a less developed country that greatly increases the hazards faced by entrepreneurs in directly *productive* lines of activity may induce them to turn their efforts to activities such as accumulation of land or advance in the government bureaucracy. And that may not just change the directions of the economy's productive efforts, but can also reduce its output and impede its growth. This sort of reallocation of entrepreneurial effort, too, can be induced by changes affecting the relative returns to more productive and less productive exercises of entrepreneurship.

Thus, there is a variety of roles among which entrepreneurs' efforts can be reallocated. And some of those roles do not follow the constructive and innovative script that is conventionally attributed to them.[5] How entrepreneurs act at a given time and place depends heavily on the prevailing "rules of the game"—i.e., the reward structure in the economy. My central hypothesis is that it is this set of rules, and not the supply of entrepreneurs, that undergoes significant changes from one period to another, and helps to dictate the ultimate effect on the economy via the allocation of entrepreneurial resources.

UNPRODUCTIVE, RENT-SEEKING, AND DESTRUCTIVE ENTREPRENEURSHIP

A key part of my story is the contention that the entrepreneur's activity can be, and as a matter of fact sometimes is, innovative and yet nevertheless makes little or no contribution to the real output of the economy. The activity can sometimes even reduce output or restrain its growth. "Rent-seeking," a concept introduced by Gordon Tullock, refers, of course, to any activity whose objective is the acquisition of some of the monopoly profit or the other economic rents currently generated or potentially available in the economy. For example, consider a regulated industry that is a bilateral monopoly. Suppose one of the monopolists finds a new way to persuade the regulatory agency to readjust prices so that a larger share of the industry's total monopoly profits flows into the coffers of its enterprise. Then it will have engaged in a successful act of rent- seeking. Such an activity can clearly be innovative. A novel legal principle may, for example, be thought of and used by the rent seeker to persuade the regulatory agency to intervene in its favor. But the activity need not contribute anything at all to economic production or productivity. Indeed, it can constitute an effective impediment to both of these, through misallocation of valuable resources into pursuits that, from the view-

5. A very similar viewpoint, stressing the allocability of persons with innovative talent among productive and less productive activities is taken by Murphy, Shleifer, and Vishny (1991) in a very illuminating theoretical and empirical analysis. The same general idea, albeit in more specialized terms, appears in the writings of Leijonhufvud (1983).

point of the economy, are useless and by forcing the targeted firm to redirect its activities into unproductive directions for the sake of self-defense.

At the extreme end of the spectrum, enterprising violence has also occurred throughout history, and continues today. The leaders of medieval mercenary armies and the early twentieth-century warlords in China were clearly businesspeople, engaged in the sale of a service as a final product or an intermediate good. Their activities were marked by innovations in strategy and technology. In short, some of them were undoubtedly entrepreneurs. But it is at least arguable that their activities reduced production and even destroyed some of the economy's capacity to produce. So, too, is modern organized crime businesslike or entrepreneurial. Thus, unlike rent-seeking, which may merely contribute nothing to production but not actually harm it except in the sense of the opportunity cost of such activity, there is entrepreneurship whose result is substantial *destruction* of both output and the capacity to produce.

It is clear, then, that entrepreneurship should not be taken as a synonym for contributions to productivity and growth. Schumpeter had already drawn attention to some types of entrepreneurial innovation whose productive contributions are questionable. He included in his list of the activities of the entrepreneur "[t]he carrying out of the new organization of any industry, like the creation of a monopoly position (for example through trustification)" (1911, 1936, p. 66).

The obvious fact that entrepreneurs engage in such a variety of tasks suggests that theory can usefully consider what determines the allocation of entrepreneurial inputs among them. Presumably the reason no such line of inquiry was pursued by Schumpeter or his successors is that any reallocation of entrepreneurial resources among the items in his basic list of entrepreneurial activities, with the exception of the creation or destruction of a monopoly, does not seem very significant. All the other activities in his list are normally beneficial to production, so that the general implications of such a shift for economic welfare are unlikely to be substantial.

More substantive results from an analysis of the allocation of entrepreneurial resources require expansion of Schumpeter's list, to include the unproductive and destructive activities that have attracted enterprising and innovative individuals throughout history. That is the approach I adopt, and I will argue that the free-market economy does a far from perfect job of attracting entrepreneurial activity into productive channels. Nevertheless, it appears to have performed far better in this role than any other type of economy.

ENTREPRENEURSHIP UNDER CAPITALISM AND ALTERNATIVE SYSTEMS: HOW PRODUCTIVE ACTIVITY BECAME RESPECTABLE

Despite the evident continuation on a substantial scale of rent-seeking and other forms of wasteful entrepreneurship under capitalism, never before has productive activity been so effective and prestigious as a method for the attainment of wealth, power, and prestige. These three goals are clearly the primary objectives of most entrepreneurs, and history indicates that many entrepreneurs are not particularly choosy about the means they utilize to achieve these ends. They, like those engaged in any other occupation, span the range of morality and dedication to virtue. So one can expect that there will be many entrepreneurs who will choose whatever activities offer the greatest promise of attaining those objectives, whatever the social consequences.

More than that, moral standards surely are not immutable. They tend to adapt themselves to current opportunities and practices, so that activities that today would be considered beyond the pale in terms of their ethics may in an earlier time have been accepted as normal and even commendable (and vice versa). As I will describe in greater detail in chapter 14, in ancient Rome and medieval China,[6] with their abundance of military and nonmilitary inventions, the pursuit of wealth and power was considered as acceptable, and even as desirable, as it is in the most greed-driven of capitalist societies. But the ideas about the means that were proper for attainment of these goals were very different from today's. Methods of wealth accumulation that were considered laudable in one or both of these societies included military aggression, ransom, bribery, and usury. Some of the great figures of Roman history, for example, were respected for having acquired vast riches by these means. The Chinese mandarins, having been appointed to powerful positions, were expected to recoup in the form of bribes the heavy expenses they incurred in preparing for the difficult imperial examinations that were requisites for such positions. No hint of scandal or disapproval attached to these means of accumulation.

But in both Roman and Chinese societies there were two types of activity that incurred unambiguous disgrace: participation in commerce or in productive activity (with the possible exception of some gentlemanly agricultural undertakings). In Rome, for example, such disgraceful endeavors were left to

6. For a very penetrating discussion of the case of medieval China, see Landes (2001).

freedmen—to manumitted slaves and their sons. And these individuals, too, strove to accumulate sufficient means so that they could afford to leave their degrading occupations, or at least make it possible for later generations in their families to achieve respectability. It is little wonder, then, that there was not much *productive* entrepreneurship in these societies. Even though the Chinese, in particular, produced an astonishing abundance of inventions, there was little innovation, in the sense of the application and distribution of the inventions. Most such inventions were put to little productive use and often soon disappeared and were completely forgotten.

In the Middle Ages, similar ideas about honorable and dishonorable means to wealth and power prevailed among the nobles, though some cracks in the edifice appeared when several monastic orders adopted the idea that labor, including productive toil, was a most virtuous activity. Still, the preferred medieval ways to wealth were the public and private wars carried on by kings and nobles alike. Also in line with the orientation of the times were the occupations of the robber barons and of the leaders of private armies whose services were for hire and who undertook aggression on their own initiative when market demand for their services was poor. In the same period, rent-seeking was also a respectable avenue to wealth. The king's friends at court who helped him against his enemies, who entertained him, and who provided him with various forms of amusement could hope for rich rewards in the form of generous grants of land, castles and other privileges. We may note again that these military activities were not merely unproductive—they were clearly destructive. They destroyed infrastructure and crops, they took into the armies people who would otherwise have engaged in fruitful labor, and they undermined production in other ways, frequently leaving poverty, misery and disease in their wake.

Destructive wars and rent-seeking activities as means to enhance wealth and power, of course, continued through the Renaissance[7] and, indeed, they

7. During the Renaissance, an ecclesiastical career could be a source of fantastic rents. A spectacular example is provided by the payoffs by the Borgia Pope, Alexander II, to those cardinals who had voted for his elevation: "Alexander set about making good his promises. . . . such practices had become common over the years in the conclaves. . . . First in line was Cardinal Sforza, the leading voter for the Pope, who became vice-chancellor. He was given the castle of Nepi, the bishopric of Erlau in Hungary, Rodrigo's annuities from the bishoprics, monasteries, and churches of Sevilla and Cádiz, and the legations of Bologna, the Romagna, and the exarchate of Ravenna. Before the election, four mules laden with sacks of silver had been seen wending their way from the Borgia palace toward Sforza's home . . . Cardinal Orsini received the cities of Monticelli and Soriano, the legation of the Marches and the bishopric of Cartagena, valued at 7,000 ducats, as well as a bonus of 20,000 ducats. For his part, Cardinal Collona was given the abbey of Subiaco with

manifestly continue today. The idea that productive activity is disgraceful continued to guide continental European nobility well into the nineteenth century. But at least in Italy, the Low Countries, and England things began to change, roughly in the thirteenth to fifteenth centuries. As capitalistic activity rose in these countries, the relative ease of wealth attainment through banking, commerce, and production seems to have become irresistible.

The attractiveness of such pursuits also grew as the constant and urgent need for funds by the royal houses made increasingly common the sale of positions of nobility to those who could afford the steep prices. As armies grew in size and arms and ammunition became more expensive, the kings found themselves repeatedly threatened with inability to finance their wars and with bankruptcy when they could not repay their vast loans. Philip II (of Spanish Armada fame) underwent bankruptcy many times because the Cortes (the bodies of nobles whose assent for additional taxes was required) proved reluctant to levy additional tax payments on themselves. The same was true of Parliament in England, where there was instituted, during the centuries following the Magna Carta, the principle of no taxation without representation (of the nobles and the gentry, of course), an issue finally settled in the seventeenth century in the battles between Parliament and the Stuarts. Edward IV, the Yorkist king, had earlier used many devices to get out of the resulting financial difficulties. For us, it is most noteworthy that among the means he employed was entry into commerce:

> Edward IV has some claim to be regarded as the first 'merchant king' in English history. From the beginning of his reign he sought to improve his finances by indulging in personal trading ventures, *an example followed by many of his great men.* Already by the spring of 1463 he was actively engaged in the wool trade. Soon after he was exporting a variety of other merchandise, notably cloth and tin, and by 1470, if not before, he was active as an importer. . . . In February 1470 no fewer than twenty-five ships entering or leaving the port of London contained goods of the king. . . . This activity continued throughout the reign. In his later years he also made use of the royal ships, when not engaged on other business, as commercial charter vessels. (Ross, 1974, p. 351, emphasis added)

Note from this passage that the king's example was quickly followed by the nobles (the king's "great men"). The royal example and the practice of the

---

the twenty-two castles belonging to it, and an income of 2,000 ducats, to which the Pope added a bonus of 15,000 ducats. Cardinal Savelli received Civitá Castellana and the bishopric of Mallorca, worth 6,000 ducats, with a bonus of 30,000 ducats [etc., etc.] . . . ." (Cloulas, 1989, p. 71). It should be noted as a suggestive standard of comparison that any person with assets of 20,000 ducats was considered extremely wealthy at that time.

elite soon dissipated the shame of such activities. By the time of Adam Smith—that is, the birth of the Industrial Revolution—many members of the higher nobility were avidly engaged in canal-building projects and in other productive and innovative pursuits. And one can surmise that it was the abundance of promising wealth-accumulation opportunities offered by the emerging free market in commerce that drew the king and his nobles into the field.[8]

Thus, it is arguably capitalism itself that brought with it the respectability of the entrepreneur's productive activity. Marx observed that it imparted an aura of virtue to the capitalist's saving: "he thus forces the development of the productive powers of society. . . . Only as personified capital is the capitalist respectable. As such, he shares with the miser the passion for wealth as wealth. But that which in the miser is a mere idiosyncrasy, is, in the capitalist, the effect of the social mechanism, of which he is but one of the wheels" ([1867] 1906, p. 649). Two implications of this passage should be noted here. The first, as Marx also emphasized elsewhere, is the change in the standards of respectable behavior brought about by capitalism. What in another society would constitute despicable miserliness becomes in a capitalist world an inescapable mode of behavior, and one that contributes materially to growth of productivity. Second, Marx asserts that this form of economy leaves no choice to the capitalist entrepreneur. He is *required* by social forces to expand the productive powers of society and is driven, moreover, "ruthlessly [to force] the human race to produce for production's sake" ([1867] 1906, p. 649). Thus, "[t]he bourgeoisie cannot exist without constantly revolutionizing the instruments of production, and thereby the relations of production. . . . Conservation of the old modes of production in unaltered form, was, on the contrary, the first condition of existence of all earlier industrial classes" (Marx and Engels, 1847).

8. Still, it is difficult for us in the twenty-first century to imagine the degree of dependence of the economy in the late medieval England of Edward IV and his successor, Richard III, upon rent-seeking and granting of such "rents" by the king to secure the seekers' services and their loyalty (an activity replicated by the great nobles in dealing with their own affinities). The primary components of this form of compensation were land and offices in the royal household and elsewhere. A curious feature of this arrangement stemmed from the fact that, because the amount of land and number of available offices were limited, the king often gained power from the resources he acquired and was able to give away after unsuccessful rebellion, as the traitors were attainted and their properties and positions forfeited. Notable examples followed the death of Warwick, the kingmaker, in battle under Edward IV and the execution of the King's brother, Clarence, after repeated acts of treason, and the execution of Buckingham under Richard III. For a detailed description of the rent-seeking structure of the society in the period, see Rosemary Horrox (1989).

It is noteworthy how different from such capitalistic behavior was the role of the entrepreneur in the former Soviet economies, which allegedly sought to follow Marxian guidelines. In the controlled economies of the old Soviet Union, entrepreneurship was driven back to its rent-seeking orientation, with gains to be sought by becoming bureaucrats and Communist Party officials.[9] Managers of economic enterprises were in effect penalized for undertaking any innovative steps that increased productivity. This happened in at least two ways. First, a manager's reward depended on the firm's success in meeting an assigned "production norm" for the year. But any disruption caused by the retooling necessary to carry out an innovation would threaten failure to meet that current production target. Second, if an innovation were carried out and promised to increase productivity, that was all too likely to lead to the assignment of a higher production target in future years, making the manager's task that much more difficult. These were just two of the obstacles to the exercise of productive entrepreneurship in the Soviet economies.[10]

These are handicaps generally absent from the free-market economies. It is true that in market economies there remains an abundance of opportunities for profit through legal rent-seeking or through outright criminal activity, much of it an impediment to growth. But the free market also offers rich rewards to the entrepreneur who successfully introduces productive innovation. And, simultaneously, it changes the standards of commendable behavior, making a role model of billionaire innovators, particularly if their earnings stem from contributions to production. For the rising wealth and power of the capitalist entrepreneurs enable them to purchase respectability, both through their impressive productive and accumulative accomplishments, and via good works they subsequently undertake with their wealth. In short, the free-market economy offers encouragement to productive entrepreneurship such as no other form of economy has ever provided. This is, then, plausibly, another crucial component underlying the dramatic growth performance of capitalism.

---

9. Of course, this happens in market economies as well, but there is a substantial difference in degree.

10. After this passage was written, I came across a much more careful and detailed analysis by Maurizio Iacopetta, a Ph.D. student at New York University ("Techological Diffusion in Market vs. Planned Economies," unpublished) that reaches essentially the same conclusion, but is based on far more sophisticated analysis than mine. Iacopetta provides clear evidence that *invention* was quite abundant in the Soviet Union, but what was missing was *innovation*, that is, the dissemination and widespread utilization of the inventions.

CHAPTER 5

ENTREPRENEURSHIP UNDER CAPITALISM: THE RULE OF LAW AND SANCTITY OF PROPERTY

I have sometimes asserted that that there is no occupation whose total economic product is greater than that of lawyers; and none whose marginal contribution is smaller. But it is the total contribution that matters most. A strong case can be made for the conclusion that without the rule of law, including the rights of property and the enforceability of contracts, the growth miracle of capitalism, indeed capitalism itself, might not have been possible.[11]

To discuss the significance of the rule of law and provide some indications of its origins, it is appropriate to return, once again, to a bit of history. In many earlier societies there was no such thing as the right of private property. At least in theory, all property belonged to the monarch, who was entitled to requisition any of it whenever it suited his purposes. This was notably true in ancient China, where not only money and physical property were subject to expropriation, but even innovations themselves were likely to be taken over by the state. For example, it is reported that "frequently . . . during the course of Chinese history . . . the scholar officials . . . gathered in the fruits of other people's ingenuity. . . . Three examples of innovations that met that fate [are] paper, invented by a eunuch; printing, used by Buddhists as a medium for religious propaganda; and the bill of exchange, an expedient of private businessmen" (Balaszs, 1964, p. 18. For more of the quotation, see chapter 13, below). Even the Church was not immune from royal takings, sometimes on a massive scale, as in the expropriation of the Templars[12] by Philip IV of France (Philip the Fair) in 1307 or that of the monasteries by Henry VIII of England, more than two centuries later.

The resulting uncertainty was surely a major discouragement to saving and to innovative activity alike. Wealth was best rapidly consumed, lest it serve as a temptation to government acquisitiveness, and it may be conjectured that this contributed to the propensity of the nobility in a number of societies to be perpetually in debt. Productive innovation, aside from receiving little recognition, much less admiration, was rarely worth the required effort. Without the rule of law, clearly, enormous obstacles prevented economic growth of any substantial magnitude.

11. See Rosenberg and Birdzell (1986) and de Soto (2001) on this subject.

12. The fact that the bulk of what Philip obtained from the Templars went to the Order of the Hospitalers rather than to the royal treasury does not matter here. Philip seems quite clearly to have been seeking a new source of funds, having run out of such conventional sources as the Jews, who had just been expelled from France (Strayer, 1980, p. 287).

Capitalism itself, even more clearly, was precluded by absence of the rule of law. Capitalism requires markets in which the participants can have confidence in any agreements arrived at. It is driven by the pursuit of accumulated and retainable wealth and opportunities to expand that wealth by devoting it to the production process. Sanctity of property and contract, and institutions that can be relied upon to enforce them both, are necessary conditions for the creation of capitalists and for effective execution of their role. That is why, without the contribution of the lawyers, the free-market economies might never have evolved. And even if they had, it is unlikely that their unprecedented growth could have occurred. It is on these grounds that I base my evaluation of the enormous total contribution of lawyers to the performance of the industrial economies.

But how was the rule of law introduced? A key to the answer arguably lies in economic pressures, together with the limited power of the kings. At various times these rulers were forced to grant (and reconfirm) privileges and protections to their subjects either under direct compulsion (as at Runnymede in the case of Magna Carta) or in exchange for needed favors. For it must be understood that the term "absolute monarchy" was always a misrepresentation of the facts. Even the most powerful kings and emperors held absolute sway only over limited geographic areas and over those subjects who were not too remote in location or too elevated in station. Primitive means of transportation, an absence of standing armies (rather than mercenaries or troops provided by powerful subjects under traditional arrangements), perpetual shortage of funds, and tiny administrative bodies meant that the medieval and Renaissance kings possessed only very limited power. They had no effective tax collection agencies, a gap, as we know, that prevailed in France until the Revolution. The kings also found it difficult to borrow, and had to pay higher interest rates than many other borrowers because there was no way they could make an enforceable commitment to repay. After all, there existed no court in which a debtor could sue the ruler.

The consequence was that in order to carry out their prime occupational duty—warfare—the kings (some historians have called them the "pauper kings") were frequently driven to beg for funds from the parliament, the Spanish Cortes, or the other bodies that held the power to tax. And those bodies frequently demanded and often received concessions in return. The century after Magna Carta inaugurated the process of conceding the sanctity of property, including immunity from taxation without representation, a process carried to its conclusion in England in the struggle between Charles I and his parliaments. In effect, the rule of law can to some degree be ascribed to the low productivity of the medieval economy, which kept even the kings in poverty in terms of what one expects of the financial circumstances of a monarch. Certainly they were constantly hampered by lack of resources for the activity on which they were expected to focus—aggressive warfare. Underpaid troops deserted and mutinied, and kings underwent repeated bankruptcies in wartime, as I have already noted. Under such pressures, and with their own nobility often themselves aggressive and unruly, the kings were forced, time after time, to agree to grant protections to various groups of subjects against certain arbitrary royal actions. The beneficiaries included not only the nobles but also the towns, which early began to acquire their traditional "liberties." As these protections evolved and accumulated, they grew into a body of law. Driven by economic forces—the low medieval productivity and the resulting royal poverty—they became the legal foundation for a free-market economy in which entrepreneurship could flourish and production could explode.[13]

CAPITALISM AND INDEPENDENT INNOVATION: OUTLINE OF THE SEQUENCE OF DEVELOPMENTS

The conclusion of this discussion is that entrepreneurs—that is, independent innovators—have played a critical role in the growth performance of the capitalist economy. They were indispensable at its inception, introducing new business methods and other innovations without which the free-enterprise system could not have prospered. They adopted new processes, ranging from the use of better ships provided by the Venetians, the Genoese, and the Dutch, to financing innovations such as the introduction of equity as a supplement to debt in the financing of business ventures,[14] and procedures such as double-entry bookkeeping. This was centuries before the Industrial Revolution in eighteenth-century England.

The conditions for the rise to economic importance of the independent entrepreneur can perhaps be ascribed to historical accident. We have seen

13. Landes (1998, p. 590) writes: "Why this peculiarly European . . . cultivation of invention—or what some have called 'the invention of invention?' . . . In the last analysis . . . I would stress the market. Enterprise was free in Europe. Innovation worked and paid, and rulers and vested interests were limited in their ability to prevent or discourage innovation. Success bred imitation and emulation."

14. It has been argued that the invention of equity was at least to some degree stimulated by the desire to evade the Church's prohibition of usury, on the argument that equity investors are actual participants in the venture and their earnings, consequently, are not merely a return on the provision of money, with no personal contribution by the investor.

how the emergence of the rule of law, the sanctity of property, and the evolving respectability of commercial activity grew out of the antagonism between the nobility and their monarchs and were solidified in the religious disputes of the seventeenth century. The kings, pursuing their own interests, did what they could to bring free-enterprising violence under control, thereby foreclosing this easy avenue for unproductive entrepreneurship. Then the upper classes, in their turn, did what they could to limit the powers of the king by restricting his ability to offer rich rewards to rent seekers.

Thus, the conditions for the flowering of productive entrepreneurship seem, ironically, to have emerged out of the struggle for power between the kings and their nobility, each side seeking to ensure its unhampered ability to pursue its natural occupation—destructive warfare. The monarchs, to succeed in their purpose, had to foreclose the route to independent military entrepreneurship by their unruly barons. The nobles, in turn, required the protection of rules such as those embodied in Magna Carta. In the seesaw battle between these two antagonists, when the power of the barons was in the ascendant, commitments such as the sanctity of property, assent to taxation by the taxpayers, and the rule of law were adopted (for themselves, of course). In a later period of ascendancy of the upper classes, they reduced the opportunities for rent-seeking by limiting the power of the king to grant monopolies and other sources of rents to his friends and others who served his purposes. When it was the king's turn as victor, it was the destructive entrepreneurship of the nobles that was curbed, foreclosing violence and aggression as an easy avenue to wealth and power. The ultimate winner was a third party, apparently not concerned in this struggle—those whom Marx had dubbed the "bourgeoisie." But the beneficiaries also included those nobles who were induced to participate in bourgeois undertakings such as commerce and production by the more restricted availability of wealth from rent-seeking and violence. From this group, whose activities were made possible by the evolving political rearrangements and by the guarantees of the rule of law, there arose the productive entrepreneurs who brought the free-enterprise economy into existence.[15]

---

15. In discussing "Why Europe?" [why Britain?] for the origins of the growth economy, Landes (1998, pp. 217–18) also stresses the institutional attributes that I emphasize in this chapter: secure private property to encourage saving and investment, secure rights of personal liberty, and enforced rights of contract, as well as stable, honest, and responsive government. See also his remark, "In despotisms, it is dangerous to be rich without power. So in [such regimes] capital accumulation proved an attractive nuisance. It aroused cupidity and invited seizure" (p. 398).

But once the conditions that nurtured capitalist entrepreneurship emerged, economic forces took over. The success of earlier innovators in commercial and productive activities encouraged other innovators to follow their lead, both by showing how it could be done and by publicizing the rewards. But it also brought political power to this class and to the capitalists who helped to finance their activities. This power was used to strengthen the rule of law and the rights of property, and to encourage other governmental measures that solidified and improved the environment's hospitality to productive entrepreneurial activity.

At the same time, in a number of industries, innovation expanded the scale of the firm required for economic efficiency. Canal building, railroad construction, steel manufacturing, and other such activities could not be carried out efficiently by the minuscule enterprises of an earlier era. These large enterprises evolved into oligopolies and their rivalry forced them to employ whatever weapons promised to preserve and perhaps enhance their market position. New products and processes were obvious tools for the purpose. Then, as described in earlier chapters, the pressures of competition forced these firms to do what they could to reduce the uncertainties of innovation. They did so by taking over much of the process as part of the routine operation of the firm.

Today we are left with an economy that derives innovations from both sources—from the routine activities of giant firms and from independent inventors and their entrepreneur partners (who are sometimes the same person).[16] But, as already observed, these are not purely substitute activities. Rather, there has been a predictable tendency toward specialization: the entrepreneurs providing the more heterodox, breakthrough innovations, and the R&D establishments of the larger firms creating the enhancements to those breakthroughs that contribute considerably to their usefulness. Thus, there is superadditive complementarity between the roles of the two types of innovating enterprise, and growth is arguably enhanced by this division of their labor.

In sum, growth in the free-market economy, from its inception (and still today), has served as a stimulus to entrepreneurship. But entrepreneurship has returned the favor, making a constant and major contribution to capitalist growth.

16. Of course, the universities and the government also make very substantial contributions.

CHAPTER 6

Voluntary Dissemination of Proprietary Technology: Private Profit, Social Gain

Conventional business wisdom says: Never let the competition know what you're doing. But at Novell, we believe the secret of success is to share your secrets. So we established the Novell Labs program to openly share our networking software technology with other companies.

—Advertisement by Novell, Inc., in *The Economist* magazine, 21 September 1991

Pretty soon, if it continues, you'll find that everyone's going to have rights to everyone else's technology, so there's not going to be any competition.

—Julie Mar-Spinola, as quoted in the *New York Times*, 11 November 2001, section 3, p. 7

The previous chapter dealt with the market's offsets to one major impediment to productivity and growth—the diversion of entrepreneurial effort and ability to unproductive activities, such as rent-seeking. In this chapter, I will examine the way in which the free-enterprise mechanism alleviates another major impediment to growth. Because firms gain competitive advantage from their possession of products and processes that are unavailable to rivals, we might expect them to do whatever they can to impede or prevent the spread of this proprietary technology. However, if every firm is denied access to the innovations that are currently employed by others, each will be condemned to activities that are at least partially obsolete, thus putting a brake on economic growth. Here I will argue that in fact competition and the pursuit of profits drive many firms to do the opposite: actually to disseminate their proprietary technology, providing it voluntarily, even to their arch rivals. Of course, they do so only if the reward is sufficient. This chapter and the next will explore the general principles underlying the resulting markets in proprietary technology and I shall offer a considerable amount of (unsystematic) evidence indicating that such technology supply occurs frequently in reality.

CHAPTER 6

THE EFFICIENCY CONTRIBUTION OF RAPID DISSEMINATION

This rapid dissemination is no minor matter for the efficiency of the economy's growth process. In his valuable article on international trade and world distribution of income, Paul Krugman (1979) takes the patterns of trade and economic growth to be governed primarily by two activities: innovation and technology transfer. The discussion in this chapter takes a similar position. It is clear that the growth of developing nations is highly dependent on the success and speed with which they can acquire and put to effective use new technology from the industrialized countries. But even growth in the industrialized economies is highly dependent on the effectiveness with which they can adopt new technology from sources foreign and domestic. That they do so to a substantial degree is surely indicated by the remarkable similarity of the technology employed throughout the industrialized world. Moreover, the vast majority of the industrial economies must rely preponderantly on technology created outside their borders because very few of them are substantial innovators themselves. For example, according to the National Science Board (2000, p. 2–40), "[t]he worldwide distribution of R&D performance is concentrated in relatively few industrialized countries. Of the $500 billion in estimated 1997 R&D expenditures for the 28 OECD [Organisation for Economic Cooperation and Development] countries, 85 percent is expended in just 7 countries [the United States, Canada, France, Germany, Italy, Japan, and the United Kingdom]." And, of these seven top R&D performers, only Japan, the United States, and Germany awarded less than 70 percent of their 1996 patents to residents of other countries (World Intellectual Property Organization). This should not be very surprising—if thirty countries all engage in invention activity, and if technology utilization is very similar in all of them, then the "average country" must be receiving 29/30ths of its innovative products and practices from abroad.

Unless technology transfer is a significant disincentive to investment in innovation, it should also be obvious that growth is promoted by the rapidity with which new technology is disseminated. The greater the share of firms and countries that make use of superior products and processes and the sooner they do so, rather than being confined to inferior substitutes, the more widespread and substantial the output and growth benefits should be. For suppose only one firm uses a new technique that increases productivity, while its competitors are forced to retain the old, less efficient technique. Then it is obvious that either output must be far lower, or (unnecessary) input use far greater, than if all of the firms engaged in the activity were able to adopt the productivity-enhancing technique.

We must, therefore, consider the market's technology transfer process in this new world in which much of innovation has become routine. Just as competitive influences have led to routinization of innovation, there are competitive mechanisms that can make dissemination of technology a part of the regular portion of the firm's *voluntary* activities. This is in direct contrast with a common view of firms as zealous guardians of the proprietary innovations in their possession, using patents, the courts, and/or secrecy to keep their technical knowledge from others for as long as possible. They supposedly do this in order to prolong the length of time during which their technological information gives them a competitive advantage and brings with it the stream of supercompetitive Schumpeterian profits.

I will show, on the contrary, that market forces frequently motivate enterprises to become active sellers of licenses for the use of their proprietary technology, or to make a variety of information-exchange arrangements ranging from implicit contracts to carefully spelled-out legal commitments. This phenomenon plays a part that is not insignificant in the continuing growth performance of the free-enterprise economies.

THE CONFLICT BETWEEN INNOVATION AND RAPID DISSEMINATION

As already suggested here, innovation and quick dissemination are two of the critical stimuli to economic growth. Each helps to increase productivity and product quality and, if one or the other were to disappear, growth would surely slow to a crawl. Yet it is widely recognized that dissemination can be the enemy of innovative activity. If a firm undertakes considerable expenditure of money and effort to carry out its innovation program, but finds that other firms, including its competitors, rapidly share in the fruits, why should that firm devote the time, effort, and funding to continue that program?

The problem is, indeed, a real one, and the amount of litigation over patent infringement indicates that it is no minor matter. Yet I will show here and in later chapters that the problem is considerably less serious than seems widely to be believed. It is relieved to a considerable degree by steps taken by many of the firms in the forefront of innovative activity to promote dissemination rather than seeking to prevent it. These firms do so voluntarily, as a source of both profit and improvement of competitive position. The result is that the market mechanism succeeds in providing a partial reconciliation of

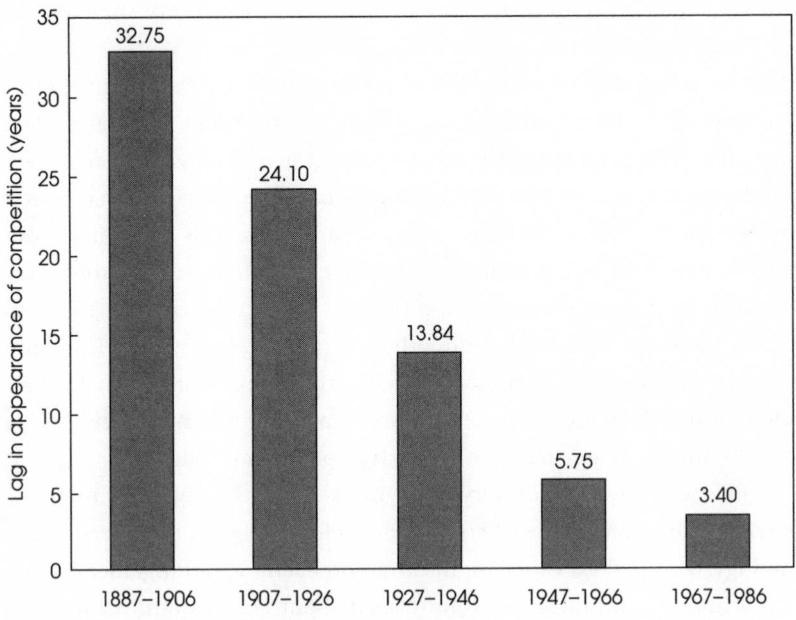

FIGURE 6.1

Interval between the introduction of an innovation and competitive entry, 1887–86. Source: Agarwal and Gort (2001).

the conflict between innovation and dissemination, adding yet another powerful growth stimulus.

Before getting to the reasons that lead enterprises to engage in dissemination of their own proprietary technology, it is worth pausing to examine some suggestive data. The evidence indicates not only that dissemination is surprisingly rapid, but that it has been growing more so with remarkable consistency for more than a century. A recent study by Rajshree Agarwal and Michael Gort (2001) examines a set of forty-six major product innovations, which they admit is not a random sample and perhaps not representative (though the list was chosen for another study and hence is not deliberately biased in relation to the current subject). They find that, in the course of a century, the average time between the commercial introduction of a new product and the entry of competitors supplying the same or similar products fell from 32.75 years at the inception of the twentieth century to 3.40 years in 1967–86. Moreover, as shown in figure 6.1, the decline was remarkably steady and persistent, and the authors report that other studies support their results.

The first suggestive implication of these striking data is that dissemination speed cannot plausibly be taken to be an accidental affair. There must be

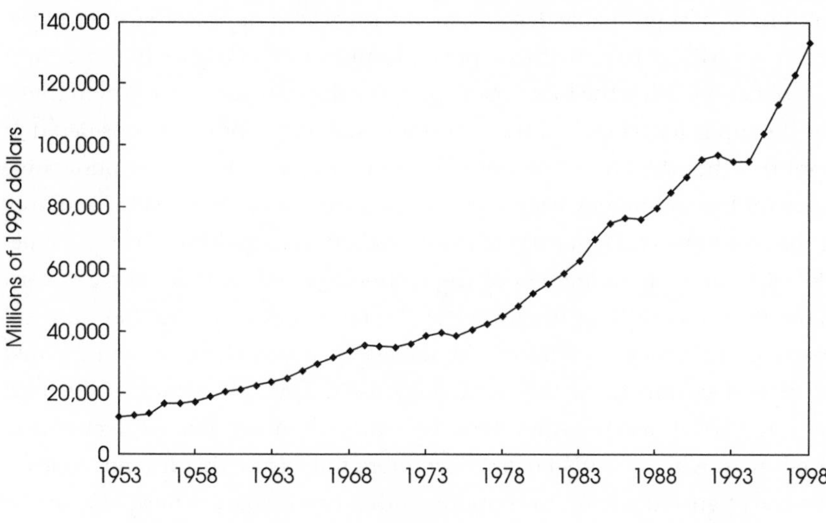

FIGURE 6.2
Real U.S. private R&D expenditures, 1953–98. Expenditures are deflated using the GDP implicit price deflator. Sources: National Science Board (2000), and *Economic Report of the President* (2001).

something systematic driving the trend, and in a market economy the natural candidate is profitability—as my analysis will suggest on other grounds. Second, at worst, this speedup of availability of new product technology to competitors has not brought the growth of investment in innovation by private industry to a halt. Figure 6.2 shows real investment in innovation by firms in the postwar period, and we see that the expansion of innovation investment has apparently been continuing unabated. In other words, although rapid dissemination may well constitute some disincentive for investment, the market mechanism has nevertheless provided incentives that at least do not make the one activity fatal for the other.

TWO INCENTIVE MECHANISMS FOR VOLUNTARY DISSEMINATION

Let us begin with a discussion of the incentive mechanism of markets in technology licenses. The logic of such markets is a straightforward matter. A firm that holds the rights to a valuable invention is, formally, in the same position as an enterprise that owns a facility with abundant capacity and superior quality. Either firm can use the property in question as an input to its own production process or it can choose to rent access to the input to other producers (who may be competitors), or it can do both. Which of these three options is most profitable depends on the price other prospective users of the input are willing to pay. If that price promises profits higher than the firm can obtain by using the input itself, then it will clearly pay that firm to transfer the input (or its use) to those customers. And a moment's consideration confirms that the other firms will be willing to pay this more remunerative price for the technology license (or for the superior raw material) if and only if they are more efficient users of the item than its proprietor is. For the superior efficiency of the renters of the technology means that they can earn more from its use than the owner of the technology can. So they can still earn a profit if they pay a license fee somewhat greater than the owner would be able to earn by using the technology itself. That, in essence, is the logic of the market mechanism's incentive for voluntary sale of technology licenses, as will presently be described more fully. Note that it tends to leave the use of an innovation to those firms that can employ it most effectively: its most efficient users.

There is another element to the explanation of the willingness of owners of proprietary technology to sell the rights to its use to others, and for others to be willing to pay the price. The purchasers of such licenses are willing to do so because such "friendly transfer" of technology is substantially more rapid than "hostile transfer," which occurs through means such as industrial espionage and reverse engineering. Because rapid obsolescence makes speed in providing the latest model so critical in high-tech industries, it becomes worthwhile for the licensee simply to pay the price rather than expend the time and effort to "create" the technology itself.

But the licensor also receives a degree of protection in the process because even friendly transfer takes some time. A year or two can pass by the time one firm has acquired another's new technology, learned to use it, installed the necessary equipment, and organized the requisite marketing. In high-tech industries that is no minor delay. In the extreme case of computers, models are often modified within six months of their introduction. Indeed, I am informed that, frequently, on the day the new model actually appears in retail stores it is no longer being manufactured! This means that a year or two of lag in the technology-transfer process still preserves a significant timing advantage for the innovating firm. In other words, by providing rivals with its latest products and processes, the innovating firm generally does not sacrifice all the advantage that priority in possession of the innovation can confer. But, clearly, all this takes the romance and mystery right out of the picture we have of wily, competitive firms!

The next chapter focuses on a second mechanism that leads to dissemination of technology. It provides a theoretical model that will enable us to analyze the benefits offered to a firm by membership in what I will call a "technology-sharing consortium." The model demonstrates that the market may impose severe penalties upon any firm that remains outside such a consortium and does not share its technical information with others. That isolated firm will be able to offer products and use processes that are improved only by its own research efforts, whereas its rivals will each benefit from their combined innovative activities. Thus, exchange of technology (in contrast to pure licensing), rather than increasing the vulnerability of the participating firms to successful "enemy attack," provides them with a degree of protection. Because each firm is given access to the others' innovations, they are insured against the possibility that one of them, or still another enterprise, will come up with an innovation that will give its proprietor overwhelming competitive superiority. In addition, despite the lags inherent in the transfer process, each firm's management can rest somewhat easier in the knowledge that it will not be denied access to the possibly superior technological developments of its rivals.

The model of the next chapter will also show that society derives welfare benefits from such sharing. This is partly because licensing or exchange of technological information can help to internalize the externalities of innovation activity, thereby reducing the spillovers problem. It will also be shown in the next chapter that technology-exchange consortia can be quite stable if the sharing game is repeated many times.

In sum, this chapter and the next argue that the dissemination of technology under free enterprise is considerably more pervasive and effective than the standard picture implies. It would, of course, be absurd to claim that no innovator firm imposes obstacles to the use of its proprietary information by others. Nor is the discussion intended to assert that the competitive mechanism dependably drives the economy close to optimality in its speed of transfer of technology. Rather, the economy's performance in this area, like its performance in investment in innovation activity, is probably substantially better than may previously have been suspected.

REMOVING THE MYSTIQUE: PROPRIETARY TECHNOLOGY IS JUST ANOTHER "BOTTLENECK INPUT"

To understand what goes on in the technology-licensing markets, it is necessary to free oneself of the preconception that firms invariably have a powerful incentive to battle determinedly against use of their proprietary technology by others. Under capitalism, whether or not that is true in any particular case depends on the *profitability* of that retention by the firm, as compared with the profitability of supplying the technology to others.

Innovation is imbued with a mystic aura that has little basis in the logic of the objectives and behavior of firms. Innovation, of course, brings us extraordinary new products and new ways of doing things—it entertains us, makes us more productive, cures what ails us—and so, appropriately, we may view its creators with awe. But, in order to pick apart how innovation figures in the workings of capitalism, we must strip it to its essence: at heart, novel technology is simply another (durable) input to the production process, one that permits better products to be produced or that enables better processes to be used. The proprietary character of the technology means simply that this input can be obtained only from a monopolist supplier. Thus, from the viewpoint of the firm's decision-making and of the market for the technology, such information is no more and no less than what, in other areas, is referred to as a "bottleneck input." We can liken it to a mountain pass owned by a single railroad that other railroads, which want to compete on partially parallel routes, will need to use as an input for their own transportation service.

A railroad in the position of the owner of this bottleneck mountain pass then has three options. It can deny access to all other railroads; it can admit other railroads for a rental fee (or in exchange for services by the other railroads) and also continue to use the pass for its own traffic; or it can close down its own operations along the route and simply earn revenue as a collector of rental fees. One cannot know, without more information, which of these three is the most profitable option for the proprietor of the pass. That depends on the size of the fee, the volume of traffic of the other railroads, its own costs, its own traffic volume, and the prices it is able to charge for transportation along the entire route. In such circumstances, a firm will often find it profitable to sell access to its bottleneck facility, even to competitors that will cut into the proprietor's own business.

The same is plainly true of the owner of a patent on a valuable innovation. The identical three options apply to this durable input, and if the market offers a license fee that is sufficiently lucrative it will pay the proprietor to go actively into the business of supplying that input. In the next section (and the next chapter), we will see that this often happens, with proprietary technology exchanged or licensed, and sometimes actively marketed.[1] And

1. Note that voluntary dissemination via a licensing market still may require the firm to rely on patents and secrecy. Otherwise users might be able to acquire the technological information without paying the proprietor for its use, and the market for licenses might then shrivel or break down altogether.

the result can be socially beneficial, actually stimulating innovation by internalizing some of its externalities and by facilitating rapid and widespread adoption of improved technology. Once it is recognized that proprietary technology is just another bottleneck input, it becomes clear that there should be nothing surprising about this phenomenon.

MARKETS IN TECHNOLOGY LICENSES: IMPROVING THE TERMS OF THE TRADEOFF

All of this shows how the market helps to ameliorate the tradeoff between the incentive for expenditure on innovation and the rapidity of transfer to others of the products of that expenditure. The market does so by inducing the users of the innovations to make payments to the owners of the technology. Whether these payments take the form of money or of compensation in kind (by granting the licensor access to other inventions in exchange), they cannot be mere tokens; they must be sufficient to induce the proprietor to permit use of the inventions by others, and to do so voluntarily. The implication is that the use of inventions by others can be a profitable activity, even one that becomes the innovator's main line of business. No longer are invention and technology transfer activities that impede one another. Rather, they become, to a substantial degree, mutually compatible.

But this is not all that the free market is able to accomplish in this arena. Among its other achievements are, first, efficiency in the selection of those firms that actually make use of an innovation and provision of an added inducement for firms to struggle to enhance such efficiency. Second, surrender of the exclusive right to use new products and processes, while providing a direct financial reward to the innovator, also leaves it with the benefits of being the first to make use of the invention, and this is an added incentive for continued investment in the process. Third, although the dissemination process does create some disincentive for investment in innovation, when done for profit it also has an influence that works the other way, at least helping to offset its recognized depressing effect. These consequences have already been hinted at in the preceding discussion, but it seems useful to end this part of the discussion with a brief review of their operation, with the three additional benefits here all described in one place.

The Market's Choice of the Most Efficient as the Users of an Innovation

The firm that creates an invention may be more efficient than others in carrying out the innovation process, yet it may not be the most efficient of the enterprises in putting an innovation to use in the subsequent process of turning out final products. As already mentioned, the profit-seeking innovator will license to a rival only if that rival can offer it a license price that is more profitable to the licensor than the gain it could obtain by keeping use of the invention to itself. But the prospective licensee can afford to pay such a lucrative license fee only if it is a more efficient user of the technology. Thus the choice between the innovator and another firm as user of the innovator's technology will depend on which of the two enterprises is its most efficient user. And, if there are several rival bidders for such licenses, the more efficient users will be able to make attractive offers and the less efficient will be unable to afford the license for use of the new product or process. Thus, the market will tend to see to it that the task of production using new technology will go to those best fitted to use it.

Moreover, since efficiency is not a once-and-for-all matter, rivalry for technology licenses serves as an additional incentive for continued investment in improvement of efficiency. The efficiency race can be encouraged only by the pressures contributed by competition among prospective licensees in the market for licenses.

The Seller of a License Retains the Early-Entry Advantage

We have noted that, even with all the help that the licensor can offer, the licensee characteristically needs many months or even several years before it can be fully up and running in the use of the technology that a license entitles it to employ. This means that, although the licensor gives rivals the opportunity to use its proprietary technology in competition with itself, it can depend on a considerable delay before effective competition materializes from this quarter. In the meantime, it can enjoy the advantages of sole employer of the technology, earning whatever monopoly profits are made possible by such exclusivity, seeking to develop customer loyalty for its product, and acquiring experience that improves its manufacture and distribution processes. Thus the technology proprietor can have it both ways—receiving money for its licenses and yet retaining the benefits from built-in unavailability of the innovation to others, at least in its early days, which can in some cases be the most profitable part of the innovation's life cycle.

Lucrative Licensing as an Incentive for Innovation Investment

Finally, the very profitability of licensing or technology trading is an incentive for investment in innovation. That is, the firm that participates in this market has an incentive for innovative effort that is lacking for the firm that does not. The obvious case is the firm that specializes in the creation and licensing of innovations. Such an innovation factory will clearly drive itself out of business if it runs out of innovative products to offer for rental. An extension of this argument shows that this inducement applies to all firms for which licensing is a profitable activity. Similarly, companies that participate in a technology-exchange consortium must have a supply of new products and processes that they can offer to the other members in order to induce them to reciprocate with their own new inventions. This will be demonstrated rigorously in the next chapter. Here, again, one must not overstate the claim. A group of colluding firms may conceivably agree to mutual disarmament—to simultaneous reduction in the amount they invest in innovation. In the absence of such an agreement, however, the market forces can confidently be expected to run the other way, to induce the firms that license or exchange their technology profitably to spend more on innovation than they would have otherwise.

The conclusion, once more, is that the market mechanism has influences that are not obviously available to non-capitalist economies. These tend to make it profitable to engage simultaneously in the innovation "arms race" and in the licensing of any new inventions obtained in the process. Imperfect though this mechanism may be, it still seems remarkably effective (see figures 6.1 and 6.2 again), and is yet another of the features that differentiate the free-market growth process from any other that we know of.

THE MARKETING OF PROPRIETARY TECHNOLOGY IN PRACTICE

I turn next to some real illustrations of the marketing of proprietary technology, to show that it is no figment of the theorist's imagination and to suggest that it is surprisingly common. First, consider some indirect evidence. A number of studies have found that innovation is disseminated far more quickly than one might expect from the hypothesis that the firm, aided by the legal system, does everything in its power to prevent or delay it. For example, a study by Mansfield, Schwartz and Wagner (1981) indicates, from data provided by a hundred American firms in a variety of manufacturing industries, that "[i]nformation concerning development decisions is generally in the hands of rivals within about 12 to 18 months, on the average, and information containing the detailed nature and operation of a new product or process generally leaks out within about a year" (p. 217). This and other evidence of impressive speed of dissemination imply that, if each of the world's private firms is striving to keep its innovations entirely or largely to itself, these enterprises are uncharacteristically ineffective in their pursuit of this goal.

In reality, the opportunity entailed in technology dissemination can and often does lead firms to engage energetically in the marketing of licenses for their technology, treating this activity as a prime profit center for the firm.[2] This is the goal of private industrial laboratories, of which Thomas Edison's firm was perhaps the most publicized example. Other firms, even those that use the technology themselves, also engage in the sale of licenses as a substantial business activity. For example, the industry producing polypropylene resin, one of the most widely used plastic raw materials, has a hotly contested market in package licenses. The package includes the basic technology, the crucial catalyst that is compatible with the selected technology, a commitment by the license supplier to update the process and catalyst technology, and a commitment to provide required inputs and technical assistance. The two principal suppliers of such package licenses are Montell (wholly owned by Royal Dutch Shell) and Union Carbide Corporation. The revenue the latter derives from the sale of package licenses to resin producers throughout the world is a substantial proportion of the revenue it obtains from its own resin production (though that is not true of Montell).

It is, then, incorrect to depict the typical firm as a determined guardian of its technology against all use by others. Licensing has become a widespread business, as illustrated by the profusion of conferences, websites, and organizations devoted to technology transfer, along with wide media coverage of licensing agreements between individual companies. Some examples include a series of conferences, beginning in 1992, organized for business firm participants by the MIT Enterprise Forum on the subject of "Entrepreneurial Technology Transfer." The initial conference offered participants the opportunity to "learn from the leaders in taking innovative technology to market." The Licensing Executives Society, an organization that claims nearly 10,000

2. The profits offered by licensing can be substantial: "The budget for IBM Research, which rose about 10 percent last year, has been growing faster than . . . the company's overall revenue, which grew just 1 percent, to $88.4 billion in 2000. IBM's profit from licensing its inventions has been growing even faster [reaching the] $1.7 billion it received last year" (B. J. Feder, "Eureka! Labs with Profits," *New York Times,* 9 September 2001, section 3, pp. 1 and 12). Comparing total company profits with these licensing revenues, which by their very nature constitute virtually pure additions to profit, IBM's licensing fees for 2000 amounted to slightly more than 20 percent of the firm's total profit!

members from over sixty countries, holds "meetings, seminars, and training sessions for education and the exchange and dissemination of knowledge and information on licensing and intellectual property . . . the Society [monitors] domestic and international changes in the law and the practice of licensing and protecting intellectual property and [encourages] articles, reports, statistics, and other materials on licensing and protecting intellectual property."[3] The Technology Transfer Society is also active in disseminating information about licensing. A recent conference run by that organization on "Leveraging Technology for Competitive Advantage" featured presentations by business executives on technology transfer as a strategy for competitiveness in large corporations. Representatives from such companies as Texaco, Advanced Micro Devices, Hewlett-Packard, and Northrup Grumman gave papers centered around the themes of industrial competitiveness, organizational technology transfer, technology transfer success factors, and R&D commercialization.[4] And there is a profusion of Internet websites offering a range of resources for technology transfer. Examples include Patent and License Exchange, Inc. (www.pl-x.com), Technology Access (www.uventures.com), CorporateIntelligence.com, Yet2.com, Pharmalicensing.com, PatentAuction.com, TechExchange Online (www.teonline.com), Knowledge Exchange Auction (Knexa.com), and Cool License (www.AnIdea.com). Surely all this implies eloquently that enterprising distribution of technology has become a widespread feature of business reality. Indeed, the National Science Board (2000, p. 2–56) reports that, for the period 1980–98, U.S., European, and Japanese firms collectively entered into almost 9,000 strategic technology alliances.[5]

3. http://www.les.org

4. http://www.t2s.org

5. Some recent examples include patent and licensing deals between Apple Computer and Microsoft (see Chris Ward, "Rivalry that Ended in Friendship," *The Times*, 13 August 1997); a technology licensing agreement in the electrical components industry between Maxwell Technologies and Siemens Matsushita Components GmbH (see Bruce V. Bigelow, "Maxwell Technologies Expects $30 Million in Device Royalties," *San Diego Union-Tribune*, 7 October 1998); a pharmaceutical technology licensing partnership between Pfizer and ArQule (see Ronald Rosenberg, "ArQule, Pfizer in 4½-Year Accord; Drug Deal May Be Worth $117 Million," *Boston Globe*, 22 July 1999); strategic technology transfer alliances in the medical imaging market made by Standard Imaging (see Maria Carlino, "Standard Imaging," *Journal of Commerce*, 23 February 1996); technology licensing of power conversion products between Vicor Corporation and NEC Corporation (see "Vicor, NEC Agree on Technology Licensing," *Boston Globe*, 5 March 1998); and technology licensing in print technology between Pitney-Bowes and Hewlett-Packard (see "Pitney-Bowes and Hewlett-Packard Settle Litigation, Announce Business and Technology Agreements," *PR Newswire Association, Inc.*, 4 June 2001).

CHAPTER 6

ON TECHNOLOGY-EXCHANGE CONSORTIA IN PRACTICE

Several studies have examined firm behavior directly, and they confirm that businesses are often prepared to share their proprietary technological information with others, their horizontal competitors included.[6] By the nature of the subject, these investigations rely heavily on samples and case studies. For one cannot expect to find systematic statistics on the extent of technological cooperation among otherwise independent business firms.

Eric Von Hippel (1988, chapter 6), for example, examined a sample of eleven (of the forty-firm U.S. total) American steel mini-mills. These enterprises, which use electric arc furnaces to recycle scrap steel, are considered world leaders in labor productivity. They have outperformed Japanese rivals and now provide a very substantial proportion of the steel output of the United States. Von Hippel found, through a series of interviews, that all but one of the firms in his sample regularly and routinely engaged in the interchange of information with the others: "reported know-how trading often appeared to go far beyond an arm's length exchange of data at conferences. . . . sometimes, *workers of competing firms were trained (at no charge), firm personnel were sent to competing facilities to help set up unfamiliar equipment,* and so on" (p. 79, my emphasis). The know-how traded was, indeed, valuable. It often entailed exchanges with direct rivals and, though engineers and technicians normally carried out the exchanges, it was done with the knowledge and approval of management. The implicit arrangement described in this study is interpretable as a predominantly ex ante exchange. Each firm stands ready to reveal technical information to the others, with the implied understanding that the others will reciprocate by providing it with information on the new technology they acquire in the future, technology whose nature is as yet likely to be unknown.

Several other studies of the subject are reported by Von Hippel. For example, Allen, Hyman, and Pinckney (1983) examined a sample of more than a hundred Irish, Spanish, and Mexican firms and found exchanges at trade shows followed by plant visits and direct supply of technical information in response to inquiries. Such studies show that technical information exchange

6. "This is not to say that there are not situations where firms license their direct market competitors. However, these seem to be industries where licensees do independent R&D, proprietary gains come directly from a head start in any case, and there is an implicit or explicit reciprocity about licensing certain kinds of technology" (Nelson, 1996, p. 70).

does actually occur. However, their limited samples and the relatively small sizes of the enterprises involved may leave open the possibility that the phenomenon is comparatively isolated. There is nonetheless reason to believe that it is much more than that.

Since I began studying the general subject of technology transfer some years ago, I have made it my business to raise this issue with every business firm that has engaged me as a consultant. This has involved perhaps twenty firms, including some of the giant enterprises of the American economy. In each case, the existence of some form and degree of technology exchange between the firm and its rivals was readily acknowledged by company management. In several cases, managements indicated that they agreed to it rather reluctantly, ascribing it to regular exchange of information among the scientists and engineers employed by them. The managerial personnel giving this report indicated that they were uncomfortable or even indignant at the giveaway of valuable information produced at company expense. However, they claimed to have little choice since, according to them, retention of their competitive position required the employment of scientists and engineers of high quality. And such able persons were unwilling to work for companies that did not permit communication with their counterparts in other enterprises (compare the quote by J. B. Say at the beginning of the next chapter).

In another instance, a retired vice president of one of America's most innovative firms described a technology-sharing arrangement with a Japanese enterprise. Representatives of the two companies meet annually to settle their "balance of payments"; a sum decided by negotiation is paid by the firm providing the less valuable innovations to its "consortium" partner, as compensation for the latter's more valuable contribution. A curious feature of this arrangement is that the two firms bargain not over the value of the innovations provided in the current year, or in the previous year, but over the innovations each expects to provide in the *following* years. A possible explanation of this ex ante orientation of the arrangement as a means to discourage cheating will be offered in the next chapter.

Another consulting assignment, in which I was engaged as this chapter was being written, entailed work for Perkin-Elmer Corporation, a firm that manufactures and sells analytical (scientific) instruments (notably those using precision optics) throughout the world. Since World War II, Perkin-Elmer has entered into many agreements with domestic and foreign firms for the ex post transfer of technology under license. The most interesting of these (for our purposes here) was an agreement in 1960 with the Hitachi

Corporation for the systematic exchange of technical information.[7] In the Perkin-Elmer/Hitachi contracts, the two firms undertook to supply regularly to one another a full menu of technical developments that had come into their possession. Each firm was authorized to produce, with full technical assistance by the other, any product on any such menu it had received, paying a royalty rate of 6.0 to 7.5 percent for items that had been invented by the other firm, with lower royalty payments on items to which the licensing firm had made a smaller innovating or development contribution. In 1971, the contract was modified to restrict the amount of information each firm was expected to supply along with its menus before the other firm had committed itself to its product selections. Evidently, the firms felt that they had been giving away too much information without compensation.

Excerpts from their contract of 10 December 1968 illustrate the spirit of the agreements:

> Perkin-Elmer . . . and Hitachi desire to insure a continuous exchange of technical information in agreed-upon fields of analytical instrumentation. . . . 3.1 To the extent permitted by other agreements to which one of the parties hereto . . . is a party, and in conformity with government security or other restrictions, (a) Perkin-Elmer agrees to make available to [Hitachi] and (b) [Hitachi] agrees to convey to Perkin-Elmer all information each has available to it during the term of this Agreement within the Product Principle List. . . . 3.2 Upon request [the firms will supply to one another] copies of all drawings available to each containing information relating to such Product Principles. 3.3 Each party may send technical representatives to the other party's premises at its own expense and at times convenient to the other party to obtain technical information related to such Product Principles. 3.4 Upon request [either firm] will send technical experts to [the other] at times and places mutually agreeable for periods not to exceed thirty (30) days. . . . In each case, the requesting company will be required to pay all travel and maintenance expense of such technical experts but not salaries. (pp. 1, 5–6)

The contract of 8 April 1971 also states:

> Each party covenants and agrees that it will at all times hereafter . . . take all reasonable steps to keep all Technical Information communicated to it by the other party secret and confidential and will not divulge any of the said Technical Information to any person or corporation other than those sub-licensed hereunder. (p. 8)

7. For more on the technology-sharing arrangements involving Perkin-Elmer, see the appendix to this chapter.

In other industries the technology-sharing arrangements differ, but they are often there. The vice president of IBM in charge of its patent portfolio[8] wrote to me that many firms in his industry licensed their patents, either in cross-licensing contracts with one another, or in limited exchanges with smaller participants in the industry. The contracts usually cover some defined field such as semiconductors or input–output devices. They are formulated in a bargaining session in which the two negotiating firms compare what each has to offer the other (larger firms being expected to provide more patents but to benefit more from each patent provided by its smaller partner), and the difference in the value of the patent offerings of the two firms is made up by a monetary "balance payment." The contract, which normally runs over several years, entitles each firm to use the other firm's current patents in the field covered (the ex post component of the arrangement), as well as other patents issued later during the life of the contract (the ex ante component). The contract covers patents but *not* know-how (i.e., information about the best ways to put a patent to use), which remains proprietary. According to the supplier of this information, the reasons such cross-licensing contracts are felt to be important by IBM are that they "level the playing field," save wasteful costs such as outlays on reverse engineering or on inventing around patents of a rival, and enhance the firm's freedom of action by permitting it to introduce new products without fear that it will be accused of infringing someone's patents.

Other examples are easily found. United Technologies' Pratt and Whitney, which manufactures aircraft jet engines and associated products, has acted as a partner with one of its principal competitors, General Electric, "in the development of an engine to power a very high speed future aircraft."[9] And, in a very different industry, a newspaper report tells us that wine making in California has been characterized by a "spirit of cooperation and communication. . . . While different wineries compete fiercely for sales, winemakers have commonly shared their technical knowledge and tricks of the trade, to their mutual benefit" (*New York Times,* 2 July 1992, p. 1). Ernesto Gallo told me that his winery helps to finance the winemaking program at the University of California, at which the latest techniques that have evolved in the company are taught to students. He also said that technical communication

8. I am deeply grateful to Vice President Howard G. Figueroa for giving me the information described here, and for editing this portion of the manuscript for accuracy.

9. Letter to me by the vice president in charge of Management Information Systems at Pratt and Whitney.

among the vineyards continues—facilitated by the very large proportion of master vintners at rival vineyards who were trained at Gallo—at least partly to make jobs at Gallo attractive to capable individuals. Finally, even in the fierce race to produce practical high-definition television technology, two of the rival groups (one consisting of General Instrument Company and MIT, and the other consisting of Zenith Electronics Corporation and AT&T) agreed to pool their efforts and to share the rights that would be provided by the U.S. patents that resulted from their combined efforts (*New York Times,* 8 May 1992, p. D1).

It is clear, then, that firms, large and small, do in many cases exchange technological information, sometimes reluctantly, perhaps more often very deliberately.[10] And a good deal of this is carried out through inter-firm exchanges.

THE PRICE MECHANISM AND RECONCILIATION OF PRIVATE AND SOCIAL GOALS IN DISSEMINATION

As elsewhere in the economy, the price mechanism can help to deal with the dissemination dilemma for society—the problem that easy dissemination reduces the incentive for innovation but facilitates its general use. Licensing and rental fees can enable the economy to attain something like the optimal compromise in this tradeoff. They can help to preserve the inventor's reward, while permitting others to use the ideas. It is this price that induces some firms to go beyond grudgingly permitting the use of some of their technology by others when forced by circumstances to do so.

If the price is right, it will pay the firm that owns any such input to permit others to use it. The question, of course, is: What is the right price? It is also natural to ask whether the price that is right for the licensor is also the one that is best for society. In particular, do there exist features of the market mechanism that drive the license fee toward the socially optimal level? We

10. Note also the following observation by George and Joll (1981, pp. 231–32) about practices in the United Kingdom: "In addition a group of firms in research-intensive industries may operate a patent-pooling and licensing arrangement by which all the firms agree to license one another but no outside firms. Indeed, Taylor and Silberston (1973) found that in the pharmaceutical industry the most important advantage claimed for the patent system was that it gave the firms something to put into such a patent-pooling system so as to gain access to the other firms' patented drugs." This is a clear example of internalization of the externalities of the R&D process that is emphasized here.

will return to these questions in chapter 13, where it will be shown that there is such a thing as an economically efficient license fee. I will also argue that this efficient fee offers benefits to both the licensor and the licensee, but that market forces support its adoption only imperfectly.

APPENDIX

SOME OTHER PERKIN-ELMER PATENT-SHARING ARRANGEMENTS

Besides its contracts with Hitachi, the Perkin-Elmer Corporation has had about a hundred other such arrangements since World War II. The following are a few examples illustrating very briefly how much their terms differed:

CSIRO. Spectroscopy uses instruments of two general types: infrared spectrophotometers, which are particularly useful for analysis of the composition of a sample whose makeup is not known in advance, and atomic absorption (AA) instruments, which are better adapted to precise measurement of components previously known to be contained in a sample. The AA technique was invented in Australia and was patented in the early 1950s by a firm whose acronym is CSIRO. Before the availability of commercially viable AA equipment, CSIRO began to license its patents, first on an exclusive basis, then, after 1959, to companies throughout the world. Perkin-Elmer was among the licensees, agreeing to pay what was CSIRO's standard royalty (depending on the country of spectrometer sale) of about 2 percent of the value of the instrument. The relatively low fee reflected the substantial development work that the licensees had to carry out to produce a salable AA instrument.

Advanced Radiation. In the 1970s, Perkin-Elmer patented a process for the manufacture of the "Microalign instrument," which uses a mercury capillary lamp to etch circuit patterns on photo-resistant semiconductor wafers. Having been a successful sole producer of the item for some period, in 1977 the firm encountered pressure from its customers to arrange for a second supplier of the Microalign lamps to ensure their continuous availability. Perkin-Elmer selected Advanced Radiation Corporation (ARC), which it described as "a small, flexible supplier," and entered into an agreement to allow ARC to produce the lamp and sell it directly to customers. Because of its blocking patent, Perkin-Elmer was able to arrange for a royalty of 48 percent of the value of ARC sales, with the arrangement apparently also proving extremely profitable to the licensee.

Laser Precision. In the late 1970s, infrared spectroscopy underwent a major improvement permitted by the growing power of computers. The new approach utilized the Fourier transform to make more effective use of the data generated by the spectroscope. Perkin-Elmer undertook its own development effort in the late 1970s, seeking to design a Fourier-transform instrument of its own. Because the effort was going too slowly, and to avoid a major gap in its product line and tardy entry into the field, in 1981 Perkin-Elmer began negotiations with the Analect Division of Laser Precision Corporation for access to Analect's Fourier-transform instrument. At the time, Analect was a tiny concern with three full-time employees, but it held the patent on a viable technique for the purpose. The license called for a payment of $1 million plus a royalty of 4 percent of sales. However, Perkin-Elmer never exercised its option to acquire the license. Instead, it chose to buy the finished instrument from Analect until Perkin-Elmer came up with a later-generation instrument of its own.

Perkin-Elmer Puerto Rico. In 1970 Perkin-Elmer founded a wholly owned subsidiary in Puerto Rico, and licensed it to manufacture a number of the products for which Perkin-Elmer held the patents. The Puerto Rican output was sold entirely to the parent company, which carried out their distribution. The transfer prices seem to have approximated the figures in the license agreement with other firms, though the U.S. Internal Revenue Service, predictably, challenged them.

CHAPTER 7

Oligopolistic Rivalry and Markets for Technology Trading

the knowledge of the man of science, indispensable as it is to the development of industry, circulates with ease and rapidity from one nation to all the rest. And men of science have themselves an interest in its diffusion; for upon that diffusion they rest their hopes of fortune, and, what is more prized by them, of reputation too. For this reason, a nation, in which science is but little cultivated, may nevertheless carry its industry to a very great length, by taking advantage of the information derivable from abroad.

—Say, 1819, 1834, p. 82

managers approached apparently competing firms in other countries directly and were provided with surprisingly free access to their technology.

—Allen et al., 1983, p. 202

BASIC THEORY

I turn now to a second mechanism that encourages and facilitates voluntary dissemination of new technology. The previous chapter discussed the profit incentive offered by the market mechanism for the licensing of proprietary technology. It also described the resulting consequences for efficiency in the use of innovations and for the rate of economic growth, arguing that the effect is generally beneficial. In the current chapter I will discuss the trading by competitors of the right to use one another's technology, rather than the unilateral sale of such a right via licenses. It may appear at first glance that there should be little difference between the two cases, the only distinction being the nature of the reward: money versus payment in kind. We will see, however, that the differences are considerably more substantial. This chapter will describe the "technology consortia" that are implicitly created by the process of technology sharing. I will examine the nature of the market incentives for their formation, their stability (in contrast with the noted instability of price cartels), and their welfare consequences.[1]

Specifically, I will show in this chapter that:

- Firms that pool their innovations gain a competitive advantage over firms that depend only on their own R&D resources. The resulting competitive handicap to nonparticipants in a sharing consortium can grow cumulatively as time passes.
- Each participant in a technology consortium has a strong incentive to comply with its agreements, giving its trading partners full access to all of its proprietary technology information that it has promised. This is because cheating, in the form of failure to provide some promised information, can result in ejection from the consortium, with all its competitive disadvantage.
- Membership in a technology consortium provides an added incentive to the member firm to invest in innovative activity.
- The result is generally a contribution to the welfare of the public.
- This implies that if antitrust policy is to serve the general welfare, in contrast to its justifiable position against inter-firm agreements on prices, it must exercise restraint in interfering with coordinated behavior by competing firms entailing the exchange of technological information on innovations.

Forms Taken by Technology-Sharing Arrangements

The arrangements for the sharing of technology that are encountered in practice are very heterogeneous. The exchange can have an explicit and formal structure, as when a trade association runs a research facility whose findings are available to all members of the association and whose expenses are divided among them on some predetermined basis. The same is true when two or more firms organize a research joint venture. Private and independent research organizations often offer the information they produce to all comers at a price. In addition, firms can, and do, exchange information that each has produced internally, by itself, and that could, instead, have been treated as proprietary.

1. For an illuminating paper that studies learning by firms from one another using a theoretical orientation somewhat similar to that employed here, see Petit and Tolwinski (1993). See also the very important articles of D'Asprement and Jacquemin (1988) and Katz and Ordover (1990).

This exchange also has many forms. The information can deliberately be disseminated on the explicit initiative of company personnel, with the knowledge and consent, or at least the toleration, of top management. Instead, company A may simply be prepared to answer inquiries from company B and to come to B's assistance when it runs into technical difficulties, always with the understanding that such assistance is a two-way process. Firms sometimes welcome highly revealing plant visits by engineers and technicians from other companies, even when those companies are direct competitors, foreign or domestic. Some enterprises even agree, on request, to train the technical personnel from another firm in the use of an unfamiliar process or technique, expecting the favor to be reciprocated in the future. There are also very formal arrangements for the exchange of technology, employing instruments such as carefully drawn contracts and cross-licensing of patents, as was illustrated by real and substantial examples in the previous chapter. Throughout the chapter, I will use the term "technology consortium" generically to describe all of the technology-exchange arrangements that have just been mentioned.

Recently, the economics literature has begun to recognize that there are a number of reasons firms may want to share some of their proprietary technical information (for an excellent overview, see Katz and Ordover, 1990). The reason that is perhaps most often given (it is also frequently cited by businesspersons) is the high cost of the innovation process, which is more easily shouldered by a group of firms than by a single enterprise. This, and several other explanations that will be noted later, seems valid enough. However, this chapter will stress an entirely different market mechanism that can provide an incentive for technology sharing far more pervasive and powerful than those previously noted.

Complements and Substitutes in Innovation

Since, in practice, many firms seem willing to participate in technology sharing, as the evidence offered in chapter 6 indicated, they presumably expect to profit by doing so. A distinguishing feature of our model describing the nature of that gain is based on the difference between innovations that are *substitutes* for one another and, hence, mutually competitive, and those that are *complementary*.[2]

2. The special role of complementarity and substitution in innovation has also been emphasized by Nelson (1990); and see also Merges and Nelson (1994). It has also been studied, in another context, by Young (1992).

When two firms are working toward innovations that are, at least to some degree, substitutes, as is implicitly assumed by many models of competition and the innovation process, then their managements may well have a strong incentive to resist leakage of their proprietary technical knowledge. But the market incentives are reversed when, as often seems true in practice in large-firm R&D, the innovations in question are heterogeneous and complementary. This scenario is very different from Schumpeter's, or from those of patent races and waiting game models in which all the competitors are after what is essentially the same technical goal: a given new product or process, say the design of a less expensive high-definition television receiver.

Here, in contrast, I will focus on an evolving product, for which innovations are small heterogeneous improvements introduced by different manufacturers of that same product. These improvements are typically complementary. In laptop computer manufacturing, for example, one producer may introduce an improved screen, another an improved keyboard, and a third may invent a way to make the laptop lighter and more compact. Each of these three firms has the choice of keeping its invention to itself. But if two of them get together and agree to produce computers combining the features each of them has contributed, they will be able to market a product that is clearly superior to what each could have produced alone. They are then likely to be in a far better position to meet the competition of the third manufacturer. Thus, I will say that the improved screen and the superior keyboard are complementary rather than substitute inventions.

In reality, both types of relationships occur. Thus, there are well-known examples of hot patent races that, by their nature, entail inventions that are close substitutes. But the normal operation of the large firm in an industry with rapidly evolving technology seems more often characterized by heterogeneity and complementarity. As has already been asserted here, the large firm is rarely the source of revolutionary new products or processes, and most of its innovative investment appears to be devoted to incremental improvements.[3] In fact, it will generally be a coincidence if the R&D activities of two suppliers of a common product hit upon similar improvements, that is, upon substitute innovations. The model that follows, then, deals with the presumably more common case of complementary innovative results.

---

3. Thus, Levin reports, on the basis of his systematic study, that "technological advance in the electronics industries has been much more 'cumulative' than 'discrete'" (1988, p. 427). Rosenberg's work (e.g., 1976, p. 66, fn) has also emphasized this point, and has provided an abundance of illustrations.

It should also be emphasized that, although the discussion will occasionally provide results that hold in the special cases of perfect competition or perfect contestability, the model does *not* assume that the markets take either of these forms.

The Technology-Consortium Model

Consider an industry containing $n + 1$ firms that are identical in all respects except that firms $1, \ldots, n$ agree to share technical information with one another, while firm $n + 1$ keeps the results of its R&D to itself. Assume, to simplify the exposition, that each firm routinely spends the same amount on R&D per period, and that the expected return to this expenditure is the same for every firm. Most important, assume that the inventions of the different members of the consortium are generally expected to be different from one another and complementary, so that none of them can be used only as a replacement for one of the others. Finally, it is assumed, also for simplicity in discussion, that innovation expenditure is devoted exclusively to cost-reducing process innovations. That is, the innovation process is taken to make final products cheaper but no better. The only purpose of this inessential premise is that it permits quantification of the immediate benefits, making them easier to represent and interpret.

The public-good character of the information derived from R&D does *not* mean that it costs nothing to transfer information from the firm, A, that has produced it, to another enterprise, B, in a technology-sharing consortium. There is, in fact, evidence that the process of imitation typically has costs that are not negligible when compared with those of the earlier innovator.[4] Nevertheless, firm B can expect a considerable net benefit from the information it obtains from the other $n - 1$ members of the technology consortium. Even if it could, eventually, get the same information through reverse engineering, industrial espionage, or other means, the empirical evidence indicates that a friendly transfer is typically far cheaper and quicker than a hostile one. In a rapidly evolving field, speed is particularly important because slowly acquired technical information is apt to be obsolete information.[5]

4. "Our respondents from the industries producing aircraft and complete guided missile systems—canonical complex systems—reported that it would cost a competent imitator more than three-quarters what it cost the innovator to come up with something comparable, even if there were no patent protection at all" (Nelson, 1996, p. 64). The survey referred to here is described in Levin et al. (1987), which contains much valuable material on the costs of imitation.

5. For more on the general subject, see Mansfield, Schwartz, and Wagner (1981) and Teece (1977).

Suppose that B's internal R&D is expected to reduce the cost of the firm's final product by r percent per year. At the same time, because of transfer costs, B can expect a cost reduction from the information it obtains from A, or from any one other single member of the consortium, of only s percent (where $s \le r$). Then, if total R&D spending by each firm is x per year, and $C_0(y)$ is the initial period's total cost of production of its output, y, its expected cost in the next period will be $C_0(y)[1 - r - s(n - 1)] + x$, that is, its expected future manufacturing costs of final products will be reduced, not only by its own efforts, but also by the R&D of each of the other $n - 1$ members of the consortium.[6] In contrast, the holdout firm, $n + 1$, which refuses to join the consortium and which, by hypothesis, starts off with the same costs as B, will incur the total expected cost $C_0(y)(1 - r) + x$ in the next period (since by hypothesis $x_{n+1} = x$), which is clearly greater than the consortium member's cost. Moreover, we will see that this expected cost disadvantage increases cumulatively with the passage of time. Beyond that, if the game is a repeated one and if the market happens to be perfectly competitive or contestable, with entry absolutely free, so that B's expected profit is zero, the holdout firm will be faced with ever-growing expected losses.

The logic of the argument, then, is clear. So long as the firms are similar in terms of expected value of information output, and technological changes are predominantly complementary, a technology consortium gives its members a considerable competitive advantage, ex ante. It apparently will pay a firm, X, to hold out from membership only if its large size or other special circumstances lead it to spend so much more on R&D than do its rivals that the cost reduction it expects to achieve for itself will enable it to stay ahead of the cost reductions its competitors can achieve in aggregate through the formation of a technology consortium that does not include firm X.[7]

Formal Characterization of the Cost of Nonmembership

Let us now examine, a little more systematically, the market's penalties upon the nonmember firm.

> **PROPOSITION 7.1.** A firm that does not join a technology consortium of members otherwise identical with itself is automatically penal-

6. In addition, such an ex ante sharing arrangement clearly provides the firm insurance against the risk that its own R&D effort will turn out to yield little of value in any given year.

7. Even then, or when a firm's R&D organization is superior in ability to that of its rivals, participation in a technology consortium can be profitable, as will be argued presently and as the example of IBM in the previous chapter clearly confirms.

ized financially by the market mechanism. (a) Its expected profits are lower than those of a consortium member; and (b) the expected opportunity losses continue through time and grow cumulatively.

That is, if two firms are identical in all other respects—in their market demand, their costs, and the returns to their R&D investment—but one has access only to the innovations it introduces itself, whereas the other exchanges information with other firms on their proprietary innovations, then the latter will be more profitable than the former. Moreover, the relative profit disadvantage of the nonmember continues and grows larger the longer it is excluded from the consortium.

This proposition is virtually self-evident, and it will be formalized only to introduce my model. To prove Proposition 7.1, as well as several subsequent results, I use the following notation, for simplicity suppressing subscripts that identify particular firms wherever that information is self-evident:

$x_k = x =$ firm k's R&D expenditure per period, assumed identical for all firms in the market;[8]

$y_k =$ output per period of firm k;

$i = 1, \ldots, n =$ the indexes identifying individual consortium member firms;

$j = n + 1, \ldots, N =$ the nonmember firms;

$\pi^i(y_i, x_i, n) =$ the total profit function of consortium member i;

$\pi^j(y_j, x_j) =$ the total profit function of nonmember j;

$R^k(y_k) =$ firm k's total revenue per period;

$C^k(y_k) =$ firm k's total non-R&D cost in period zero;

$f^k(z_k) =$ the cost reduction factor for firm k in the subsequent period, where $\partial f^k/\partial z_k < 0$ and where $z_i = nx_i$ for consortium member i,

$z_j = \alpha nx_j$ for nonmember j (so z_k is a measure of the new information available to firm k);

$\alpha < 1 =$ benefits lost from an information transfer because it is "hostile" rather than "friendly"; and, finally,

's' and 'p' are superscripts referring to profit-maximizing values of the variables in question for those firms that share their information (s) and those that hold it proprietary (p), respectively.

8. Later, in Proposition 7.2, the choice of value of x is calculated explicitly on the premise that each firm follows a Cournot strategy. Except in the model used to derive Proposition 7.3, the premise that the value of x is the same for every firm plays no essential role.

Here I use $\alpha < 1$ to represent the fact that, though the spillovers of innovative activity bring benefits to nonmembers of the technology consortium as well as to members, the costs and benefits to the former are generally smaller, because it is more difficult to obtain technological information without the cooperation of its proprietor, and because such hostile technology acquisition takes longer and therefore is closer to obsolescence when the information is finally obtained by the nonmember. We may note also that we can, if we wish, take the variables in the model to refer to *expected values,* so that all of the calculations become ex ante in character.

Proof of Proposition 7.1. Part (a). Since, generally, for a technology-sharing firm, I, y^p_i and x^p_i are not the profit-maximizing values of y_i and x_i, we now have immediately

$$\begin{aligned} (7.1)\qquad \pi^i(y^s_i, x^s_i, n) &\geq (\pi^i(y^p_i, x^p_i, n) \\ &= R^i(y^p_i) - f(nx^p_i)C(y^p_i) - x^p_i \\ &> R^i(y^p_i) - f(\alpha nx^p_i)C(y^p_i) - x^p_i \\ &= \pi^i(y^p_i, x^p_i). \end{aligned}$$

This is our desired result; the firm will lose out in terms of profits (or expected profits) if it declines to become a member of the technology consortium when all members spend the same amount on R&D.

Proof of Proposition 7.1. Part (b). The profit (opportunity) loss of the firm that finds itself excluded from the consortium is not just a once-and-for-all matter. Rather, it is an intertemporal stream of losses that grows cumulatively with time. This is easily proved by rewriting the two central expressions in (7.1) with the addition of time subscripts (and the omission of subscripts and superscripts that are obvious). We obtain for the consortium member and nonmember, respectively,

$$(7.2)\qquad C_t = f(nx_{t-1})C_{t-1} \text{ and } C_t = f(\alpha nx_{t-1})C_{t-1},$$

so that $\Delta\pi_t$ and $\Delta\pi_{t+1}$, the profit loss in periods t and $t + 1$ resulting from ejection from the consortium in period $t - 1$, become

$$\Delta\pi_t = [f(\alpha nx_{t-1}) - f(nx_{t-1})]C_{t-1}$$

$$(7.3)\qquad \Delta\pi_{t+1} = [f(\alpha nx_t) - f(nx_t)][f(\alpha nx_{t-1}) - f(nx_{t-1})]C_{t-2} > \Delta\pi_t,$$

as we wanted to show.[9]

9. The discussion has described the model in terms of ex ante sharing, in which each consortium member agrees to supply information on the output of its R&D activities over the selected future period. However, it should be noted that the mathematical discussion

It should be emphasized that, although the motivation for membership in a technology consortium that has just been described is important and pervasive, the literature has offered other reasonable explanations for technology sharing. Reduction in the cost burden of R&D to each of the sharing enterprises has already been mentioned. This incentive is clear in the case of research joint ventures, but in arrangements such as royalty-free cross-licensing of patents its role is less obvious. The literature also mentions sharing incentives such as network externalities that only a group of enterprises can achieve, the benefits of standardization and compatibility that a consortium can arrange to have built into the new products of its members, and the possibility that the mutual benefits of an outward shift of the demand curve facing the industry as a whole may be achievable only by products that share all of the available improvements. For further discussion, the reader is once again referred to the admirable overview of the subject by Katz and Ordover (1990).

Welfare Consequences

I come, next, to some of the welfare consequences of technology consortia, where my mathematical model begins to pay off. In a sense, it is obvious that a technology consortium can generate welfare benefits by permitting wider and more rapid use of innovations, unless the sharing of information undercuts the incentive for R&D investment or leads horizontal competitors to engage in monopolistic types of behavior. It may seem plausible, for example, that colluding competitors will all agree to cut their expenditures on innovation to save the trouble and expense.[10] But it will be proved next that if the innovations of the firms are complementary then information sharing will *increase* the profit-maximizing oligopolist's spending on innovation.[11] More-

is not dependent on that assumption in any way. It is equally applicable, for example, to a consortium that operates through cross-licensing of the patents it holds on its past inventions. Thus, the results derived so far, and (except where otherwise noted) those that follow, apply to a broader spectrum of technology-sharing consortia, and not only to those with ex ante sharing.

10. For a fuller discussion of these problems, see Shapiro (2001).

11. The model assumes that the firm's behavior is of the type described by Cournot (1838). However, it is not difficult to show that the result is more general.

Levin's evidence seems to provide some empirical underpinning to this result, even though it has sometimes been suggested in the theoretical literature that (unintended) information sharing should discourage expenditure on innovation by the firm. Thus, note Levin's comments on the prediction of Spence's model "that spillovers discourage R&D investment but may be conducive to rapid technical progress." Levin indicates that his results, "though only suggestive, give some support for the latter hypothesis, but none for the former" (1988, p. 427).

over, the cost saving, in turn, will increase the profit-maximizing output per firm.

I emphasize that neither Proposition 7.2 nor Proposition 7.3, which follow along the same lines, implies that a technology consortium yields a socially optimal outlay on innovation by the firm. It still remains true that the externalities of innovation can be expected to lead to outlays that are generally less than optimal. I claim here only that the technology consortium tends to move matters in the right direction. It internalizes part of the externality by enabling an innovating firm, A, to obtain a substantial reward for its own innovation effort in the form of cheaper and quicker access to the innovations of other enterprises that are beneficiaries of A's technology. Specifically, we have,

PROPOSITION 7.2. With a fixed number of profit-maximizing firms producing a single product and investing in cost-reducing R&D, if each firm in the consortium behaves like a Cournot oligopolist and there is complementarity among the research outputs of the technology-sharing firms, then a rise in the number of consortium members will increase each member's outlay on innovation, as well as its output of the final product, and shift its total cost function downward.

Here, I assume that the number of firms in the industry is expected by the Cournot firm to be fixed, so that an increase in $n + 1$, the number of consortium members, entails an equal reduction in the number of nonmembers. On the Cournot assumption, this means that each firm will expect the total output of the remainder of the industry to be unaffected by a change in n. For convenience, n will, unrealistically, be treated as a continuous variable.

Proof of Proposition 7.2. Let the profit function of a consortium member (firm 1) be given by

$$\pi = R(y, Y) - f[x + \alpha X(n)]C(y) - x, \tag{7.4}$$

where R, C, y, x, and f have the same economic connotation as before, and

Y = the total output of all firms in the industry other than 1, which Cournot firm 1 assumes to be constant,

$X(n)$ = the sum of the expenditures on innovation of the n other members of the consortium,

α = a constant, $(0 < \alpha < 1)$, this time representing the cost of "friendly" technology transfer, and

D = the Jacobian determinant of the derivatives of π.

Then we expect, by assumption,

(7.5) $R_y \equiv \partial R/\partial y > 0,\ f_x < 0,\ f_n < 0$ and $C_y > 0.$

By the second-order conditions

(7.6) $D > 0,\ \pi_{yy} < 0,\ \pi_{xx} < 0.$

Finally, define complementarity between x and $X(n)$ (where $dX/dn > 0$) as

(7.7) $f_{xn} < 0,$

that is, a rise in $X(n)$ increases the marginal cost saving yielded by a rise in x, firm 1's expenditure on innovation.

Then the first-order maximization conditions for (7.4) are

(7.8) $\pi_y = R_y - fC_y = 0, \qquad \pi_x = -f_xC - 1 = 0.$

Setting the total differential of each of these equal to zero to determine what changes in y and x are needed to restore equilibrium after an exogenous change in n, we obtain

(7.9a) $d\pi_y = \pi_{yy}dy - f_xC_ydx - f_nC_ydn = 0$

(7.9b) $d\pi_x = -f_xC_ydy + \pi_{xx}dx - f_{xn}Cdn = 0.$

Thus,

(7.10a) $\partial y/\partial n = (f_nC_y\pi_{xx} + f_{xn}Cf_xC_y)/D$ and

(7.10b) $\partial x/\partial n = (f_xC_y^2f_n + \pi_{yy}f_{xn}C)/D.$

By (7.5), (7.6), and (7.7) it follows directly that (7.10a) and (7.10b) are both positive.

Moreover, the effect of a rise in n on firm 1's total production cost for a given volume of output, y, is

(7.11) $dfC/dn = Cf_n + Cf_x\ \partial x/\partial n < 0.$

This completes the proof of Proposition 7.2. It is also clear that the same results all hold if the inventions are very weak substitutes, so that f_{xn} is positive but relatively small. We can also prove, analogously:

PROPOSITION 7.3. Under the assumptions of Proposition 7.2, but if each consortium member expects every other member will make exactly the same decisions that it does,[12] any increase in n, the num-

12. This term can be interpreted to mean either that the outcomes are symmetric or that the choices are made jointly. Here I mean the former—that, because the firms are all

ber of firms that share the results of one another's R&D, will shift the production cost curve of each firm downward. *Each* information-sharing firm will increase its output when n rises,[13] and, if the marginal-cost-reducing returns to x, the firm's investment in R&D, are increased by an increase in the technical information it receives from other consortium members (complementarity in their innovations), a rise in n will increase the firm's R&D outlays.

Proof of Proposition 7.3. For simplicity, rewrite the profit function of a member of the technology consortium as

$$\pi = R(y) - f(z)C(y) - z/n, \quad C' > 0,\ f'<0, \tag{7.12}$$

where $z = nx$ is the total outlay on R&D by all the members of the consortium together. Differentiating in turn with respect to z and y, we have the first-order maximum conditions

$$-f'C - 1/n = 0, \quad R' - fC' = 0. \tag{7.13}$$

Equating to zero the total differential of the LHS of each equation yields

$$\pi_{zz}dz - f'C'dy = -dn/n^2 \tag{7.14a}$$

$$-f'C'dz + \pi_{yy}dy = 0. \tag{7.14b}$$

We obtain our comparative-statics results directly, using inequalities corresponding to (7.5), (7.6), and (7.7):

$$dz/dn = -\pi_{yy}/n^2D > 0, \qquad dy/dn = -f'C'/n^2D > 0. \tag{7.15}$$

Recalling that C is the initial total cost function for the firm and that f is the function indicating the proportion by which that cost is reduced by invention, we also have $\partial fC/\partial n = (\partial fC/\partial z)(\partial z/\partial n) = f'C\partial z/\partial n < 0$, so that the firm's production cost, fC, is, *ceteris paribus,* a decreasing function of n. We can complete our proof by substituting $x = z/n$ in (7.12) and obtain, by then repeating all the preceding steps, the result that $\partial x/\partial n > 0$ iff f'' is negative, zero, or positive and sufficiently small. This can be interpreted as the premise that the innovations are complementary, independent, or very mild

similarly situated, their profit-maximizing decisions on outputs and investment in R&D will be the same, and that experience will have led each firm to recognize the identity of its own behavior and that of the other members of the consortium.

13. For a similar result for the case of cooperation in R&D activity (in contradistinction to the sharing of the results of independent R&D activity), see the very nice paper by D'Aspremont and Jacquemin (1988).

substitutes. That is, in all such cases, technological information exchange will actually stimulate each firm's outlays on innovation.

The result that, under the premises of either proposition, an expansion in the number of members of the consortium reduces production cost is not, by itself, conclusive evidence that efficiency is increased. For, with a given y, it is still conceivable that spending on R&D will increase by more than the cut in production cost. When n increases, so long as the resulting rise in x (the firm's innovation outlay) does not exceed the reduction in its cost contributed by access to the technology of the new consortium member(s), this, obviously, will not happen. However, if a larger value of x were selected, this would presumably indicate that the yield of the incremental R&D outlay more than covers this enhanced expenditure. Certainly that must be true if the markets are perfectly competitive or contestable, and there is at least a presumption that the same conclusion holds in a considerably broader range of market conditions. This, then, is the sense in which a rise in the number of members of the consortium can be presumed to be welfare increasing.

It is important to observe that the same conclusions, as well as the results of Propositions 7.2 or 7.3, must necessarily also apply to the formation of a technology consortium. This follows because the decision of n firms to create a technology-sharing consortium can be interpreted simply as an increase in the number of its members from zero to n, and the result then follows directly. The creation of a new technology-sharing consortium can increase spending on innovation, increase output, and reduce cost.

None of this is, however, meant to imply that it is impossible for a technology consortium to harm the general welfare. On the contrary, it raises at least two (closely related) dangers. If such a group learns to coordinate its decisions closely, one cannot rule out the possibility of perversion of the technology consortium into a conspiracy either to fix prices or to suppress innovation outlays, or both.

There is one apparently characteristic feature of such consortia in practice that seems to reduce these dangers substantially. In every technology-exchange program of which I am aware, the negotiation and supervision of the arrangements are strictly bilateral. That is, even though firms A, B, C, and D are members of the same consortium, in the sense that they all trade information with each of the others (and each is well aware that the others are doing so), A, for example, will have a separate agreement with each of the others. Its exchange contract with B may be very different from that with C or D. The four firms will never meet together nor will the group as a whole share communications. Such a pair-wise mode of operation seems unlikely to permit the degree of coordination that is necessary for effectiveness in fixing prices or in agreeing to hold down R&D outlays.

It should also be noted that the welfare issues raised by my discussion of technology-sharing consortia go well beyond the subject of innovations and their use. In particular, my analysis raises the obvious questions about the dangers to the public interest of inter-firm agreements. It is generally accepted, for example, that price-setting coordination by horizontal competitors is damaging to the public interest, and that it will normally end with final-product prices higher than they would have been if those prices had been arrived at independently. It is on these grounds that the U.S. courts hold such price fixing to be a per se violation of the law, that is, one for which there can be no justification, no matter what the circumstances.

But this does not mean that *all* coordinated acts by independent enterprises are damaging to the public interest. Indeed, the preceding discussion has demonstrated that this is not always so. This general issue, with its important implications for antitrust activity, particularly in relation to innovative activity and growth, is examined more fully and in more general terms in the appendix to this chapter.

THE STABILITY OF TECHNOLOGY-SHARING CONSORTIA

Incentives and Disincentives for Cheating

The economic literature is replete with discussions of the inherent instability of price cartels—the difficulty of getting agreement on the output quotas for the individual members, the incentives for cheating, the monitoring difficulties that encourage cheating, and the resulting vulnerability of the entire enterprise. To get at the stability issue for technology consortia it is instructive to contrast these consortia with price-setting cartels.

Despite the loss of profit resulting from exclusion from a technology consortium (Proposition 7.1), it does not follow that incentives for cheating are absent. Such incentives do exist, for both price and technology agreements, at least in the short run. In a horizontal pricing cartel, a member can clearly profit by surreptitious price cutting to achieve sales above its quota, even though it shaves the monopoly profits offered by the cartel price and harms other members. In a technology consortium, the obvious cheating scenario involves a member that hopes to be able to profit from the information that the other members provide, but at the same time tries to retain a competitive advantage by keeping (some or all of) its proprietary technology to itself. Thus, in both cases dishonesty can be the most (immediately) lucrative policy.

In the long run, however, the stability properties of price cartels and technology-exchange consortia are very different. Here I must first note that the prospects for success in cheating are far from identical. In a horizontal price cartel it pays the customer to act as co-conspirator with the cartel member that wishes to cheat. The reduced price will be reason enough for the customer to avoid revealing the defector's secret. So cheating is not always easy to detect.

In a technology consortium, in contrast, there is no customer whose acquiescence is required for successful cheating. Technology exchange is normally a game that is played many times, and this is a powerful force for stability. Firms have many ways to monitor one another's technology, and a variety of clues can indicate cheating: low prices suggesting an undisclosed process innovation that permits long-lasting cost reductions, or changes in product characteristics, or industry gossip, or other signals. These can all arouse the suspicion that the firm in question is not giving out all the information it claims to be ready to provide. In such cases, other members of the technology consortium can readily reciprocate by becoming more selective in passing information about their own technological advances to the suspect enterprise, or by ceasing to do so altogether. As in so many situations, reputation becomes an invaluable asset in a much-repeated game of technology exchange (see below).

So far, I have merely pointed out that information-exchange cheating is apt to be discovered eventually, and that the firm that does cheat is likely to be deprived of the benefits promised by consortium membership when that happens. But that is also true of a price cartel. However, there are at least two special features of a technology consortium that can be more effective in discouraging cheating and another that protects the consortium from collapse, even when some cheating occurs.

The first of these special features is the option available to the consortium members of abandoning an informal information-exchange arrangement that relies largely on mutual trust, and substituting a more formal program in which the trades are specified explicitly. Perhaps the most straightforward form this can take is cross-licensing of patents, so that each party knows exactly what it is getting from the other. Such an agreement clearly restricts the opportunity for cheating, and may help to explain the apparent recent rise in patenting.

There are other formal arrangements that can be used to discourage cheating. For example, a real-world arrangement, which I have not found in the economic literature, is used by at least several real firms of which I am aware in negotiating their technology-exchange program. Any two such firms (call them A and B) meet at intervals to negotiate the monetary compensation to be paid by A to B (or vice versa) for any shortfall in the value of the innovations that A expects to provide to B in the period before the next negotiation, in exchange for B's innovations that will be given to A. Such an arrangement gives each firm a strong incentive to reveal all or most of the inventions currently being worked on in its R&D facilities and almost ready for direct use or commercial introduction. Any such invention whose existence is concealed by A simply increases the amount it must pay to B on the balance equalization account, and increases A's payment obligation to B by an amount approximating the expected value of the undisclosed innovation. There is, of course, an adverse selection problem here, because the innovating firm is apt to know more about the value of the invention than the purchaser of its technology does. Yet, if such negotiations are repeated at regular intervals, each firm will learn the trustworthiness of the other party's evaluations of its own inventions. The value of a reputation for integrity in such a bargaining process can, then, reduce the adverse selection problem.

The second attribute of a technology consortium that discourages cheating is more automatic than the various options for formalization of the exchange arrangement, two of which have just been described. Proposition 7.1's proof that nonmembership in the consortium constitutes an ever-growing opportunity loss implies that ejection from the consortium in a repeated game is likely to be very costly, particularly in the longer run.[14] That is, the penalty of ejection for discovered cheating can be far harsher than in a price cartel. Indeed, in those special cases where markets are highly competitive or highly contestable, so that maximum long-run profits are close to zero, the ejected technology consortium member will be condemned to growing losses and to eventual insolvency. In such circumstances, firms with a considerable investment at stake and with an ambition for the long-term future will find it essential to cultivate a reputation for integrity, just as is pointed out in the literature on product quality in markets with imperfect consumer informa-

14. The contrast of the cost of nonmembership in a technology consortium, relative to a price cartel, is significant here. Nonmembers of a price cartel benefit from any price increase the cartel is able to impose, and the nonmember may even be better off than the member, because the former makes no commitment to reduce its output. The nonmember of a technology consortium benefits only via the innovation spillovers and, as we have seen (Proposition 7.1), it suffers a growing competitive handicap.

tion. Thus, technology consortia have a strong and growing incentive against cheating.

This leads immediately to another distinctive and pertinent feature of technology consortia: their striking invulnerability to defection, in sharp contrast to a horizontal price cartel. In the latter, as is well known, once the members begin to suspect cheating on the part of the others, it becomes dangerous for them to continue to obey the cartel's decisions. The horizontal cartel member that continues to insist on the high product prices specified in the cartel agreement is likely to find itself without customers, all attracted away by defecting price cutters. That, ultimately, is why horizontal price cartels are considered to be so unstable.

In a technology consortium, in contrast, we see that even when some members defect, each remaining member will continue to enjoy the benefits of access to the R&D of the other remaining members. That is the obverse implication of Proposition 7.1—that the members of even a small consortium will derive an advantage over nonmembers. If one member is suspected of cheating, the rational reaction is to eject that firm from the consortium and to continue exchanging information with the remaining members. And, certainly, a defection by one member does not eliminate the danger to another member when it does anything that risks ejection from the consortium. Consequently, a technology consortium can easily survive a case of (discovered) cheating. So it is far less vulnerable to the prospect that one or a few members will succumb to this temptation.

Still, technology consortia are not absolutely immune from destabilizing cheating. A prime source of temptation is the fact that even routine R&D can sometimes turn out ex post to yield a breakthrough of enormous and unusual value, even where the firm had no reason to expect it ex ante. When such an extraordinary advance occurs the innovator firm may be strongly tempted not to share it with others, particularly with its horizontal competitors. Two things weaken this temptation to some degree. First, the fact that the imitation process usually entails some lag means that the original innovator often can enjoy a period with no competition in the invention and can therefore obtain considerable benefit from it, even if it provides information about it to the other consortium members promptly and fully. In addition, as we have seen, the costs of permanent exclusion from the consortium as the penalty for cheating can be very great. Consequently, only if the value of the development is *very* substantial will it be rational to succumb to the temptation to defect because it transpires ex post that the R&D investment has been unexpectedly successful.

Toward Formalization of the Stability Issue

The stability of a technology-sharing consortium can be investigated somewhat more formally in terms of repeated games.[15] I start off with a structure that resembles a prisoners' dilemma game. If the members share information they all get higher payoffs than if they all fail to do so. However, firm j will obtain a reward that is even higher if the other firm, k, really shares whereas j succeeds in hiding its invention and in concealing the fact that it is doing so. This situation is illustrated in the payoff matrix of the stage game, Payoff Matrix 1, in which the notation, as well as the discussion that follows, is based on the work of Abreu, Milgrom, and Pearce (1991).

Here, the two available strategies for each player are Share (h) and Hide (H); π is the return to each sharer if both players share, and excess profit, g, is earned by the firm that is able to exploit the other enterprise's sharing of its technology but succeeds in hiding its own. Let us take π, g, and b all to be strictly positive, with $-b < -h$. Then the symmetric pure strategy profile (S,S) clearly yields payoffs that dominate or Pareto-dominate the other symmetric pure strategy profile (H,H). However, the mutual concealment strategy profile (H,H) is the unique dominant strategy equilibrium, that is, either firm will do better by choosing H, given any fixed decision by the other enterprise.

But if this is a repeated game that is played at $t = 1, 2, \ldots$, and the payoffs in Matrix 1 are per period payoff values, then the payoff (π,π) can be sustained in the long run. One equilibrium strategy pair in the repeated game that can in suitable circumstances yield the collusive payoff (π,π) is the "trigger strategy" profile.[16] This strategy is a decision by each firm to play "Share" so long as the other does so, but to play "Hide" forever after, once the other enterprise fails to share. If one firm, say j, expects to conceal in some period, call it the initial period, and it believes that the other firm has adopted the trigger strategy that will come into play after period 1, when j's concealment is discovered, then it will no longer earn $\pi + g$, or even π, per period forever. Instead, taking δ as the pertinent discrete period discount factor, j can expect a stream of earnings whose net present value (NPV) is

$$\text{(7.16)} \quad \text{NPV} = (\pi + g) + (-h) \sum_{t=1}^{\infty} \delta^t = (\pi + g) + (-h)\delta/(1 - \delta),$$

15. For help in the formulation of this section, I am deeply indebted to Professors Dilip Abreu and Zsuzsanna Fluck.

16. Throughout, I measure payoff in terms of a constant per period equivalent. That is, if a stream of payments has an expected net present value (NPV), and δ is the per period discount factor, then the constant per period flow equivalent of that stream is an amount, E, whose discounted present value summed for $t = 0, 1, 2, \ldots$, is also equal to NPV.

		Firm k	
		S	H
Firm i	S	π, π	$-b, \pi + g$
	H	$\pi + g, -b$	$-h, -h$

PAYOFF MATRIX 1

so that, taking this to be equivalent to the constant per period flow of earnings, E for $t = 0, 1, 2, \ldots$, we obtain

$$\text{NPV} = E \sum_{t=0}^{\infty} \delta^t = E(1/(1 - \delta)), \text{ or}$$

(7.17) $\quad E = (\pi + g)(1 - \delta) - h\delta.$

Adoption of the trigger strategy will induce two profit-maximizing firms to act in a manner that yields the sharing equilibrium and renders that equilibrium stable iff $E \leq \pi$, that is, if and only if the earnings expectable from this course of action exceed those that can be expected from concealment of proprietary technical information.

From the point of view of the potential defector, the story, so far, can be summarized in Payoff Matrix 2, where g represents a "one-shot" gain. However, as it stands, with no explicit role assigned to the other members of the consortium, the logic of the construct is the same as that of the prisoners' dilemma game. It is only the presence of the other consortium members that changes the argument and carries it beyond the prisoners' dilemma/repeated game story, which asserts merely that the one-shot gains from cheating do not exceed the future loss from punishment.

	Inclusion in Consortium	Exclusion from Consortium
Share	0	—
Hide	g	$-b$

PAYOFF MATRIX 2

One drawback of the preceding construction is that it is not "renegotiation proof" (on this, see, e.g., Bernheim and Ray, 1989; Farrel and Maskin, 1989; and Pearce, 1987/1990). After a defection in the two-player case, both firms receive low non-cooperative payoffs in the punishment phase that follows. Might they not then be tempted to promote their mutual interests by renegotiating to achieve a more cooperative mode of operation? However, if that is anticipated, the entire incentive structure of the supposed equilibrium unravels. More sophisticated structures are needed to evade this problem (see the papers just cited).

In our setting, the issue has a nice resolution that rests on the multiplicity of other firms in the consortium. A defecting firm is punished upon detection (though this may occur only with a lag) simply by exclusion from the consortium. The special feature that characterizes this case is that the non-defecting firms have no need to break up their profitable sharing arrangement. They can go on indefinitely, sharing their information, while the defector continues to suffer the consequences of exclusion. In contestable markets, this argument can be strengthened further, because the place of the defecting firm can be taken over by a new entrant.

In short, this formal analysis lends some systematic support to an assertion in the previous section about sources of stability of a technology-sharing consortium. This is the argument that the likelihood of continued profitability of membership in a technology consortium, even after defection of one or even several of its members, contributes stability to this form of association of a sort that is absent in a horizontal price cartel.

Of course, this discussion is a simplified treatment of its subject. A richer model is a dynamic Markov game in which the state variable (the accumulation of each firm's technical information) increases during periods when sharing goes on. The other main oversimplification is that concealment of information is treated here as though it were perfectly or nearly perfectly observable, though it is in fact likely to be recognized by other firms only imperfectly and only after some delay. Exploration of these effects leads us to the analysis in Abreu, Milgrom, and Pearce (1991), to which the reader is referred for further details.

CONCLUDING COMMENTS

This chapter, along with chapter 6, has shown that firms have much to gain by licensing their technology at a suitable fee or by joining a technology consortium, and that they can suffer severe competitive penalties if they refuse to do the latter. However, one must not jump to the conclusion that the market mechanism offers no impediments to the dissemination of technology. In practice, a substantial number of firms seem to hold out and try to keep the results of their R&D proprietary. The number of patent infringements lawsuits (e.g., Polaroid v. Kodak, Lotus v. Borland, and Litton v. Honeywell) is clear evidence that firms do sometimes take this position. This can be rational for a number of reasons, most notably because of market imperfections.

For example, resistance to technology sharing can benefit firms financially if product innovations result in product heterogeneity that permits the coexistence of several islands of (perhaps moderate) monopoly power. If the innovation process yields distinctive products to each firm in the industry and each of the products commands some degree of customer loyalty, then every firm may be able to charge a price above its competitive level. In contrast, where circumstances impede successful collusion and similar products are offered simultaneously by several rival enterprises, supercompetitive profits are generally precluded. This may be one of the more compelling explanations for unwillingness to join a technology consortium—the desire to ensure that one's own product remains quite different from those of other firms. Sometimes that may be the only way of obtaining and keeping a degree of market power sufficient to yield substantial and continuing economic profits.

More generally, we may recognize that unwillingness to provide a technology license to a competitor in a final-product market constitutes a form of vertical foreclosure. In effect, it is a case in which the (upstream) proprietor of a valuable input (the innovation) is motivated to prevent its use by a downstream competitor firm—a rival supplier of the final product in which that input is used. The reader is referred to the substantial literature on vertical foreclosure for extensive discussion of the circumstances in which this type of behavior is to be expected. Here, it is important, however, to take note of the general conclusion that concerted pricing and other related types of behavior by horizontal competitors are much the more serious anticompetitive threat, and that the market generally offers business substantial incentives for reasonably desirable behavior in its vertical relationships.

In this and the previous chapters, enough evidence has been reported to give credence to the view that the market does a far better job of technology dissemination than is, by implication, credited to it in the literature of economic theory. It has also been shown that, by internalizing the spillovers of knowledge production, technology consortia can even help to reduce the market's incentives for underinvestment in innovation.

All in all, the analysis suggests once again that we need to reconsider the judgment that the market performs quite well in terms of static economic efficiency but that, because of inadequacy of expenditure on innovation and unwillingness to share technology, it is highly defective in the intertemporal sphere. Still, the discussion up to this point has said little about what is most frequently cited in the literature as an obstacle to efficiency in investment in innovation—the externalities (spillovers) that are generated by the activity. The next chapter will turn to that issue.

APPENDIX

WHEN IS COLLUSION SOCIALLY BENEFICIAL?

On the open range it was first come, first served, a principle that invited abuse . . . all involved understood that they faced the dilemma of the commons, where each individual's pursuit of self-interest, in the form of grass for more of his cattle, threatened the ruin of all, in the form of degradation of the range . . . [Theodore] Roosevelt addressed this issue . . . [creating a stockmen's organization] to deal with overgrazing, and other shared concerns.

—Brands, 1997, p. 186

We are used to the idea that collusion among firms is (often quite legitimately) presumed to be damaging to the public interest, and that the antitrust authorities are fully justified in taking coordination of prices to merit prohibition per se—as inexcusable in any circumstances. One reaches that conclusion when considering price as the matter being decided upon and when the coordinating parties are horizontal competitors. But, as has been shown in this chapter, and as those who have studied the issue know, joint decisions can in some general cases materially promote the public interest when those decisions deal with matters other than price. Even coordination of prices can be desirable if the firms involved are vertically, rather than horizontally, related. Indeed, this is widely recognized by antitrust authorities, who, for example, take a more favorable view of vertical coordination than of horizontal coordination and have frequently avoided interference in research joint ventures. The central point of this appendix stems from the key welfare observation in the body of this chapter that, with important exceptions, coordination on innovation and on the supply of proprietary technical information to competitors can be highly beneficial to the economy, enhancing both its static efficiency and its growth. The policy implication is that regulatory agencies and the courts should exercise extreme restraint in interfering with such joint decision-making, though they should maintain some degree of vigilance to ensure that it does not transform itself into anti-competitive behavior that profits those who undertake it at the consumer's expense.

Preliminary: Vertical Price Coordination as an Illustration of Virtuous Collusion

It is generally recognized that the prices adopted by horizontal competitors will normally be higher than those arrived at independently. However, the opposite has long been known to hold where the firms are related vertically. To demonstrate that inter-firm coordination *can* sometimes be desirable, it may be useful to begin with an explicit recapitulation of the vertical price coordination argument. For this purpose, I provide a formal proof—with no pretense to novelty—confirming that the coordinated final-product prices of two firms that are vertically related profit maximizers will be lower, in total, than the sum of the independently adopted prices of the two final-product components they supply and that together constitute the final-product price paid by the consumer. The proof is simple and compares the price that maximizes the combined profits of the two firms with the Cournot equilibrium prices individually arrived at.[17]

Let

p_j = the price charged by firm j for its component of the final product,

$p = p_1 + p_2$ = the final-product price,

$f(p)$ = the final-product demand function,

$c_j(p)$ = the cost function of firm j, and

T, T_j = the corresponding profits.

We can assume

$$f' < 0,\ c_j' = f'\mathrm{d}c_j/\mathrm{d}f < 0. \tag{7A.1}$$

17. The argument may seem similar to the "double marginalization" analysis based on Spengler's justly noted article (1950). However, the derivation here deals with a more general situation, and does not depend on the firms constituting a succession of production stages, with a compounding of markups on successive stages. Rather, as Ruffin points out in an extremely valuable paper (forthcoming in 2002), the result stems from the work of Cournot ([1838] 1897, pp. 99–103). It entails two firms, each of which produces a component of the final product that may or may not represent different stages of production. In this scenario, each firm neglects the external damage to the other firm in the form of lost sales when the former raises the price of its component, so that the sum of the individual component prices exceeds the profit-maximizing price of the final product. Ruffin extends the result to a general multi-firm case.

Then, differentiating firm j's profit function partially with respect to its own price, we obtain the first-order Cournot maximum condition for j:

$$(7A.2)\quad f + p_j f' - c_j' = 0.$$

Similarly, the combined profit maximum requires

$$(7A.3)\quad T' = f + pf' - c_1' - c_2' = 0, \qquad \text{or } p = (-f/f') + (c_1' + c_2')/f',$$

where both terms of the RHS of the last equation are positive, by (7A.1). Thus, (7A.3) gives us the final-product price that maximizes the combined revenues of the two firms. To find the corresponding price in the independent-decision Cournot equilibrium, add the equations (7A.2) for the two firms, $j = 1, 2$, and solve for p, yielding immediately

$$(7A.4)\quad p = (-2f/f') + (c_1' + c_2')/f'.$$

Substituting this price into the LHS of the first equation in (7A.3) we obtain after straightforward manipulation

$$(7.A5)\quad T' = -f < 0,$$

so that at the Cournot price the marginal combined profit is negative. In other words, if the profit function is concave, a reduction in the final-product price from the Cournot level is necessary for maximization of the combined profit of the vertically related firms. Q.E.D.

Here, then, we have a clear case in which coordinated action—shall I say collusion—is socially beneficial. This confirms that coordination of the decisions of several firms is demonstrably not necessarily damaging to the public interest. (For an intuitive explanation of the result, see footnote 17 above. The discussion will return to this explanation in the following section.)

We have already seen that beneficial welfare results can follow from coordination on decisions related to innovation. Evidently, coordinated decisions and activities by otherwise independent firms, even between horizontal competitors, can sometimes be damaging, sometimes beneficial, in terms of the public interest. Let us consider whether more can be said toward generalization of the discussion.

When Is Inter-Firm Coordination Beneficial? Toward a Common Thread

The discussion has provided several examples in which "collusion" among the suppliers of a product can enhance economic welfare, the general presumption to the contrary notwithstanding. The examples may seem to be totally unrelated. The case of pricing decisions by vertically related suppliers is different from that of the providers of innovation and of access to their private intellectual property—and both of these differ substantially from the example (in the brief opening quotation on page 114 about Theodore Roosevelt) involving prevention of overgrazing by the herds of cattle of competing beef suppliers.

Yet there is a common element that seems to help explain them all and that may well indicate why there exist such significant exceptions to the well-grounded presumption against coordination by rival enterprises. In theoretical terms, the answer is suggested by the literature that culminated in the Arrow–Debreu theorems, asserting that, in the absence of externalities, perfect competition will yield equilibria that satisfy the requirements of economic efficiency and Pareto optimality. Since inter-firm coordination can be interpreted as a move away from a competitive regime, this immediately suggests that it will be beneficial only where externalities are present. The well-understood overgrazing issue supports this observation. It is the case of the tragedy of the commons, in which overuse results when users do not give full weight to the external damage their usage imposes on the others who depend on the availability of the common property.

Once this is recognized, it is easy to see that the externalities issue is critical for both of my other illustrations of beneficial coordination. The price of the final product of two vertically related firms will exceed the profit-maximizing level and, incidentally, will presumably reduce consumer welfare because each of the two firms takes no account (or at least inadequate account) of the external damage that a rise in its own price does to the sales volume of the other. For example, when considering a rise in its prices, an independent producer of pharmaceuticals will ignore the loss to a maker of the capsules in which the former's medications are enclosed, and the capsule manufacturer will behave in the same way. But, to maximize their joint profits, the price decided upon must take these detrimental external effects of too high a price into account, and so coordination will result in a lower price for the final product than would emerge from independent decision-making.

In the case of innovation, the role of the pertinent externalities is even more obvious. For innovation is a prime example of a product with enormous beneficial externalities. Coordination among the innovative firms helps to internalize the externalities, increases the incentive for investment in the innovation process, and reduces the avoidable costs that must be incurred by firms that might benefit from the innovations if their acquisition of these benefits is prevented or impeded by the proprietor of the innovative intellectual property, or even if the proprietor chooses not to help the other firms in the process of obtaining the requisite information needed to adopt innovations and to put them to effective use.

This suggests a general hypothesis about the circumstances in which the effects of inter-firm coordination will have beneficial consequences. Such benefits can be expected when the activities of each or most of the firms in question generate substantial externalities whose victims (or beneficiaries) are or include the other firms in the group. As is well recognized in the literature, where such externalities are present and substantial, uncoordinated behavior can result in substantial static inefficiency and, because of the crucial role of innovation in the growth process, it can also lead to substantial intertemporal inefficiency as well. Such a case is patently an opportunity for material enhancement of the general welfare via beneficial coordination, using any of a number of mechanisms ranging from Pigouvian taxes and subsidies through voluntary coordination, that is, "good collusion" among the affected firms.[18]

It may perhaps appear that, by tying the possibility of desirable coordination to the presence of externalities, I have reduced it to a very special case. But a moment's consideration will confirm that it is inappropriate to treat this case as an exception. Rather, to paraphrase Marx, it may be more to the point to consider it as an instance where the rule becomes the exception and the exception (frequently) becomes the rule. Nowadays, we are well aware of the importance and pervasiveness of externalities in the economy. The dangers of overuse of public goods as common property are also well recognized. But, above all, the significance of the issue for innovation and growth, which, in turn, are so crucial for future economic welfare, means that it cannot be deemed to be a special issue of limited general importance.

Implications, Particularly for Antitrust Policy

There is much more that can be said about the subject. For example, a good deal can be reported about the magnitude of efficient technology-licensing fees and about the extent to which one can or cannot rely upon market forces to yield fees of that magnitude. But this is not the appropriate place to go into these details (for fuller discussion, see chapter 13). Enough has been said to enable us to offer some tentative conclusions.

First, it would appear from the discussion that the performance of the market in terms of the quality of resources devoted to innovative activities,

---

18. This is a point I have argued for literally half a century, when I suggested in my first book that externalities are the primary underpinning for any economic role of government (Baumol, 1952).

and the market's dissemination of the results of those activities, is considerably better than standard economic analysis may suggest. In particular, the degree of internalization of the externalities of innovation that technology trading and licensing permits may contribute substantially to economic efficiency. Second, it follows that innovation is an activity in which inter-firm coordination, even among horizontal competitors, can bring substantial welfare benefits. If further exploration supports this conclusion, it follows that the antitrust authorities' willingness to show forbearance in their toleration of research joint ventures and technology licensing is fully justified.

Yet two amendments of the prevailing approach may well prove desirable. Where there has been no explicit announcement of policy by the authorities, indicating as specifically as possible what types of coordination and of what degree will meet with no interference by the agency, and in what circumstances they will so forbear, firms may well feel that a threat overhangs activity that they have reason to consider benign. I have heard businesspersons assert that this continuing threat has a chilling effect on legitimate inter-firm cooperation, despite the tolerance of the authorities in the past. If so, something may be gained from an attempt by the regulatory authorities to minimize this sort of uncertainty.

Finally, it may be equally desirable to have a public pronouncement indicating just what the authorities will seek to prevent. In particular, when there is reason to fear that industry expenditure on R&D is less than optimal, they should make it explicit that any attempt by the participants in a technology consortium to fix industry expenditure on innovation will be looked upon as unfavorably as price fixing.

CHAPTER 8

Tradeoff: Innovation Incentives versus Benefits to Others (Distributive Externalities)

External economies are an important aspect of the production of knowledge. The greater the externality, the more inefficient is the final equilibrium. If inventions are completely inappropriable, no profit-maximizing competitor will produce an invention because increases in productivity would be instantaneously erased by a fall in price, and the firm would suffer losses to the extent of its research outlay.

—Nordhaus, 1969, p. 39

[If] everyone received the full measure of his marginal product and no joint inputs existed, the benefits generated by great entrepreneurs and inventors would accrue entirely to them. There would be no "trickle-down" of progress to the masses. . . . The trickle-down of benefits is a merit of capitalism in the real world, and it works insofar as the distribution of income departs from the strict standard of reward for personal contribution to production.

—Okun, 1975, pp. 46–47

The central conclusion of this chapter will be that, despite the substantial spillovers (externalities) of innovation, expenditure on R&D in the free-market economies may nevertheless be quite efficient. There is a tradeoff between the welfare contribution of the spillovers and the welfare gain forgone because of the resulting limitation of the payoffs to innovators. Such a tradeoff has already long been recognized from the Dupuit (1853)/Samuelson (1954) analysis of public goods, and its implication that any nonzero price for the use of such a good is inefficient if it decreases such use. This is so because an additional user of such a good, as in the case of an innovation, does not deplete its usability by others. So, with the true marginal cost equal to zero, any use forgone because of a positive usage fee is a wasted opportunity. On the other hand, with a zero usage fee, *all* of the benefit of an innovation must become spillover and none of it will go to the innovator, which plainly constitutes a major disincentive for innovation. This, then, is the well-known tradeoff between the static efficiency benefits offered by (zero-priced) spillovers of innovation deriving from their public-good attribute on the one side, and the contribution to welfare stemming from the growth deriving from a generous payoff incentive for innovation investment on the other side. However, the beneficial attribute of spillovers involved in the tradeoff that will be emphasized here is more specific, and it entails no basically static efficiency gain. I will argue that, because of the distributive benefits of the spillovers through time, on balance the externalities of innovation need not significantly damage the welfare contribution of the growth process, even if they materially reduce its speed. The standard theoretical analysis implies that only zero spillovers are compatible with optimality in innovative activity, which leads us to expect that externalities as great as claimed here will reduce investment in innovation in the free-enterprise economies far below the optimal level. But I will contend that this is not so, because the resulting impediment to growth has a tradeoff with the beneficial distributive consequences of the externalities. The result can be a balance between abundant innovation, entailing rapid but not maximal growth, and widespread dissemination of the benefits, entailing prosperity that, although it is hardly universal, is more widespread than ever before.

I will also argue that the total uncompensated external benefits of innovation activity probably are surprisingly large, but that even this does not undermine the preceding conclusion. There are reasons to believe, in fact, that individuals who have invested directly or indirectly in the economy's innovation processes can be estimated, conservatively, to obtain less than 20 percent of the total economic benefits contributed by new technology and new products.

The reason a zero spillover level is not optimal is that, though spillovers are a disincentive for investment in innovation (as most of the literature contends), they are at the same time significant benefits in themselves. A major component of these innovation spillovers is the resulting (spectacular) increase in the economic welfare of the population as a whole, so that innovation does not just benefit direct participants in the innovation process. Indeed, these spillovers, in the form of resulting rises in general living standards, are arguably the prime social benefits of innovation. In the real world, however, these distributive benefits can be obtained only by some sacrifice in innovation investment resulting from the reduced payoffs to the innovators.[1] Thus, there is a tradeoff between an increased flow of invention and the distribution of benefits to others—the resulting rise in *overall* living standards—because of which zero externalities cannot be optimal. Moreover, there is no one level of spillovers that is unambiguously optimal. Instead, there is a range of values of what I will call the "spillover ratio"—the share of the benefits of innovation that goes to persons other than the investors—within which all values of the ratio are Pareto optimal. Or rather, they are what I will call non-lump-sum (NLS) Pareto optimal, meaning that they are all optimal in a world in which persistent lump-sum redistribution is impossible. Thus, I will be dealing with what may be considered second-best Pareto optima, subject to a constraint that rules out hypothetical but totally infeasible redistributive arrangements.

The results of this chapter may, perhaps, be viewed as another step in our attempt to reconcile the market economies' allegedly inefficient innovation performance, which the standard theory leads us to expect, and their historically unprecedented growth record, which is clearly documented by the economic historians. The problem arises because the theory has failed to deal with the implications for the distribution of income and wealth.

Welfare economics—the theory of economic policy—has sedulously avoided these issues. And it has excused itself from this task by repeatedly leaning on a fairy tale: the legend that one can somehow aim for efficiency in the allocation of resources to the growth process, and afterwards rectify any resulting damage to the desirable distribution of wealth and income by means of what are called "lump-sum" redistributions of income and wealth—forms of redistribution that somehow have been cleansed of all incentive or disincentive effects.[2] In an appendix to this chapter, I will deal in general terms with the

---

1. The disincentive to innovation has long been recognized by economists:

> [The general argument for the system of natural liberty or laissez faire] implicitly assumed that the individual can always obtain through free exchange adequate remuneration for the services which he is capable of rendering to society. But there is no general reasoning for supposing that this will always be possible; and in fact there is a large and varied class of cases in which the supposition would be manifestly erroneous. . . . [S]cientific discoveries . . . however ultimately profitable to industry, have not generally speaking a market value; the inventions in which the discoveries are applied can, indeed, be protected by patents; but the extent to which any given discovery will aid invention is mostly so uncertain, that, even if the secret of a law of nature could be conveniently kept, it would not be worth an investor's while to buy it, in the hope of being able to make something of it. (Sidgwick, 1887, pp. 406–7)

2. Of course, economists are aware that the assumption is artificial, and their use of the premise has been helpful in theoretical analysis. However, the point here is that it has distracted attention from the fundamental tradeoff with which this chapter deals.

tradeoff between efficiency and distributive equity that results because, as will be shown, lump-sum redistributions are impossible in a wide variety of significant circumstances. The main body of the chapter will deal with these same issues, but only as they relate to the innovation activity that is the main concern of this book. The discussion will show why, in the absence of lump-sum corrections, substantial spillovers may be compatible with Pareto optimality, whereas zero spillovers may prevent it altogether.

APPLICATION: THE NON-LUMP-SUM PARETO-OPTIMAL LEVELS OF INNOVATION EXTERNALITIES

I turn now to the key question here: what range of magnitude of the spillovers (externalities) from innovation, if any, qualifies as NLS Pareto optimal? I will argue that zero externalities probably do *not* qualify and that the plausible range of optimality may include spillovers that are very large. Thus, it is at least possible that the volume of innovation activity experienced in free markets often does not violate the optimality requirements to anything like the extent that much of the theoretical discussion leads us to expect.

All this is, of course, in direct conflict with the view that only zero externalities are consistent with an optimal allocation of investment to innovation activity. The reason a zero spillover level in innovation is not optimal is, as I have just said, the tradeoff between an increased flow of invention and the distribution of benefits to others that has occurred in reality, i.e., the resulting rise in *overall* living standards. And, there is no single level of spillovers that is unambiguously optimal. Instead, there is a range of values of the spillover ratio, within which all values of the ratio are NLS Pareto optimal. They are all what may be considered second-best Pareto optima, subject to the constraint that rules out hypothetical but infeasible lump-sum redistributions.

My analysis takes off from the pathbreaking work of Paul Romer (1994a), which introduces a more profound view of the spillovers generated in the innovation process. He observes that general gains in real wages that result from innovation must constitute spillovers, since they are social benefits that are not private benefits to the innovator. Along with this, it can be argued that the bulk of the unprecedented rise in the developed world's living standards since the Industrial Revolution could not have occurred without that Revolution's innovations.[3] Consequently, a very substantial share of the benefits of innovation must have gone to persons other than the innovators in the form of spillovers.[4]

Romer studies the role of these differences between private and social benefits—the spillovers of innovation—as an impediment to innovative activity, discussing the difficulty innovators face in covering their sunk costs and the resulting dampening of innovative activity and output. That is part of the story that I retell in this chapter. However, Romer alludes only in passing to the central issue of the chapter: the inevitable tradeoff between the number of innovations actually produced and the standard of living of the majority of the population. In this scenario, as overall GDP is raised by innovation, any resulting increase in workers' standards of living constitutes a rise in the spillovers from innovation, which depresses the flow of further innovation. Thus, the more the general public benefits from such growth in GDP, the slower that growth must be.

This is more than just an embellishment of the old story of the tradeoff between output and distributive equality. The mechanism under discussion here is very different, and does not involve the disincentive to work that results from a reduction of the marginal return to worker effort. Rather, I am concerned here with the heart of the capitalist growth process: the private payoff to innovation and the speed with which new technology and new products become available.

My scenario is far more dramatic. Romer notes in passing that, if the innovators had not had to forgo *any* of the benefits they generated—if spillovers had been zero—then real wages would hardly have risen from their levels before the Industrial Revolution![5] It is almost impossible to imagine how

3. Many observers have emphasized the leading role of innovation in the growth process. In addition to Romer, there are, of course, Solow (1956), Nordhaus (1969), and Nelson (1996), among others.

4. Some writers on innovation use the term "spillovers" in a more restricted sense to refer, for example, to direct gains of knowledge by customers of the industry that supplies the R&D in question (see Griliches, 1979). Such use of the term is, of course, entirely legitimate. Here, however, the term is taken as synonymous with *total* external effects. It represents all the social benefits of innovation that do not accrue as private benefits to the inventor or to those who invested in or otherwise contributed to it. This connotation is clearly required by the issue under discussion—the disincentive to innovation activity resulting from the difference between its social and private rewards.

5. A reader of this chapter has argued that this conclusion is unrealistic because innovations do benefit workers. That is, of course, correct. By definition, however, zero externalities amount to the counterfactual state of affairs in which no such benefits go to the workers. What this implies is that zero externalities simply cannot occur in the world of reality—that it is an unattainable goal. The question that remains is whether that imaginary goal, if it could somehow be achieved, could be accepted as optimal. The answer of

great a difference that would have made. What are probably the best available estimates put U.S. per capita GDP in 1820 at less than one-seventeenth of what it is today, and even as late as 1870 real per capita GDP is estimated to have been less than one-ninth its current level.[6] If one assumes the most extreme case—that the spillovers from innovation could somehow have been reduced to (anywhere near) zero—the living standards of the vast majority of the citizens of today's rich countries would have stalled at pre–Industrial Revolution levels. One can hardly accept the notion that it would be socially preferable to achieve a total GDP far higher than today's through maximal incentives for innovation while, simultaneously, condemning most of the population to abysmal living standards. But that is the world that a zero-spillovers premise depicts.

MARGINAL COST, TOTAL COST, AND THE ADOPTION OF SOCIALLY BENEFICIAL INNOVATIONS

Before constructing a more formal model of the socially optimal level of spillovers from innovation, I must briefly review an important issue for the analysis that, as Romer notes, goes back to Dupuit. This is the role of total cost relative to that of marginal cost in "lumpy" decisions, such as the decision to build a bridge or to launch an innovation process. Where such an activity has substantial fixed and sunk costs or where scale economies make small-scale entry infeasible, one cannot rely on marginal analysis, because marginal data relate only to small adjustments.[7]

This means that, when deciding whether to build a bridge or to launch a large-scale research project, the pertinent criterion is whether the total yield

---

this chapter, emphatically, is that it would not be optimal, contrary to what may be inferred from the literature. Though it would increase the number of beneficial innovations, it would, tautologically, preclude any of the benefits from going to persons other than the innovators. Romer puts the matter very clearly: "This pattern of industrialization without wage gains is what it would take to ensure that the industrialist captures all of the benefits he creates when he introduces machinery. . . . [This] cannot be a historically accurate description of the process of development in industrial countries, for if it were, unskilled labor would still earn what it earned prior to the Industrial Revolution" (Romer, 1994a, p. 29).

6. Maddison (1995, pp. 196–97).

7. That is not to deny the important role of marginal considerations in the theory of innovation. For example, in deciding how much to increase or decrease the budget for R&D on improvement of a particular invention, or how much longer to work on it before releasing it to the market, the usual sorts of marginal calculation apply, as I, among many others, have shown elsewhere (see Baumol, 1993).

will exceed the total cost. A profit-seeking firm will not undertake an innovation unless the total revenue is expected to be greater than the total cost, and society should not undertake it unless its total benefits are expected to exceed total costs.

The very legitimate argument conventionally linking this to the spillovers of innovation, then, is straightforward. It suggests that there are many prospective innovations that promise total net social benefits but will nevertheless not be carried out by private enterprise, even if marginal spillovers, at whatever margin is relevant, are all zero. Although many potential innovations have prospective total benefits (including their contributions to consumers' surpluses) greater than their total costs, no one will find it profitable to carry them out because a considerable proportion of the total benefits would go to persons other than the innovator (in the form of spillovers). Here, I will carry on with the story from this point, and provide a somewhat different ending.

A MODEL AND GRAPHIC ANALYSIS OF OPTIMAL SPILLOVERS

For this purpose, I turn to a formal analysis of the relation between the spillover ratio and optimality and will demonstrate graphically the possibly wide range of NLS Pareto-optimal spillover ratios. I adopt two premises to facilitate the discussion. First, production uses only two inputs, labor and innovation, so that income earners are divided into innovators and (non-innovating) workers. Second, with a given labor force, the production frontier can be shifted outward only by innovation.

Let S represent the spillover ratio—the share of the benefits of innovation that do not accrue to the innovator, relative to the total benefit contributed by innovation. Consider two scenarios. In the first, the value of S is assumed to be fixed exogenously. In the other scenario, it is treated as a modifiable parameter.

The model follows Romer in recognizing that there is a vast set of potential innovations, and that they offer society different amounts of total net benefit over and above their sunk costs. Each such innovation, I, also requires a sunk expenditure, $C(i)$, where i is the index assigned to invention I, as described below. Assume that both benefits and costs can be translated into money terms and that the total gross benefit, $B(i)$ (before deduction of sunk costs), is given by the discounted present value of the stream of the benefits and other costs expected from invention I from now to eternity.

Then, clearly, maximization of the direct benefits from innovation requires that at any given time the economy carry out every recognized prospective innovation, *I*, for which $B(i) - C(i) > 0$. However, given the spillover ratio, private enterprise will undertake only those innovations for which $B(i)(1 - S) - C(i) > 0$. This means that the beneficial innovations, *J*, for which $C(j)/(1 - S) > B(j) > C(j)$, will be lost to society. That is, roughly speaking, where the story stands in much of the literature.

To take it further, I use a few simple graphs. Figure 8.1 is a standard depiction of the relationship between the benefits from innovation and the share of innovations that are actually carried out from among those that are currently considered possible by prospective innovators. It shows how spillovers limit the number of prospectively useful innovations that are actually undertaken. In this graph it is assumed that the spillovers are a fixed percentage (for example, $S = 0.75$) of the total future benefits of an innovation. The potential innovations currently recognized as possibly worth carrying out are taken to be a continuum (or one can assume that they can be approximated by one). It is also assumed that the sunk investment required to carry out a single innovation is fixed at the level *C*.[8] The horizontal axis, which extends from zero to unity, represents the share of currently recognized innovation possibilities that is actually carried out. Innovations are indexed in descending order of incremental gross benefit, *B*. Here, gross benefit is defined as the discounted present value of all the current and future gains an innovation provides, minus the discounted value of all current and future costs other than the sunk costs needed to carry it out. The descending order of benefits, then, means that $B(i) > B(j)$ iff $i < j$. For simplicity of presentation the gross benefits curve, *B*, is taken to be linear. It must have a negative slope throughout by construction (because of the way in which the potential innovations are ordered).

Then, with *S* a given constant, one can easily also draw in the innovator's gross benefits curve, the lower straight line $(1 - S)B_0$. Point *N*, where the B_0 and *C* lines intersect, represents the exhaustion of all recognized innovations that currently promise a net gain to the economy. That is, at *N* the economy has adopted every recognized innovation that offers benefits that exceed its sunk costs.[9] However, private enterprise will be unable to go beyond point *M*,

8. Jean Gadrey has noted in correspondence that *C* is unlikely to be horizontal in reality; more beneficial innovations are perhaps apt to incur a higher sunk cost, so that the line (curve) may well have a negative slope. It is easy to see that this change leads to no fundamental modification of the analysis.

9. The association of point *N* with optimality in the set of innovations that are carried out forces me to use the very broad definition of spillovers employed in this chapter, rather

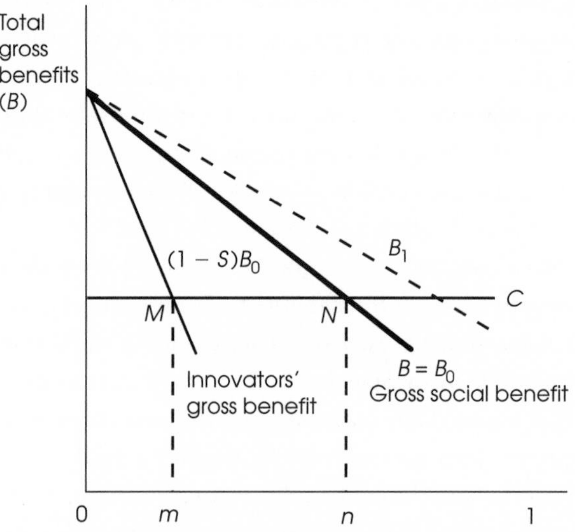

FIGURE 8.1
The Spillover Ratio, Optimality, and Equilibrium

with its much lower output of innovation, because spillovers, SB_0, will prevent it from covering the sunk costs of any additional innovations.[10] The implication is that the actually realized level of innovation can be much below the socially efficient level, *n*.

It should be noted, incidentally, that this is not a problem of private enterprise alone. The public sector can fare no better without financing the shortfall out of the gain that would otherwise accrue to the labor force. Of course, private innovators can do just as well if at the margin they can be subsidized or use some other source of revenue to offset the share of total benefit that escapes them as spillovers.

Next, consider what happens in figure 8.1 when there is a change in the spillover ratio. Obviously, as *S* increases, if the *B* line remains fixed in its ini-

---

than a more restricted concept, such as one including only unpaid-for benefits obtained by an innovator's competitors. Clearly, in itself, an innovation is beneficial to society if its costs are exceeded by the sum of the benefits to anyone, including consumers in other countries, unrelated producers, and members of future generations.

10. More generally, it is easy to prove that, so long as there is no shift in *B*, $\mathrm{d}i/\mathrm{d}S < 0$ at the least remunerative invention I whose production causes no loss at the given *S* value. For zero profit requires $(1 - S)B(i) - C = 0$, so that $(1 - S)B'\mathrm{d}i = B\mathrm{d}S$, or, since $B' = \mathrm{d}B/\mathrm{d}i < 0$ by construction, $\mathrm{d}i/\mathrm{d}S = B/(1 - S)B' < 0$.

tial position, B_0, the line $(1 - S)B_0$ will simply move steadily lower and become steadily steeper, with the curve rotating clockwise. However, this overlooks the possibility that, at least up to a point, the spillovers themselves will contribute to productivity and innovation and, hence, to the total benefits the economy derives from innovation.

In reality, there are at least two ways in which this can occur. First, the spillovers from innovation facilitate further innovation. They do so by cutting down the need for and the expenses involved in the design of duplicative technology by competing firms. Moreover, to the extent that technical advance is cumulative, with one step facilitating the next (as is certainly true in many fields), today's technological advance by one firm lays the groundwork for tomorrow's advance by different firms or by others. In addition, spillovers increase the number of inventors who can work effectively from the base provided by the new technology.[11]

Second, zero spillovers, as the term is interpreted here, mean that the labor force is condemned to extremely low nutritional and educational levels. The evidence indicates, however, that the transfer to workers of some of the benefits of innovation in the form of improved nutrition and education can contribute materially to labor productivity. Consequently, in figure 8.1, as S increases above zero, say to S_1, at least initially line B can be expected to shift upward or rotate counterclockwise, sufficient to yield a social benefit line, B_1, that lies above B_0. This can result in a rise in the private benefits line, $(1 - S_1)B_1$ (not shown), which also lies above the corresponding line's initial position. However, when S becomes sufficiently large, further increases in S will indeed lower and steepen the line $(1 - S)B$ monotonically.

The relationships and their implications yield more interesting insights with the aid of figure 8.2, which focuses on the effects of changes in the spillover ratio. In the figure, the horizontal axis represents S, the size of the spillover ratio. Like the i on the horizontal axis of figure 8.1, it ranges between $S = 0$ and $S = 1$. The upper curve, B^*, is the integral of $B(i) - C$ from $i = 0$ to the profit-maximizing value of i in figure 8.1, where $(1 - S)B(i) = C$. In the region to the right of n in the graph, the slope of the B^* curve must be negative since, by construction, $dB^*/di = B - C > 0$ and, from footnote 10, $di/dS = B/(1 - S)B' < 0$, so

$$(8.1) \qquad dB^*/dS = (dB^*/di)(di/dS) = (B - C)B/(1 - S)B' < 0.$$

11. I owe the observations in this paragraph to Richard Nelson. Indeed, most of the paragraph is a lightly edited quotation from a letter he sent to me (10 June 1998).

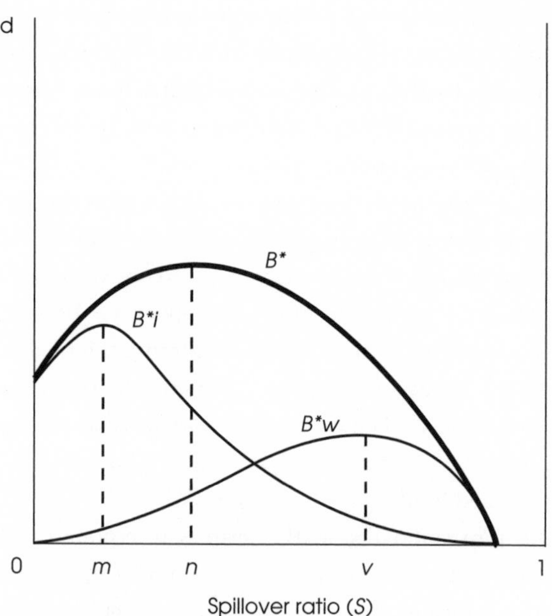

FIGURE 8.2
Benefits as a Function of the Spillover Ratio

It is also easy to verify, by taking the second derivative, that in this region the B^* curve is normally concave, as drawn.[12]

The negative slope would persist throughout the graph if innovation were the only direct input to productivity growth or if innovation were not facilitated by spillovers from other innovations. However, as has been noted, in reality productivity growth *is* enhanced, up to a point, by the improved nutrition and education of the labor force, which are severely reduced as the value of S approaches zero, and by the spillovers from innovation that facilitate and stimulate further innovation. Consequently, the B^* curve begins by initially rising toward the right as S begins to increase above zero, so that the state of health of the workers increases and the innovation process begins to benefit from the growing spillovers from other innovations. That is, toward the left of the graph, $dB^*/dS > 0$; this portion of the B^* curve has a positive

12. Continuing to assume $B'' = 0$ for simplicity, and writing $b = dB^*/di = B - C$, so $b' < 0$, equation (8.1) indicates that $d^2B^*/dS^2 = [(b'B + bB')(1 - S)B'di/dS - bBB']/K^2 = (b'B^2)/K^2 < 0$, where K is the denominator of dB^*/dS and, as shown in footnote 10, $di/dS = B/(1 - S)B'$. However, to the right of $S = 1 - C/B(0)$, at which any investment becomes unprofitable, there will be no investment, no costs, and no benefits, so that the B^* curve will follow the horizontal axis.

slope. All of this together yields the shape of the B^* curve depicted in the graph. It has a unique maximum at $S = n$. Here, current investment in innovation maximizes the net total gain to society.

However, the rest of the story differs for the two classes into which society is divided: the innovators and the workers. For example, the benefits added by innovation that go to the workers are shown by the B^*w curve given by the expression SB^*; that is, the workers' benefit equals the total social benefit, B^*, multiplied by the share, S, that goes to these (assumed) non-innovators. This lower curve, SB^*, must start off at zero at its left-hand end, where $S = 0$, and it must approach steadily closer to the B^* curve as S increases toward unity, with the two curves meeting at or before the extreme right, where S equals or is close to unity (see footnote 12). B^*w has the derivative

$$(8.2) \qquad dSB^*/dS = B^* + SB^{*\prime},$$

which is positive at the maximum, n, of the upper curve, B^*, where derivative $B^{*\prime} = 0$. This means that v, the maximum of B^*w, must occur to the right of n, the maximum of B^*. The intuitive explanation is that slightly to the right of the maximum of B^*, although the total size of the social output pie is decreasing, the workers' share of that shrinking pie increases sufficiently to make them better off, on balance. Eventually, however, the size of the social output gain shrinks so much that further increases in S are damaging even to workers. The workers' benefit maximum requires $B^* = -SB^{*\prime}$, which has a straightforward intuitive interpretation in terms of the total benefit pie and the size of the workers' slice. B^* is the workers' gain from a unit increase in their *share* of the pie, while $SB^{*\prime}$ is the loss to them from the accompanying decrease in *total size* of the pie, $B^{*\prime}$, and maximization requires this marginal loss to equal the marginal gain.

Similarly, the graph depicts an innovators' benefits curve, B^*i. Its equation is $B^*i = (1 - S)B^*$. Its relation to the B^* curve is perfectly analogous to that of the workers, except that the innovators' curve's behavior going from right to left (as $1 - S$ increases) corresponds exactly to that of the workers' curve going from left to right (as S increases). Thus, $S = m$, the maximum[13] of B^*i, must always lie to the left of n, the maximum of the social gain curve B^*.

Several substantive conclusions follow from this discussion. First, it is clear that innovators do not obtain their maximum reward if they receive *all*

13. This can conceivably be a corner maximum at $S = 0$. That will occur if at this point $B^* > B^{*\prime} > 0$, so that at $S = 0$ the slope of the innovators' benefit curve, $(1 - S)B^{*\prime} - B^*$, is negative.

of the benefits their innovations can yield—that is, if spillovers are zero. Rather, their gain is maximized at $S = m > 0$. Their preferred value of S may even be higher than this, if, for example, they derive some utility from altruistic egalitarianism or if higher wages reduce crime and thereby increase the safety of the innovators.

For the same reason, the welfare of workers will be reduced if *all* of the benefits of innovation go to them in the form of spillovers, because then, of course, there will be no innovation and so there will be no innovation benefits to accrue to them. They will be better off if $S = v$, corresponding to the maximum point on their benefits curve. They may derive indirect gains from a value of S somewhat lower than v if greater innovator wealth leads to such outcomes as increased donations to hospitals, from which workers benefit.

Thus, point n (at which productive efficiency is maximized) is not preferred by either party and, although n is a possible compromise between the two groups, it is hardly the only available compromise position. Every point in the entire range $m \leq S \leq v$ is a possible solution, since any change from a point within that range must harm one of the groups while benefiting the other. In other words, the corresponding range of a utilities-possibility frontier for the two groups, which can easily be derived from our model, must have a negative slope throughout. So there is a range of S values all of which are (NLS) Pareto optimal,[14] rather than a unique and clearly definable global optimum. And, it should be emphasized, if the value of S is anywhere in that range the interests of the two groups will be in conflict: any change in S that benefits one of the groups will necessarily harm the other.

PIGOUVIAN SUBSIDIES, CONSUMERS' SURPLUS, AND LUMP-SUM TRANSFERS

The preceding analysis naturally prompts the question of whether, at least in theory, one cannot have it both ways, somehow providing the incentive for the socially optimal amount of innovation, with a subsequent redistribution of the resulting gains, thereby making all parties better off. But, even if all socially beneficial innovations could somehow be obtained through the market, the lump-sum transfers needed to distribute the benefits to the general population without distorting the equilibrium would remain a figment of the

14. The issue here and my conclusion have close analogies in the literature on optimal patent life, notably in the work of Nordhaus (1969) and Scherer (1965). There the issue is the tradeoff between reward to the inventor (before the time of patent expiration) and the transfer of subsequent benefits to the general public.

theorist's imagination. In the appendix to this chapter I show why, in general, there can be no such thing as a lump-sum transfer in the real world. In the particular case of innovation, the unreality of the proposal is far more striking. If, as the next section argues, actual spillover ratios probably exceed 0.75, their elimination would give innovators a huge addition to their current earnings. If the remainder of the population were subsequently to be compensated by ostensibly lump-sum transfers, the resources could not conceivably come from anyone except the super-rich innovators who would be the recipients of the bulk of the economy's GDP. They could hardly avoid noticing that most of their innovation payoff was being taxed away. Surely, this would affect the amounts of resources and effort they were willing to invest in the innovation process. The idea that lump-sum transfers are pertinent to the problem, even in theory, is tantamount to assuming the problem away.

Another attribute that makes innovation spillovers different from other beneficial externalities, as Romer rightly emphasizes, stems from the heavy sunk costs of the innovation process. These mean that, even if the prices of the products of innovation are adjusted to cover the marginal costs of supplying them, the sunk costs will generally not be covered. Thus even if Pigouvian subsidies are added to those prices, so that they cover all of the pertinent marginal costs, private enterprise will not be willing to invest in every socially beneficial innovation. Here, the obvious test of social desirability is whether the total benefits of the innovation, including consumers' surpluses now and in the future, can be expected to cover the total costs, both those that are sunk and those that are not.

It is tempting to argue that one can in theory induce the market to provide all innovations that are expected to be beneficial ex ante by means of a patent system that perfectly protects intellectual property rights and enables innovators to acquire all consumers' surpluses by perfect price discrimination. Romer, however, shows how difficult (if not impossible) such price discrimination is to carry out in practice.

The bottom line, simply, is this: there is no way *in reality* to escape the tradeoff between the incentives required to elicit the "optimal" level of investment in innovation and the desire for the resulting rise in real productivity to benefit everyone, and not just the innovators.

HOW LARGE ARE THE SPILLOVERS?

As already indicated, the total size of the spillovers from innovation is hardly negligible. If one provisionally accepts the conclusion that the bulk of the rise in per capita GDP and the rise in productivity since the Industrial Revolution ultimately could not have occurred without innovation, it is possible to arrive at a very crudely estimated lower bound for the spillover ratio. As noted earlier, per capita GDP has increased almost ninefold in the United States since 1870. This implies that fully eight-ninths, or nearly 90 percent, of current U.S. GDP was contributed by the innovation carried out since 1870.[15] The total contribution of innovation is certainly even greater than that, since pre-1870 innovations, such as the steam engine, the railroad, and many other inventions of an earlier era, still add to today's GDP. Moreover, the difference between the increase in productivity (estimated to have risen thirteenfold since 1870) and the increase in GDP is attributable in good part to enhanced leisure, surely a benefit over and above reported GDP, and a benefit also made possible largely by innovation.

At the same time, the share of total investment income in GDP during this period was certainly less than 30 percent. But investment in innovation is only a part of total investment. In 1999, R&D expenditures made up only 15 percent of total investment in the United States.[16] Thus, if the return on innovation investment had been the same (after adjustment for risk) as the return to investment of other types, the return on innovation would have been less than (30)(0.15) = 4.5 percent of GDP. Compare this with the 90-odd percent of GDP we have just shown to be attributable to innovation. It follows that *S*, the spillover ratio, may well have been as high as 0.8. That is,

---

15. The discussion of the amount that innovation has added to growth may seem to argue that contributions to economic growth from all other sources must have been negligible. No such assumption, however, is intended (nor is this or any related premise critical for my main argument). It is clear that enormous contributions have been made by education and other forms of investment in human capital, by investment in plant and equipment, and by other stimuli. Still, the enormous expansion of outlays on education and physical productive capacity in the world's industrialized countries themselves would not have been possible without the resources provided by innovation in the course of the Industrial Revolution. In this sense, a burst of innovation constituted a necessary condition for the economic expansion that has occurred since the eighteenth century. If new technology in agriculture, mining, and manufacturing had not appeared with the Industrial Revolution and the centuries that preceded it, it is arguable that miserably low per capita income levels would have prevented any substantial savings. Therefore no significant increase in investment in plant, equipment, or the education or health of the labor force would have been possible. If so, innovation must be considered the ultimate source of most of the investment in human and physical capital that, along with the innovation itself, is surely responsible for most of the growth in production, production per capita, and productivity that followed the Industrial Revolution.

Moreover, the cross partial derivatives of national output growth among the input variables are undoubtedly substantial. For example, innovation surely stimulates educational expenditure both by providing the necessary resources and by increasing the returns to education. But education, in turn, clearly facilitates innovation.

16. U.S. Census Bureau (2000).

some 80 percent of the benefits may plausibly have gone to persons who made no direct contribution to innovation. The rather startling implication of all this is that the spillovers of innovation, both direct and indirect, can be estimated to constitute well over half of current GDP—and it can even be argued that this is a very conservative figure.

The very crude estimates offered here are not out of line with the available estimates of private and social returns to innovation.[17] Edward N. Wolff, for instance, estimates the social rate of return to be 53 percent (in line with previous work on the subject) and the private rate of return to be between 10 and 12.5 percent or less (a figure slightly below earlier estimates) (1997, p. 16). These yield a spillover ratio of about 80 percent. For our story, the precise figure does not matter. What is noteworthy is that the spillover ratio seems clearly to be surprisingly large.

THE RELEVANCE OF THE ANALYSIS FOR REALITY

At first glance the optimality arguments of this chapter may appear farfetched and remote from the real world. However, a little reflection will suggest that this is not true. I have never come across a discussion of the consequences of the Industrial Revolution that did not stress that its main social benefit was its ultimate contribution to the living standards of the population as a whole—fostering improvements in health, longevity, education, reduction of poverty, and so on. Yet these are the main spillovers from innovation, and the focus of this chapter.

One can only begin to suggest the shocking levels of poverty to which the labor force would be condemned in a world without the spillovers from innovation. Histories of Europe confirm that for many centuries before the Industrial Revolution the vast majority of the population struggled simply to exist. Most families spent nearly half their food budgets on "breadstuffs." As late as 1790 in France, according to Robert Palmer (1964, p. 49), "The price of bread, even in normal times, in the amount needed for a man with a wife and three children, was half as much as the daily wage of common labor." Still more commonly, the breadstuff took the form of gruel (in good years) consumed in life-sustaining quantities. But there were many years when even gruel was unavailable. Devastating famines threatened Europe as late as the beginning of the nineteenth century, and before that had been a fact of life.

17. See, for example, Nadiri (1993), Mohnen (1992), and Wolff (1997).

Fernand Braudel's remarkable history of Europe documents the depths of human misery before the Industrial Revolution:

> A few overfed rich do not alter the rule. . . . Cereal yields were poor; two consecutive bad harvests spelt disaster. . . . Any national calculation shows a sad story. France, by any standards a privileged country, is reckoned to have experienced 10 *general* famines during the tenth century; 26 in the eleventh; 2 in the twelfth; 4 in the fourteenth; 7 in the fifteenth; 13 in the sixteenth; 11 in the seventeenth; and 16 in the eighteenth. . . . The same could be said of any country in Europe. In Germany, famine was a persistent visitor to the towns and flatlands. Even when the easier times came, in the eighteenth and nineteenth centuries, catastrophes could still happen. . . .
>
> The poor in the towns and countryside lived in a state of almost complete deprivation. Their furniture consisted of next to nothing, at least before the eighteenth century, when a rudimentary luxury began to spread. . . . Inventories made after death, which are reliable documents, testify almost invariably to the general destitution . . . a few old clothes, a stool, a table, a bench, the planks of a bed, sacks filled with straw. Official reports for Burgundy between the sixteenth and the eighteenth centuries are full of references to people [sleeping] on straw . . . with no bed or furniture, who were only separated from the pigs by a screen. . . . Paradoxically the countryside sometimes experienced far greater suffering [from famines than the townspeople]. The peasants . . . had scarcely any reserves of their own. They had no solution in case of famine except to turn to the town where they crowded together, begging in the streets and often dying in public squares. (Braudel, 1979, pp. 73–75 and 283)

Surely, none of us would be prepared to argue that it would be optimal to multiply the wealth of the world's richest innovators far above their current levels while condemning the rest of the population to miserable living standards. But that is just what zero spillovers would mean.

INNOVATION EXTERNALITIES: UNDERINVESTMENT VS. OVERINVESTMENT INCENTIVES

So far, I have argued that, although the externalities of innovation may impede growth, they may nevertheless be desirable, at least up to a point, because of their distributive consequences. But recent analysis has indicated that there are externalities of innovation that tend to drive this activity *above* its optimal level. Schumpeter's expression, "creative destruction," involves one such type of externality that has received a considerable amount of attention as a mechanism that may lead to excessive innovative activity. This felicitous term is useful because of both its clear message and its stimulating ambiguity. Its message is that innovation and growth force obsolete technical prearrangements to be swept away. Specifically, it refers to the replacement of obsolete products, processes, and firms by their more up-to-date and superior successors. The concept, however, tells us nothing about the desirability of this process and offers no basis on which to judge how far economic efficiency requires the process to go. Schumpeter does imply that without creative destruction we would be condemned to stagnation. But even he must have recognized that, at least in some cases, the old ways still offer some benefits, which progress nevertheless sweeps aside just as effectively as it removes procedures that are unquestionably inferior to their replacements. More important, in terms of both the current literature and, probably, policy, are the associated quantitative issues. Does the economy engage in too much or too little creative destruction? How can one tell?

As has already been noted, until recently most economists who dealt with the subject held that the substantial spillovers of innovation probably led to considerable underinvestment in innovation activities from the viewpoint of economic efficiency. But more recent writers, notably Aghion and Howitt, have raised the opposite possibility. Because the creators of innovation and those who suffer the resulting (creative) destruction are different individuals or groups, the process involves an externality that will tend to induce overinvestment by innovators.

Dasgupta and Stiglitz (1980) demonstrate that R&D expenditure can be excessive in terms of social welfare for another reason. Overinvestment in innovation can also occur when competing firms duplicate and rush to get ahead of one another's innovation programs, in an attempt to win an innovation race. It must surely be concluded that some of these externalities tend partly to offset the others, producing on balance a result that may well be better for economic efficiency. Thus, the externalities stemming from creative destruction or innovation races may be doubly beneficial, not only offsetting some of the disincentive effects of the distributive spillovers, but also permitting preservation of their beneficial consequences.

If creative destruction, for example, were the only source of externalities, it is indeed plausible that it would lead to investment in innovation in excess of the amount required for economic efficiency. This is the conclusion to which the Aghion-Howitt analysis correctly leads. But, as we know, this is by no means the only source, and it is also very plausible that the sizes of these externalities are relatively modest in comparison with the enormous beneficial spillovers of innovation. Since the creative destruction externalities go in the opposite direction from the redistributive spillovers—in terms of their expected effect on innovative activity—three conclusions follow:

1. The creative destruction externalities are an offset to the beneficial spillovers, and may bring the economy, on balance, somewhat closer to the requirements of efficiency and the incentives for the optimal quantity of innovation activity.
2. If the creative destruction externalities are, indeed, the smaller of the two, their effect cannot be an over-correction. That is, the net result will be an increase in innovative activity that is still insufficient to bring us to the efficient level, but moves the economy in a beneficial direction.
3. The improvement in efficiency will have been achieved with no offsetting deterioration in distribution. For the distributive benefits discussed in this chapter are not a monotonic function of the *net* magnitude of the externalities, after one has partially offset the other. Rather, the distributive benefits depend on the size of the externality that is quantified by the spillover ratio and on the amount of innovation, whose magnitude will, if anything, be increased by the creative destruction externality.

THE SIZE OF THE RANGE OF POSSIBLE OPTIMA

The graphic analysis has not yet dealt with one relevant issue. I have concluded that there generally exists a range of values of the spillover ratio, all of which are NLS Pareto optimal. But I have not considered how wide that range is likely to be, or how the width of that range is determined.

This is significant for at least one reason. If the range of (NLS) Pareto-optimal S values is narrow, then the interests of innovators and workers will be relatively close and conflict in their interests will be minimal. On the other hand, a wide range will make it more difficult for policy makers to determine to what degree it is best to tighten intellectual property rights and the strength of their enforcement. I will show next how the length of the range of NLS Pareto optima can, theoretically, be determined. The conclusion will be that, the flatter the B^* curve in figure 8.2 is near its maximum, the wider that range will be.

A simple intuitive explanation helps to bring out the logic of the issue. Flatness of the B^* curve means that changes in the distribution of the benefits from innovation do not materially undercut those benefits—the size of the total benefits pie shrinks slowly with changes in distribution. This can

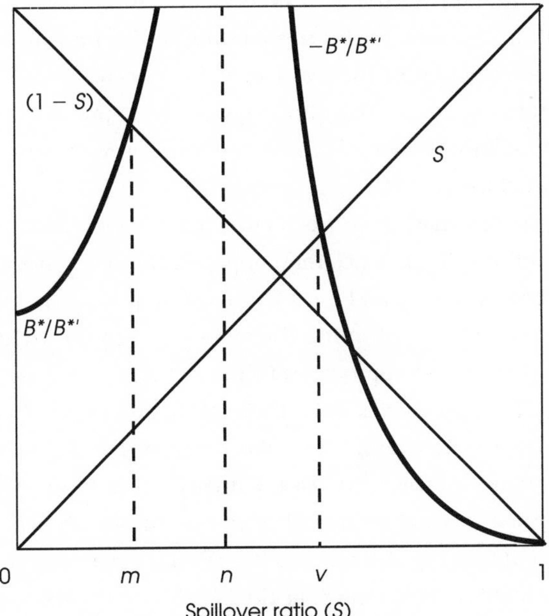

FIGURE 8.3
Determination of the Pareto-Optimal Range

occur, for example, if a substantial rise in the spillover benefits to workers does not greatly discourage investment in innovation, or if the innovations that will be lost will be ones that offer a relatively modest productivity contribution, or because there are some other offsets. So, since a flat B^* curve means that changes in income distribution will reduce the social output pie very slightly, each of our two groups can benefit substantially at the expense of the other if it manages to get a considerably larger share of that fairly fixed-sized pie. In that case, the innovators' optimum and the workers' optimum will be far apart. The opposite will be true if B^* curves downward sharply from its maximum.

This result can be demonstrated graphically. The points *m* and *v* in figure 8.2 and, thereby, the length of the range of possible optima, can be determined in the following way. For the workers' maximum, $dB^*w/dS = dSB^*/dS = SB^{*\prime} + B^* = 0$. Thus, the maximizing S is obtained from

$$S = -B^*/B^{*\prime}.$$

The calculation indicated by this equation is carried out graphically in figure 8.3, where the 45-degree line represents S and the negatively sloped heavy curve toward the right of the graph represents $-B^*/B^{*\prime}$, which has a vertical asymptote at n, the value of S corresponding to the maximum of B^*, where $B^{*\prime} = 0$. The intersection of the two loci at $S = v$ occurs at the point that satisfies the workers' maximum condition given by the previous equation.[18] The analogous calculation is carried out for the innovators[19] using the negatively sloping diagonal for $(1 - S)$.

We have noted that $-B^*/B^{*\prime}$ is a curve that approaches the vertical line above n asymptotically as S declines, approaching B^*_{max} from the right. So, the interval between $S = n$ and $S = 1$ is the relevant range in which to seek v, the maximum of B^*w, confirming that v must lie to the right of B^*_{max}. We have seen that the curve approaches infinity at B^*_{max} because near there the denominator, $B^{*\prime}$, approaches zero. Then, at its other end, $S = 1$, where $B^* = 0$, the curve approaches zero. The intersection of the S line with the curve $-B^*/B^{*\prime}$ will increase if the curve rises. But this will result from a flattening of B^*. The flattening raises the value of B^* in any subregion near B^*_{max} and, by definition, the flattening also reduces $B^{*\prime}$. With the numerator raised and the denominator lowered, it is clear that the $-B^*/B^{*\prime}$ curve will rise except at the end points where $S = 1$ and where $B^* = B^*_{max}$. Thus, its intersection with the 45-degree line will move to the right, demonstrating our result: a flattening of B^* near B^*_{max} will bring B^*w_{max} further from B^*_{max}. Exactly the same argument holds for B^*i. It confirms that a flattening of the B^* curve near its maximum will increase the distance between the maximum of B^*i and that of B^*w.

This completes the graphic discussion of the determination of the NLS Pareto-optimal range of the innovation spillover ratio.

CONCLUDING COMMENT

It is worth noting that the externalities of innovation on which this chapter has focused are not unchangeable. There *are* ways in which policy makers can modify them and affect the outcome of our story. Either they can partially offset the effects of the spillovers or they can adopt measures that increase or decrease them.

---

18. An obvious alternative construction uses the B^* curve from figure 8.2 and superimposes the curve $-SB^{*\prime}$. The intersection of these two curves gives the workers' optimum, v, with a similar construction for the innovators' optimum, m. This second construction is a bit more complicated graphically, but it is a little easier to interpret economically as equating $-SB^{*\prime}$, the effect of a very small increase in S on the workers' loss via the reduced size of the "benefit pie," with the associated marginal gain, B^*, from their increased share.

19. This assumes that, at $S = 0$, $B^* < B^{*\prime}$ so that m is an interior maximum. See footnote 13, above.

Policy makers can obviously decrease the innovation-inhibiting effects of the spillovers without reducing the distributive benefits materially by providing public sector assistance to cover at least part of the sunk cost of innovation. We do not know whether the implied role of government in deciding which innovations to subsidize and the large amount of financing that would then have to flow through the public sector would themselves significantly inhibit growth and innovation. Still, it seems widely agreed that government's financing of basic research, whose spillovers are particularly large, is quite appropriate. But where most R&D is carried out by private industry, as in the United States, the government support is probably far from sufficient to make a fundamental difference.

The government can also affect the magnitude of the spillover ratio by legislating greater (or smaller) rights to the creators of intellectual property and it can increase or reduce the resources devoted to enforcement of those rights. For example, Japanese patenting laws are far less favorable to inventors than are those in the United States and probably increase greatly the spillovers from Japanese innovation. No obvious and substantial decline in Japanese innovative activity appears to have resulted from this less protective atmosphere.[20] Even more important, the paucity of protection available from the patent system appears to have strengthened the incentive for Japanese innovators to enter technology-sharing agreements with competitors and others. That, in turn, has insured that inventions are rapidly disseminated and put to use throughout the Japanese economy, enhancing Japanese productivity growth (on this general subject and for more details on the relevance of the Japanese rules, see Baumol, 1993, chapter 12). This also illustrates another way in which a spillover ratio substantially different from zero may be desirable in reality and not only in theory.

Returning, finally, to the central point of this chapter, the crucial fact is that most of us *do* recognize the beneficial spillovers that innovation has contributed and we all seem to agree that this enhancement of living standards is very desirable. In other words, perhaps without realizing that we were discussing the spillovers of innovation, we have concluded that they are a very good thing. It follows immediately that, even if zero spillovers were possible and did increase innovation, they would certainly be far from optimal.

20. Wolff, in conversation, has suggested the hypothesis that this may have resulted because more rapid dissemination resulting from decreased effectiveness of patent protection reduced the sunk cost of innovation sufficiently to offset the effect on profits from the increase in spillovers.

Here, the standard reaction of many economists—that disinterested academicians cannot take a stand on income distribution on any basis of rigorous analysis, whatever their personal feeling—just will not do. Of course, no one aspires to a world in which innovators receive incomes in the trillions of dollars (putting Mr. Gates' income into the shade), while the remainder of the community languishes in seventeenth-century poverty. But if this is so, then we must also go on to reject the conclusion that spillovers are incompatible with optimality in the growth process. Once that is recognized, the remainder is a matter of haggling about the degree of deviation from zero. My own value judgment on this issue is summed up by George Bernard Shaw's dictum that there is no crime greater than poverty, which leads me to believe that the most desirable value of *S* is very much large than zero. For, surely, it is widely and appropriately accepted that the main benefit of the Industrial Revolution is the remarkable increase in average per capita incomes and, more particularly, in real wages.

Of course, those innovations that have never been born do constitute a loss to society. But the point in the analysis here is that there is an inescapable tradeoff between two desirable phenomena: further increases in innovative activity versus diversion of the benefits to bring society out of poverty, to spread education and health care, and to finance the better life not just for the fortunate few but for the population as a whole. Given such a tradeoff, we are back in the realm in which economists are most comfortable. In Lionel Robbins' justly noted words, we are back at the allocation of scarce resources among competing (and desirable) ends. And the analysis of such tradeoffs is the meat and potatoes of our professional activity.

The range of choices for society under discussion here can perhaps better be thought of as possible movements along an efficiency-distribution frontier, rather than as a choice among alternative and second-best Pareto optima. The issue is a matter of determining an optimal tradeoff between economic efficiency and the variance of income, subject to the constraint that the only feasible way to achieve substantial transfers is by means of spillovers.

This brings us to the end of the discussion of the reasons for the unprecedented growth record of the capitalist economies. Undoubtedly there are both contributory influences and impediments that have been omitted. But the five elements that I have stressed seem by themselves sufficient to make this performance less puzzling: oligopolistic competition that uses innovation as a weapon and engages in an innovation arms race, that routinizes the innovation arms race to reduce its uncertainties, and that engages in systematic innovation exchange and licensing for profit. Together, these plausibly constitute a large part of the story. The relative decline in the opportunities for destructive and rent-seeking entrepreneurship as compared with productive entrepreneurial activity, along with the emergence of the rule of law from the struggles between the kings and their nobles, arguably also played a particularly critical role in the rise of capitalism. They continue to be important today. Finally, the socially beneficial side of the spillovers from innovation serves as a very valuable offset to any resulting disincentive to innovative activity. All of these features are, in part or in their entirety, attributes of the free-enterprise economies that other types of economy either do not share or do so to a very limited degree. That is, I believe, a persuasive explanation of why even the most inventive of non-capitalist societies has fallen so short in terms of innovation.

APPENDIX

THE EFFICIENCY–EQUALITY TRADEOFF AND LUMP-SUM REDISTRIBUTION

Limited Relevance of Lump-Sum Redistributions: The NSL Pareto Optimality Concept

Fairy tales indisputably have their value, but there are times when it is appropriate to go beyond them. The concept of lump-sum transfers as a mode of redistribution that can preserve economic efficiency unscathed is such a legend.[21] Here, I will show why in certain significant circumstances such transfers cannot occur, and illustrate what can be learned if one is willing, at least sometimes, to abandon the premise. This is not just another tedious and counterproductive plea for greater realism in economic models, as an end in itself. For I hope to show that much of substance and importance can be learned by dropping the lump-sum redistribution premise from the theoretical analyses. Once it is recognized that a desired distribution cannot be achieved without some sacrifice in economic efficiency, one is led to study the nature of the tradeoff and the means to minimize its cost to society.

If for purposes of analysis society is divided into different groups, it can be expected that one group will prefer an efficiency–distribution combination

---

21. Akerlof (2000) comments that applied economists are well aware that, generally, lump-sum transfers are simply not possible. I certainly agree. More than that, even most pure theorists must know this in their hearts. But this does not stop them from using this mythical device in their formal writings to focus exclusively on allocative efficiency, assuming away the implications for distribution.

different from that preferred by another. To simplify, let Y be some index of total net output of the community (or, alternatively, its rate of growth) and E be an index of the degree of equality of distribution (as measured, perhaps, by the reciprocal of variance). Assume that there are incentive compatibility constraints making Y decrease monotonically as E increases. Suppose that the maximum amount of Y the economy can produce, consistent with incentive compatibility constraints, is $Y = e$. Let society be divided into two groups: group I most strongly desires the combination (Y_1, E_1), whereas group II's optimum is (Y_2, E_2). Then, if each group's valuation of an outcome decreases steadily as its distance from its preferred (Y, E) increases, every intermediate (Y, E) combination must be Pareto optimal, though for many such combinations $Y < e$. That is, from any such point in (Y, E) space it will be impossible to make one group better off without harming the other. To emphasize that these are *constrained* Pareto optima, I have referred to any such outcome as "NLS Pareto optimal"; that is, it is optimal so long as no lump-sum transfers are possible, at least if they are attempted pervasively and repeatedly. This chapter has applied these observations to the economy's investment in innovation and examined the effects of the difference between its social and private benefits.

On the Impossibility of Repeated and Pervasive Lump-Sum Transfers

It is, of course, sometimes analytically convenient and even, occasionally, basically harmless to assume that lump-sum transfers are possible and that they can be carried out systematically. But, as has just been indicated, there are issues whose analysis is substantially distorted by such a premise—if it is in fact untrue. And it is easy to argue that the assumption is, in reality, often false.

By a lump-sum transfer is meant an income or wealth transfer with absolutely no efficiency-damaging incentive effects. That is, those persons from whom the transfers are derived must not wish to or must not be able to do anything that damages the economy's efficiency in order to reduce the magnitudes of their losses. Similarly, the recipients of the transfers must not be led by their windfall to change their behavior in a manner that impedes efficiency. But even a once-and-for-all transfer cannot plausibly be expected to be free of any distortion in incentives if we suppose that it depends on any aspect or consequence of market activity.

The likelihood of distortion is far greater if the ostensibly lump-sum transfers are to be adopted as a long-term corrective of any objectionable distribution consequences resulting from the choice of the pattern of resource allocation required for allocative efficiency. Then, simply by definition of a correction of an undesired distributive effect, those whose activities have contributed to their excessive income or wealth must provide the resources to be transferred, and those whose incomes or wealth are considered inadequate must become the recipients. In such a repeated game, members of each group will soon learn that their economic activities—those that contributed to their pre-transfer wealth or income levels—also condemn them to the role of transfer payer or recipient. Clearly, this is an incentive to the payers to cut back on the activities that force them into that position, and an incentive for the recipients to do the reverse.[22]

It is important to recognize, however, that such a transfer can nevertheless be lump-sum if the effects of the transfer include no externalities or deviations from perfect competition. The Arrow–Debreu theorems state that, if the economy is perfectly competitive and there are no externalities, then a change in the distribution of wealth will simply lead to a new equilibrium that can also be Pareto optimal. Prices and the allocation of resources can all be changed in a manner compatible with the new Pareto optimum.

So much for the theory, but reality is generally different. There is no need to remind the reader that real markets are not perfectly competitive, and externalities in the real world are arguably far from zero (see below). More important for the discussion of this chapter is the fact that the very act of reducing an externality, whether marginal, average, or total, is tantamount to a redistribution of real income between the recipients of those benefits and the agents whose activities generate them. For an externality, by definition, is simply a matter of the distribution of the costs or benefits of an activity between those directly involved in the activity and those who are not. Consequently, if a decrease in externalities is necessary for an increase in efficiency, then there clearly must be a redistributive effect. And any measure that undoes that distributive effect must automatically re-create the external-

22. Even a transfer unconnected with wealth or income cannot easily be made lump-sum. A clearly silly example will bring out the point. Suppose a fixed and substantial tax payment is imposed upon the birth of a child to a family whose surname begins with a letter in the first half of the alphabet. The tax payment is to be transferred upon each birth to families with names later in the alphabet (with name changes prohibited by law). This would surely entail an incentive affecting family sizes in the two groups. More important, such a scheme could not be used to correct what was deemed to be a maldistribution of income resulting from the requirements of economic efficiency or from the behavior of the market. It could not be used for that purpose precisely because it would be designed to have no connection with any choices of economic behavior. There is no reason for the members of the alphabetically disadvantaged group to be the same as those who have acquired what is deemed to be excessive wealth.

ity. Such offsetting changes in distribution must patently affect efficiency and so, by definition, they cannot be lump-sum.

The difficulty, in short, is this. Suppose one starts with an acceptable distribution accompanied by externalities that prevent efficiency. One then undertakes a two-stage approach toward optimality, first eliminating the externalities and then correcting any undesired redistribution effects. The very act of distributive modification re-creates the externalities indirectly because, at the end, those who were better off as a result of the externalities still end up with benefits for which they made no contribution;[23] and those who initially were deprived by the externalities of part of the benefits generated by their activities still suffer the same damage as before. Thus the externality is simply reconstituted by the redistribution, this time via a two-stage process rather than a direct one. One simply cannot eliminate the distributive consequences of preventing the externalities without restoring the unearned rewards and burdens initially stemming from the activities that generated the externalities. They are inseparable Siamese twins. The elimination of externalities and the restoration of the initial distribution by means of lump-sum transfers are therefore inherently self-contradictory notions. This problem for the lump-sum transfer scenario was brought out concretely by my application of the analysis to the enormous (and arguably beneficial) spillovers of the innovation process.

The Range of Non-Lump-Sum Pareto Optima

I turn now to a graph to describe the locus and possibly wide range of NLS Pareto optima that emerge in a world in which lump-sum distributions are ruled out. It is simply a generalization of figure 8.2 and its direct application to the subject of innovation. The vertical axis in figure 8.4 indicates some scalar measure of the total welfare benefits, Y, that are currently attainable by the two-group economy.[24] Y can be thought of as total output in a one-good

23. The concept is unfamiliar, so an example may be needed to bring out the point. Let individual A be the generator of, say, a beneficial externality worth D dollars to both parties in question. Assume that B receives the externality. Suppose the resulting distribution of benefits is desirable, but the efficiency effects are not. Accordingly, we take step 1 and eliminate the externality. In step 2, we use a tax to get back to the previous distribution. This requires taxing A the amount D dollars and giving the D dollars to B. If A and B recognize what has happened and why, are we not back at the previous inefficiency incentives?

24. In effect, this assumes that utility is transferable so that efficient behavior is independent of the distribution of benefits. This is a heroic assumption, to be sure, but one that does no real damage in this context. I adopt it only to facilitate a simple graphical exposition.

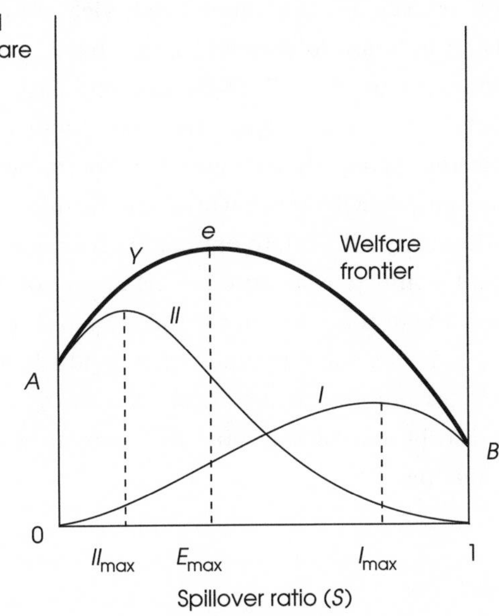

FIGURE 8.4
The Range of NLS Pareto Optimality

economy, and the two groups as producers and non-producers. The horizontal axis measures (from left to right) S, the share of the total benefits that accrues to group I. The share of the benefits to group II, $(1 - S)$, is measured from right to left along the same axis. In the absence of lump-sum transfers, suppose that incentive compatibility constraints on individual behavior imply that the maximum Y depends on S. For instance, there may be no feasible contract that is able to separate the incentive to work from the level of compensation. Let point e denote the (S, Y) combination at which Y is maximized. At this efficient point E_{max} is the share of the benefits that happens to accrue to group I, so that $1 - E_{max}$ is the share of group II. In the absence of lump-sum transfers, any other distribution—that is, any other value of S—must reduce Y, because of the decline in allocative efficiency, ignoring the incentive compatibility constraints. For simplicity, I assume that the remaining distribution share values, S, yield values of Y that are bounded from above by a smooth, hill-shaped welfare frontier, the heavy solid curve *AYeB*, which, for brevity, will be called curve Y.

Next, it is easy to derive from the overall benefit–distribution frontier Y the two corresponding upper frontiers for groups I and II, exactly as was done in figure 8.2. For these obviously are given by the expressions SY and $(1 - S)Y$

for groups I and II, respectively, and immediately yield the corresponding two curves labeled *I* and *II*. It also follows, as before, that $I_{max} > E_{max} > II_{max}$, that is, group I's maximum must lie to the right of group II's.

The range between the maxima for the two groups clearly is a region in which it is impossible (along the efficient frontier) to benefit either group without harming the other. In other words, the frontier points within this range are all, indisputably, NLS Pareto optima. Such a range must always exist where the efficient point, *e*, is an interior maximum of *Y*, the measure of social welfare, and where the *Y* frontier is hill-shaped. For then, any change in distribution that favors some group(s) of individuals must do so at the expense of others, because the change must decrease *Y* (the total size of the pie available for distribution), and it must also decrease at least some group's share of that smaller pie.

PART II

Integration of Innovation into the Mainstream of Microtheory

CHAPTER 9

Oligopolistic Competition, Pricing, and Recoupment of Innovation Outlays

[in] the sacred precincts of theory, the price variable is ousted from its dominant position. . . . [I]n capitalist reality, as distinguished from its textbook picture . . . [the] kind of competition which counts [is] the competition from the new commodity, the new technology, the new source of supply, the new type of organization . . .—competition which commands a decisive cost or quality advantage and which strikes not at the margins of the profits and the outputs of the existing firms but at their foundations and their very lives.

—Schumpeter, 1947, p. 84

. . . innovations are rarely the dramatic breakthroughs that Schumpeter may have had in mind but rather small improvements in a new process or product in which genuine novelty and imitation-with-a-difference shade imperceptibly into one another.

—Blaug, 1997, p.110

Part II will, to some extent, look further into the growth process of the free-enterprise economy. Notably in chapter 13, I will return to the discussion of licensing and the voluntary dissemination of proprietary technology, considering the magnitude of license fees, deriving necessary conditions for consistency of this price with economic efficiency, and obtaining an explicit pricing formula. That chapter will also consider whether market forces lead to the adoption of such efficient licensing prices, and will conclude that the market does provide such incentives, though perhaps not always sufficiently powerful, in reality, to lead to prices that approximate optimality.

But the central focus of part II is not the efficiency of the free-market growth process. My main objective, rather, is to illustrate, by means of concrete analyses of a number of significant issues, how readily the standard toolkit and results of microanalysis can be adapted to the study of routine innovation. This evidence invites us to examine the possibility of going one step further: explicitly to incorporate innovation into the basic models of the firm and the industry, not as a mere side issue but as an activity that lies at the heart of the models. In chapter 4, I took a first step toward that goal, in an elementary model of oligopolistic competition as a force that promotes expenditure on invention and innovation. In this chapter and those that follow I continue this sort of analysis. Yet, although I accept the Schumpeterian observation that nowadays it is innovation rather than price that is characteristically the main concern of competing oligopolists, this part of the book will devote a good deal of attention to the interrelation between innovation and pricing. I will consider how innovation affects the price of the final products that employ its technology, how prices are adapted to the requirements of the recoupment of outlays on innovation, and how to set the prices of access to innovations when the proprietor of such intellectual property permits its use to others.

This chapter and the next two will consider the pricing and recoupment of investment in innovation. In this discussion we will find ourselves driven to go beyond the theory to consider an important policy issue. I have already emphasized that the oligopolistic sectors of the economy, and the competition among these large firms, play a major role in the spectacular growth performance of the free-market economies. Oligopolies, traditionally, are nevertheless the prime targets of attention by the antitrust authorities. There is, of course, good reason for this. Market forms populated by smaller firms are unlikely to entail any market power, and so the weak enterprises they contain will be unable to carry out anticompetitive acts or even to attempt to do so. On the other hand, unregulated pure monopoly is a rare bird, if it is to be found at all. So it is the oligopoly markets where any attempt at anticompetitive activity by private and largely unregulated firms is to be expected. Still, exploitation of the public through anticompetitive actions is surely not something undertaken by every oligopoly firm, any one of which must be deemed innocent until proven guilty. It has been common to offer evidence of at least the possession of monopoly power in the form of data showing that an oligopoly firm's prices differ from the (perfectly) competitive level and, in particular, that it engages in differential (discriminatory) pricing practices. Chapter 10 will end with a discussion of this sort of argument, showing that oligopoly firms, particularly those engaged in substantial innovative activity, may well be forced by competitive pressures and the necessities of survival to adopt prices very different from those that could be expected under perfect competition, and, indeed, prices that are markedly discriminatory. Without this, they might simply be unable to recoup their continuing outlays on innovation. Indeed, rather than constituting manifestations of monopoly power, such investment-recouping prices may well be thrust upon the innovative firms, which may consequently be price takers, not price makers, in the sense that market forces may impose upon them the particular prices they adopt.

WHY INNOVATION IS CRUCIAL FOR MODELS OF OLIGOPOLISTIC COMPETITION

I believe, with Schumpeter, that it is not merely desirable for innovation to be incorporated into the microtheory of oligopolistic competition. Without that component, I believe the theory is deprived of much of its applicability to the modern free-enterprise economy. Anyone with any intimate knowledge of the operation of the firms that constitute the modern sector of an industrialized economy will recognize that pricing is not the primary competitive issue in management's deliberations. Its hopes and fears instead relate primarily to the redesign of its current products, to the new products it plans to introduce, and to the more productive and reliable production processes it hopes to adopt. In short, the continued exile of innovation to the suburbs of microtheory does not merely mean that there is room for improvement in that body of analysis. Rather, the theory is thereby deprived of what should be one of its most critical components. That is why this book devotes so much attention to suggesting ways in which innovation can be incorporated into the heart of microanalysis, and to emphasizing attributes of the activity that improve the prospects for success in this task. That, then, is the primary purpose of this second part of the book.

THE EFFECTS OF INNOVATION ON FINAL-PRODUCT EQUILIBRIUM: THE COMPARATIVE STATICS

Let us turn now to how the magnitude of the R&D activity determined by competition affects the variables more usually studied in the theory of the firm and industry. I will consider the effects of an increase in the amount of innovation on final-product outputs, prices, and the welfare of consumers and producers.

To obtain determinate results about prices and outputs, the discussion leaves the oligopoly situation discussed up to this point and focuses instead on a single firm whose decision-making is independent of the activities and decisions of other enterprises (and is presumably a pure monopoly).

Definitions

Process and Product Innovations. A *product innovation* is defined here as one that shifts the demand curve for the affected final product to the right, while a *process innovation* is one that shifts the pertinent cost curves downward. In the discussion that follows I assume that there is a clear distinction between process and product innovations and that any particular innovation can unambiguously be assigned to one of these two categories.

Successful Innovation. I define an innovation to be successful (commercially) if it increases the producer's profit. We will see that a successful *process* innovation can be expected to expand output, reduce product price, and enhance welfare. Thus, it can be considered beneficial in terms of all three of these attributes. A successful *product* innovation will also increase final-product output, but its general effects on price and welfare can go either way.

The Effects of Process Innovations

The results for a process innovation now follow trivially on the assumption that it shifts the marginal cost curve downward.[1] A graph will suffice to demonstrate them. Figure 9.1 shows the firm's initial marginal revenue and marginal cost curves, MR_1 and MC_1, this time for the supply of its final product rather than for its investment in R&D, as in chapter 4. The broken lines MR_2 and MC_2 are the corresponding curves after the introduction of an innovation.

We see at once that:

> PROPOSITION 9.1. (a) If a process innovation shifts the marginal cost curve downward, it must increase output because of the negative slope of *MR*, moving the equilibrium point from *B* to *A*. (b) Because there is no shift of the demand curve, its presumably negative slope means that the product's price must fall. (c) If the invention is successful, as defined, it follows that the producer's surplus will not fall and, because of the fall in price, consumers' surplus[2] must rise. This confirms our results for the case of a process innovation.

1. Of course, there can be exceptions—cases in which a rise in marginal cost is accepted in return for a large cut in fixed costs.

2. Here, I obviously refer to the simplest measure of the surplus, that of Alfred Marshall (1920, pp. 125–33).

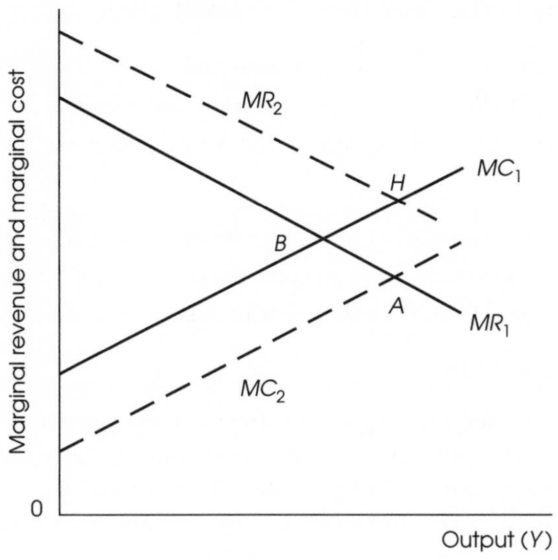

FIGURE 9.1
Effects of an Innovation

The Effects of a Product Innovation

The case of a product innovation follows the same sort of logic, but the arguments are considerably less straightforward, except for the analysis of the effect on output. The innovation results in an upward shift of the marginal revenue curve to MR_2 (and, presumably, also of the demand curve). That will lead to a rise in output even if the marginal cost curve is downward sloping, so long as its slope is less than that of the marginal revenue curve—as stability of equilibrium requires. All this assumes that the cost curve does not also shift as a result of the product innovation, a possibility that will be considered later.

It will presently be shown that price may either rise or fall as the result of a product innovation. That is because price is now affected by two influences working in opposite directions. The upward shift in the demand curve will push price upward, but the increase in output and the negative slope of the demand curve will have the opposite effect. Once again, the area between the *MR* and *MC* curves may well increase, so that, with output expanding, consumers' surplus may also rise. However, once we consider the possible changes in demand elasticity as well as the sunk costs of the innovation, the effect on welfare is no longer clear. Next, I will look at the price and welfare effects of a product innovation more carefully.

Product Innovation and Price. Let us next prove:

PROPOSITION 9.2. A product innovation may either decrease or increase the firm's profit-maximizing price, depending at least in part on the effect of the innovation on the price elasticity of demand for the product.

To prove this, it is sufficient to show that either result is possible in the simplest case in which marginal cost does not vary with output in the relevant range. The firm's objective is to maximize profit

(9.1) $$\pi = R(p,\mu) - C(p),$$

where R and C are, respectively, the total revenue and cost functions, p is the final-product price, and μ is the shift variable representing the contribution of the innovation to total revenue.

Next, we note that first-order and second-order maximum conditions are

(9.2) $$\pi_p = R_p - C_p = 0, \qquad \pi_{pp} < 0.$$

By our simplifying assumption, we have $C_p = C_y y_p$ = a constant. Setting the total differential of the first-order condition in (9.2) equal to zero, we have

(9.3) $$d\pi_p = \pi_{pp} dp + R_{p\mu} d\mu = 0.$$

Thus,

(9.4) $$\partial p/\partial\mu = -R_{p\mu}/\pi_{pp}$$

has the same sign as $R_{p\mu}$.

But $R_p = y + py_p = y(1 - E)$, where E is the initial (absolute value) elasticity of demand at the initial price, p. We know that profit maximization requires $E > 1$. And we have

(9.5) $$R_{p\mu} = y_\mu(1 - E) - yE_\mu.$$

This, and therefore $\partial p/\partial\mu$, is clearly positive iff $E_\mu < (1 - E)y_\mu/y < 0$, which is our result. Thus, a product innovation can, indeed, either raise or reduce price, as Proposition 9.2 asserts. The role of demand elasticity is clear intuitively. If the innovation substantially increases the elasticity of the demand curve, the increased direct revenue contribution of a rise in price is more than offset by the loss in quantity sold resulting from the price increase.

Product Innovation and Welfare. A product innovation can, indeed, add to welfare but, like all innovations, the validity of this result depends on the real cost of the innovation. Other things being equal, if it has a sufficiently large sunk cost it can obviously cause a net loss in welfare. In the case of a process innovation we avoided this difficulty by assuming that the innovation was successful, meaning that it must still yield an increase in the producer's surplus, however small. Since in the process innovation case it is trivial to show, as we did, that consumers' surplus must also increase, the rise in welfare then becomes unambiguous.

The same can be shown for product innovation in special, but not necessarily unrepresentative, cases. However, because of the plausible resulting rise in price that has just been demonstrated, total consumers' surplus will not necessarily rise, as will be shown presently. Consequently, even if the producer's surplus is increased slightly, it is possible for a product innovation to reduce welfare. Further, a product innovation can lead to shifts in the cost curves as well as in the revenue curves, unlike a process innovation, which can reasonably be assumed to affect only the cost side. Since costs as well as revenues are affected by product innovation, and those costs can either be raised or lowered, we have a second influence that prevents unambiguous results about the welfare effects.[3]

Before demonstrating the negative result, let us prove:

PROPOSITION 9.3. Where the marginal and average curves are all linear and the shift in the marginal and average revenue curves as the result of a product innovation does not change any slope or affect the marginal cost curve, then consumers' surplus must be raised. In that case, a successful innovation (as defined here) must be welfare enhancing.

Proof: Let

$a - by + \mu = p$ = the average revenue function

$c + ky$ = the average cost function.

Then the firm's total profit function is

$$\pi = (a + \mu - c)y - (b + k)y^2, \tag{9.6}$$

whose first-order maximum condition yields as the profit-maximizing value of y

3. If the new product has a lower marginal cost than the old product, that may lead to a fall in the product price, further weakening Proposition 9.2. Thus, shifting cost curves can make the price effect of a product innovation even more ambiguous.

(9.7) $y^* = (a + \mu - c)/2(b + k)$.

Marshallian consumers' surplus at that output is given by

(9.8) $$\int_0^{y^*} (a + \mu - by)dy - (a + \mu)y^* + by^{*2} = (a + \mu)y^* - by^{*2}/2 - (a + \mu)y^* + by^{*2}$$
$$= by^{*2}/2 > 0.$$

Thus, under the linear and parallel shift assumptions, a product innovation must increase Marshallian consumers' surplus. Therefore, if it is successful, meaning that it increases the producer's surplus, it must enhance welfare.

Product Innovations and Welfare: The Generally Ambiguous Result. A graphic counterexample will suffice to prove:

PROPOSITION 9.4. Even if a product innovation is successful, it can decrease welfare.

This will happen if the innovation reduces consumers' surplus because of its effect on the slope of the demand curve, and the sunk cost incurred by the innovation yields a negligible contribution to the producer's surplus.

I will, once again, deal with linear average and marginal revenue curves (in the graph the marginal cost curve will also be drawn as a line segment, but that is unnecessary for the argument). However, in this case I will take the innovation not to shift the left-hand end of the revenue curves. In figure 9.2 I assume that, without the innovation, the marginal and average revenue curves are HMR_1 and HAR_1, respectively. With the innovation, the right-hand end of the old marginal revenue curve moves rightward, so that the new *marginal* revenue curve, HMR_2, coincides with the old *average* revenue curve. Consumers' surplus then clearly changes from triangle *ABH* to triangle *abH*, where *B* is the point on AR_1 directly above the intersection of *MC* with MR_1, and *b* is the corresponding point for *MC* and MR_2. It is clear that if the *MC* curve were vertical then the second triangle would be considerably smaller than the first: the horizontal sides would be identical but the vertical side of the second triangle would be much smaller than that of the first. By continuity, this must still be true (though the difference will be smaller) if the *MC* curve is upward sloping but not quite vertical. Thus, in this case, the product innovation will reduce consumers' surplus by a substantial amount (call it *s*), because it will raise the profit-maximizing price considerably, reduce the slope of the demand curve, and not add much to the quantity purchased. Let *r* represent the corresponding increment in the producer's surplus. Then, so long as $r > 0$, no matter how small, the innovation will be successful on our

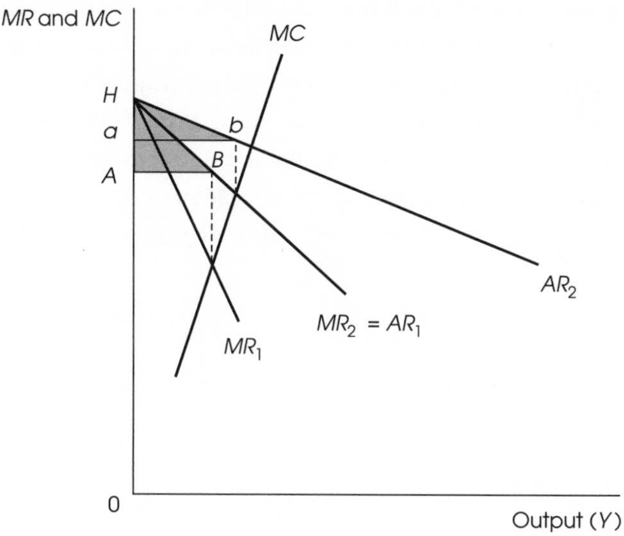

FIGURE 9.2
Effects of Product Innovation on Welfare

criterion. By increasing the sunk cost, the magnitude of r can be reduced as close to zero as desired without making the innovation unsuccessful. In particular, there will be a magnitude of sunk cost beyond which $s > r > 0$. This proves Proposition 9.4: a successful product innovation can yield not only a negative consumers' surplus but also a welfare loss.

The key to construction of the counterexample is a resulting shift in the demand curve that reduces its absolute slope, rather than leaving it unchanged as before, and a rapidly rising marginal cost curve. The decreased slope of the demand curve means that the innovation will increase price considerably, while keeping the rise in the area under the *AR* curve to a minimum. The sharply rising marginal cost curve ensures that any contribution to consumers' surplus resulting from an increase in sales will remain small. The graph shows that these two conditions together can ensure that the innovation will decrease welfare. Obviously, if the product innovation increases marginal cost because it provides a better product that is more costly to supply, that can exacerbate any resulting loss in welfare, or it can transform what would otherwise have been a net gain into a net loss.

The next chapter continues the use of elementary microtheory, returning to the implications of routinized innovation for the pricing of final products. In particular, it will focus on the influence of the repeatedly sunk outlays that routinization requires of the firm, and will show the crucial role of discriminatory (differential) pricing in this process, demonstrating that in these circumstances differential prices do not imply possession of monopoly power by the enterprise. Indeed, it will be shown that in these conditions not only may the firm be forced by market pressures to engage in differential prices, but it may have little choice in the magnitudes of those prices.

CHAPTER 10

Microeconomic Theory of Industrial Organization in the "Innovation-Machine" Economy

Casual observation suggests that price discrimination is common in many industries that appear to be extremely competitive. . . . [F]irms in the airline, car rental, moving, hotel and restaurant businesses practice common types of price discrimination, and much evidence suggests that high-valuation consumers pay higher average prices than low-valuation consumers. Yet these markets are not characterized by unusually high entry costs, economies of scale, product differentiation, or market concentration.

—Dana, 1998, p. 395

There is nothing sinister about high gross margins. Nor does their presence suggest any monopoly power.

—Shapiro, 2000, p. 10

This chapter provides an overview of the way in which the "invention-machine" economy requires us to modify our vision of the microeconomy, in particular of the firm and of industry. I will show that the differences from the traditional scenario are profound.

Although no one has claimed that the world is perfectly competitive in the textbook sense, traditional microeconomic theory implies that the depiction provided by the perfect competition model is sufficiently pertinent to enable us to understand the workings of real-world market forces.[1] And that

1. Economists all recognize the limited relation to reality of the model of perfect competition, and I am fully aware of the shift of attention in the literature to game-theoretic analysis of oligopoly. But the game-theoretic analysis, with all its analytic power, is not designed to offer any integrated overview of industrial organization in the economy as a whole. Since such an overview is the goal of this chapter, it is with perfect competition, which also provides such an overview, that my depiction must be contrasted.

model *is* arguably pertinent to the world of the early nineteenth century, when a firm with a hundred employees was a rare giant and economists such as Adam Smith and David Ricardo saw no need to provide any substantial discussion of innovation and the process by which it is generated. In the model of perfect competition, there is also no role for determination of firm size, because all firms are assumed to be minuscule, as in fact they generally were then. As a result, there was no need to determine when market forces would lead to oligopoly or monopoly. Indeed, a monopoly was usually something granted by a monarch to reward a favorite, rather than a result from the workings of the free market. The model generated well-recognized predictions about prices, asserting that the price of the (assumedly single) product was equal to both marginal and average cost, so that it could be expected to enable the firm just to recover its costs, yielding on average exactly the competitive rate of return on their investments to those providing the financing it needed. Discriminatory pricing, in which the same product is supplied to different customers at different prices, was an issue that did not arise. Sunk costs were occasionally mentioned, but mostly the discussion was designed to demonstrate their irrelevance.

Today's innovation assembly-line economy is very different. The competitive model that is helpful in indicating how it works is the perfectly contestable market, where entry and exit are instantaneous and costless. Not that the world is perfectly contestable—any more than Ricardo's economy was in reality perfectly competitive—but the contestability model does allow us to deal explicitly with the pertinent issues in the growth-machine economy. In this economy many firms are driven to be large, and some to be huge, arguably by market forces, which implies that the affected markets are led to an oligopoly industry structure. Sunk costs, notably the sunk costs required to fight the innovation battles, are substantial, mandatory, and constantly repeated. As a result, prices above marginal costs and price discrimination become the norm rather than the exception because, as I will show, without such deviations from behavior in the perfectly competitive model, innovation outlays and other unavoidable and repeated sunk outlays cannot be recouped.

Traditional microeconomic theory gives the impression that, once the firm is in a position to charge prices above marginal cost and to engage in discriminatory pricing, it can exercise free will in selecting those prices and price patterns that best suit its purposes. In other words, firms are no longer the "price-taker" entities of perfect competition, in which market forces determine price magnitudes that the firm has no option but to accept. I will show, however, that even in the world of oligopolistic innovators the market can continue to exercise substantial power over their decisions and behavior. It can decide how large the firm will be and how much more than marginal cost it will charge, it can force the firm to engage in price discrimination, and, at least in theory, it can even impose each and every one of the different prices the firm charges to different customers. Moreover, my analysis shows how those prices will, in principle, be determined, just as unequivocally as the perfectly competitive model does for its world. In other words, the markets of the growth-machine economy can also make firms into price takers—albeit discriminatory price takers—and can force their other decisions upon them as well. This, then, is the new industrial organization story of the innovation assembly-line economy, and shows how innovation does indeed fit at the center of pertinent microanalysis.

FULLY EFFECTIVE COMPETITION: THE CONTESTABLE MARKETS MODEL

"Contestability" refers to a market into which entry is quick and easy and which faces a multitude of potential entrants, each one vigilant for any opportunity to earn profits by opening up for business in the field. A number of industries clearly approximate these conditions. For example, the restaurant industry is a contestable market, even though, to set up a business, an entrant must incur substantial sunk costs. Barge lines are perhaps a better example. A firm that provides barge service on the Ohio River may easily transfer barges and tow boats to the Lower Mississippi if profits are higher there. Moreover, such transfers can, in effect, be made virtually instantaneously and at negligible cost, if barge owners enter into contracts with large shippers via email or fax.

A market with such attributes is "contestable"; in the theoretical extreme case, where entry and exit can be carried out instantaneously and at zero cost, it is "perfectly contestable." This assumption is also one of the requirements of the model of perfect competition. However, the perfect competition model entails several other assumptions that are absent in the analysis of contestable markets, a difference that makes the perfect competition model inapplicable to an economy of innovation assembly-lines but permits at least rough compatibility with the contestability model. Specifically, perfect competition assumes the absence of any economies of scale. Consistent with this, the perfectly competitive industry is assumed to be populated by myriad firms, each providing only a minuscule share of total sales in the market. Neither of these is assumed in contestable market analysis and, clearly, neither holds even approximately in the oligopolistic markets of the capitalistic growth machine. Thus, the contestable markets model is the more applicable to that world. Perhaps more important, because this model (unlike that of perfect competition) does not preordain by sheer assumption the size and number of firms in the market, contestability analysis permits investigation of the determination of these matters and the consequent determination of the form of industry organization—whether or not, for example, the industry will be driven by market forces to oligopolistic structure.

Only one feature of the growth-machine economy seems to conflict fundamentally with contestability analysis: the substantial sunk investment that is characteristic of the relevant markets of reality. But this conflict is not nearly as substantial as it appears. Contestable market analysis takes the need for substantial sunk investment as the primary form of barrier to entry—as the prototype impediment to contestability. If a new firm must risk huge outlays before it can open for business, that clearly can be a substantial disincentive to entry. But innovation, as has been noted earlier in this book, often does not require large *initial* sunk investments. Rather, the requirement is for *repeated* sinking of funds—substantial outlays year after year—if the firm, once established, is to retain its place in the continuing innovation arms race. This is not something that prevents entry. Rather, its primary effect is on the firm's continued operation once its entry has been carried out successfully. And it is crucial to recognize that these sunk outlays are not barriers to entry in Stigler's pertinent sense, because they continue to be equal burdens for the entrants and the incumbents. That is, they offer no competitive advantage and, hence, no monopoly power to an incumbent firm.

When and where such entry is possible, a number of consequences for the behavior of incumbent firms follow immediately:

- They cannot adopt prices that yield supercompetitive profits overall, because that would automatically invite entrants to come in with lower prices. That threat will be particularly effective where business is conducted by contract, because contract facilitates rapid entry.
- No firm can charge a price for any of its products so high that entry by a specialized supplier of that product becomes profitable at prices that undercut the incumbent's. That is (in the economist's jargon), the price of a product cannot exceed the stand-alone cost of that product.
- No firm will be able to operate inefficiently. In particular, its scale of operation cannot fall short of or exceed the cost-minimizing level, be-

cause that, too, would make it vulnerable to takeover of its customers by entrants.

- With each firm forced to produce something close to its cost-minimizing volume of output, the number of firms in the market will be the number required to meet demand at minimum cost.
- In such an effectively competitive market, customer demands will be fully met; otherwise prices would rise and attract the entrants who are prepared to satisfy whatever demands have not initially been satisfied.
- Often (but not always) such markets will be characterized by many cases of entry. However, that will often be followed by many cases of failure and withdrawal, because entry is always a very risky undertaking.

The bottom line here is that markets into which entry is so quick and easy are patently highly competitive. The perpetual threat of entry forces competitive behavior upon incumbent firms whether they like it or not: they cannot expect to earn profits above the competitive level; they cannot adopt prices that offer monopoly profits; they cannot operate wastefully or inefficiently; they must be prepared to meet all consumer demands; they cannot prevent the establishment of the number of firms that can serve consumer demands at lowest costs. In such a market it is at least arguable that there is no monopoly power.

I will use elementary analysis to shed more light on the behavior to be expected of the innovative firm, and I begin with the pricing practices of innovative firms in the sale of the final products that make use of the inventions.

RECOUPING SUNK INNOVATION COSTS WITH COMPETITIVE PRICES THAT EXCEED MARGINAL COSTS

I have already emphasized that one of the prime attributes of operation in a competitive and innovative industry is the need to sink outlays repeatedly into research and development (R&D) and other innovative activities. These outlays are substantial, amounting to more than 10 percent of total annual revenue in industries such as communications and pharmaceuticals (Lichtenberg, 1998). In the computer software industry they may well be higher—Microsoft is reported to have spent some 17 percent of its sales in 1997 on research and development (National Science Board, 2000, pp. 2–26). These outlays must somehow be recouped if the firm is to have the incentive to continue its activities.

As we know from standard microeconomic theory, under perfect competition the price of each and every product will in the long run be driven to the level of the product's marginal cost. This must be true because, if price is above marginal cost, the production of an additional unit will bring in more money than it adds to cost, so firms will be induced to expand their production until price is driven down to the level where further expansion is unprofitable. By definition of marginal cost, that will occur only when price is reduced to where it is no longer any higher than that cost.

But it is equally well known that, where the firm's production is characterized by scale economies, prices equal to marginal cost cannot bring the firm sufficient revenue to cover its total cost. That is true, in particular, if fixed and sunk costs are the source of the scale economies. Since marginal cost by definition is the added (variable) cost incurred by the supply of one additional unit of output, by that same definition the marginal cost includes no iota of either fixed or sunk costs, because neither of these is varied in total when output increases. Hence, a price equal to marginal cost at most covers only variable costs and makes absolutely no contribution to the recovery of either fixed or sunk costs. Such a price, clearly, is a recipe for insolvency.

This is strikingly clear in the case of computer software, for example. Once a new computer program has been created, its marginal cost, that is, the cost of providing the program to an additional user, is the cost of producing and distributing a disk that contains the program. That cost is virtually zero. But a product price close to zero can hardly provide income large enough for recovery of the large outlays that are typically required to construct a complex computer program, debug it, ensure its user friendliness, and so on.

Even with the big firms that may be present in a contestable market, freedom of entry can provide the competitive pressures required to deprive all firms in the industry of any monopoly power—the power to set prices that yield monopoly profits to the firms. In an industry into which entry is quick and easy and in which a multitude of potential entrants are vigilant for any opportunity to earn profits by opening up for business in the field, the firms cannot get away for very long with prices that yield supercompetitive profits overall, because that will automatically invite entrants to come in, offering lower but still profitable prices.

Despite the absence of the power to earn monopoly profits, the threat of entry will not prevent the innovating firms in the field from recovering their sunk costs. That is because no firm will enter if no feasible prices will enable that entrant to cover its fixed or sunk common costs. Entry will occur and drive down prices *only* if those prices are above the levels needed to cover these costs. Thus, entry will drive prices to the levels that just permit competitive returns overall, but it will not depress them down to marginal costs. And, although such prices exceed marginal costs, they are patently not evidence of the absence of effective competition.

RECOUPMENT OF INNOVATION COSTS AND THE PRESSURES FOR DISCRIMINATORY PRICES

Competitive pressures often constrain the final-product prices of the oligopolistic routine innovators in another significant way. I will show that price discrimination—the sale of products at prices that vary from one customer to another, relative to the applicable costs—can be expected to occur (and to occur frequently) in the pricing of the products of innovation, not *despite* relative ease of entry (or other competitive forces) but *because* of it. This discussion, then, offers a drastically revised view of competition, one that may be particularly pertinent to the economy's most innovative industries, though hardly to them alone. It provides an explanation of the pervasive prevalence of price discrimination; I will undertake to reconcile this with the evidence that, in many of the industries in which price discrimination occurs, earnings do not yield more than normal profits; and I will argue that, in a wide range of cases, firms that employ discriminatory prices are, nevertheless, powerless price takers, forced by the market to adopt, at least approximately, every one of the high discriminatory prices and each of the low discriminatory prices that management appears to select by design.

Once again, it is the need to recover continuing and repeated sunk costs that accounts for the prevalence of discriminatory pricing in the innovative industries. There is nothing new in this observation. Much of the literature on price discrimination (see, e.g., Varian, 2000) cites fixed and sunk costs as a prime reason forcing firms to eschew uniform pricing.[2] But what is new here is my argument that, in the pertinent markets, firms can often be expected to earn no more than competitive profits from their discriminatory prices, that such pricing can be expected to occur even when firms have no monopoly power, and that firms may even prove to be price takers, adopting just those discriminatory prices that market conditions assign to them.

2. Of course, the primary reason firms adopt discriminatory prices is that they generally increase profits (or reduce losses). But the need to incur sunk and fixed outlays can supplement this influence powerfully if such prices are indispensable for survival.

Such discriminatory pricing takes a variety of forms in innovative industries. Educational discounts are only the most obvious. Large customer firms may be offered products at special discounted prices that bear little relation to what the supplier saves on these larger-volume sales. Special tie-in prices are also offered to customers that simultaneously purchase a number of products from the same supplier. And products are sold in foreign markets at prices very different from those that prevail domestically.

I will demonstrate a proposition about price discrimination that is significant both for the theory of competition and for associated policy, and that differs markedly from standard views. This proposition asserts that, if price discrimination is feasible for a firm with substantial fixed costs or a continuing need to sink substantial investment, free and unimpeded entry—substantial contestability of the market—can be expected virtually always to force the firm to adopt such prices. As just noted, it has long been recognized that a firm will sometimes be unable to recoup its sunk costs and its fixed costs if it employs only uniform pricing (depending on the size of those costs and the happenstance of demand and competitive conditions). But I will show that this is neither a pathological case nor a fortuitous matter, but a normal result. Free entry can be expected to force *all* affected firms that are in a position to do so to adopt discriminatory prices. Moreover, each firm in a market with no impediments to entry and exit will be forced not only to adopt discriminatory prices but to select the set of such prices that maximizes the company's profits and, at least in this hypothetical scenario (which arguably is often approximated in reality),[3] those maximal economic profits must nevertheless always be zero.

3. The prevalence of price discrimination is most obvious in passenger transportation where, according to Ordover (2000), "literally hundreds of thousands (!) of [airline] price changes . . . are filed *each day.*" But even more common throughout the economy are discounts for students, for senior citizens, for isolated users of telecommunications (in "universal-service" rates), for bulk users of products, for large corporate purchasers of services and inputs, etc. Indeed, virtually all products whose prices are negotiated between sellers and buyers are sure to entail discriminatory prices. For example, chemical products sold to large firms for further processing are widely negotiated customer by customer. The list of markets with discriminatory prices is easily expanded.

Perhaps more surprising is the fact that many of the enterprises that use discriminatory prices do not earn profits that exceed competitive levels, despite the monopoly power that is often said to be necessary for the imposition of such prices. This is well known to be true of commercial theaters, with their student discounts and a variety of other special deals. The evidence also shows that the major airlines have earned, over any substantial period of time, less than the bulk of industries in the U.S. economy. Certainly, their investments earn a lower return than an investment in a comprehensive stock index, such as the S&P 500 (Kalt, 2000). Even the computer industry (encompassing both hardware and software), with its widely offered educational discounts and the like, has been estimated, as a whole, to have provided no economic profits overall since its inception, as

The argument is summarized in the following central result:

PROPOSITION 10.1. Entry enforces discrimination. In a perfectly contestable market in which a seller can separate customers into distinct groups with different demand elasticities, and can prevent its product from being transferred from one customer to another, the firm's equilibrium economic profits will be zero. But, aside from very exceptional cases, avoidance of losses will require discriminatory prices.

Proof of the proposition follows directly from three elementary observations.[4] I refer to them as "observations" rather than assumptions because they themselves follow from basic economic analysis:

1. Where discriminatory pricing is possible, and the demand curves of different customer groups have different price elasticities, there will always be a set of discriminatory prices for a given product that yields higher profits than any uniform price for that product.[5]
2. Zero entry barriers will preclude positive economic profits, but they will not prevent incumbent firms from covering all of their costs, including common costs, fixed costs, and continuing sunk costs. For, even if entry is completely unimpeded, no firm will be willing to open for business in the market if it does not offer returns sufficient to enable it to recoup its investment. Hence, only returns higher than this will be precluded by the threat of entry.
3. The zero profits that the firm can earn in equilibrium can be obtained only from a profit-maximizing price vector, which is normally discriminatory.[6] For, if there were prices that yielded maximal profits greater than

---

we saw in chapter 3 (footnote 6). It does, of course, have its spectacular success stories, but these are apparently fully balanced by the profusion of failures.

4. The proposition is foreshadowed by the Baumol, Panzar, and Willig (1988, chapter 8) weak invisible hand theorem, which asserts that in a monopoly market that is perfectly contestable the discriminatory Ramsey prices are sustainable against entry.

5. To summarize the elementary argument, assume for simplicity that the marginal cost (MC) of serving any customer is the same, and that the products at issue are neither complements nor substitutes. Then profit maximization requires for any two customers, j, k, $MR_j = MC = MR_k$, where MR represents marginal revenue. But we also know that $MR_x = p_x(1 - 1/E_x)$, so that $p_x = MC/(1 - 1/E_x)$, $x = j, k$, where p_x and E_x are, respectively, the price and elasticity of demand for product x. So, maximum profits will entail uniform prices $p_j = p_k$ if and only if $E_j = E_k$. That is, uniform pricing will maximize profits only in a set of measure zero. The proposition seems to be due to Joan Robinson (1960, pp. 181 and 187, fn 2). She apparently was the first to work out the formal diagrammatics of Pigou's price discrimination analysis.

6. In a perfectly contestable market, the concept of an equilibrium that entails price discrimination would appear to conflict with the theorem that in such a market, if it con-

zero, firms would adopt those prices and entry would then be attracted into the field until all such opportunities were eliminated.

It should be clear, intuitively, that these three observations yield Proposition 10.1. If market conditions require the firm to charge its profit-maximizing prices in order to break even, and those prices permit it to do so, then those are the prices it will select in equilibrium. But if there exist discriminatory prices that yield profits higher than those that are possible under uniform pricing, it then follows that the equilibrium profit-maximizing prices must be discriminatory. Moreover, if the profit-maximizing set of prices is unique, those are the prices that the firm will be forced to charge in order to survive.

This is not mere theory and it applies not only to innovative industries. In practice, we see marginally surviving firms scrambling for every perceived source of potential revenue, and adopting for every such source the price it believes necessary to capture that revenue. Neither the impecunious theater nor the marginal airline can tolerate empty seats. Each seeks desperately to fill them with whoever can help its finances—students, leisure travelers, and others who are unwilling to pay high prices but who will pay a price that contributes something in addition to marginal cost. Similarly, that airline cannot forgo the higher price it can impose on business travelers who book at the last minute, because without their contribution to total cost recovery the firm's financial problems would be exacerbated.

To the best of their ability, these firms will select the prices that promise to maximize profits, that is, to minimize losses. Experience may well enable them to come close to selecting the most lucrative prices and, if they do not succeed in this, they will be replaced by others who can do so more effectively. Thus, market forces impose selection of approximations to the profit-maximizing discriminatory prices. The computer firm that charges a lower price to educational institutions or to foreign buyers does this not out of charity, but because market conditions force it to do so. Of course, one cannot doubt that firms would want to adopt higher discriminatory prices if entry were difficult and those prices could bring in substantial economic profits. Even if that were not so, entry would still force them to adopt differential prices, whose magnitude is dictated by the rule that maximum profits are zero

---

tains two or more firms, the only prices sustainable against entry must be equal to the corresponding marginal costs. However, this result will presently be used to show that the discriminatory price equilibrium will not normally be stationary, because it will constantly be vulnerable to entry. Such "churning equilibria" seem close to what we see in reality, with frequent entry and frequent failures.

(economic) profits. That is not a sign of a breakdown of contestability but rather a manifestation of its normal functioning. And only the firm that is more efficient in finding and carrying out better pricing strategies will survive against less creative firms.

The firm that charges discriminatory prices in such an environment is, in effect, a price taker not a price maker, because there is no substantial range of prices from which management can select.[7] Rather, it is the need to survive that makes those selections, selections that may well be unique. Where entry is sufficiently easy, it can deprive the firm of choice in the setting of even discriminatory prices. To see this, we need only consider the likelihood that, in practice, the profit-maximizing price vector for the firm will be unique. If that is so, where that price vector and no other yields zero profits, the firm will have no choice. Any enduring deviation from that vector must be suicidal. The firm will, in effect, be a price taker, though not one that follows a posted price that emerges publicly on a market such as that for, say, pork bellies.[8]

---

7. Two things need to be said here to adapt this conclusion to reality. First, as has already been noted, in markets of the sort in question it is not unusual for prices to change frequently, indeed, sometimes with astonishing frequency. The fact that the airlines adopt hundreds of thousands of price changes every day may well elicit skepticism about the assertion that the firms have little choice about the prices they adopt. Yet it should be noted that in the most competitive of markets—the commodity and securities exchanges—price change is virtually continuous, varying from moment to moment; yet no one is led by this to suspect that a relatively small wheat farmer is really a price maker. Indeed, it is mostly in industries where there is reason to suspect that the firms possess market power that prices tend to persist unchanged, often for many months. Sticky prices are not a hallmark of industries in which pricing is controlled by the market.

Here, however, I must not exaggerate. Unlike a farmer or a purchaser of stocks, the executives in charge of pricing in an airline cannot communicate with any organized market electronically to determine what fares current circumstances impose. These people must constantly do their best to determine the current profit-maximizing prices for their firm, but at best they do so very imperfectly. They do not have access to current demand functions for their products or even a set of accurate demand functions for some time in the past. Neither they, nor anyone else, know their marginal costs or even their average costs, as is confirmed dramatically by examination of the records of any substantial antitrust trial in which predatory pricing is an issue. In these trials, in the absence of the pertinent cost data in the records of the firms, specialists on both sides are commonly employed at great expense to determine their own greatly differing and admittedly imperfectly accurate cost estimates. Given the unavailability of the requisite information and the speed with which the firm finds it necessary to respond to changing market conditions, the prices selected will at best be rather imperfect approximations to the profit-maximizing prices toward which they are driven by market pressures. But that is still very different from the leisurely and considered pricing choices available to the firm that is really a price maker, protected by lack of competition from having to obey the dictates that emanate from a powerful market.

8. Because, so far, only the price-taker side of the firm's activities has been discussed, there is little room for insights from game theory. However, we will see presently that there is more to the story because the market's equilibria are vulnerable to constant disturbance.

CHAPTER 10

FREQUENCY OF ENTRY IN INDUSTRIES WITH SMALL BUT RECURRING SUNK COSTS

Many of the industries under discussion are characterized by dramatically frequent entry in reality. This is clearly true of restaurants and theaters. Still more striking is the frequency with which start-up software enterprises are born (and, of course, many of them, like restaurants and theaters, die while still very young). In airlines, the frequency of entry (and exit) is substantial. For example, a witness for the U.S. Department of Justice in an antitrust case reported that "the top 500 U.S. domestic airline routes experienced 543 entry episodes, over a 6 year period" (Berry, 2000, p. 3). Perhaps the clearest and most pertinent examples of profuse entry and exit are the "dot-com" enterprises, those associated with computer software, the Internet, and other activities of the "new economy." Their rapid entry surely helped to engender the rapid rise in stock market prices in the 1990s, and their rapid exit has been associated with the subsequent stock decline.

If something close to zero economic profit is really the expected ceiling for these firms, the frequency with which they find themselves forced to exit should not really be surprising. Such a ceiling does not leave much margin for error. A little inefficiency—that is, efficiency or product quality just a bit lower than that of what we may refer to as "best-practice firms"—can then easily be fatal. This is certainly the plausible story for the dot-com firms, the airlines, and restaurants, and there is little reason to doubt that it is far more extensively applicable.

THE CHURNING EQUILIBRIA

If the scenario that has been described here represents a state of equilibrium, one may well ask why, as described earlier, the real markets to which the description is claimed to apply experience so much entry. After all, even a market into which entry is easy and costless will be shunned by potential entrants if the competitive behavior of the incumbents drives profits to zero and so offers no incentive for the creation of new enterprises. I will argue next that these equilibria have a peculiar attribute: their very structure makes them constantly vulnerable to entry, with firms frequently being born and both incumbents and entrants dying off with about equal frequency. These equilibria are not stationary and subject to change only in response to exogenous shocks. On the contrary, they are inherently in a continuous state of churn, with change encompassing not only entry and exit, but also the hundreds of thousands of daily price moves that have already been mentioned.

The most obvious inducement for such entry is the fact that an industry whose overall profits are zero still characteristically contains winners and losers. Entrants can be attracted by excessive optimism or by some special advantage, such as particularly able personnel or a promising new product that leads the entrepreneurs to expect that their profits will be well above the industry norm. Such entrants are often inexperienced, poorly informed, and inadequately financed, and frequently do not survive very long.

Second, discriminatory pricing itself always seems to attract niche entrants who skimp on the sunk costs that would enable them to compete with full effectiveness in the longer run. They hope that they can find a segment of the business in which they can undercut the incumbent and earn a profit by operating there alone, while the incumbent with its larger recoupment requirement cannot, because the entrants employ much less costly plant and equipment. Their goal is to survive and accumulate enough to expand their investment, ultimately growing into fully effective rivals. For a variety of reasons, many relating to their own limitations, they often do not succeed.

In addition, at least theoretically, there is a feature of the equilibrium prices themselves that generally makes profitable entry possible. Normally, at least some of an incumbent firm's prices must exceed marginal costs in order to permit sunk, fixed, and common costs to be covered. But, in theory, any market prices that exceed marginal costs, and that enable the incumbent firms to earn competitive profits, always permit profitable entry whenever there are two or more incumbents offering the same product (among other products) to one particular subgroup of their consumers at the same price, p, that exceeds marginal cost. For, then, an efficient entrant whose costs are no higher than those of the incumbents can earn profits higher than those of one of the incumbents (call it firm S) by adopting prices slightly different from those of firm S.[9] The entrant need merely shave the above-marginal cost prices by a minuscule amount, leaving the essentially unchanged prices still above marginal cost, and to sell more than the quantity, y_s, that firm S sold at price p before entry took place. The entrant can sell this amount, $y_s + k$,

9. It is the fact that, in a perfectly contestable oligopoly market, a price above marginal cost is not sustainable against entry, which leads to the theorem that any stationary equilibrium in such a market must entail marginal cost pricing (see Baumol, Panzar, and Willig, 1988, chapter 11; and ten Raa, 1984). But it is this unsustainability of prices above marginal costs that helps to produce the churning equilibria under discussion.

without materially depressing the market price, by taking part of its newly acquired business from firm S and part from another incumbent firm, thereby not increasing the total amount sold to the set of customers in question. The entrant must earn more, because sale of the additional quantity k will bring in more revenue than it adds to costs, thereby increasing the entrant's profits above the nonnegative profit that firm S was earning before entry.

Specifically, we have

PROPOSITION 10.2. Prices that exceed marginal cost invite entry. If two or more incumbents with nonnegative initial profits offer the same product to a given set of customers at a price that exceeds marginal cost, then, if these incumbents do not reduce this price in response to entry, it will be possible for a new firm to enter profitably.[10]

Proof:[11] Let

j, k, indicate different products or a given product sold at different prices to different consumer groups;

y_{js} = the quantity of product j sold by firm S;

p_j = the initial price of j;

$\mathbf{p}$ = the vector of initial prices;

$\mathbf{y}_s$ = the vector of initial output quantities of firm S;

$Q_j(p)$ = the quantity of j demanded; and

$C_s(y_s)$ = the cost function of firm S, with C_{js} the marginal cost of j to S.

Then let $y_{js} < \Sigma_x y_{jx} = Q_j(\mathbf{p})$ and $p_j > C_{js}(y_s)$ and define

$$F(k) = \mathbf{p}(y_s + k) - C_s(\mathbf{y}_s + k),$$

where $\mathbf{y}_s + k$ is the original output vector of firm S but with the amount of product j increased by quantity k. $F(k)$ is clearly the profit earned by an entry plan in which the entrant replicates all the outputs of firm S except for a k-unit increase in the output of good j. Evaluated at $k = 0$, $F(0) \geq 0$ is the nonnegative profit earned by firm S before entry. Direct differentiation gives us

$$F'(k) = p_j - C_{js}(\mathbf{y}_s) \text{ at } k = 0,$$

10. This proposition as it stands has limited applicability to practice because the opportunity for profitable entry it describes requires the entrant to replicate the incumbent's product line almost completely. That is why the threat of entry can reduce profits to zero without precluding discriminatory pricing.

11. The following proof is taken from Baumol, Panzar, and Willig (1988, p. 317n).

which is positive by hypothesis.

Thus, the entrant's prospective profit increases with k starting at firm S's initial output. Hence, there exists some $K > 0$ for which $F(k) > 0$ for all $0 < k < K$. The entry plan is feasible for $0 < k < Q_j(\mathbf{p}) - y_{js}$, so that the entrant's output of good j is no greater than the amount demanded by its customers at price vector $\mathbf{p}$. Q.E.D.

This proposition clearly exaggerates the ease of entry that one finds in reality, where risk and uncertainty, the likelihood of price responses by incumbents, and other impediments can be expected to require more than a small difference between price and marginal cost before entry actually becomes attractive. On the other hand, excessive optimism and entrepreneurial propensity to seek out risky ventures can easily work the other way.

The conclusion, then, is that the structure of the equilibria described here invite entry, despite the zero expected profits for any pertinent industry as a whole. But those zero profits mean that the market has no room for both incumbents and entrants, so that, after entry, the demise of some of the firms can confidently be expected. Consequently, a constant strategic battle for survival must be the order of the day, with the time trajectory characterized by an unending inflow of entrants, followed by a stream of exiting enterprises composed in part of entrants, in part of former incumbents.

CONCENTRATION OF MARKETS AND INNOVATION: TECHNOLOGICAL IMPERATIVES

Market concentration—roughly, smallness of the number of firms that account for the bulk of the sales in a market—is widely used in antitrust proceedings as an indicator of market power. If entry into innovative activity is indeed relatively easy, then firm size will be heavily influenced, if not altogether dictated, by technology and cost. As already noted, the crucial role of technology stems from the efficiency property of contestable markets, where long-run equilibrium requires that the industry's set of outputs be produced at minimum cost. The reason is simple. If output is produced by a firm at a cost significantly above the attainable minimum, then that constitutes an invitation for current competitors or entrants to take the business away from the inefficiently operating incumbents.

The consequence of this for the number of firms in the market is that, given the set of industry output quantities selected by the market, determination of the sizes of the outputs and the input quantities of the individual firms becomes, in principle, a straightforward and mechanical minimization computation. And the number of firms in the market then is equal to total industry output divided by average output per firm. Moreover, in markets without too much difficulty of entry, an increase in concentration in the longer run may not be ascribable to attempts by firms to achieve monopoly power but, rather, to innovation and the resulting technological changes that make it efficient for output to be provided by firms that are larger than previously was the case.

All this is shown quite clearly, if somewhat misleadingly, by the most elementary model of the output of the firm. This model assumes that the industry produces a single homogeneous product, that the firms have average and marginal cost curves that are well defined and U-shaped, and that rent payments to more efficient inputs make the average costs (inclusive of rents) identical for all of the firms. It will also be assumed that there is a well-defined demand curve of normal shape for the industry.

Let y_m represent the cost-minimizing output of the firm—an output level that is identical for all of the industry's firms, given the assumption that they all have identical cost curves. At the equilibrium price p, let the quantity of output demanded from the industry be $Y(p)$. First, we have the following, fairly obvious, result:

> **PROPOSITION 10.3.** If $Y(p)/y_m = n$ is an integer, then the efficiency property of long-run equilibrium requires the industry's output to be produced by n firms, each producing average cost(AC)-minimizing output y_m. If there is a shift in the industry demand curve, say one that moves the demand curve to the right, but the increased n remains an integer, then the number of firms, n, producing the industry output will increase, but the size of each firm will remain absolutely unchanged. Proof of this result is trivial, and need not be recapitulated here.

Where $Y(p)/y_m = n$ (the ratio of industry quantity demanded at price p to the AC-minimizing output) is not an integer, then only a minor modification of our previous result is required. We have

> **PROPOSITION 10.4.** Where n is not an integer, the industry output in an efficient equilibrium will be produced by a number of firms no less than $n - 1$ and no greater than $n + 1$.

The proof by contradiction is straightforward, and it will be only sketched. Let us focus on the upper bound upon the number of firms. There is obviously an integer n^*, with $n < n^* < n + 1$. Consider a possible equilibrium with industry output Y, in which the number of firms is $n^{**} > n + 1$. Then the average output of the firm at price p will by $Y/n^{**} < Y/n^* < Y/n$. Since the average cost curves are assumed to be U-shaped, we must have $AC(Y/n^{**}) > AC(Y/n^*) > AC(Y/n) = AC_{\min}$. Thus, the number of firms n^{**} cannot be compatible with cost minimization.

The implication of Proposition 10.4 is that the *average* output of the firms will be close to y_m. Moreover, we see next that competitive market forces will push the outputs of all of the firms to close proximity to the output that minimizes average cost. Indeed, we have

PROPOSITION 10.5. If the marginal cost curves of all the firms are (also) identical and U-shaped (i.e., the second derivative of total cost is positive everywhere in the relevant range), then, where industry output is not an integer multiple of y_m, efficiency requires the output of every firm to deviate equally from its AC-minimizing level.

Proof: Let industry output be $(n + v)y_m$ with n an integer and $0 < v < 1$. By Proposition 10.4, the number of firms must be either n or $n + 1$. If there are n firms in the industry, and each firm produces $y_m + (v/n)y_m$, this will clearly yield the industry output. But suppose firm j produces more than this amount. Then, given industry output, there must be another firm, i, that produces less than this quantity. In that case, rising marginal cost means that the marginal cost of j must be greater than that of i and this clearly is incompatible with cost minimization. A similar argument applies in the case where the number of firms is $n + 1$.

COROLLARY. Efficiency requires the deviation of the output of the firm from the AC-minimizing output to be a decreasing function of the number of firms in the industry.

Proof: The preceding discussion indicates that the deviation is $(v/n)y_m$ (or it is equal in absolute value to $y_m(1 - v)/(n + 1)$). Either of these is a decreasing function of n.

Propositions 10.3 through 10.5 indicate for this simple model how little effect demand *may* have upon the size of firm dictated by the efficiency requirement of competition, and the corollary places an explicit bound on this influence. Shifts in demand largely affect the number of firms in the single-product industry with U-shaped average cost curves, but demand does not affect their size, except to the extent that shifts lead to an industry output that deviates from an integer multiple of y_m. Competition forces firms to remain near their cost-minimizing output level. In particular, where the number of firms in the industry is large, the effect of demand on firm size must be negligible—at most, it must yield a deviation close to $(1/n)y_m$ in the case where v in the proof of the corollary approaches its maximum value, unity.

We will see presently that only in the simple model with which we have dealt so far is demand assigned such a negligible role in the determination of firm size. Nevertheless, considerable validity remains for the conclusion most directly pertinent to our analysis: in competitive industries, if one observes any substantial and enduring changes in the size of the outputs of firms, or in the magnitude of their labor forces, one should expect changes in technology to play a critical role in the change. A clear example is the decrease in the average size of firm in freight transportation, which is surely a reflection of the partial replacement of railroads by trucks, rather than a consequence of any decline in demand for transport services.

EFFICIENCY AND HETEROGENEITY IN FIRM SIZES

Propositions 10.3 to 10.5 are patently not quite realistic as they stand. They imply that efficiency requires all firms in an industry to be approximately equal in size. But casual observation confirms that in reality firm sizes within an industry do vary, sometimes considerably. The explanation is that the equal-size feature of my results is simply a consequence of the simplifying assumptions adopted so far. The argument has used three premises: (a) all firms in the industry have identical average cost curves; (b) these curves are U-shaped; (c) the firms in question supply only a single product. Abandonment of any one of these assumptions permits considerable heterogeneity in firm size without undermining my main conclusion about the primacy of technology in the determination of firm size under competitive conditions. Let us consider these premises in turn.

Inter-Firm Differences in Cost Curves

The premise that all the firms in an industry have identical average cost curves was justified by the argument that differences in (non-rent) costs from one firm to another are ascribable to differences in the quality and performance of their inputs. However, according to the standard argument, under competition the gains from superior efficiencies of this sort will be captured in the prices of the responsible inputs, in the form of efficiency rents. So far as the firm is concerned, such a rent payment is no different from any other cost, and so, once rent is included, the inter-firm cost differences will be eliminated.

But this argument is not quite right. Even if all efficiency rents go to the inputs responsible for a firm's superior performance, this means that all firms in an industry will have the same minimum average cost. But the minimum for one firm, *v*, can easily occur at an output different from that for another firm, *w*, that supplies the same product. For example, firm *v* may have a labor force particularly skilled in dealing with a small number of units of product, whereas in firm *w* the labor force may be more attuned to mass production. So, though each may have the same minimum average cost, that cost will be attained by firm *v* at a lower output than it is by firm *w*. The preceding propositions require only minor modification to take such diversity into account, and do not materially affect the technological determination of the sizes of firms in long-run equilibrium.

U-Shaped versus Flat-Bottomed Cost Curves

Much of the preclusion of differences in firm size can also be attributed to the assumption that the average cost curves are perfectly U-shaped. Business experience, however, seems to indicate that, in reality, flat-bottomed average cost curves are reasonably common, perhaps much more so than average cost curves with unique minima.[12] A flat-bottomed AC curve is one in which, after an initial declining segment, the average costs level off and remain horizontal for a considerable range of output before beginning to go back uphill. In such a case, efficient firms can vary in size between the lowest output in the horizontal portion of the AC curve (the point of minimum efficient scale) and the largest output in this range (maximum efficient scale). This range can, of course, be substantial. And, where it is large, the size of a firm and its labor force plainly will be influenced by the demand for its product. Thus, when technological influences have a range of neutrality in terms of efficient firm size, demand becomes the determining influence.

12. See, e.g., F.M. Scherer and David Ross (1990, chapter 4, pp. 106–7). Scherer cites petroleum refining, petroleum pipelines, steel manufacturing, automobile manufacturing, beer manufacturing, and fabric manufacturing as examples of industries in which empirical studies have shown such AC curves (personal correspondence with Frederic M. Scherer, October 2001).

Multi-Product Firms

The range of firm size compatible with equilibrium grows larger still when one turns to multi-product enterprises that, over some ranges of outputs and product lines, benefit from economies of scale and scope.[13] Here, it is important to note that virtually all, if not all, firms in reality supply a number of products—at least their principal product is carried in different sizes, colors, and so on—meaning that a multi-product analysis is applicable to them. But in the multi-product case it can be shown that the sizes of the firms in an efficient industry configuration can vary very substantially.[14] It can be efficient for some firms to specialize in a small number of products, seeking to produce the amounts of these few items called for by efficient scale, while others are characterized by wide diversification, benefiting appropriately from economies of scope.

The relationships are illustrated in figure 10.1, which represents the situation in a two-product industry. The axes measure the quantities of the two products, y_1 and y_2. The point labeled $\mathbf{Y}(\mathbf{p})$ represents the industry output vector, and the output vectors of the firms in the industry can be indicated by different points in the graph (not shown), whose vector sum must be $\mathbf{Y}(\mathbf{p})$. In this model, the counterpart of a U-shaped average cost curve in the single-product case is what has been called "U-shaped ray average cost" (see Baumol and Fischer, 1978). That is, consider any ray, such as $0w$, that clearly represents all vectors of the two outputs in which the output proportion remains constant and equal to the slope of $0w$. Then, with constant output proportions, one can define an unambiguous measure of the quantity of output and, correspondingly, a measure of average cost along that ray. If, proceeding from the origin along this ray, this ray average cost first declines, then reaches a minimum, and thereafter begins to rise, we clearly have a case of U-shaped ray average cost. Suppose the point of minimum ray average cost along the ray occurs at point v, where $0w$ intersects the heavy curve, M. Repeating this process for all other rays we obtain the (possibly irregular) curve M, which is the locus of the minima of all the ray average costs. It should be clear that efficiency requires the firm to be located not too far from the M locus. But this can occur on the axes, where firms specialize in only one product, or in the

13. For a fuller discussion of some of these size variants, see Baumol, Panzar, and Willig (1988, chapter 5).

14. See Baumol, Panzar, and Willig (1988) for a discussion of this case. It should be emphasized that, for the multi-product firm, average cost cannot be defined or measured except by arbitrary apportionment of fixed and common costs or by adoption of an arbitrary index of the firm's total output.

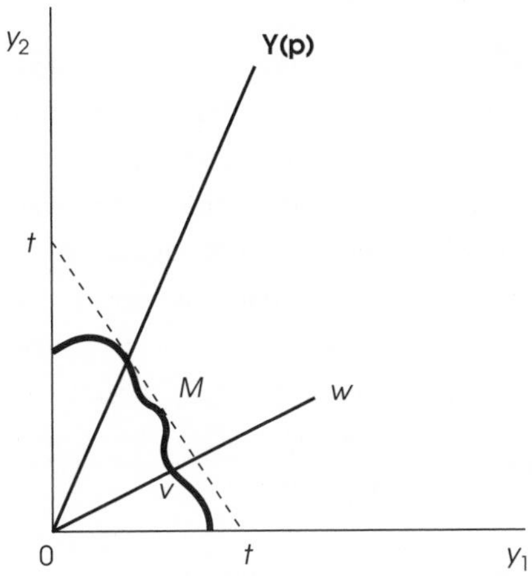

FIGURE 10.1
Determination of Firm Size in a Multiproduct Industry

center of the graph, where a firm's production is quite unspecialized. Moreover, it can be shown that efficiency is not incompatible with the location of some multi-product firms' output vectors at a considerable distance from the *M* locus. Of course, in any particular case, the set of multi-product firms that together produce the industry's output most efficiently may be uniquely determined, but such a unique solution may well entail a set of firms whose output vectors are represented by points scattered throughout the region surrounding the *M* locus that has just been described.

Thus, my analysis is compatible with the reality of the dispersion of firm sizes within industries. But, in showing this, I may seem to have proved too much. I seem to have demonstrated that there is little that is universal about the firm size results of the very simple model with which I began. I have, however, shown a great deal. Nothing said here has questioned the fundamental conclusion that, in a highly competitive market, the firm's size and its level of employment of labor must satisfy the efficiency requirement that, in long-run equilibrium, the distribution of firm sizes must be such as to produce the industry output vector at minimum cost. And there is no reason to assume that this cost-minimizing configuration of firm sizes is not unique, even though it may entail a considerable dispersion of firm sizes. Competitive forces, if sufficiently powerful, should drive the actual vector of firm sizes toward that cost-minimizing configuration.

CONCLUDING COMMENTS

In this chapter, I have sought to describe how the industrial organization of the innovation-machine economy can be expected to differ from that of the traditional textbook model. In carrying out this task, the discussion has indicated more concretely how the important role of innovative activity can be incorporated into standard microeconomic analysis. Here, I have focused on the big picture, offering what may perhaps be considered a macroeconomic description of the consequences of assembly-line innovation activity for microeconomic theory. The chapters that follow, in contrast, will deal with particular microeconomic issues, and show in greater detail how innovation can be dealt with in relation to these issues.

Implications for Antitrust and Growth Policy

Before closing the chapter, I want to point out that the models described here have substantial implications for antitrust policy and for issues related to innovation and growth. For antitrust policy, the model offers a drastically revised view of the nature of monopoly power and the kinds of evidence that can legitimately be used to support or refute an accusation that a particular firm possesses monopoly power. For issues related to innovation and growth, the model is significant because firms engaged in substantial R&D and other innovative activities are, inherently, prototypes of the enterprises on which this chapter has focused. It is easy for new enterprises to embark on innovative activities in competition with established firms. Characteristically, firms in these fields dare not fall behind in their continuing sunk expenditure on innovation. Moreover, the marginal costs of their final products are frequently very low, and prices anywhere near those costs are a recipe for financial disaster. Innovation can force concentration in a market to rise without necessarily increasing monopoly power and not as a result of attempts by firms to acquire such power through increases in their market shares. The point is that we must beware of precedents that make such firms targets for antitrust prosecution simply because their prices are discriminatory or are not close to marginal costs. Of course, individual innovative firms may or may not behave in ways that violate the antitrust laws, and they should be treated accordingly. But they should not be deemed vulnerable to prosecution simply on the claim that their pricing patterns show them to be the possessors of monopoly power. Such a course can easily constitute a major handicap to the steadily growing expenditure on innovation by private industry, which is arguably a mainstay of the U.S. economy's unprecedented growth record.

CHAPTER 11

Recouping Innovation Outlays and Pricing Its Products: Continued

technological knowledge is itself a kind of capital good. It can be used in combination with other factors of production to produce final output, it can be stored over time because it does not get completely used up whenever it is put into a production process, and it can be accumulated through R&D and other knowledge-creation activities, a process that involves the sacrifice of current resources in exchange for future benefits. In all these respects knowledge is just a kind of disembodied capital good.

—Aghion and Howitt, 1998, pp. 25–26, summarizing Frankel's analysis

This chapter continues with analysis of the financing of innovation, treating expenditure for this purpose as just another of the firm's portfolio of investments. It focuses on the intertemporal pattern of final-product prices that returns the investment in a manner compatible with economic efficiency. The analysis will illustrate once again the ways in which our theoretical work becomes easier when we recognize that decisions on routine investment in innovation are very similar to those on other types of business investment; indeed, many parts of those decisions are formally identical. In particular, this is because the grand budgeting decisions of the firm weigh the alternative investment options using similar and obvious criteria for them all: costs, probable returns, risks, and length of time before the returns can be expected. Investment in plant and equipment and investment in research facilities and activities clearly are among these competing demands for the resources of the firm. Both types of investment inherently entail "waiting," that is, the passage of time before the funds tied up begin to generate revenues. In addition, if management foresees the need to increase output in the future, it can plan to do so either by acquiring new plant and equipment or by adopting innovations that increase productivity. Consequently, at least to a degree, the two types of investment are substitute inputs for the production process.

This chapter focuses on such productivity-enhancing process innovations. It is convenient to think of an innovation of this sort as a modification of equipment design or production procedures that increases the productive capacity of a given plant and set of equipment. There are many real examples. Some of these innovations have enhanced capacity directly, for example the technical advances that have increased the amount of petroleum that can be extracted from an oil well, or those that permit the spectrum used in telecommunications to carry data as well as voice, without any crowding of the latter. However, *any* innovation that increases the productivity of capital can clearly be interpreted as I do here.

These observations suggest that one can turn to a standard model of capacity-increasing investment to analyze a number of the basic decisions of the firm on its research and development (R&D) activities. This chapter describes one such model and shows how the model can be used to calculate the optimal intertemporal trajectory of R&D investment outlays, how those outlays affect the pricing of the firm's final products, and how the investments are, optimally, amortized and depreciated. Thus, the chapter will study the fundamental financial decisions involved in that investment process. Using examples somewhat more sophisticated than that of the previous two chapters, the discussion will also show how standard analysis lends itself directly to study of the economics of routine innovation.

PRELIMINARY: PRICES, INNOVATION, AND THE INFORMATION REQUIREMENTS OF THE MARKET MECHANISM

Before turning to the central material of this chapter it is well to deal briefly with a more general issue. Earlier, I made two assertions that require some assessment, and whose role is suggested by the analysis that follows here. The first, following Schumpeter, is that, in many firms, innovation has replaced price as the primary instrument of competition. The second assertion is the claim that innovation belongs at the core of microeconomic analysis, rather than on its periphery.

But here we must face up to the critical role that price plays in standard microeconomics and general equilibrium theory. The price mechanism is surely the bloodstream that keeps the economic body in operation and guides its workings. In particular, theorists have repeatedly pointed out the extraordinary efficiency and effectiveness of price as a conveyor of the information that decision makers need in order to make rational choices. We all know the story: at its most elementary level, if, say, production of good X exceeds the amount that is demanded on the market, its price will automatically fall, demand will be stimulated, and the incentive for production will decline, moving both quantity demanded and quantity supplied toward equilibration.

Nothing to be said here is intended to replace that story, but only to supplement it. The point is that, even at this elementary level, the mechanism is not moved by price alone. Instead, the scenario really deals with the interaction between price and resource allocation. In other words, there are two starring actors here, not just one. Indeed, as the story of the previous paragraph is recounted in elementary economics textbooks, this often comes out clearly. The initial fall in prices may bring the quantity supplied and the quantity demanded closer together. But, if the supply still exceeds demand, this forces prices to fall still further, and so on, in the familiar sequence of steps toward equilibrium. What is fundamental here is not the movement of price or that of quantity, by itself. It is their interaction that constitutes the mechanism.

In a dynamic setting, the same is true of the interplay of prices and innovation investment, among other variables. It is this interaction that determines the profitability of the allocation of resources to innovation and other growth-promoting activities. In any defensible microeconomic analysis of the growth process as a general equilibrium or a general disequilibrium construct, then, innovation, but not innovation alone, must be given an explicit and prominent role. Price is not to be excluded from the story. Rather, it is the interaction of price and investment in innovation that, I maintain, is fundamental. The analysis that occupies the remainder of this chapter is meant to provide a preliminary indication of a way in which such interactions can be approached.

ASSUMPTIONS OF THE MODEL

Because of the direct substitutability between investment in (certain types of) innovation and investment in the capacity of the firm's plant and equipment, it is legitimate and convenient in the discussion of this chapter to think of R&D expenditure as just another means to increase the output capacity of the firm. Since the outcomes of even routine innovation outlays can be highly uncertain I will, without constantly noting that I am doing so, deal in expected values of the stochastic variables rather than with magnitudes known with certainty. In terms of risk and uncertainty, of course, the difference of innovation expenditure from other types of investment is a matter of degree, since the future returns to investment in plant and equipment are also far from riskless. There are, of course, well-known deficiencies in the use of expected values to deal with risk, which, it is sometimes suggested, amount to sweeping the complications of uncertainty under the rug. However, here it does not seem essential to face up to the problems explicitly.

More troublesome is the characterization of the innovation process as something that only adds to the firm's output-producing capacity. Obviously, innovation often does much more than that, most notably providing new products or valuable modifications of existing products. However, if I treat the result as an expansion in the firm's ability to produce revenues rather than as tangible physical outputs, it should be possible to apply the model to routine innovation more generally. That is, it can be applied to product innovations as well as to process innovations.

An important feature of an investment is its impermanence. It is generally durable, but it does not last forever. Plant eventually deteriorates, but so do inventions, by becoming obsolete. This erosion in the productive powers of an investment can follow many patterns. An extreme scenario is the one-horse–shay model, in which the productive power of the investment does not decline at all with the passage of time, until the date of its demise. At that point the investment suddenly becomes totally useless, in one moment being transformed from a perfectly operational item to a piece of junk. This scenario is easily dealt with in a model very similar to the one that follows.[1] However, here the discussion will focus on a more gradual intertemporal trajectory of the decline in productive powers of an innovation investment. It will be assumed that the rate of decline is constant, so that the capacity contributed by an asset falls by a fixed percentage every period (call it "a year") in the life of the asset. The parable underlying this illustrative choice of intertemporal trajectory is straightforward. We can think of an innovation that increases the productivity of capital as one that leads to modification of the design of new equipment produced at the time the innovation becomes available, and for a limited period after that. Further innovations of this sort continue to emerge from the R&D activities of private firms, and lead to gradual retirement of the equipment that used the earlier innovation. In that way the productivity contribution flow of each such innovation undergoes a gradual decline, approaching zero asymptotically.

1. Such a model is, in fact, constructed in Baumol (1971). Most of this chapter is based on that article.

The discussion will also be simplified by assuming that there are constant returns to scale in investment in R&D (though a remark will indicate how that premise can easily be eliminated). In that case the rules that the mathematics yield on the optimal timing of investment outlays, on optimal pricing, and hence on depreciation policy are easily described.

1. Investment in the innovation process should, of course, be carried to the point where the present value of its expected marginal revenue yield is equal to its marginal cost.
2. During any years in which the flow of innovation produces unused capacity, because either demand proves to be low or the capacity contributed by the R&D process is great,[2] the optimal price of the firm's final product should cover only operating costs (i.e., short-run costs). For, in such a period, long-run marginal cost is equal to short-run marginal cost. Therefore, that price includes zero contribution to depreciation and amortization.[3]
3. During the years when the asset is used to capacity, the depreciation charge should be determined by the demand function, and consumers should be charged the price that just induces them to purchase the asset's capacity output. The difference between that price and marginal operating cost constitutes the depreciation payment for the period in question.
4. This peak-period price is apparently determined by demand relationships rather than by cost (since the price is the one that *just* reduces the quantity demanded to the capacity level). Nevertheless, over the lifetime of added capacity, the sum of its depreciation contributions will just add up to the marginal R&D cost of an increase in capacity. Where there are constant returns to scale, such pricing of the products of the innovation will bring in, over the asset's lifetime, total revenues whose present value just suffices to cover the investment outlay.

The rationale for the second and third rules is straightforward. For this purpose it is useful to think of the depreciation problem as an intertemporal peak-load pricing problem. The years in which the capacity provided by investment in R&D is fully utilized are the peak periods. It follows that, dur-

2. Where there are economies of scale in R&D investment, excess capacity may also occur in some periods because it is economical to anticipate growth in demand by means of large early investment outlays. With the premise of constant returns to scale this source of excess capacity is absent.

3. This assumes that there exists no price at which demand during this period will suffice to utilize the capacity fully and still more than cover the marginal operating cost.

ing "off-peak" years, increased use of (the excess) capacity is always desirable so long as marginal operating costs are covered. That is precisely why no contribution to depreciation is included in price for such a period. However, once the quantity demanded exceeds capacity at a price that makes no contribution to recovery of investment outlays, price becomes the required rationing device. It equalizes the quantity demanded and the amount of output that the firm's physical assets and the innovations contributing to their productivity are able to produce.

The irrationality of a depreciation policy that demands the same contribution toward the cost of an asset in periods of both heavy and light usage is now easy to see. It is not too dissimilar in character from the curious commuter discounts that, in effect, make it cheapest to travel through tunnels or over bridges precisely at the times of day when they are most crowded. Both simply compound congestion and offer no incentive for increased utilization when there is unused capacity.

I shall later discuss the intuitive explanation of the fourth rule: the paradox that a set of prices apparently determined exclusively from demand information turns out, ex post, always to cover exactly the cost incurred in creating the capacity-yielding innovation.

DERIVATION OF THE RULES FROM THE BASIC MODEL

This section derives the preceding rules. The model's basic assumption is that the firm can add capacity during any period by increasing its investment in R&D. I use the following notation:

p_t = the present value of the anticipated price of output during period t;

x_t = the quantity of output during t;

y_t = the output capacity created during t;

i_t = the total remaining capacity in period t of all assets purchased before period 1;

$c(x_1, \ldots)$ = the present value of the stream of total operating costs;

$g(y_1, \ldots)$ = the present value of total R&D investment costs;

$u(x_1, \ldots)$ = an (unspecified) money measure of the total (social) utility of outputs.

I take maximization of total *net* benefit (consumers' utility minus the capital and operating costs of output) as the social welfare objective. To deal with the profit-maximizing firm we need merely reinterpret the utility function as a total revenue function. I will note later how this modifies the analysis. For now, the objective is to maximize

$$(11.1) \quad u(x_1, x_2, \ldots) - c(x_1, x_2, \ldots) - g(y_1, y_2, \ldots)$$

subject to the production capacity constraints that take into account the decrease in net productivity of past R&D investment with the passage of time as a result of obsolescence.[4] I assume that, because of retirements of assets incorporating the innovation in question, the assets whose capacity was y_1 in the initial period have only capacity $y_1(1 - k)$ in the next period and a capacity $y_2(1 - k)^2$ in the period after that, and so on. Then the constraints of our maximization problem become

$$x_1 \leq y_1 + i_1$$

$$x_2 \leq (1 - k)y_1 + y_2 + i_2$$

$$\ldots$$

$$x_t \leq (1 - k)^{t-1} y_1 - (1 - k)^{t-2} y_2 + \ldots + y_t + i_t.$$

$$\ldots$$

Observe that the set of constraints is not finite in number since, under my assumptions, the productivity of an R&D investment never erodes completely, though a horizon date can be built into the model without great difficulty. After t periods of aging, an investment's capacity contribution will be reduced from its initial value, y, to $(1 - k)^t y$, which approaches zero only asymptotically. We then have as our Lagrangian for the Kuhn–Tucker calculations

$$L = U - c - g + \Sigma_{j=1}^{s} \lambda_s [i_s + \Sigma_{j=1}^{s} (1 - k)^{s-j} y_j - x_s],$$

where s is a time period not necessarily the same as t. Assuming that some output is sold in each period (all $x_t > 0$), this yields the following first-order conditions:

$$(11.2) \quad \partial L/\partial x_t = \partial u/\partial x_t - \partial c/\partial x_t - \lambda_t = 0$$

In addition, assume that some R&D investment occurs in period t, so that $y_t > 0$. We then have

4. Much of the material that follows is, essentially, a slight modification of Littlechild's (1970) work.

(11.3) $\partial g/\partial y_t = \lambda_t + (1 - k)\lambda_{t+1} + (1 - k)^2\lambda_{t+2} + \ldots,$

or

$$\lambda_t = \partial g/\partial y_t - (1 - k)\lambda_{t+1} - (1 - k)^2\lambda_{t+2} + \ldots.$$

Last, we have the Kuhn–Tucker conditions

(11.4) $\lambda_s(\partial L/\partial \lambda_s) = \lambda_s[i_s + \Sigma_{j=1}^{s}(1 - k)^{s-j}y_j - x_s] = 0.$

Let us now eliminate the undefined utility function from our analysis by noting that, for the usual reasons,[5] $\partial u/\partial x_t = p_t$ [(relative) marginal utility equals (relative) price]. Substituting this into (11.2) we obtain

(11.5) $p_t = \partial c/\partial x_t + \lambda_t$

This states that optimal prices must include a nonnegative payment, λ_t, over and above the operating cost of the output in question. This payment will be interpreted as a depreciation charge—the contribution to recovery of investment outlays, including interest.

From (11.4) we see that in a year in which output is not up to capacity, that is, in which $x_t < i_t + \Sigma_{s \neq t} (1- k)^s y_s$, we must have $\lambda_t = 0$; in other words, in that year there will be a zero depreciation charge. This is the first of the depreciation rules of the preceding section.

Equation (11.3) now is readily interpreted as the fourth depreciation rule: the sum of the depreciation payments on the additional output made possible by a unit of investment in R&D is equal to the marginal R&D investment cost of that output. Consider an R&D investment that occurs in period t. The sum of the discounted depreciation payments on its outputs is $\lambda_t + \lambda_{t+1}(1 - k) + \lambda_{t+2}(1 - k)^2 + \ldots$. But since $y_t > 0$, we know that (11.3) must be an equation, so that these depreciation payments will then equal $\partial g/\partial y_t$, the marginal cost of y_t. This is the last part of the optimal depreciation rules of the preceding section.

All of these results are essentially affected in only one way if, instead of maximization of social welfare, we consider maximization of the profits of the firm. As already noted, in this case we need merely interpret $u(x_1, \ldots, x_n)$ to be total revenue. Then our maximand $u(x_1, \ldots, x_n) - c(x_1, \ldots, x_n) - g(y_1, \ldots, y_n)$ obviously represents the firm's total profit. This leaves unchanged

5. Strictly speaking, this implies the absence of externalities of consumption. Note that I am dealing here not with an "absolute marginal utility" but with a marginal utility measured in money terms, i.e., with the marginal rate of substitution between x and money, which is, of course, equal to p_x/p_m, where $p_m = 1$ is the "price" of money.

every one of the equations except (11.5), in which the product price, p_t, appears. For, except where price is fixed and independent of the size of output, we now have, in general, instead of $u_t = p_t$,

$$u_t = \partial u/\partial x_t \equiv MR_t,$$

where MR_t is the marginal revenue of output x in period t.

However, it is not implausible that, for a wide variety of products, elasticity of demand does not change very rapidly over time. In the possibly special case where the elasticity, E_t, is (approximately) constant over time and cross-elasticities are relatively small, then, by the standard relationship,

$$MR_t = p_t(1 - 1/E_t).$$

So prices and marginal revenues will vary proportionately from period to period. In that case, (11.5) and all subsequent relationships that contain p_t will be affected only by multiplication of p_t by a constant. In terms of relative inter-period prices, absolutely nothing will have changed. The firm will then find it most profitable to set relative prices and depreciation rates exactly as is required for maximization of social welfare.

THE EFFECTS OF INFLATION, INTEREST RATE, AND TECHNICAL CHANGE WHERE INNOVATION OCCURS IN EACH PERIOD

I will now derive some remarkably simple depreciation rules that apply in the special case where demand grows so rapidly that assets are used to capacity in the period in which they are installed, and new capacity will be needed in each succeeding period. In terms of the innovation model, this assumption means simply that R&D investment in process innovation is nonzero in every period, a premise usually satisfied in reality by high-tech firms. Since, by assumption, $y_t > 0$ in every period, (11.3) is an equation rather than an inequality. Comparing this equation (11.3) for period t with the corresponding equation for period $t + 1$, we obtain at once as an expression for the present value of the depreciation payment

$$\lambda_t = \partial g/\partial y_t - (1 - k)\,\partial g/\partial y_{t+1} \tag{11.6}$$

Equation (11.6) can be considered the fundamental relationship in the model in which the productivity contribution of an innovation declines with age at a constant rate. Its interpretation helps to explain the logic of the entire analysis. Suppose output increases by dx_1 units above current capacity. This means that capacity in period 1 will have to be increased by $dy_1 = dx_1$ units at a cost $(\partial g/\partial y_1)dy_1$. In the following period, however, $(1 - k)dy_1$ units of this new capacity will still be available. This will permit a corresponding reduction in next period's R&D expenditure, yielding a saving in that period of $(1 - k)dy_1(\partial g/\partial y_2)$.

Following Turvey (1969), in this case I define the long-run marginal investment cost of output as the R&D cost it incurs in this period minus the investment cost it is expected to save in the following period. For $dx_1 = dy_1 = 1$, this marginal cost is $\partial g/\partial y_1 - (1 - k)\partial g/\partial y_2$, and, for any period t, this marginal innovation cost is given by the right-hand side of (11.6). Thus (11.6) tells us that in the model, assuming the R&D process increases capacity in every period, the optimal depreciation charge, λ_t, is equal to the present value of the expected marginal R&D investment cost of output in period t. Similarly, we may now interpret (11.5) to state that price should equal long-run marginal cost, which is equal to the sum of marginal operating cost, $\partial c/\partial x_t$, and marginal investment cost, λ_t.[6]

So far, the analysis has all been expressed in terms of discounted present value. Since, in practice, investments and prices are all expressed in current dollars, it will be useful to translate some of the relationships into current dollars to examine explicitly how they are influenced by the discount rate and other relevant parameters. For this purpose, let r be the discount rate and let v_t be the value of $\partial g/\partial y_t$ expressed in dollars of period t so that

$$\partial g/\partial y_t = v_t/(1 + r)^{t-1}$$

and[7]

$$(11.7) \quad \lambda_t = \mu_t/(1 + r)^t,$$

where μ_t is the number of dollars of depreciation accumulated in period t. By substitution of expressions (11.7) into the depreciation equation (11.6), we obtain

$$(11.8) \quad \mu_t = (1 + r)^t \lambda_t = v_t(1 + r) - (1 - k) v_{t+1}.$$

6. It should also include marginal user cost, that is, wear and tear of capacity. However, because it adds no insights, user cost has been omitted from this chapter. It is included in the earlier article on which this discussion is based (Baumol, 1971).

7. This defines the period, so that the investment outlay, v_t, is made at its beginning while the depreciation, μ_t, is collected at the end of the period. Consequently, to obtain the corresponding present values at the initial period $t = 1$, we divide the former by $(1 + r)^{t-1}$ and the latter by $(1 + r)^t$.

By the definition of $\partial g/\partial y_t$ and (11.7), v_t is the marginal dollar cost of capacity in period t. Suppose that because of technological progress in R&D activity the real marginal cost of a unit of capacity is expected to decrease at the annual rate h, but because of price inflation this is (at least) partly offset by a rise in money cost at rate m per year. We then have

$$v_{t+1} = (1 + m - h)v_t. \tag{11.9}$$

Substitution of (11.9) into (11.8) gives

$$\mu_t = v_t(1 + r) - v_t(1 - k)(1 + m - h),$$

so that multiplying through and dropping the terms mk and $-kh$, which are presumably small,

$$\mu_t \approx v_t(\mathrm{r} - m + k + h), \tag{11.10}$$

or, if we wish to put the matter in terms of the real rate of interest $r^* = r - m$, we obtain

$$\mu_t \approx v_t(r^* + k + h). \tag{11.10$'$}$$

This rule, it must be emphasized once again, is valid only if growth is sufficiently rapid for capacity to be needed in each period so that R&D investment, $y_t > 0$ for every t.

INTERPRETATION OF THE RESULT

Equations (11.9) and (11.10′) are the basic rules determining the optimal depreciation policy if innovation occurs in every period. It may be helpful to discuss them further in more intuitive terms. Equation (11.10′), which is a little easier to interpret than (11.10), gives μ_t, the depreciation component of the period t price of the final product produced with the aid of the innovations in question. It asserts that this should be proportional to v_t, the dollar R&D cost per unit of added capacity in that period. Obviously, the ratio between the two is required by (11.10′) to vary directly with h, the annual rate of reduction in the expected R&D cost of additions to capacity, and with k, the rate of decrease in the net productivity contribution of R&D investment. It also varies directly with the real rate of interest, r^*. Finally, it varies directly with m, the annual rate of increase in the price level, since v_t is raised correspondingly above v_{t-1}.

Intuitively, the rationale of the relationships is easily described. Technological changes that reduce the costs of added capacity with the passage of time make it desirable that demands be postponed until less expensive capacity becomes available. Hence, the optimal current depreciation charge is increased by a rise in the value of *h* as a means to discourage current demand. Similarly, a high real discount rate, r^*, calls for postponement of investment since it makes a future R&D investment less expensive relative to an earlier investment, and so, like a high value of *h*, a high r^* increases optimal depreciation charges. Rapid deterioration in the productivity contribution of an innovation (a high value of *k*) and higher prices (higher *m*) simply mean that more money must be collected each year of its life to cover the cost of investment.

SOME REMARKABLE PROPERTIES OF THE SOLUTION

This solution of the depreciation problem seems reasonable enough in terms of economic principles. Perhaps the only surprising property to emerge so far is the conclusion that the depreciation payments called for by the calculation appear to add up, automatically, to the marginal cost of capacity. They do so even though that was not imposed in advance as a requirement for the solution, and even though the magnitudes of the depreciation contributions, in the peak periods in which they occur, are determined not by costs but by demands. Here, demands enter through the requirement that final-product prices be those that reduce the quantities demanded to available capacity. The reason the depreciation payments always add up to the cost of capacity is because the model is set up to determine, not only the optimal values of prices and depreciation payments, but also, for each period, the size of the optimal addition to capacity. That is, the act of magic consists of dealing not with some arbitrary level of investment, but with the amount of investment that satisfies the optimality conditions.

Here, it is helpful to think of the sum of the depreciation payments, $\Sigma(1 - k)^t\lambda_t$, as the total rental values of the investments. Obviously, if the R&D investment program is optimal, its marginal cost, $\partial g/\partial y_t$, must be equal to its total lifetime rental revenue per unit; otherwise it would pay either to increase or to decrease the quantity of investment. So it is only because investment in innovation is carried to the optimal level that the demand-determined depreciation payments per unit of capacity must always add up to innovation costs per unit.

Under my assumption that the expected magnitude of added output capacity increases linearly with R&D investment, rental prices equal to *mar-*

ginal (= average) investment cost will yield total revenues just equal to the total R&D investment outlay. However, if there are increasing or diminishing capacity returns to investment in R&D, total revenues at rental prices equal to marginal costs will obviously not equal R&D investment. In that case, second-best optimal rental prices that do cover total investment cost will of course have to be Ramsey prices.

There are (at least) three other noteworthy properties of the solution, the first two perhaps of interest primarily for pure economics. The third, rather remarkable, characteristic, which Kenneth Arrow has called "the myopic property," may also be important for application.

The first of these three properties is the conclusion that the λ_t, the depreciation payment in period t, is equal to the marginal net social yield of added capacity in period t. That is, the unit depreciation payment in any period is equal to the marginal productivity of added capital in that period. This is, of course, what neoclassical analysis should lead us to expect: optimally, an input will be paid its marginal yield, and that is how I conclude that the λ's are the rental values of the capacity in question. The proof of the property follows at once when we recognize that the λ_t, the Lagrange multipliers of the Kuhn–Tucker maximand, are necessarily the structural variables of the dual program. Since, as is well known, the dual variables are the marginal yields corresponding to the limited inputs of the primal problem, we have the first of the three results.

The second of the solution properties is equally easy to derive. It states that two apparently independent definitions of the depreciation problem are both satisfied by the solution. The economic depreciation problem can, clearly, be defined as the answer to one or the other of the following questions. First, how much has the economic value of a given (earlier) addition to capacity (derived from an R&D investment) decreased in the period in question? Second, during the period, what is the (optimal) payment to be charged to consumers toward recovery of the cost of the R&D investment, over and above its marginal operating cost? So far, the discussion has addressed itself to the second of these questions, and the solution may at first glance appear to have no necessary relevance for the first. However, once having selected a set of consumer prices that satisfies the requirements implied by the second question, it is easy to show that the first is easily answered, at least for a marginal unit of capacity, and that the answers to the two questions then coincide. For I have decided to charge during the (infinite) useful lifetime of the addition to capacity a stream of prices given, according to (11.5), by $p_t = \partial c/\partial x_t + \lambda_t$. The net gain from the marginal unit of output is then $p_t - \partial c/\partial x_t = \lambda_t$.

Hence the marginal value of a unit of capacity added in period t is (since the λ^*_t are all present values)

$$v_t = \lambda_t + (1 - k)\lambda_{t+1} + (1 - k)^2\lambda_{t+2} + \ldots .$$

By the next period, the residual value of that piece of equipment will have fallen to $(1 - k)v_{t+1} = (1 - k)\lambda_{t+1} + (1 - k)^2\lambda_{t+2} + \ldots$. Consequently, the amount by which the value of the marginal unit of equipment will have declined in period t is precisely

$$v_t - (1 - k)v_{t+1} = \lambda_t,$$

in other words, it is exactly equal to the period t depreciation payment calculated in answer to the optimal depreciation problem. Thus, so long as the revenue requirement is met by prices given by (11.10), the two interpretations of depreciation turn out to be identical. Where, in addition, a revenue requirement must be imposed on the analysis, prices will presumably be different from long-run marginal costs, and so the two answers will no longer be identical.

Finally, I turn to the so-called myopic property of the solutions. This remarkable property, which Arrow (1964) attributes to earlier writers, applies in the special case where some R&D investment occurs in each of two successive periods, i.e., when $y_t > 0$ and $y_{t+1} > 0$. In that case, it is necessary to forecast only one single period in the future in order to determine the correct magnitude of depreciation or long-run marginal cost. Moreover, in that case, the depreciation figure can be determined simply from four data: (1) the R&D cost of an added unit of capacity in the current period, v_t; (2) that of the next succeeding period, v_{t+1}; (3) the calculated rate of loss of physical productivity of the capacity, k, and (4) the discount rate, r. This follows at once from (11.6) and (11.7). From these I calculate immediately the *long-run* marginal cost figure

$$\frac{\partial c}{\partial x_t} + \lambda_t = \frac{\partial c}{\partial x_t} + \frac{\mu_t}{(1 + r)^t} = \frac{\partial c}{\partial x_t} + \frac{v_t}{(1 + r)^{t-1}} - (1 + k)\frac{v_{t+1}}{(1 + r)^t} .$$

This is the correct long-run value of marginal cost, since it includes both the marginal operating cost and the period's assigned contribution toward capacity replacement.

The rules given by (11.8), (11.10), or (11.10′) are called “myopic” because they permit depreciation of R&D investment to be calculated correctly with the aid of a forecast extending over only one period and not over the entire life of the added capacity. Moreover, they refer not to some average of one-year cost differences but to the actual difference in cost between this year and the next. For example, suppose that, because of technological progress, the costs of added capacity decline 5 percent per year on the average. However, this year happens to be particularly slow on innovation in R&D procedures, so that the expected R&D cost of added capacity is going down at a rate of only 2 percent. Then the latter is the correct figure to use in the myopic formulas for long-run marginal cost!

The reason the rules work has already implicitly been explained. If some R&D investment is going to have to take place next year in any event, the marginal cost of increased R&D today is simply the added cost of carrying it out one year earlier, all other decisions remaining unchanged. After that (say, in the third year), since the innovations provided by the R&D would have been in existence in any case, the only difference it makes if the R&D takes place today rather than next year is the one-year reduction, $(1- k)$, in its productivity. That is, in computing the marginal cost of its provision today, we perform the calculation

> [total present and future cost of carrying it out today] minus [total present and future cost of doing so next year] plus [cost of replacing the portion that decays from this year to the next].

Since any associated third-year cost is already contained in each of the three terms in brackets, it simply cancels out in subtracting. All that remains after subtraction is the cost difference over the one-year period beginning today, clearly $\partial g/\partial y_t - (1 - k)\partial g/\partial y_{t+1}$, the right-hand side of equation (11.6).

The myopic decision rules can be helpful in practice because, where they apply, they can simplify the calculation of marginal costs and depreciation charges. Unfortunately, the conditions for their applicability are somewhat more demanding than they may seem at first glance. It is not enough for a firm as a whole to invest in R&D in every period. The products of the R&D in different years must all be substitutable for one another as additions to capacity, otherwise the argument does not work.

If this condition—the investment in new substitutable innovations each period—does not hold, the myopic depreciation rules (11.10) and (11.10′) need not be valid as they stand. In that case, we may have to employ instead conditions such as (11.3) in which all relevant future periods must be considered in the depreciation calculation.

WHAT HAS THIS CHAPTER ACCOMPLISHED?

The analysis just provided has illustrated how the analysis of routine innovation activity can be carried beyond the elementary level of the previous two chapters in theoretical analysis that answers the sorts of question that conventional value theory investigates. It has done this simply by using analysis taken directly from capital theory and transferring it to R&D activity. It has shown how the optimal time path of investment in R&D can be determined, considering both the social optimum and the profit-maximizing solution for the innovating firm. It has described how the process affects the pricing of the commodities in whose production the (process) innovations in question are utilized. It has indicated how one can analyze the effects of parameters such as rate of obsolescence and discount rate on the optimal intertemporal trajectories. Finally, it has examined how pricing and recoupment of the R&D outlays are interrelated.

Still, a good deal remains to be done. Most notably, the model deals with process rather than product innovations, and any theory of routine innovation that neglects the latter obviously is seriously incomplete. Perhaps even more important, the analysis of this chapter and that in the next is fundamentally static, incorporating nothing about the active competition of business firms that forces them to keep abreast of their rivals in their innovation efforts. As a result, the discussion here has told us only a little about innovation as the engine of capitalist growth, which is presumably the prime reason for increased attention to the mechanism of capitalist innovation and enhancement of its incorporation into the central economic theory.

However, there are a number of tasks that the static theory can carry out. It can explain such things as the timing of the introduction of an innovation into the market, that is, its emergence from the R&D laboratories, or the circumstances in which firms will select cooperation with other firms rather than rivalrous activity for some or all of their innovative activity. Some of this has already been discussed. The next chapter carries on with this process, turning to the optimal timing of innovation introduction.

CHAPTER 12

Models of Optimal Timing of Innovation

Puzzle: Suppose that, because of innovations in the production process, a computer model with unchanging features has been falling in price at a rate of r *percent per year. A prospective buyer decides that* t *is the optimal purchase date, the best tradeoff between deferral of benefits and declining cost. Then, after a research breakthrough, the rate of cost decline increases to* $q > r$. *Is the new optimal purchase date,* s, *sooner or later than the old purchase date,* t, *or is* s *related to* t *in some other systematic way?*

This chapter provides another illustrative application of the standard tools of microeconomic analysis to innovation—this time to timing issues. In particular, it focuses upon the optimal length of time a product or process undergoing continued improvement via research and development (R&D) should continue to be kept in the firm's R&D facilities before it is released to the market. Unlike the previous two chapters, the issues raised here are not at the heart of mainstream microtheory. But the discussion shows that the standard microeconomic tools can offer concrete results that are far from obvious and that may have substantial applications. Thus, the main purpose of the chapter is to illustrate the capacity of the formal analysis to provide unsuspected insights, showing that some of the issues are far less straightforward than they may seem.

The spirit of the discussion is indicated by the puzzle at the head of this chapter, which also brings out the logic of much of the material that follows. This is a puzzle with which I have repeatedly challenged audiences, offering a (very modest) cash payment to anyone who arrives at the answer intuitively within the time of my lecture. So far, no one has qualified for the prize.

It is routinization of the innovation process that also permits timing decisions to be analyzed by the standard tools of optimization. Innovation entails many such timing decisions. For example, the choice between racing to be the first and playing a waiting game, which has been emphasized in recent literature, is clearly a matter of timing. But this is hardly the only way timing decisions arise.

In any major innovative step there is an obvious tradeoff between haste and deliberate delay. Early introduction of a novel product or process offers several clear benefits. It speeds the date when the stream of benefits begins. Two years of delay can mean two years of benefits forgone. In addition, speed can head off rivals who might otherwise get there first, or narrow the opportunity for others to invade the innovator's market. Third, in an industry where products change constantly, if a product is brought out in 2002 instead of delaying it to 2004, the company can be protected in 2003 from having to market a model that has almost become obsolete because of advances by competitors. But there is a tradeoff. Delay in introduction also offers significant benefits. It can permit further improvement in the design or reliability of the new item or reduction in its cost and avoidance of the high costs of a "crash" development program. Thus, some dates can be too early for maximization of profits, while other dates constitute excessive delay. As usual, this suggests that there is an optimal intermediate introduction date that yields the greatest profits to the innovator.

This chapter will provide several simple models describing the analytics of this optimization process. In addition to the formal conditions for optimality and their economic interpretation, the discussion reports some comparative-statics analysis. It shows how changes in some of the parameters, such as speeding-up of the rate of improvement of the process or product or of the rate of reduction of their costs, affect the optimal timing decision. The timing consequences of such an exogenous change will turn out to be somewhat complex, sometimes delaying the optimal introduction date, sometimes hastening it. This conclusion, however, is not as amorphous as it sounds, for it will be possible to derive a formal but easily interpretable expression that shows when and why each of the two possible outcomes results.

To help the intuition, I will discuss this issue in terms of a perfectly analogous and familiar timing decision, the one that underlies the chapter's puzzle. Any reader who has recently been in the market for a personal computer will understand the timing dilemma all too well. Too great a delay means depriving oneself of the computer's benefits for an excessive period, but too much haste risks early obsolescence. This tradeoff is, in fact, precisely analogous to the one involved in the decision about the date to take an improved product from the firm's R&D facilities into the market. To see where these countervailing influences leave the optimal timing of a computer purchase and the perfectly analogous decision about when to introduce an innovation, we need a formal model.

THE TIMING OF PURCHASE OF A PERSONAL COMPUTER

Case 1: Falling Price

The formal analysis that follows is readily interpretable in either of two ways. The first is as the choice of the optimal date, T, for the introduction of an innovation that is undergoing continuing improvement until date T. Alternatively, it can be interpreted as the determination of the optimal date, T, for the purchase of a product such as a computer that is improving steadily. The following discussion is expressed in terms of the computer purchase, leaving the translation to the optimal time of introduction of an innovation for the next section. The case that is simplest to describe, and with which I begin, is the one in which the only effect of progress is to reduce cost and, hence, purchase price. This permits direct quantification of the rate of technical progress and, therefore, simplifies the discussion.[1] Once it is bought, the computer is assumed to yield a (constant) stream of benefits (revenues) to the purchaser, with those benefits measurable in money.

I use the following notation:

R = (the money value of) the flow of benefits per unit of time, before the purchase;

S = the flow of benefits per unit of time, after the purchase date (where $S > R$);

Ce^{-wT} = the purchase price of the improved product at time T;

r = the (continuously compounded) rate of interest (discount);

w = the rate of cost reduction through technical progress, $0 < w < 1$;

T = the purchase date; and

$B(T)$ = the present value of the net benefits obtained by the purchaser, as a function of the date of purchase.

1. Nevertheless, it would be inappropriate to ignore the important case of product improvement. As Nathan Rosenberg has pointed out to me (personal communication), "when American firms are asked about their R&D expenditure plans, they classify most of it as product innovation or improvement, not process innovation." Consequently, the case of product improvement will be discussed separately.

Then, the consumer's objective is to maximize

$$(12.1)\quad B(T) = \int_{t=0}^{T} Re^{-rt}\,dt - Ce^{-(r+w)T} + \int_{t=T}^{\infty} Se^{-rt}\,dt,$$

that is (by straightforward integration), to maximize

$$(12.2)\quad B(T) = R/r + (S/r - R/r)/e^{-rT} - Ce^{-(r+w)T}.$$

Thus, the first-order condition for maximization becomes

$$(12.3)\quad B_T = (R - S)e^{-rT} + (r + w)Ce^{-(r+w)T} = 0,$$

where I write B_T for the partial derivative of B with respect to T. As is to be expected, equation (12.3) simply tells us that profit maximization requires that marginal cost equal marginal revenue. It requires the marginal opportunity cost of delay, in the form of forgone gain per unit of time, $S - R$, to equal the associated marginal cost-reduction yield achieved through continuing improvement in technology, as well as through postponement of expenditure.

There is nothing surprising here. But matters are less obvious when I turn to the comparative-statics question on which my analysis focuses: does a speeding-up of the rate of technical progress lead to a hastening or to a postponement of the optimal purchase date? We will see that

> **PROPOSITION 12.1.** An increase in the rate of technical progress, w, will generally change the optimal date for purchase of a rapidly improving product (or the optimal date for introduction of a product or a process innovation). There will be a critical date, I, such that, if the initially optimal date, T, was less than I, then $dT/dw > 0$, whereas if T was greater than I, then $dT/dw < 0$.

I will first prove this for cost-reducing process improvements, and then turn to the case of product improvement. An intuitive explanation will also be provided. To find the response of T, the optimal purchase date, to a change in w, I employ the usual procedure of comparative statics. I calculate the total differential of (12.3), obtaining from the requirement that equilibrium condition (12.3) must be satisfied both before and after the change in w,

$$dB_T = B_{TT}dT + B_{Tw}dw = 0$$

or

$$(12.4)\quad dT/dw = -B_{Tw}/B_{TT},$$

where we know $B_{TT} < 0$ by the second-order condition. Consequently, the sign of the derivative in (12.4) will be the same as the cross-partial derivative

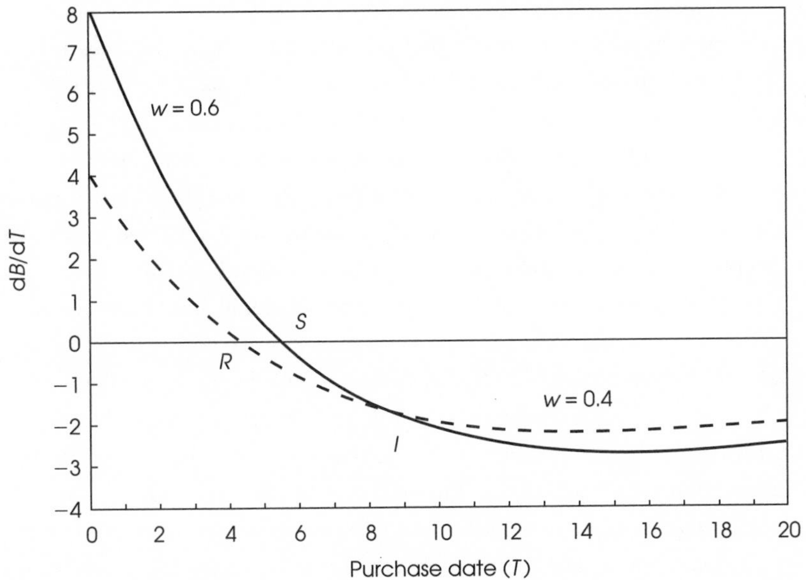

FIGURE 12.1
Derivative of Net Benefits with Respect to Purchase Price

of B with respect to T and w, that is, the numerator of (12.4). Direct differentiation of (12.3) tells us that this equals

$$B_{Tw} = Ce^{-(r+w)T}[1 - T(r + w)], \quad (12.5)$$

which will take the sign of the expression in square brackets. That is, dT/dw will be positive if T (the [initially] optimal purchase date) is sufficiently small to yield $1 - T(r + w) > 0$, or $T < 1/(r + w) \equiv I$, and it will be negative if T is sufficiently large to reverse that sign, as Proposition 12.1 asserts.

Thus, (12.5) tells us that the rise in w calls for postponement of the optimal purchase date of the product if, before the rate of technical progress increased, that date was relatively early and for a hastening of that purchase date if the date previously was relatively late. Next, I provide an intuitive explanation of this apparently curious result.

Here, a graph is helpful. Figure 12.1 plots (12.3), the curve of *marginal* benefits of waiting, taken as a function of T; that is, it shows the behavior of B_T, the partial derivative of B with respect to T. To see why this curve has a negative slope throughout, I note first that in this model when there is a marginal benefit of waiting longer before purchasing the computer (when $B_T > 0$), this results from the constant decrease in the computer's cost. However, the cost of the computer will never fall below zero, so that the *total* cost as a function of T must approach the horizontal axis asymptotically. This means that dC/dT must approach zero as T increases, so the benefits of waiting are steadily decreasing, While this is happening, the (un-declining) marginal opportunity cost of further postponement of the purchase continues to be deducted from the marginal net benefit. As a result, the marginal benefit curve in figure 12.1 must have the negative slope shown in the figure, and must ultimately cut the horizontal axis at the value of T that is optimal.

The graph also shows the effect on that marginal benefit curve of a change in the value of w. We see that a rise in w has two consequences. First, it raises the vertical intercept of the B_T curve—it adds to the initial benefits of delay. That is, the marginal benefit of a unit addition to the delay before buying is initially enhanced because the rise in w increases the cost saving the consumer obtains by waiting an additional unit of time. Second, the rise in w must ultimately reduce the height of the marginal benefits curve, B_T. It must do so because it causes the total cost of the computer to approach zero more quickly than before, so that this cost figure must begin to level off at a lower value of T than it does when the w value is smaller. This means that thereafter there remains relatively little more to be gained through further postponement of the purchase date.

The initial raising and later lowering of the B_T curve amounts to a clockwise rotation of that curve. This observation permits us to compare the new, high-w B_T curve with the previous, low-w curve. The rotation of the benefits curve when w is increased implies that the new, high-w curve must intersect the low-w marginal benefits curve at some point, I. This means that, if the optimal value of T, corresponding to the first-order requirement $B_T = 0$ (point R or S), lies to the left of I, as in figure 12.1, then the high-w curve will lie above the low-w curve at that point. In that case, the rise in w will have increased the reward of additional waiting before buying. Thus, the optimal point, corresponding to the intersection of the B_T curve with the horizontal axis, will move to the right (the move from R to S, where B_T now equals zero). However, if the optimal point had been to the right of I, then the effect of the rise in the value of w would have been the reverse. This is because, for high values of T, the marginal reward of additional waiting is thereby reduced.

Finally, I can suggest what determines whether the optimal value of T will be relatively low or relatively high. That can be studied directly from (12.3), which tells us that when this equilibrium condition is satisfied we must have

$$e^{wT} = C(r + w)/(S - R).$$

In other words, a rise in purchase cost, C, relative to the net benefits, $S - R$, of the improved (more economical) computer, or a rise in the rate of reduction, $r + w$, of the present value of that cost, must raise the optimal value of T. It has this effect because it shifts the B_T curve upward, that is, because it raises the marginal benefit of delay to some degree, for every value of T.

My graphic discussion suggests that the conclusion of Proposition 12.1 on the timing consequences of a change in the rate of technological progress does not depend on the particular functional forms selected here for illustrative purposes. Thus, the conclusions apparently have some degree of robustness. Intuitively, this must be so because a rise in the (percentage) rate of cost reduction will generally make the cost curve fall more rapidly, initially. But it will also cause that curve to level off earlier than before because our computer's production cost can never be reduced to a negative level. But it should be clear that these two qualitative effects of a change of w on the time derivative of cost—the initial rise and the later fall in the rate of decline of product cost—are all that is needed for our results.

Case 2: Product Improvement

I can easily modify the preceding model to deal with the case where delay in purchasing gives the consumer an improved computer and does not merely make it cheaper, as assumed so far. That is, the model can readily be extended to cover product innovation in addition to cost-reducing process improvement. Then, letting v be the rate of improvement per unit of time of a newly purchased computer, we need merely replace S by Se^{vT} in (12.1), so that the last term in the expression for B becomes

$$Se^{vT}\int_T^{\infty} e^{-rt}\,dt.$$

Thus (12.2) changes to

$$(12.6)\quad B(T) = R/r - (R/r)e^{-rT} - Ce^{-(r+w)T} + (S/r)e^{(v-r)T},$$

so that

$$(12.7)\quad B_T = Re^{-rT} + (r + w)Ce^{-(r+w)T} + S[(v - r)/r]\,e^{(v-r)T} = 0.$$

Consequently,

$$(12.8)\quad B_{Tv} = (S/r)e^{(v-r)T}[T(v - r) + 1].$$

It now follows immediately, analogously with (12.4), that dT/dv will have the same sign as B_{Tv}, which, in turn, will take the sign of the bracketed term in (12.8).

First, one must discard a bizarre possibility, the case in which $v - r$ is positive. Then dT/dv must always be positive, because then the rate of progress will increase the stream of revenues more rapidly than the discount rate erodes its present value. Consequently, a rise in v will then *always* make it worthwhile to wait longer before purchasing, as is easily verified from (12.7), because when $v - r > 0$ every term in the expression for B_T must be positive. This leads to the absurd conclusion that it pays the consumer to wait forever before buying a computer because the rate of product improvement interminably swamps the opportunity cost of further delay in purchasing.

Rejecting that case as unrealistic (to put it mildly), I conclude that $v - r$ must be negative. Then we immediately obtain a comparative-statics relationship identical to that in Proposition 12.1, this time for changes in the value of v instead of w. That is, we see now that, if the optimal value of T was relatively small before the rise in v, dT/dv will be positive. In that case it will pay to wait longer before making the purchase when the product improves more rapidly. In contrast, if the initially optimal value of T was sufficiently large, that derivative will be negative, and the rise in the value of v will lead to an optimal purchase date earlier than it would have been otherwise. Intuitively, the explanation is only slightly different from that of the cost reduction case considered earlier in this section, though it is now rather more convoluted.[2] This completes my discussion of the consumer's optimal timing of the purchase of a rapidly improving product, and leads us directly to my models of the timing of innovation.[3]

---

2. My objective is to show that, as the value of v rises, the curve of the marginal benefit of waiting, B_T, rises with T for small values of T but falls for large T, leading to an intersection between the low-v and high-v B_T curves, as in figure 12.1. To understand the reason, first note that, with r (the interest rate) greater than v (the rate of improvement of the product), every increase in T must lead to some erosion of the present value of the product improvement. This by itself would always lead to $T = 0$ as the optimal purchase date. However, the other influences in the remaining terms of the objective function work in the opposite direction. For example, a premature purchase is likely to give the buyer a product that is still very primitive. These influences together normally yield an optimal value of $T > 0$. However, any such positive T entails some forgone contribution to the present value of marginal benefit of waiting, as given by the negative last term in (12.7). This loss is proportionate to $(v - r)/r$, which clearly declines when the value of v rises toward that of r. But the loss also erodes with the passage of time because it is divided by $e^{(r - v)T}$. That loss-erosion rate is obviously also cut by a rise in v. Thus, an exogenous increase in the value of v will lower the deduction from the marginal benefit of waiting at the left-hand end of the curve, but it will lower the rate at which the present value of the deduction subsequently declines. Consequently, the rise in v will raise the left-hand end of the marginal benefit curve, but will lower its rightward end, just as in the case of cost-reducing process innovation illustrated in figure 12.1.

3. The result of Proposition 12.1 has other immediate applications. For example, it tells us about the optimal length of time for which a new product such as a new pharmaceuti-

MODELS ON THE OPTIMAL DATE FOR LAUNCHING AN INNOVATION

Let us turn from computer purchasing to innovation timing. First consider this decision in isolation, abstracting from the influence of competition. For that simple case, we will find that the preceding models of the timing of purchase take us most of the way, at least so far as the formal characterization of the optimal choice is concerned. I begin, then, with the case of the innovator decision process in which no rivalry is involved. Here, I will combine the cases of product innovation and cost-reducing process innovation. For our decision maker, the choice between an earlier and a later date of introduction may balance off some or all of at least five effects. If the later date is chosen it can be expected to: (a) postpone the date when increased net revenues (benefits) flowing from the innovation begin; (b) reduce the length of the period during which the enhanced revenues are earned; (c) increase the period during which outlays on innovation, such as R&D spending, continue; (d) increase the post-innovation net benefit per period because the delay permits improvement in quality or a reduction in cost of the innovative product or process; (e) reduce the present value of the costs (such as marketing costs) of introducing this item.

Obviously, not all of these consequences will always result from postponement, and other effects are conceivable. Still, this list seems fairly comprehensive, and it is easy to see that the following profit function encompasses all of the items in that list. For simplicity it will be assumed that there is a fixed terminal date, h, for the flow of enhanced net revenues generated by the innovation, say because a better product that will make the new item obsolete is scheduled to appear at date h. This artificial premise is easily modified, for example by changing that terminal date to $T + h$, where T is the date of introduction of our firm's new product. However, the fixed-horizon case is useful because it includes the possibility that delay of the innovation date could shorten the total economic lifetime of the new item.

I now use π to represent the total profit from the innovation as a function of its date of introduction. The other symbols require no explicit definition since they correspond to those in the previous model of the purchase

cal should be tested for safety before sales to the public are permitted. The mathematical argument of this section can be used to show directly that a technical improvement in the testing process will increase the optimal length of the testing period, T, if the optimal value of T had been relatively low before the technical change. But such an improvement in the testing methods will lead to a reduction in the optimal length of testing period if the initial value of T had been relatively high.

timing decision. The objective of the innovator is assumed to be maximization of

$$(12.9) \qquad \pi = R\int_{t=0}^{T} e^{-rt}\,dt - Ce^{-(r+w)T} + Se^{vT}\int_{t=T}^{h} e^{-rt}\,dt.$$

It is not difficult to show that (12.9) can include some or all of the five consequences of delay in the innovation date, T, that were just listed. Postponement obviously means that the increased post-innovation revenues, S, will be delayed by precisely the amount of time equal to the rise in T. The reduction of the length of time during which the enhanced revenues are received corresponds to the decrease in the period from T to h in the last integral in the equation. If pre-innovation revenue, R, is taken to be net of cost, including outlays on the innovation process, the lengthened period of innovation outlays is represented in the first term of (12.9). The increased post-innovation rate of net revenue flow is shown by the e^{vT} by which S is multiplied in the last term in (12.9). Finally, the cut in introduction cost, C, permitted by delay is clearly represented by the middle term in the equation. Of course, other expressions can be used to represent similar relationships, but (12.9) is at least one reasonably simple function that contains them all.

There is a clear formal similarity between this profit equation and the objective function used earlier for the benefits from the purchase of an innovative product (equation [12.1] and the maximand corresponding to [12.6]). It follows that little or nothing is added by formal manipulation of (12.9) similar to that in the discussion of the timing of the computer purchase. The results are essentially unchanged, both in formal and in intuitive terms. In particular, we see that Proposition 12.1 applies, unmodified, to the optimal date of introduction of both process and product innovations. This must be so unless the calculation yields an optimal introduction date that is finite; that is, if v, the rate of technical progress (the rate of intertemporal revenue growth resulting from the product improvement) is not larger than the interest (discount) rate, r.

TIMING COMPETITION WITHOUT INTERACTION: IS IT BETTER TO BE AN INNOVATOR OR AN IMITATOR?

I end the chapter by adding to the preceding material a primitive first step toward analysis of another of the firm's innovation timing choices—the choice between seeking to be first (innovation) or second (imitation). It should be noted first that, in reality, the distinction between the two is hardly clear-cut. Many imitations of new products or processes include modifications and improvements to make the imitator's product more attractive or to adapt the imitated product to special features of the imitator's market. Moreover, products regarded as true inventions almost always build on earlier technology. Perhaps the most striking example is James Watt's steam engine, which really was only(!) an improvement in design over steam engines that had been widely available for many decades.

This discussion represents a start toward the study of rivalry in innovation and what determines whether it will turn into a race or a waiting game. However, this book will not deal with competitors' timing interactions. To simplify the analysis, the rival's launching time will be taken as given, never moving in response to our firm's choice of the launching date of its own product. The device is clearly artificial, though perhaps not always unrealistic.

Here, then, the firm's total profit, $\pi = \pi(T, h)$, is a function of its own launching date, T, conditional upon the competitor's hypothetically fixed launching date, h. Calculation of this function yields two main results:

> **PROPOSITION 12.2.** The graph of the profit function will not generally be a single-peaked hill. Rather, it is likely to have two substantially separated peaks.

> **PROPOSITION 12.3.** In contrast to behavior in the Hotelling location model, where a second entrant gains by positioning itself as close as possible to its predecessor, the most profitable date, T, for the firm to launch an innovation can be substantially separated from the corresponding date, h, of its rival.[4]

The argument for the two propositions is based on an example using particular functional relationships with selected numerical parameter values. But

---

4. This result seems generally consistent with the record of innovation in practice. Although imitation seems often to follow innovation with considerable speed, usually a few years (perhaps on the order of one to four) do typically to separate the two. On the timing of imitation in practice, see Mansfield, Schwartz, and Wagner (1981).

There are nonetheless cases where the improved model of the imitator followed almost immediately after the initial innovation. One example is the seventeenth-century introduction by Rev. Edward Barlow of the repeater watch. This is the watch that, until about World War I, was the substitute for an illuminated dial. It struck the current hour any time the appropriate lever was depressed, and some rather expensive later versions even chimed the current time correct to the minute. The introduction of Barlow's repeater was followed almost immediately by Daniel Quare's improved model. On the other hand, the dramatic few hours that separated Alexander Graham Bell's and Elisha Gray's telephone patent applications are surely an example of an astonishingly close patent race, rather than a Hotelling sort of innovator-imitator timing equilibrium. As a matter of fact, even the Barlow–Quare affair turned into a battle—if not a race—for the patent, which the King awarded to Quare.

reasoning by example *is* legitimate here since neither proposition claims to provide a result that is universally valid. It is convenient to deal with a period of limited duration, H, and to assume that the rival has selected a launch date $h < H$, which is known to our firm's management (in the illustrative graphs I take $h = 10$, $H = 22$). Using this information, management then chooses its own introduction date, T, the value of T that maximizes the present value of the firm's prospective profit flow, π. If it turns out that $T < h$, then a profit-maximizing management will choose the role of innovator, whereas if we obtain $T > h$, then the firm will find it more profitable to be an imitator.

The form of the profit function follows the form in (12.9) of the previous section. But there are two new complications. First, it is necessary to build in the effect of the launch of the rival's product on date h. This is assumed always to reduce our firm's rate of profit flow, at least temporarily. Second, it is necessary to formulate two types of profit function: one for the innovator case and one for the imitator, though the two functions turn out to be similar in form. Using notation like that of (12.9), but with K representing the reduced rate of profit flow after the rival's entry date, we have as the profit function for the case of the innovator firm, where $T = T^* < h$,

$$\text{(12.10)} \quad \pi_{in} = R\int_{t=0}^{T} e^{-rt}\,dt - Ce^{-(r+w)T} + Se^{vT}\int_{t=T}^{h} e^{-rt}\,dt + K\int_{t=h}^{\infty} e^{-rt}\,dt.$$

Figure 12.2 shows the time path of the undiscounted values of these profit flows as the solid curve. For example, it takes the value R for the interval $0 \leq t < T$. At time T^* (in the graph I arbitrarily set $T^* = 5$), the height of the graph is equal to $R - Ce^{-wT^*}$, thus yielding the downward spike at T^*. Then, in the interval between T^* and h, the height of the graph equals Se^{vT^*}, and so on.

Correspondingly, we have as the profit function of the imitator, with the later introduction date $T = T^{**} > h$,

$$\text{(12.11)} \quad \pi_{im} = A\int_{t=0}^{h} e^{-rt}\,dt + B\int_{t=h}^{T} e^{-rt}\,dt - De^{-(r+w)T} + Ee^{bT}\int_{t=T}^{H} e^{-rt}\,dt + A\int_{t=H}^{\infty} e^{-rt}\,dt.$$

which is similar to (12.10) in structure and interpretation. Figure 12.2 also illustrates the time path of the undiscounted profit flows corresponding to (12.11). The dashed curve shows these imitator's profit flows, with T arbitrarily placed at $T^{**} = 12$, merely for illustration.

The integrations in (12.10) and (12.11) give the discounted present value of total profit as a function of T, our entrepreneur's selected entry date. The calculation, precisely analogous to that of $B(T)$ earlier in this chapter, enables

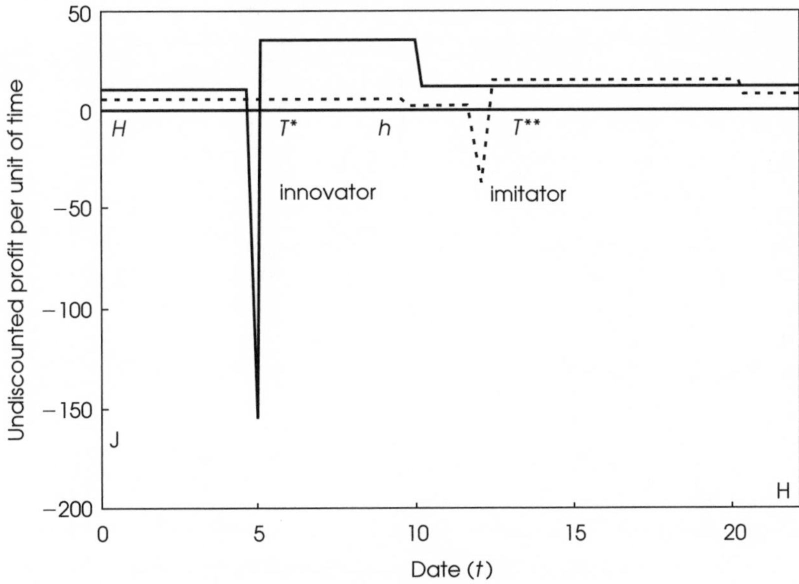

FIGURE 12.2
Undiscounted Profit Flows: Innovator vs. Imitator

us to plot the graph of $\pi(T, h)$. This graph is shown in figure 12.3. It is seen to be composed of two hills, as Proposition 12.2 asserts, with a discontinuity at $T = 10$. A little experimentation with parameter values, always keeping them within plausible bounds, shows that it is easy to vary the curvatures and the relative heights of the two hills. It is, of course, possible for the portion of the graph to the left of h, or that to its right, to have a positive or a negative slope throughout. In that case, it can possibly yield a corner solution at $T = 0$ (immediate launch) or $T = h$ (the Hotelling solution, in which the second entrant crowds the incumbent as closely as possible).[5]

In the graph, the peak, M, of the innovator's profit hill, to the left of $T = h$, lies below N, the peak of the imitator's hill. Thus, in this case, the profit-maximizing firm will choose to be an imitator. Management will then select launch date T_N.

Note also that, in the case shown in the graph, T_M and T_N (the optimal launch dates of innovator and imitator, respectively) both lie relatively far from h within the range of pertinent dates. This confirms the assertion of

5. I ignore the implausible case where the segment of the profit curve to the right of h has a positive slope throughout, so that the optimal launch date is infinity.

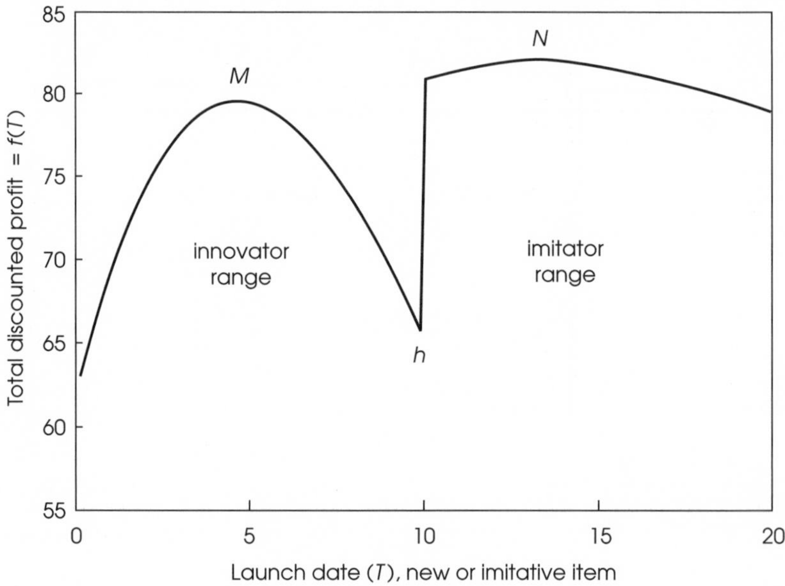

FIGURE 12.3

Total Discounted Profit: Innovator vs. Imitator (as a function of T)

Proposition 12.3 that, in the relation of innovator and imitator, it is at least theoretically possible to obtain an anti-Hotelling case in which the two firms, far from attempting to select neighboring launch dates, try instead to keep a considerable interval between them.

This is not merely a formal possibility. The original innovator has every reason to try for a long interval between the date of launch of that firm's new product and the date at which the imitator enters and begins to erode the innovator's profits. A glance at (12.10) confirms that this is indeed built into the profit function, and can contribute materially to its decline as T approaches h from the left.

But there can also be good reason for the imitator to keep its distance from the launch date of the innovator. Delay saves capital cost, for the usual reasons. It offers the imitator a longer period to carry out R&D and to come out with a more marketable product. It permits additional free-riding upon the improvement efforts of the innovator, thereby possibly avoiding the worst problems and risks of the earliest models. Finally, the possibility that the original innovator will go bankrupt, as has so often happened, means that waiting may enable the imitator to acquire the innovator's assets at bargain prices. Not all of these considerations have been built explicitly into (12.11), but enough of them are implicitly there to account for the distance between T^{**} and h.

I still need to consider what determines the relative heights of M and N, that is, the relative profitability of "pure innovation" and imitation. Here, there seems little to be said beyond listing some major influences. This does not provide any formal analysis, but it shows why one cannot readily generalize about the relative advantages of the positions of "original innovator" and imitator. Certainly, history provides examples of sometimes the one, sometimes the other, turning out to have made the more profitable choice, and suggesting that luck played a large role in the outcome.

The state of competition among the firms is one of the key determinants. A large pool of potential imitators favors an attempt to get there first—as the innovator—because effective competition will limit the returns to imitation. On the other hand, if early entry by a few imitators is likely, that will cut down the relative and absolute returns to innovation. The comparative costs of the R&D in the two processes are clearly also important, notably the imitator's cost of product modification sufficient to get around any patents held by the innovator. The durability of the product, too, can be significant, for it can delay the date at which an imitator can hope to enter the market successfully with a product that is only a moderate improvement. Risk can make it more attractive to play the imitator, in the hope that someone else will take the chance of entry into an unexplored market with an unproven product. The preferred choice is also affected by the magnitude of the spillover benefits that the innovator provides to imitators, through generation of information about the market, the technology, and relevant R&D techniques.

This list of variables affecting the relative profitability of innovation and imitation at least shows that there is no a priori reason to expect the advantage always to go to the one choice or the other. Consequently, it is difficult to predict whether any particular case will turn out to constitute a race or a waiting game.

CONCLUDING COMMENT: OLIGOPOLISTIC COMPETITION IN INNOVATION

This chapter has described several analytic models that offer concrete results about timing issues in the innovation and imitation processes. The comparative-statics results of the first timing model in the chapter are surely difficult to obtain by intuition alone.

The absence of strategic interaction among firms competing in innovation that was assumed in the previous section obviously prevents us from studying an important feature of reality. Where the kinked profit curve analysis of chapter four is deemed inappropriate, game theory is clearly the correct approach for analysis of such strategic interaction and there is an extensive and illuminating literature dealing with the subject in this way. Here, the work of Dasgupta and of several co-authors is appropriately singled out (see, e.g., Dasgupta, 1988). As is often true in such game-theoretic analyses, general conclusions are difficult to arrive at, since small changes in the structure of the game can affect the solution substantially. Nevertheless, the game-theoretic work on innovation has produced extremely illuminating results and has greatly increased our understanding of the interactions of innovators and imitators. For example, Dasgupta is able to draw the following conclusion from two of his models, one dealing with an innovation race and the other with a waiting game:

> For a given level of industrial concentration . . . the greater the imitation possibilities the less will each firm be expected to conduct R&D. . . . Furthermore, there is a positive chance that no innovation will occur. . . . And this chance increases with greater competition, growing to [a determinable] limit . . . as the number of firms increases without limit. By the same token, there is a positive chance that an innovation *will* occur, and this decreases with increasing competition. There is thus a positive relationship between industrial concentration and the probability that an innovation will occur. Notice as well that each firm's *expected* R&D expenditure increases with the pure profitability of the innovation. . . . Thus, the larger the market, or the greater the innovation opportunities, the larger is the volume of R&D investment expected to be.
>
> These results are congenial to intuition. Spillovers hold firms back from investing in R&D. But they do not hold them back completely, even when spillovers are so large as to make it positively beneficial to be an imitator. For if all hold back forever there will be no one to imitate! (1988, p. 78)

The reader is referred to this paper and other contributions on the subject for further insights into the results in the game-theoretic literature on innovation and the methods by which they are derived.

CHAPTER 13

Licensing for Profit: Efficiency Implications

There was general agreement at the time that Beta technology could give better picture quality, but Sony did not license anyone else to use its patented Beta technology, and thus more VHS recorders were sold by different companies. In time it became much easier to find the VHS version of movies and other tapes in video rental stores, and it became the standard.

—Petroski, 1996, p. 112

In this chapter, I provide a final illustration of the ways in which innovation and growth theory can be adapted to standard microeconomic analysis. But this case will not involve mainstream value theory, and the related theory of the firm will be used only toward the end of the chapter. Rather, I will use another well-developed body of analysis—the theory of the economic regulation of business firms. This material deals with what is referred to as "parity pricing" of bottleneck inputs (see, e.g., Laffont and Tirole, 2000).[1] These are inputs owned by a single proprietor firm, which uses them in its own production of final products; and without these inputs, competitors cannot operate successfully in the markets for those products.

Chapter 6 dealt with the lucrative business activity of direct sale or rental of access to proprietary technology. It was argued that, contrary to widespread impression, if the license price is right, it is never most profitable for the owner of such technology to prevent others, even its most direct com-

1. The basic theorem on the efficiency of parity pricing, as well as the concept itself, is attributable to my colleague Robert Willig (1979).

petitors, from using it. But that chapter ended with several unanswered questions: What price is "right" from the point of view of the proprietor? Is there a price that is economically efficient, and is that price profitable for the licensor? And, if there is an efficient price, can the market mechanism be relied upon to yield a price at or close to that level?

This chapter explores these questions, and I will conclude that there is such an efficient price. Moreover, I will argue that at this price it will be possible and profitable, at least theoretically, to provide such licenses to competing producers of the commodities that use the technology. Such profitable license fees will exist provided there are rival suppliers of the final products that are no less efficient than the proprietor of the technology. However, we will see that there may exist license fees even more profitable to the licensor than the (lowest) efficient price. Even so, it will not pay the owner of the technology to deny its use to others that are willing to pay either the efficient price or the profit-maximizing price. In practice, management can sometimes even misunderstand its own best interests in the licensing market and may consequently end up with a license fee that is less profitable and less desirable socially. Alternatively and perhaps more commonly, it may be altogether unwilling to license even at a price that can increase profits, a profit opportunity that it fails to recognize.

It is clear that there are levels of price that are materially too high or substantially too low for a social optimum. Prohibitively high licensing fees are really the same thing as outright refusal to license to anyone, while inadequate fees, which can easily occur if licensing is compulsory, constitute a strong disincentive for investment in innovation. Fees that are excessively low can also lead to use of the technology by some firms at the expense of others better qualified to do so, as will be explained below. Although we can recognize some fees as patently excessive, and others as clearly inadequate, that still leaves unsettled the determination of the best intermediate level of that fee.

The proper magnitude of licensing fees becomes an issue of immediate significance in practice when courts of law adopt compulsory licensing to limit the monopoly power conferred by patents.[2] For, unless a licensing edict is accompanied by restrictions on the size of the fee, compulsory licensing is

2. See, e.g., Scherer (1980, pp. 456–57). He reports that a number of European countries and Japan, unlike the United States, have laws containing general compulsory licensing provisions. But grants of such licenses have been quite infrequent in those countries, whereas in the United States they have often been granted by the courts at "reasonable royalty rates" (and occasionally free of charge) as a remedy in antitrust cases.

an empty gesture—it does not constrain the patent holder from preventing use of the invention by others through prohibitive charges. Pricing is, clearly, also a critical issue in voluntary licensing agreements.

This chapter approaches the optimal pricing issue by focusing first on a little-discussed efficiency loss that can result if the licensing fee is inappropriate.[3] After deriving the formula for an efficient license fee, I will turn to the price that can be expected to emerge in an unregulated market for technology licenses. We will see that in some circumstances arm's-length negotiation in a free market may lead to adoption of something approximating that efficient price, if the patent system offers the innovator an appropriate reward incentive for investment in innovation.

EFFICIENCY IMPLICATIONS OF THE LICENSE FEE

To determine what level of license fee is consistent with economic efficiency it is necessary to identify the activities that are affected by this price. Just what resources will be misallocated if an inappropriate royalty is selected? Three activities are directly affected by the license fee: (1) the allocation of resources to research and development (R&D) and to other parts of the innovation process; (2) the allocation of resources to technology transfer, that is, to imitation and dissemination of inventions; and (3) the allocation (among competing suppliers) of the task of production of final goods and services that use the invention as an input; in other words, which firms—the licensees or the licensor—will produce how much of a technology-using final product?

The Fee as Incentive for Innovative Activity: The Role of Spillovers

The economy's innovating activity has been discussed extensively in the literature as well as here, and only a few further comments on the subject are necessary. The major point is self-evident: if innovators are forced to license their discoveries and to do so at bargain prices, it creates a strong disincentive to investment in the expensive and risky innovation process. This will exacerbate the effect of the spillovers from technological advances. Anything that facilitates the diffusion of technology at excessively low prices aggravates the

3. For a discussion of the issue in general terms, see Laffont and Tirole (2000).

free-rider problem. We will see in this chapter that a proper license fee for a patent can help to alleviate the free-rider problem.

The Costs of Dissemination

Technology transfer also competes with innovation, because dissemination uses substantial quantities of resources, thus reducing those available for innovation (or any other purposes). Despite the public-good property of information, dissemination is not costless. The magnitude of the license fee has a role in determining whether, taking account of this cost and other considerations, the allocation of resources to dissemination is excessive or inadequate for economic efficiency.

The Allocation of Innovation Use among Final-Product Producers

Besides its role in the allocation of resources between innovation and dissemination, the license fee has another allocative task. When an innovation has been offered for license, there will, as already emphasized, generally be firms that consider using it as an input to produce final outputs similar to those of the patent holder. The question is, what share of that final output should be produced by each of these firms? Or, if that output will be produced by only a single firm, which of the firms should get the job? License fees will influence that allocation, and the efficiency of the industry's activities will obviously be affected.

Clearly, the royalty rate will influence the allocation of the task between innovator and licensee. The lower the fee (which is commonly expressed as a percent of the price of the final innovation-using product), the more of the final product we can expect the licensees to supply, because a reduction of the license fee cuts their relative production cost. And, if license fees are negotiated separately with each licensee, the allocation of final output production among those firms will also be affected. An optimal set of fees will, then, be one that permits efficient allocation of the task of final-product supply among the competing providers. We will see below what price meets this efficiency requirement and we will see that the solution is not immediately obvious. Certainly, it is not the price traditionally chosen by government agencies dealing with precisely analogous issues in other arenas.

WHY THE DETERMINATION OF AN OPTIMAL LICENSE FEE IS DIFFICULT

The efficiency problem just discussed is most difficult when the holder of the patent is also the supplier of some or all of the final products in whose manufacture the invention is to be used. Then the patent holder becomes the direct competitor of other suppliers of these same or close substitute final products. Too high a license fee is clearly a handicap to more efficient competitors of the patent holder, whereas too low a fee is a relative (competitive) disadvantage to the patent holder, even if it is the more efficient supplier of the remainder of the final-product manufacturing process.[4] The issue, then, is whether a pricing rule exists that prevents either of these types of inefficiency, which can conceivably substantially increase the social costs of the use of inventions.

The obvious solution, though one that is not very helpful, is to require all users, including the technology owner, to pay the same license fee. Reality, however, does not provide such an easy way to prevent discrimination among final-product suppliers that unequally affects their ability to compete. The difficulty arises because the price that the patent holder *really* charges itself for use of the invention as an input is far from clear. This price may be specified in the firm's accounting records, but it is generally an artificial and arbitrary number that tells us nothing about what the owner really gives up financially (that is, what the firm really pays) when it supplies that invention input to itself. After all, a rise in that price merely moves money from one of the firm's pockets to another. It is necessary to search further to determine what price the patent holder is really paying for the invention input it provides to itself.

THE PARITY PRINCIPLE FORMULA FOR ACCESS PRICING

The economics of price regulation provides a pricing principle that can be used to determine an efficient technology licensing fee. This principle has been referred to as the *efficient component-pricing rule* (ECPR) or as the *parity principle.* Despite its distinctive nomenclature, the rule is merely a variant of familiar elementary principles for efficiency in pricing. The parity principle tells us that the price that the patent-holder firm charges itself for the use of its own innovation input is the same price the firm charges to a final-product customer, minus the incremental cost[5] to the patent-holding firm of the

4. In particular, if the license price is not sufficient to enable the innovator to cover its continuing sunk outlays, that price will clearly constitute a subsidy from the innovator to the licensee.

5. The term "incremental cost," though widely used in regulatory arenas, is less familiar to economists. It refers to the addition to a supplier's total cost that results from any given addition to the output of one of its products. Thus, it is analogous to marginal cost

remaining inputs of the final product—that is, the other, non-innovation inputs that go into the production of the final product, including the requisite capital costs. The parity principle tells us that this is the price that the monopoly owner of any bottleneck input (such as a patent) that is indispensable to the activities of all the final-product competitors implicitly charges itself for that bottleneck input. It is, consequently, the price at which the competing final-product providers should be entitled to purchase the bottleneck input.

The logic of the proof that the parity-pricing formulas (given below) satisfy this requirement is not difficult to understand. Since we cannot directly observe the fee that the licensor is charging itself, we need an alternative test, with observable components, to determine whether or not the licensor is charging others the same fee that it pays itself. Such a substitute test is provided by the following observation. If, and only if, two independent producers of a commodity pay the same license fee for the technology they employ, the difference between the prices at which the two firms can afford to sell a unit of the final product will be exactly equal to the difference between the costs of their remaining inputs. This obvious proposition can be extended directly to a patent holder that is a provider both of licenses for use of the patented invention and of final product in which the invention is used. For it is clear that this firm will really be selling use of the invention to itself at the same price that it sells that input to a rival final-product provider if and only if, at that input price, the rival can afford to sell the final product at a price that differs from the patent holder's by precisely the amount that the rival's incremental remaining-input cost differs from the patent owner's. If the remaining input cost of the competitor is X cents lower per unit of final-product output than the patent owner's, then both of them are paying the same price for use of the invention if the rival can afford to provide the final product exactly X cents cheaper than the patent owner can.

All of this can be described formally, giving explicit formulas for an efficient license fee. I use the following notation:

$P_{f,i}$ = the invention owner, I's, given price per unit of final product;

$\min P_{f,c}$ = the competitor, C's, minimum viable price of final product;

P_i = the price charged for a license to use the invention, per unit of final product;

but refers to larger increments in output. Most commonly it refers to the incremental cost of an entire product; that is, if the firm is producing x units of good X and a number of other products, it refers to the amount that supply of these x units adds to the firm's total outlays.

$IC_{r,i}$ = the incremental cost to the invention owner of the remaining final-product inputs, per unit of final product;

$IC_{r,c}$ = the corresponding figure for the competitor;

IC_i = the incremental cost to the invention owner of use of the invention by itself or by others.[6]

As will be demonstrated presently, the efficient component-pricing rule requires that the licensing price satisfy either (and, hence, both) of two equivalent rules. The first is expressed in the formula

(13.1) $P_i = P_{f,i} - IC_{r,i}$ [license price = I's final-product price – I's incremental cost of remaining inputs].

Alternatively, and equivalently (as will be shown), the ECPR price of the bottleneck input must satisfy

(13.2) $P_i = IC_i$ + the invention owner's profit per unit of final-product output.

Equation (13.1) tells us that the ECPR establishes a tight link between the price, $P_{f,i}$, that the invention owner charges for its final product and the price, P_i, it charges its rivals for the license to use the invention. If incremental production costs do not change, efficiency requires that a rise in one of these prices must be matched dollar for dollar by a rise in the other. Equation (13.2) tells us that the efficient price of the license is the direct incremental cost to the owner of the invention resulting from use of the invention by others, plus the associated incremental opportunity cost. This opportunity cost is the loss of profit made possible because the invention has been licensed to the rival, which can then take final-product business away from the licensor. Thus, the second form of the ECPR asserts that the price of the license should equal any direct incremental cost incurred in supplying it to a competitor, plus any incremental opportunity cost incurred as a result of that transaction.[7] Stan-

6. Sometimes that cost may vary from one user to another. For example, if the personnel of the owner of the invention learned how to use it during the development process, but rivals need training for its use, the incremental cost of use by the two types of firm will clearly differ. Then the parity-price formula must be modified in a straightforward way, with the prices to different users of the invention differing by the variation in the cost to the patent owner of their usage.

7. Notice that the relevant opportunity cost here is *average* profit forgone—the total profit forgone by the patent holder as a result of the transaction, per unit of final product sold. It is not the *marginal* opportunity cost, which is likely to be zero, because a profit-maximizing patent holder that produces the final product in which the innovation in question is used will produce the quantity of final product at which marginal profit falls to zero. For a fuller discussion of the issue, see the appendix to this chapter.

dard economic analysis tells us that this is a proper way to price—that is, the price should equal marginal (incremental) cost including marginal (incremental) opportunity cost—so that, at least at first, this result should not be surprising.[8]

Then the task is to prove the following:

PROPOSITION 13.1. The "Level-Playing-Field" Theorem. The parity price, as given by (13.1) or (13.2), for use of a bottleneck input such as a patented innovation is both necessary and sufficient in order for the playing field to be level. This means that the maximum difference between the remunerative prices of the perfect-substitute final-products of the two firms, the invention owner (I) and its final product competitor (C), is exactly equal to the difference in the firms' remaining incremental costs (other than the license fees).

Proof: The level playing field is defined by

$$\min P_{f,c} - P_{f,i} = IC_{r,c} - IC_{r,i}. \tag{13.3}$$

That is, the lowest compensatory price the competitor can afford to charge should differ from the invention owner's exactly by the amount (positive or negative) that the competitor's remaining costs are below the invention owner's. But the lowest price that is financially viable for the competitor clearly is given by

$$\min P_{f,c} = P_i + IC_{r,c}. \tag{13.4}$$

That is, the price must cover the patent licensing cost plus the remaining cost of supplying the final product (of course, including the cost of the required capital, made up of depreciation and normal competitive profit).

Comparing the two equations, we see at once that the level playing field condition (13.3) will be satisfied if and only if

$$P_i = P_{f,i} - IC_{r,i}. \tag{13.5}$$

8. Yet the opportunity cost element of this result is the focus of current debate over use of ECPR in the regulation of firms deemed to possess monopoly power. The problem is that the bottleneck owner is a monopolist, and its final product price may therefore be set at a level that yields monopoly profits. These monopoly profits are among the profits forgone as a result of a lost sale of final product. Consequently, they constitute a part of the opportunity cost for which, according to (13.2) (at least without further modification of the ECPR regime), the bottleneck owner should be compensated when it sells bottleneck input to a rival. The subject will be considered again later in this chapter.

But this is the parity-pricing formula (13.1). Thus, parity pricing is both necessary and sufficient for a level playing field. Q.E.D.

The parity-pricing formula (13.5) is also identical to the opportunity-cost variant of the rule, (13.2), since, by definition,

(13.6) $P_{f,i} = IC_i + IC_{r,i}$ + I's profit per unit of final-product output,

or, by (13.5),

(13.7) $P_i = P_{f,i} - IC_{r,i} = IC_i$ + I's profit per unit of final-product output.

This is the parity-pricing formula (13.2).

This completes the proof that parity pricing of a patent license is necessary for economic efficiency in the provision of a final product by competing suppliers. If this rule is violated, a less efficient supplier of the remaining inputs can win the competition for the business of supplying those inputs, instead of the task going to a more efficient rival. That is, violation of (13.1) or (13.2) permits a less efficient supplier of nonbottleneck inputs to underprice its more efficient competitors.[9] The proof is readily extended to cases with three or more competing firms.

INTERTEMPORAL EFFICIENCY AND ECPR PRICING

It must be confessed, however, that the ECPR price, though necessary for efficiency, is by itself not only insufficient for that result but also, in a deeper sense, literally incompatible with static efficiency. This is because technical information, in particular, information about an invention, is surely a prime example of a (nearly) pure public good, one whose use by an additional individual does not deplete its technical capacity to be used by another person. As Dupuit brought to our attention in the nineteenth century and as Samuel-

9. Here we should pause to admit that, where scale economies mean that marginal cost pricing is not feasible, theory calls for adoption of a Ramsey price for the license as well as for final product, and that Ramsey price can be expected to violate ECPR. It should be noted, however, that a frequent complaint against ECPR in regulatory arenas such as telecommunications and electricity is that it yields bottleneck-input prices that are disturbingly high. Yet the Ramsey-adjusted ECPR prices can be expected to be even higher. Specifically, so long as any rents are left to a competitor of the bottleneck owner, the rival's demand for the essential bottleneck service will be (perfectly?) inelastic. Thus, the Ramsey rule requires the price of bottleneck service to be raised possibly until all such rents accrue to the bottleneck owner, whereas ECPR leaves competitors' efficiency rents to them.

son demonstrated in his noted paper on the theory of public expenditure (1954), efficiency in the employment of such an undepletable resource requires its use to be priced at zero. That means that any positive license fee that deters anyone from using an invention is preventing a use that offers a positive marginal benefit but incurs zero marginal cost.

The fundamental problem here is that such a zero price, although required for static efficiency, is incompatible with intertemporal efficiency, because of its very significant disincentive effect on investment in innovation. If inventors are to be compensated for their contribution by any nonzero price based on usage, the preceding analysis indicates that this price must satisfy the efficient component-pricing rule if it is to be compatible with (second-best) efficiency. There is a tradeoff here between static and intertemporal efficiency analogous to the tradeoff between the optimal incentive for innovation investment and the distributive spillover benefits that was the focus of chapter 8, and, as in that case, the best of the available options may be a second-best solution.

In theory, there is an alternative that is suggestive, though it may not often be very helpful in practice. Something like a two-part tariff can solve the problem if one of the parts can be levied on something for which the price elasticity of demand is zero, or very close to it. Then it becomes possible to use that part's tariff revenues to compensate the innovator, while leaving the license fee for use of the innovation at zero.[10] Under such an arrangement, the zero license fee will, moreover, satisfy the ECPR, because the innovator will receive suitable compensation from another source, and will no longer be able to derive any of that compensation out of monopoly profit from the sale of the final product whose supply makes use of the innovation. In a competitive industry, the innovator will then be unable to earn any profit from this source because, with a zero license fee, competition by licensees can be expected to drive the final product price down correspondingly. With the innovator's profit from this source driven down to zero, additional use of the innovation by others will incur a zero opportunity cost, and so the ECPR price will also be zero unless the innovation is not a pure public good, in which case its use by others imposes some cost upon the innovator. But, even in that case, the ECPR will constrain the license fee to cover no more than that cost, and it will still be compatible with static efficiency.

10. Something like this arrangement does actually occur when two firms decide simply to trade access to one another's innovations, with no charge for additional usage but with an equalization payment by the firm with the less valuable technology to compensate the other for its more valuable innovations (as described in chapter 6).

These remarks are intended only to shed a bit more light on the analytical issue, not to constitute a workable procedure for dealing with the problem.[11] For that, it seems necessary to make use of the ECPR in the form described earlier in this section.

ON THE INNOVATION-DISSEMINATION TRADEOFF AGAIN: THE EFFICIENT COMPONENT-PRICING RULE AS "INDIFFERENCE PRINCIPLE"

Let us turn next to efficiency in the allocation of resources between innovation and dissemination. The license fee by itself cannot carry out this task because its rate is already determined by the requirement of efficiency in the allocation of output among the innovation-using firms, as the previous sections described. It is convenient, then, that there is another price, *P*, that of the final product that still remains to be determined. We will see that *P*, together with the royalty rate, can do the job, at least in principle.

The Royalty Rate and the Innovation-Dissemination Tradeoff

A royalty rate that follows the efficient component-pricing rule already makes some contribution toward solution of the problem by reducing the conflict between dissemination and innovation. The fee ensures that both the sale of licenses and the sale of final product by the patent holder can contribute to recovery of the sunk innovation cost. The final-product sales can make such a contribution because the competitors' prices will have to be high enough to cover the license fee in addition to their other input costs.

But what has so far been said here is true of any level of royalty payment. The parity-pricing rule, however, selects a price that benefits the patent holder in a second way. It sets the license fee to recover the incremental opportunity costs that result from licensing of the invention to rival final-

11. Yet there are other examples demonstrating that sometimes something like the two-part tariff that has just been described may be feasible in practice. This is shown, for instance, by an analogous situation involving the debate among U.S. telecommunications firms over the pricing of access to use by the long-distance carriers of the facilities of local service providers, including the latter's wires into household and business premises. To help cover losses on the low-priced local service required by regulation to be provided by local carriers to very poor subscribers and others deemed to merit such subsidized usage, the long-distance carriers have agreed to contribute what can be interpreted as lump-sum payments into a fund (called the "universal-service fund") while pricing access to the local carrier's facilities at something like marginal cost.

product suppliers. As a result, the patent-holder firm is just as well off financially if it makes the final product itself or if, instead, some or all of the (same quantity of) sales are made by rival suppliers of the final product. Because of this attribute, ECPR has sometimes been called the "principle of indifference." That is, it sets the royalty rate at the level that makes the innovator firm indifferent between production by licensees and production of the same quantity of final product by itself. We will see below, however, that, with a license fee set in accord with ECPR, efficient licensees will generally *not* produce the same quantity of final product as the owner of the patent. Indeed, competitive and efficient licensees will generally produce more than the licensor would have, and as a result, with the fee set per unit of final product output, ECPR will generally make the patent holder better off if it agrees to license than if it refuses to do so.

The Role of the Final-Product Price

To complete the story, it would be desirable to produce an illuminating insight on the determination of the optimal final-product price and the resulting return (incentive payment) to the patent holder. Presumably, the bottom line is that the proper price is one that includes the appropriate Pigouvian subsidy calculated to offset the distorting effects of the externalities generated by innovative activity. This is undoubtedly true, but it must be admitted that it offers very little guidance in practice, particularly given the lack of agreement among economists about the nature of these externalities, with no one claiming to offer any reasonably exact method of calculating their magnitude in any particular case.

Whatever the magnitude of the incentive payment that, implicitly, has been agreed upon, its payment currently primarily comes from one source. It is the surplus obtained by means of the monopoly power given to the innovator by patents or by some substitute, such as maintenance of secrecy on the technical specifications of an invention. Policy can, if so desired, enhance this power, for example by facilitating the grant of patents, by strengthening their enforcement, by extending the life of the patent, and so on. All this is quite obvious and adds nothing new. It does suggest the nature of the relevant tradeoff and the corresponding considerations that should be weighed in trying to determine an optimal arrangement.

The nature of the tradeoff is clear: it is a direct balancing of static efficiency losses caused by the monopoly power against prospective gains in economic growth. The incentive for innovation is increased by enhancement of the inventor's temporary monopoly power. But that power and the resulting increase in final-product price will interfere with static economic efficiency and reduce welfare. The increase in the monopoly power conferred upon an inventor will tend to shift the production frontier outward more rapidly, but it will simultaneously move the economy to a point on this higher frontier that is less than optimal. One can readily show that this tradeoff can be pushed inadequately or, alternatively, that it can go too far. If the monopoly power granted to a patentee is strengthened, it can reduce welfare even if it shifts the economy's production frontier further outward. If the added monopoly power permits output to be restricted sufficiently by the patent holder, then welfare will be decreased even if productivity has risen considerably. I conclude that, in principle, there is likely to be some intermediate degree of patent or other form of protection of the inventor's intellectual property that constitutes the optimal tradeoff, though this observation is hardly likely to be very helpful for policy design. The discussion suggests only how difficult it is to design a patent system that can be claimed to approximate optimality even very roughly.

We do, however, end up with one helpful observation. As already noted, for most regulated industries it is generally agreed that an ECPR price that includes any monopoly profit component in its opportunity cost figure is incompatible with economic efficiency. In the case of a license fee for an innovation, this is surely *not* so. Efficiency requires that whatever temporary monopoly profit is selected as the best incentive reward for innovations must also be included in the opportunity cost that the ECPR license fee covers.

THE MARKET, THE ROYALTY RATE, AND EFFICIENCY

Given a defensible policy decision on the strength of legal protection to the innovator, if royalty rates are set in accord with the ECPR everything will fall into place. A set of resources commensurate with the selected innovator-protection policy will be devoted to innovation. Patent licenses will be acquired only by firms that can make efficient use of them, and the production of innovation-using final products will be allocated efficiently among firms. There remains only the question of whether something has to be done to ensure that royalty rates set in the marketplace for licenses at least approximately satisfy the efficient component-pricing rule. There is some a priori reason to suspect that the market mechanism can produce something close to that result without intervention, because, in theory, this is the way that analogous input prices will be set in a market that is perfectly competitive. There, as we know from elementary theory, equilibrium prices will equal incremental or marginal cost, including incremental opportunity cost (and, of course, including exactly the competitive return on the required incremental capital), just as the ECPR requires.

This immediately raises the question whether or not the incentive exists for the pertinent oligopoly firms of reality to arrive at something like an ECPR figure when negotiating bilaterally over a license fee. It has been argued at regulatory hearings and elsewhere by myself and others that in appropriate circumstances there is such an incentive, though the argument has been hotly disputed. First, it is clear that the proprietor of the patent or some analogous bottleneck input has no financial incentive to offer the license to competitors at any price that does not at least cover incremental cost, including incremental opportunity cost. Thus, the ECPR yields the lowest price that one can expect from such voluntary negotiations. But at that price the proprietor of the bottleneck's services should (at least) be indifferent between their use by itself and their use by competitors, since that ECPR price just covers average opportunity cost. This means that the bottleneck owner receives the same net compensation whether a unit of the final product and its nonbottleneck components are supplied by itself or by a rival. That is, payment of the opportunity cost compensates the bottleneck owner fully (and, as we will see, very likely more) for any profit forgone by use of the invention by rivals, so that at that price the owner firm should at worst be indifferent between the option of supply of the final product by itself or by others.

The argument is still stronger where the bottleneck owner faces a fixed final-product price. It does not matter whether the price is set by regulation, by the market, or by other forces. Indeed, the result holds when the market fixes the profit-maximizing monopoly price—the price the owner of a patent is presumably entitled to charge. Here, it is convenient to deal with the case where the remaining inputs for the final product are supplied under competitive market conditions. Given the market price for the final product, the resulting revenue will be divided between the supplier of the bottleneck input and the suppliers of the remaining inputs. Then it will benefit the patent holder if the remaining inputs are supplied by the most efficient providers of those inputs. The lower these input costs, the less of the revenue from sale of the final product goes to the input suppliers in their competitive market, leaving more for the bottleneck owner. Moreover, it will clearly not pay the bottleneck owner to supply those remaining inputs itself if its own incremental cost of doing so is higher than the price at which it can obtain them from others. In this case, because in effect the bottleneck owner faces a make-

or-buy decision for the remaining components of the product, rationality requires the owner to buy the remaining inputs from the more efficient competitors rather than making them itself. Since pricing in accord with the ECPR allocates the task of supplying the remaining inputs to the most efficient provider, it serves the interests of the bottleneck owner. And that owner will not find it profitable in the long run to extract a fee that prevents licensees from earning at least the bulk of their efficiency rents and obtaining the competitive return on their capital, because that would deprive the licensor of an efficient supplier of the remaining final-product inputs. As we have seen, such a loss of efficient suppliers must reduce the maximum net profits the licensor can hope to obtain. ECPR pricing permits the licensee to earn the competitive rate of return, as well as its efficiency rents. So the patent holder may lose out if it drives the fee substantially above this level. Since no lower fee and no much higher fee may be more profitable to the patent holder, one can expect voluntary negotiations to yield a fee not very far from the ECPR level.[12]

The workings of the market mechanism in this case can be put in terms of the incentives of the two parties, showing that both licensor and licensee have some incentive to carry out the transaction at an ECPR fee.

The Licensor's Incentive. It will pay the owner of proprietary technology to license its use to rivals whenever those rivals are prepared to offer a license fee that gives the technology owner a return an iota higher than it can obtain by using it itself. But if the competitor's price corresponds to its costs, such a price offer will be profitable to the licensee when and only when it is a more efficient user of the technology than is the owner of the technology. And then the price can cover the owner's opportunity cost incurred by the act of licensing. That is, suppose the owner of the technology earns, say, $100 in profit for every unit of final product it turns out itself with the aid of the innovation and then sells. Then it is clearly better off if the technology is licensed to a rival that pays a parity-price license fee yielding $101 per unit of final product sold by that competitor.

Indeed, if the licensees operate in highly competitive or highly contestable market for the final product in which the innovation in question is

12. The patent holder may, of course, be tempted to extract some of the rents. If these are true economic rents, their transfer to the patent holder will not affect the outputs of the licensees. However, as will be argued presently, these "rents" can be expected to affect the behavior of the licensees. Where their technology is considered to be somewhat superior to those of their rivals, they can and do include a premium in their fee, but that premium is, allegedly, severely limited by the market and the competition of the close substitutes.

employed, the licensor can be expected to gain by licensing even at a fee that does not exceed the \$100 opportunity cost per unit of output. For more efficient licensees will have lower marginal costs than the licensor's at the latter's output, y, of final product but, at that output, the market price, $p(y)$, of the final product will be the same as the licensor would have charged. So the licensees' marginal profit from an increase in output above y will be positive and equal to their cost advantage, so competition or entry will force price down and output to increase (say to $y^* > y$). This means that the licensor will obtain total license revenue (\$100y^* in the example) greater than the total opportunity cost (\$100y) that it incurs by licensing.[13] All of this will be explored further below. The discussion will examine the final-product output of the licensees at an ECPR royalty rate, where the final-product market is competitive and where it is monopolistic, as well as the licensor's profit-maximizing license fee and its relation to ECPR. The troublesome implication of this last observation is that, although, as will be shown later, it always pays the holder of the patent to license to an efficient and competitive final-product producer at the ECPR fee, there are generally other levels of fee that will make the licensor's profits even higher.

The Licensee's Incentive. A licensee more efficient at turning out the final product than the technology owner should, by definition, earn a gross return greater than the \$100 per unit of final product in the previous illustration. If, for example, it earns \$120 in the process, an ECPR fee of \$101 will obviously leave it with a net gain of \$19 above the normal profit on its capital. But of course, as will be emphasized later, if the final-product market is competitive, none of this matters for a licensee if the profit in question is above the normal profit level, because competition will take the excess away in the long run, whatever it may be.

But that is not the end of the story. Normally in licensing markets an innovation-access purchase is not a one-shot affair. Rather, the licensee is often also interested in acquiring rights to a future stream of innovations from the licensor. Assume that the licensor earns only competitive profits overall, so that the ECPR fee is a component of the revenues that enable it to cover its fixed and common costs, including the costs of investment repeatedly sunk in the innovation process. If the licensor is more efficient than the

13. As we will see below, this is not necessarily true if the licensee is a monopolist, because there are cases in which the monopolist maximizes profits by producing an output $y' < y$. But then the licensor is free to produce some final product itself, in competition with the licensee.

licensee in the innovation process (but not in the *use* of the innovation in creating final products), then it will be profitable to the licensee if the licensor earns an amount sufficient to induce the latter to continue to invest in innovation. The logic of the allocation of the task of final-product supply applies equally (but in reverse) to the *production* of innovation. The more efficient licensor can supply innovation more cheaply than the licensee can do it for itself. In that case, the ECPR price will be profitable to the licensee in the long as well as the short run.

For analogous reasons, it will not be rational for the licensor to seek a license fee so high that it drives the licensee from the field in the long run. That will simply deprive the licensor of the profit contribution it gains from the licensee's efficiency. In short, it pays innovation users to ensure the survival of efficient innovation producers, and it profits the producers of the innovation to ensure the continued existence of efficient innovation users. A price in the neighborhood of the efficient component-pricing rule level can help to achieve both these objectives, and can therefore serve the interests of both parties in a licensing transaction. However, as implied in footnote 12, some deviation from ECPR may well result from conflict between licensors and licensees over efficiency rents or from an attempt by the patent holder to extract more of the rents generated by the competitive final-product producers that license the patented innovation for the purpose.

That, in essence, is the logic of the argument asserting that the market mechanism automatically provides incentives for voluntary dissemination of technology by its owner, and for agreement by all parties involved to a price that approximates the requirements of economic efficiency.

LICENSING PROFITS AND OUTPUTS: ECPR VS. THE PROFIT-MAXIMIZING LICENSE FEE

This section will use the most elementary approaches of the theory of the firm and industry to explore the output of a final product that makes use of a patented innovation that may or may not be licensed to others than the proprietor, and how the magnitude of that output is affected by the choice between the ECPR license fee and the fee that maximizes the licensor's profits. The discussion will employ some very elementary mathematics and a diagrammatic analysis. In particular, it will be shown under not very restrictive assumptions that:

PROPOSITION 13.2. The ECPR license fee is generally not the fee that maximizes the licensor's profit, the ECPR fee being the lower of the two.

PROPOSITION 13.3. At either an ECPR license fee or a fee that maximizes the profits of the patent owner, the final-product output of the efficient competitive licensees will be greater than the profit-maximizing output of the patent holder that refuses to license.

PROPOSITION 13.4. If the downstream users of the innovation are competitive final-product producers and more efficient at producing the final product than the patent holder, then the patent holder will always increase its profit by licensing either at the ECPR price or (a fortiori) at the profit-maximizing price.

PROPOSITION 13.5. If the downstream licensee is a monopolist, its final-product output may or may not be larger than that of the patent holder that refuses to license.

For expository simplicity, I will assume that the demand and average cost curves are all linear and that the final-product average cost curves of the efficient downstream firms as a group, AC_{effic}, are below but parallel to that of the patent holder, AC_{innov}, so that the two differ only by a constant. I also assume that the demand curve for the final product is downward sloping, while the average cost curves are all upward sloping (figure 13.1).

In addition, costs sunk in creation of the final product are taken to be zero, as is the cost to the patent holder of use of its innovation by a licensee. This last premise means that the ECPR license fee is equal simply to the loss of profit per unit of final output that the patent holder incurs when the innovation is used by a licensee to supply a unit of the product that the patent holder would otherwise have provided.

It is important to recognize that the validity of the four propositions containing the results of this section does not depend on the validity of the linearity assumption. They hold (qualitatively) so long as the demand curve slopes monotonically downward, the average cost curves slope monotonically upward, and both the zero profit points and the maximum profit points are unique. Nevertheless, the linearity assumption permits several easy simplifications. First, the output of the competitive licensees will obviously be that at which profit is zero, where the demand curve and the relevant average cost curve intersect. For example, in figure 13.1, if the license fee were zero this would entail a competitive output corresponding to point e'. Sec-

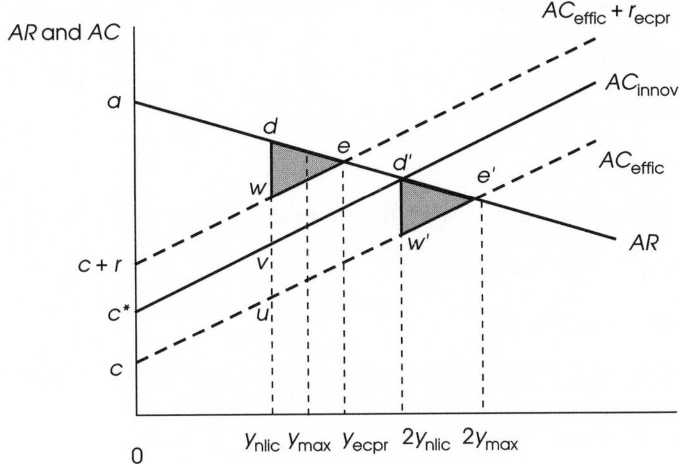

FIGURE 13.1
ECPR Pricing and Efficiency

ond, as is well known, the profit-maximizing output will be exactly half the competitive output. Third, at this output the profit per unit will be exactly one half the distance between the intersection of the demand curve and of the *AC* curve with the vertical axis. For example, if AC_{innov} is the pertinent AC curve, the profit-maximizing output of final product will be y_{nlic} and profit per unit will be $vd = 0.5(a - c^*)$. This is particularly important for the discussion that follows, since it is also the ECPR license fee per unit of final-product output, because that is the profit the licensor forgoes if it loses the sale of a unit of final profit—it is the per unit opportunity cost of replacement by another supplier.

The basic relations are

(13.8) $p = a - by$ (demand curve)

(13.9) $AC_{effic} = c + ky + r$ (efficient suppliers' AC curve)

(13.10) $AC_{innov} = c^* + ky, \quad c^* > c$ (patent holder's average cost curve)

where p and y are final-product price and output, respectively, and r is the patent license fee per unit of final-product output by the licensee. Then at license fee r a competitive set of final-product producers will produce the quantity $y(r)$ that satisfies

(13.11) $a - by(r) = c + r + ky(r) \quad \text{or} \quad y(r) = (a - c - r)/(b + k).$

The earnings of the patent holder will then be

(13.12) $ry(r) = [(a - c)r - r^2]/(b + k)$,

which are maximized when

(13.13) $a - c = 2r_{max}$,

yielding a licensor's maximum profit at output

(13.14) $y_{max} = 0.5(a - c)/(b + k)$

and a maximum profit of

(13.15) $\Pi_{max} = r_{max}y_{max} = 0.25(a - c)^2/(b + k)$.

We see at once from (13.13) that

(13.16) $r_{max} = 0.5(a - c) > 0.5(a - c^*) = r_{ecpr}$.

That is, the ECPR license fee is always lower than the fee that maximizes the patent holder's licensing profit, as Proposition 13.2 asserts.

By (13.11), final-product output under the ECPR license fee is

(13.17) $y_{ecpr} = (0.5)(a - 2c + c^*)/(b + k)$.

We know that $y_{ecpr} > y_{max}$ by direct comparison of (13.17) with (13.14). But this is true more generally, and not just in our linear model, because competitive output is generally a monotonically decreasing function of the license fee, which, for reasons analogous to those just seen, is lower under ECPR.

Finally, if the patent holder refuses to license, the profit-maximizing output will be half of that which reduces its profit to zero, i.e.,

(13.18) $y_{nlic} = 0.5(a - c^*)/(b + k) < y_{max}$ since $c^* > c$.

This completes the proof of Proposition 13.3.

Turning to Proposition 13.4, if the patent holder refuses to license, its profit will be

(13.19) $\Pi_{nlic} = (\text{per unit profit})y_{nlic} = [0.5(a - c^*)]^2/(b + k)$,

which is clearly lower than maximum profit by (13.15). More to the point, it is also lower than profit under ECPR since

(13.20) $\Pi_{ecpr} = r_{ecpr}y_{ecpr} = 0.5(a - c^*)(0.5)(a - 2c + c^*)/(b + k) > \Pi_{nlic}$

by (13.17) and (13.19). And this, too, is true more generally than just in the linear case. At the profit-maximizing output for the patent holder that chooses not to license, the per unit profit will equal r_{ecpr}, and the per unit cost of the efficient producers is lower than the patent holder's by some amount $\Delta C > 0$ unless the patent holder is the most efficient producer of final product. Therefore, since both face the same demand curve, at y_{nlic} the efficient producers would earn a per unit profit of $r_{\text{ecpr}} + \Delta C - r_{\text{ecpr}} = \Delta C$, if the licensees were permitted access to the patented innovation at the ECPR rental fee. In a competitive final product market with monotonically rising average cost, this will lead to an increase in output beyond y_{nlic} by the licensees, to a level we may designate general $y_{\text{ecpr}} > y_{\text{nlic}}$. This immediately implies that the patent holder will always be better off licensing to more efficient producers of the final product at fixed license fee r_{ecpr} than it would be if it refused to license, because, as has just been shown, in general

$$(13.21)\quad y_{\text{ecpr}} > y_{\text{nlic}},$$

so that

$$(13.22)\quad \Pi_{\text{nlic}} = r_{\text{ecpr}}\, y_{\text{nlic}} < r_{\text{ecpr}}\, y_{\text{ecpr}} = \Pi_{\text{ecpr}} < \Pi_{\text{max}}.$$

At least in the linear case, and presumably more generally, y_{max} will be greater than y_{nlic} because these are, respectively, half the outputs that yield zero profits at cost c and c^* (points e' and d' in figure 13.1)—the lower AC curve must intersect the AR curve to the right of the AR curve's intersection with the higher AC curve.[14]

I have now demonstrated all the propositions with which this section began, except for the last, which deals with the case where the prospective licensee is the only producer (except perhaps for the patent holder) in the final-product market. This case can be formalized in a Cournot model in which the patent holder and the downstream licensee are both monopolists.[15] Proposition 13.5 is most easily demonstrated diagrammatically. In figure 13.1, note again that the output of the patent holder that refuses to license will be half the abscissa of point d', the output at which the patent holder's profit would be zero. For the downstream monopolist, the argument

14. Indeed, in my simple model we must have $y_{\text{ecpr}} - y_{\text{max}} = y_{\text{max}} - y_{\text{nlic}}$, i.e., y_{max} must be at the midpoint between the other two. Proof: the shaded triangles *wed* and $w'e'd'$ in figure 13.1 must be congruent because they are clearly similar and are drawn so that $wd = w'd' = c^* - c$. But then we must have $y_{\text{ecpr}} - y_{\text{nlic}} = 2(y_{\text{max}} - y_{\text{nlic}})$.

15. Here the profit of the patent owner is $(\Pi_{\text{nlic}} = ry^{\text{d}} + [(a - c^* - ky^{\text{p}}) - b(y^{\text{p}} + y^{\text{d}})]y^{\text{p}}$, where y^{p} and y^{d} are, respectively, the output of the patent holder and of the downstream licensee. A similar expression can readily be written for the profit of the downstream licensee. The patent holder's profit-maximizing license fee and output are then obtained by partial differentiation of its profit function with respect to these two variables, to determine whether it pays the patent holder to produce any final product in competition with the licensee.

is analogous. For this purpose let us now reinterpret the AC curve labeled $AC_{effic} + r_{ecpr}$ simply as $AC_{effic} + r$, that is, as the average cost curve of the monopolist licensee at whatever license fee, r, the patent holder chooses to charge. Then e becomes the licensee's zero profit point, and its profit-maximizing output in the linear case will be just half of that. Hence, the output of the monopolist licensee will be greater, equal to, or less than that of the non-licensing patent holder as e lies to the right of, at the same abscissa, or to the left of d'. But it should be obvious that, if c and r are sufficiently low relative to c^*, e will lie to the right of d', whereas if, as in the diagram, c and r are relatively high in relation to c^*, e will be to the left of d'. This completes the demonstration of Proposition 13.5.

The bottom line of the discussion of this section is that the ECPR is not generally the value of the license fee that maximizes the profits of a patent holder. Second, and perhaps most important, it has been shown that it generally does pay the patent holder to license rather than to keep others from using the innovation. Third, although the license fee that maximizes the patent holder's profits is generally higher than the ECPR fee, there is no reason to expect the two to differ substantially. As (13.16) shows, the two will be very different only if the patent holder is a very inefficient producer of the final product, so that c^* is materially greater than c, meaning that the patent holder benefits primarily by gathering the efficiency rents of the efficient producers.

We may note that failure of the market mechanism to enforce ECPR license fees results only from the patent holder's monopoly power. A competitive market in innovation licenses will enforce a fee equal to the marginal (average) cost to the patent holder of use of the license by others, where that cost, of course, includes opportunity cost. But that is precisely the ECPR fee. And, in reality, the licensors may typically not have as much monopoly power as they appear to possess. In practice, sellers of licenses often face competition from suppliers of (imperfectly) substitutable technology. I have seen a number of sworn depositions in the course of lawsuits (depositions declared secret by the courts) in which large-firm sellers of technology licenses claim that they are, for all practical purposes, price takers because their license fees are in effect constrained by those of their competitors.

All of this adds up to one central conclusion about the role of the market mechanism in efficiency in the dissemination of technology. Whether or not the markets are competitive, the market does provide an incentive for efficient allocation of the two tasks at issue here: the creation of innovations and their use in the supply of final products. The task of innovation will tend to go to the most efficient innovators, and the task of supplying final products will go to the most efficient producers of these items (where some firms may be efficient in both activities and may participate in both).[16] But, although the market provides the incentive for satisfaction of this efficiency requirement, the spillovers entailed in innovation and its use mean that there is no market mechanism that automatically drives either the amount of innovative activity or the output of the associated final products toward optimality. The best that can be said with respect to those, as already indicated in chapter 7, is that the market's performance in these two arenas probably is considerably better than the standard literature leads us to think.

RATIONALITY OF BUSINESS FIRMS AND INCENTIVES FOR VOLUNTARY ACCEPTANCE OF ECPR FEES

Casual observation suggests that, in reality, patent license fees are frequently not set in ways that resemble an ECPR guideline. There are many reasons for this. For example, as described in the previous section, there is the incentive for the profit-maximizing bottleneck owner to extract rents from more efficient suppliers of the innovation-using final product by charging a license fee somewhat higher than called for by ECPR. Second, and perhaps even more important in practice, the firms themselves cannot always be counted upon to see the logic of the argument indicating the benefits they can derive from licensing, even at an ECPR license fee, and to act accordingly. For, in reality, firms do not always possess the rationality and insights that economic theory sometimes assumes them to have.

Over the years I have encountered many types of irrational action by business management, as is to be expected of the members of any profession. Some of these types of behavior appear to be quite widespread and systematic. As a result, patent owners may not always voluntarily choose to do business with the most efficient suppliers of the final products that can use their innovations, and they may choose not to license their proprietary technology even when this entails a substantial profit sacrifice.

16. However, if there are substantial scale economies or substantial advantages to early entry, an activity may go to the firm that got there first and may be retained by it despite attempts at entry by prospective rivals that could supply the output more efficiently than the incumbent if only they could replicate the incumbent's advantages of size and early entry. On the general subject of retainability by less efficient suppliers, see Gomory and Baumol (2000, esp. pp. 16–22).

The following anecdotal evidence is suggestive and represents just one of a number of analogous cases in which I participated. Some years ago, a major U.S. railroad contemplated the acquisition of a barge line that had been carrying some of that railroad's freight from its rail terminal on a waterway. Competing barge owners complained to the Department of Justice. I was approached by the railroad to consider serving as a witness on its behalf. At a meeting attended by the railroad CEO and some of the other officers of the railroad and the barge line, I called attention to the profit advantage to the railroad, particularly with a ceiling on its final-product rates fixed by regulation, if it always used the services of the lowest-cost barge carrier, whether that happened to be its own barge line or a competitor. This assertion was greeted with restrained derision by the assembled executives, who described it as an argument usable only by lawyers. They commented that, in the real world, any railroad would always favor directing business to its own subsidiary. I thought that was the end of the story until a telephone call came from the CEO some weeks later. As I recall it, he said, "You will never believe what happened after that meeting last month. When we returned to our offices that day, my colleagues went on arguing among themselves for hours. Finally, they ended up having convinced themselves that you were right after all. Their conversion was complete. 'Choose the low-cost barge line' has become an article of religion at our company, and anyone who violates the rule faces summary execution!"

CONCLUDING COMMENT

The theory of pricing for allocative efficiency in innovation and technology dissemination tells us a good deal about the optimal value of the license fee. When a court or a regulatory agency chooses to intervene, economic analysis is consequently in a position to offer concrete guidance for the determination of the fee and to show how the choice of fee affects economic efficiency. Here, as so often happens, the economist's rules turn out to call for fees very different than those regulators have tended to favor in analogous arenas.

The basic conclusion is that, although managerial and entrepreneurial contributions to technology transfer undoubtedly serve the public interest, they can be carried out in a manner that is efficient or one that is inefficient. Price, as usual, plays a key role here, and this chapter offers some insight on the nature and determination of an efficient price.

This chapter has thus provided another illustration of the ease with which innovation theory and other parts of microeconomic theory can be brought together. It has also continued with the theme in earlier chapters that licensing is a business in itself. The market for licenses, too, undoubtedly contributes to the growth performance of capitalism by speeding and facilitating the spread of technology and by helping to internalize the externalities resulting from innovation spillovers. Even though the potential recipients of spillover benefits often can obtain these benefits without payment of the license fee, the license market offers them the advantages of speed and lower cost that "hostile technology transfer" denies them. In an industry with rapid innovation, in which lagging transfer frequently means that the transferred technology is obsolete, the market mechanism is able to impose some degree of efficiency. Whether the prices that are determined by this market in reality are generally close to their efficient levels is, however, a question that is still requires study.

APPENDIX

MARGINAL VS. AVERAGE INCREMENTAL OPPORTUNITY COST AND SCALE ECONOMIES

In the discussion that follows, it will be convenient to use the term "direct costs" to refer to all costs other than opportunity costs. The ECPR principle tells us that the price of access to a bottleneck input should cover both of these. Their relative size is a matter of some interest here. The direct cost to the licensor of licensing an innovation can be negligible, unless it requires substantial training of licensee personnel or other such outlays to carry out the technology transfer. However, the opportunity costs can be large. This is clearly true if a patent holder's grant of the license to actual or prospective rivals permits those rivals to take much profitable business away from the patent holder. A high opportunity cost is also likely if the resulting rivalry forces prices down or increases the patent holder's advertising or other costs. Thus, it is plausible that the costs relevant to efficient pricing of a patent license may consist largely, and sometimes almost entirely, of these sorts of opportunity costs.

However, there is a subtle complication that does not seem widely recognized. In some cases, although total opportunity costs are substantial, they are likely to be close to zero at the margin. There will, of course, normally be a marginal opportunity cost when some fully utilized facility or other input with limited total capacity is sold or rented, so that the more the seller supplies to others, the less is left for its own use. A firm that lets others use a bridge whose capacity was already fully employed in transporting its own products can be expected to incur such an opportunity cost. But the public-good attribute of an innovation means that the grant of a license to others need not have such a capacity limitation.

So, when innovative activity is routinized, the profit-maximizing firm's investment in innovation will be expanded to the point where its expected marginal economic profit is zero. It can therefore be argued that the relevant opportunity cost of patent licensing or sale of any other bottleneck input by such a firm will also be close to zero.

This argument, however, misses the nature of the pertinent margin. If the licensee is able to take away a high proportion of the sales of the patent holder's competing final product, more than just the zero-profit marginal unit of its original sales volume is likely to be lost. That is, a substantial infra-marginal opportunity cost is then likely to result for the licensor firm. That is why the average incremental opportunity cost rather than the marginal opportunity cost is what I have taken into account in my discussion of the setting of the license fee.

But there is another reason—scale economies—why the opportunity cost of the licensing of a patent can play an important role in the determination of an efficient price for use of an invention. As we know, in an output-producing activity that is characterized by declining average incremental cost,[17] the market will, in equilibrium, assign the entire output to a single producer. For, if production of the output were divided up among several enterprises, the total resources cost must be greater than if production is carried out exclusively by the most efficient possible producer. Then the efficiency issue is not how much of the total output should be produced by each participating firm (as in the interior solution that one expects in the diminishing returns case most often considered in the literature). Rather, the issue is which of the firms can produce the entire output at lowest resources cost (in the scale economies corner solution). The most efficient producer in the scale economies case is a single firm that can produce the entire output at the lowest total incremental cost (or, what amounts to the same thing, at lowest average incremental cost).[18]

---

17. In a multi-product firm or industry with costs that are fixed and common to several of its products, average total cost is not even definable, because the fixed and common costs can be divided only in an arbitrary manner among those products. However, even then, each product does have uniquely defined total and average incremental costs—that is, the addition to cost that occurs, *ceteris paribus,* as a result of the addition of the product in question to the entire product line.

18. This statement assumes that total industry output of the commodity is fixed so that the most efficient firm is the one that can provide that given output with lowest

Thus, where there are scale economies, average incremental cost replaces marginal cost as the cost standard pertinent to efficiency in production.

More than that, if the product has declining average incremental cost (AIC), efficiency requires that the firm's price not be lower than its average incremental cost. For, if firm A sets the price of Y below its AIC, that low price can prevent production by more efficient firm B, whose AIC for Y is less than A's but is above A's price. In other words, the textbook efficiency rules must be modified in this case, with AIC playing at least part of the normal role of marginal cost (MC) in the case of diminishing returns.

---

resources use. In practice, of course, different firms have different cost functions, and a firm will consequently produce an output quantity different from another firm's when the former is the exclusive producer of the item in question. This still need create no difficulties in defining and identifying the more efficient of the candidate producers unless there are, say, two firms, A and B, with A having the lower average incremental cost (AIC) at the output quantity, y_a, of good Y that it would produce if it were sole producer of Y, and with B having the lower AIC at its output level, y_b.

PART III

On the Macrodynamics of Capitalism

CHAPTER 14

Capitalism's Unique Innovation Machine: Historical Evidence

The bourgeoisie . . . has created more massive and more colossal productive forces than have all preceding generations together. . . . The feudal organization of agriculture and manufacturing industry . . . hindered production instead of developing it. . . . [I]nto their place stepped free competition accompanied by a social and political constitution adapted to it.

—Marx and Engels, 1847

[by 1920] the astonishing thing was that the son of the millionaire ever succeeded in graduating, for previously ignorance had been one of the privileges of the wealthy classes. Now, however, they were forced to apply themselves to their studies like everyone else. The leveling process was equally noticeable in the life of the aristocracy and the great families. Sons of these families now made their careers in offices, or went into banking, the export trade, shopkeeping, or the liberal professions. A half-century earlier, any such careers would have been thought dishonorable.

—de Meeüs, 1962, p. 357

This third part of the book takes a preliminary look at the bottom line of our discussion: What does it all add up to for the economy as a whole? Part I and portions of part II have sought to contribute some analysis of the free-enterprise growth process, viewed from the microeconomic side. I have contended that this is where one *must* look to discover the critical attributes of the capitalist growth process that account for its unparalleled accomplishments. But that is not enough. Even if we were to prove that each of the components, individually, works in the right direction, it would not follow that taken together they still do so. At least abstractly, it is surely possible that the success of one of these components can turn out to interfere with the effectiveness of another. To get to the heart of the matter, we are forced to abandon the microscope and turn to the telescope. We have to consider how the pieces hang together, recognizing that here the macroeconomic orientation must take control.

Accordingly, part III provides both theoretical models and historical evidence related to the capitalist growth process. As it turns out, there *are* relationships among elements of the macroeconomy in which success of one of capitalism's growth components handicaps the success of another key attribute. But before we get to the modified macromodels in the following two chapters, which show this and offer other insights, I will review some pertinent historical material that deals with economies, some ancient and some more recent, some with outstanding records of invention but generally poorer performance in terms of subsequent innovation. This historical material provides further insights into the nature of the influences that affect innovation and its contribution to growth in economies of different types.

This chapter looks at some of the most relevant historical episodes in order to explore the relation between the record of invention of the past few centuries and the extraordinary growth performance of the competitive market economies. There were apparently no forces in any earlier society comparable to those that promote innovation in the capitalist economies. Although, as is so well known, several previous societies have had remarkable records of invention, none of them seems to have had institutional arrangements capable of driving decision makers forcefully toward the next stage—the innovation step that puts the invention to substantial economic use. Indeed, in China and the classical world, powerful influences were at work in the opposite direction, most notably sabotage by governmental institutions and the low esteem accorded commercial and productive activity (at least outside of agriculture). In other periods, competition was systematically, if imperfectly, suppressed—as under the guild system—so that there was little role for an aggressive weapon such as rivalrous innovation. What incentive remained was severely handicapped by the fact that the notion of progress of any sort, let alone technical progress, was foreign to the ways of thinking for long periods of time, for example during the early Middle Ages.[1] Historians have suggested that in such periods, if the attention of a contemporary had been drawn to the change that was actually going on, that person might well just have denied it.

1. Moreover, that period was characterized by severe distrust of any inquiry into facts and explanations, let alone anything that might be considered to resemble research. Such activity was suspect because it constituted "prying into God's secrets."

The historical episodes that will be reviewed also underscore a critical point. The availability of human capital may be necessary but is surely not sufficient by itself to ensure a firm connection between invention and economic growth. This requires, in addition, a set of powerful incentives, such as the free market provides, to ensure a continuous flow of inventions and their transformation through the innovation stage into a direct contribution to productivity and output growth.

I begin with a review of some remarkable facts about relatively recent European economic history that suggest not only why earlier forms of economic organization failed to provide the powerful pressures that enforce innovation under modern capitalism, but how these alternative economic systems systematically *impeded* innovation. This surely helps to explain why the Industrial Revolution required so much more time to take over the economies of a number of countries on the European continent, and why their growth lagged that of the United Kingdom for so long.

THE SERVILE ECONOMIES OF EIGHTEENTH- AND NINETEENTH-CENTURY EUROPE

Noted historian Jerome Blum, who is the primary source of the material in this section, referred to the bulk of the nations in continental Europe before the mid-nineteenth century as the "servile states" (Blum, 1978). By this he meant that these countries, including France (up until the revolution), the Germanic states, the Habsburg lands, Denmark, Poland, and Russia, retained the institution of serfdom, a number of them until the 1850s. This was not a peripheral phenomenon because some 80 percent of the labor force was then employed in agriculture, and most agricultural workers were subject to rules of serfdom of varying degrees of severity. It will not surprise the reader that, according to contemporary reports, when serfs carried out the labor obligations they owed to their lords they did so with a minimal outlay of effort. Serfs determinedly resisted any attempts at change, fearing that it was just a way to reduce their meager incomes or to extract additional work from them. What may be more unexpected is that the vast preponderance of seigniors (the nobles) also resisted innovation, including those innovations that promised substantial increases in productivity.

As I review the history of these "servile states" to look for an explanation of the resistance to innovation by the noble landed proprietors, I will note the marked contrasts with institutions in England, where the local version of serfdom had, in fact, largely disappeared by the end of the fifteenth century. Similarly, in the American colonies and, afterwards, in the United States—apart from the institution of slavery and a limited number of indentured servants—agriculture was carried out on a free-market, competitive basis from the beginning of European white settlement.

In the eighteenth and nineteenth centuries the vast majority of the labor force everywhere was agricultural. That was true in the United States as well as in Great Britain. This helps to explain why the first half-century of the Industrial Revolution in Britain achieved such negligible growth rates (estimates run to 0.03 percent per year growth in per capita GDP from approximately 1780 to 1830). Certainly, in the countries where serfdom still prevailed, pursuits that were not agricultural engaged a small minority of the labor force:

> Estimated ratios of rural populations: France, 85 per cent in 1789, Switzerland, 68 per cent in 1800, Germany, 80 per cent in 1800; Denmark, 80 per cent in 1769, Poland, 72 per cent ca. 1800, Hungary, over 90 per cent ca. 1800, Estonia, 84 per cent in 1782, Russia, 92 per cent in 1851. (Blum, 1978, p. 3; Blum's references omitted)

Even in these countries there were some free laborers, but the great preponderance of the workers who were employed in agrarian pursuits were subject to some sort of serfdom. This generally meant that the individual was tied to the land and was not permitted to change location or occupation without permission of the lord who held that land. Moreover, a serf generally owed the seignior a variety of services, notably a fixed period of labor per week on the lord's own land.

> The explanation for the inefficiency of the labor obligation in all of the servile lands lay in the fact that it was compulsory and that the workers received no pay. The peasants knew that no matter how poorly they performed the labor service, the seignior had no recourse. There were no wages for him to reduce or withhold, nor could he discharge the workers, since then he would lose whatever labors they did accomplish for him. The peasants took no interest in the task assigned to them; they tried to do as little as they could; indeed, according to Albrecht Thaer, they considered it a point of honor to cheat the seignior in the performance of the obligation. (Blum, 1978, p. 319)

Blum also reports the remarkable determination of the serfs to resist productivity-enhancing change. To put it in modern terms, both product and process innovations were opposed and long delayed, if not thwarted altogether. Workers fought the adoption of new and soil-regenerating crops, whose rotation with the more usual agricultural produce vastly enhanced output over what the traditional fallow field system could provide. They battled the introduction of new products such as the potato and other migrants from the New World, which offered far more nutrition per hour of labor and per unit of land than the traditional bread grains. They sought to prevent the introduction of foreign breeds of sheep, even though they demonstrably offered more wool as well as more meat. This resistance can be attributed to massive ignorance and conservatism. But it can also partly be ascribed to fear that any change would increase the exploitation of the serf by the master, as it had in the past.

> The endeavors of parish priests, and of seigniors, agricultural societies and governmental agencies to spread the practices of progressive farming met with even less success among the peasants than it did among the masters. Most seigniors met the recommendations with apathy. Peasants actively resisted them. Those who had insecure tenures, or who lived in villages that periodically redistributed holdings, saw no advantage in investing time and money to make improvements whose benefits they might not enjoy. Anyway, few of them, no matter what their tenure, had the available capital resources needed to make improvements. They reasoned, too, that most of the increased product that improvements might bring would be taken from them by increased demands from their seigniors. They were suspicious of the propagandists, who were all of the upper orders of society. Experience had taught them to be wary of those who for so long had exploited and scorned them, and who now suddenly assumed the guise of their benefactors. They realized that enclosure of common lands, and consolidation of scattered strips, would work severe hardships on the poorest villagers, who depended so much upon the right to pasture their few cattle on commons and fallow fields. Ignorance and superstition, and their constant companion, fear of anything new, also had much to do with their rejection of any and all improvements. An official of Zurich reported in 1787 that the peasant's "preconceived opinions bristle at everything which lies outside his obsolete way of thinking, and through hardheadedness, obstinacy, and uncooperative behavior, he often makes even the best arrangements ineffectual and useless." The pressures of conformity had considerable influence, too. The adoption of a change, even a relatively minor one, involved abandonment of customs and traditions that formed part of the fabric of village life. It took a strong will to withstand the criticism, and even the opprobrium, of neighbors that an innovation would bring, and to survive their ridicule if the innovation did not succeed. (Blum, 1978, p. 292)

As already noted, it was not only the peasants who resisted innovation; their masters did so as well. The seigniors' rejection of productivity-increasing innovation has at least two explanations. The first is found in the historical circumstances of the era, which encompassed both the pretensions of the rulers to absolute monarchy and the spread of enlightened despotism. Both of these goals created a chasm between the kings and their aristocracy. It was, after all, only the nobles who could possess power sufficient to curb or even thwart the absolute rule of king or emperor, and it was they who perceived themselves as having most to lose when an enlightened monarch undertook to reduce the harshness of the institution of serfdom or sought to abolish it altogether. The seigniors had every reason to fear any change as yet another opportunity for the monarch to curb their powers.

For us, the second reason for aristocratic opposition to innovation is more directly to the point. There was no competitive market mechanism to force the landed nobility to battle for superiority of performance in terms of productivity or product quality. Their lands continued to yield income that was largely unaffected by direct rivalry of other landed proprietors. Although this income was often insufficient for their prodigious spending habits—leading to frequent bankruptcy, impoverishment, and forced sales of properties, particularly in the nineteenth century—this seems to have provided little incentive for competitive marketing behavior. There was a group of "improving landlords" who adopted new methods, new breeds, and new products, sometimes with substantial financial reward. But, unlike in England, on the Continent these were relative rarities; they had little effect on the market for agricultural products and did not distract most of the nobility from their customary pursuits by forcing them into a competitive innovation race.[2]

> Whether directly involved in agricultural production or whether the receiver of rents and seigniorial dues, the usual noble of the servile lands did not look upon his property as an enterprise to be run for profit. He considered its primary function to be the support of his household—his family and domestic staff. Only the surplus left after meeting his needs went to the market. That included the surplus from his payments in kind, as well as the surplus from his own production. . . . Conspicuous consumption and

2. Still, something surely did happen to increase agricultural output on the Continent before the end of serfdom, since the famines that caused regular widespread starvation throughout continental Europe as late as the end of the seventeenth century seem largely to have ended by the eighteenth. The explanation can perhaps be found in rising productivity in the Netherlands and England and the resulting availability of cheaper products from abroad, though in an economy making little use of money this explanation is not very persuasive. There also seems to have been an improvement in the climate at the time, which may have made a major contribution to agricultural productivity.

> ostentatious display were matters of great moment to a nobleman. They could determine his social and political status among his peers and affect his own and his family's fortunes. And so the usual noble showed scant interest in investment in improvements to increase the productivity of his property. That would postpone present consumption, and most nobles did not think in those terms. In any event, the many petty seigniors who in the best of times barely managed to make ends meet, and who lived always in fear of ruin, could not afford to invest for future gains. . . .
>
> There were, of course, proprietors who were market-oriented and who wanted to make a profit from their estates. Nobles invested in business enterprises, too; some of the great families of France had money in Flemish mines, forges and iron works, and in the colonial trade. Many proprietors in Schleswig-Holstein, in the Baltic lands, in Prussia and Silesia and in Bohemia were active producers of grain and other commodities for the domestic market and for export to western Europe. The provincial nobility of Bordeaux, Rennes, and Toulouse had long been actively engaged in production for market and were shrewd, profit-oriented businessmen. And there was a small, but as history was to prove, a very influential group of noble proprietors scattered through the servile lands who led in the introduction of innovations designed to increase the productivity of agriculture as well as the revenues of the proprietors.
>
> Whatever their interest or lack of it in commercial agriculture, the fact was that in every land nobles or large renters were by far the chief suppliers of farm goods to the market. The peasants, overburdened by their obligations, were barely able to support themselves from their labors, and usually had little left over for sale. (Blum, 1978, pp. 160–61)

> As with innovating entrepreneurs in other fields, the numbers of these "improving landlords" were strikingly small. Careful examination by Michael Confino found only seven instances in all of Russia of efforts to introduce improved agriculture in the last three decades of the eighteenth century. The number increased during the first half of the nineteenth century, but was still a tiny fraction of the many thousands of Russian proprietors. In Hungary in the first half of the nineteenth century, not more than twenty to twenty-five landowners employed progressive methods on their properties. A small number of French proprietors, principally from the highest levels of the nobility, applied the teachings of the new husbandry to their land. Most landowners showed no interest in the innovations. (Blum, 1978, p. 285)

The bottom line is that the servile states of the European continent emphatically lacked the competitive market pressures for innovation that in England and, later, the United States arguably drove the economy toward rapid growth.

CHAPTER 14

TECHNOLOGICAL ACHIEVEMENTS IN ANCIENT ROME

A second instructive historical case is that of ancient Rome, a society that apparently produced a good deal of invention but little innovation. A variety of inventions are credited to Rome, notably in construction. The vestiges of Roman roads, Roman aqueducts, and Roman baths continue to impress tourists. Roman water mills were fairly sophisticated devices. The society even produced a working steam engine. However, none of these seems to have been employed systematically for productive purposes.

The explanation appears to be reasonably clear. Several respectable avenues were open to those Romans who sought power and prestige. Indeed, they had no reservations about the desirability of wealth or about its pursuit (see, for example, Finley, 1985, pp. 53–57). So long as it did not involve participation in industry or commerce, there was nothing degrading about the acquisition of wealth. Persons of honorable status had four primary and acceptable sources of income: landholding (not infrequently as absentee landlords); booty and ransom from aggressive military enterprises; money lending ("usury"); and what may be described as political payments, including what we would call "bribery." Finley writes:

> The opportunity for "political moneymaking" can hardly be overestimated. Money poured in from booty, indemnities, provincial taxes, loans and miscellaneous exactions in quantities without precedent in Graeco-Roman history, and at an accelerating rate. The public treasury benefited, but probably more remained in private hands, among the nobles in the first instance. . . .
>
> Nevertheless, the whole phenomenon is misunderstood when it is classified under the headings of "corruption" and "malpractice," as historians still persist in doing. Cicero was an honest governor of Cilicia in 51 and 50 B.C., so that at the end of his term he had earned only the legitimate profits of office. They amounted to 2,200,000 sesterces, more than treble the figure of 600,000 he himself once mentioned (*Stoic Paradoxes 49*) to illustrate an annual income that could permit a life of luxury. We are faced with something structural in the society. (1985, p. 55)

On the Romans' attitudes to the promotion of technology and productivity, Finley cites Vitruvius' monumental work on architecture and technology in whose ten books he finds only a *single* and trivial reference to means of saving effort and increasing productivity. Finley then reports:

> There is a story, repeated by a number of Roman writers, that a man—characteristically unnamed—invented unbreakable glass and demonstrated

> it to Tiberius in anticipation of a great reward. The emperor asked the inventor whether anyone shared his secret and was assured that there was no one else; whereupon his head was promptly removed, lest, said Tiberius, gold be reduced to the value of mud. I have no opinion about the truth of this story, and it is only a story. But is it not interesting that neither the elder Pliny nor Petronius nor the historian Dio Cassius was troubled by the point that the inventor turned to the emperor for a reward, instead of turning to an investor for capital with which to put his invention into production? (1985, p. 147)[3]

The vigor of inventive activity that nevertheless characterized Roman society has already been noted. By the first century B.C., Alexandria, the center of technological invention in the Roman empire, possessed virtually every form of machine gearing that is used today and, as already noted, had a working steam engine! But these seem to have served largely as what amounted to elaborate toys. The steam engine was used only to open and close the doors of a temple. Rome also had the water mill, arguably the most critical pre-eighteenth-century industrial invention, because it provided the first significant source of power other than human and animal labor: "[I]t was able to produce an amount of concentrated energy beyond any other resource of antiquity" (Forbes, 1955, II, p. 90). Like steam in more recent centuries, the water mill promised a leap in productivity in the Roman economy—and apparently actually delivered it during the eleventh, twelfth, and thirteenth centuries in Europe. Yet, according to Reynolds (1983, p. 17), the knowledgeable Vitruvius, writing in about 25 B.C., listed water mills in a section of his great work devoted to "rarely-used machinery." And Finley (1985, pp. 35–36), citing White, reports that "though it was invented in the first century B.C., it was not until the third century A.D. that we find evidence of much use and not until the fifth and sixth of general use. It is also a fact that we have no evidence at all of its application to other industries (i.e., other than grinding of grain) until the very end of the fourth century, and then no more than one solitary and possibly suspect reference to a marble-slicing machine near Trier."

In an economy in which commerce and industry were disreputable activities, in which rent-seeking and destructive enterprise were the respectable

3. To be fair to Finley, we may note that he concludes that it is *not* really interesting. North and Thomas (1973, p. 3) make a similar point about Harrison's invention of the ship's chronometer in the eighteenth century (as an instrument indispensable for the determination of longitude). They point out that the incentive for this invention was a large governmental prize rather than the prospect of commercial profit, presumably because of the absence of effective patent protection.

avenues to wealth, and in which one hears nothing of markets characterized by vigorous competition entailing innovative commodities and production processes, the evidence suggesting substantial technical stagnation does not seem extremely surprising.

THE ASTONISHING INVENTIONS OF MEDIEVAL CHINA

The impressive set of inventions produced in ancient China, mostly in the T'ang (A.D. 618–906) and Sung (A.D. 960–1126) dynasties, constituted one of the earliest prospective revolutions in industry. Among the many Chinese technological contributions one can list paper, movable type, the water wheel sophisticated water clocks, and, of course, gunpowder. But those are only the beginning of the list. Mokyr (1990a) adds the spinning wheel, which "appeared about the same time in China and the West—the thirteenth century (possibly somewhat earlier in China)—but advanced much faster and further in China . . . a small multispindle spinning wheel, not unlike Hargreaves' spinning jenny" (p. 212); a mechanical cotton gin; hydraulic trip hammers (eighth century); ship construction techniques that permitted the production of vessels "much larger and more seaworthy than the best European ships"; the sternpost rudder; superior sail designs providing far greater maneuverability than Western ships could muster before the fifteenth century; porcelain; the umbrella; matches; the toothbrush; playing cards; and many, many others.[4]

But in China, as in Rome, these inventions strikingly failed to serve as the basis for the growth and spread of industry throughout the economy, even during the times of the country's greatest prosperity (see, for example, Liu and Golas, 1969).[5] Commerce did flourish, but there seems to have been little upheaval in the production of nonagricultural goods, such as a switch in production from the artisan's shop to the factory. It would, no doubt, be

4. Needham (1964a, 1964b, 1981) provides the classic description and analysis of Chinese technology and invention. A briefer but excellent discussion is in Mokyr (1990a, chapter 9).

5. Also, as in Rome, none of this was associated with the emergence of a systematic body of science involving coherent theoretical structure and the systematic testing of hypotheses on the basis of experiment or empirical observation. Here, the thirteenth-century work in England of Bishop Grosseteste, William of Henley, and Roger Bacon was an early step toward that unique historical phenomenon—the emergence of a systematic body of science in the West in the sixteenth century (see Needham, 1956).

unreasonable to expect to find the satanic mills of nineteenth-century Birmingham and Manchester in medieval China. But the remarkable number and variety of water mills that crowded the banks of the Seine and dotted the landscape of southern England in the later Middle Ages (see below) seem also to have been missing from the Chinese countryside. It is noteworthy here that, as in Rome, the technical know-how was available in impressive abundance but seems never to have led to any commensurate addition to the ability and willingness of industry to make use of that knowledge.[6]

The explanations for this lack parallel those I offered for the case of Rome, but include others as well. Perhaps most notable was the propensity of government to expropriate and exploit for its own purposes any inventions that the bureaucracy had not succeeded in suppressing. In China, as in many kingdoms of Europe before the guarantees of the Magna Carta and the revival of towns and their acquisition of privileges, monarchs commonly claimed ownership of all property in their lands. Consequently, and particularly in China, when the sovereign was in financial straits, confiscation of the property of wealthy subjects was considered appropriate. It has been claimed that this led those with resources to avoid investing them in any sort of visible capital stocks, and that this, in turn, was a substantial impediment to economic expansion.[7]

Innovation of a practical sort was also frowned upon by the bureaucracy, which was, however, willing enough to take over for its own use any novel product or process that had escaped its vigilance. Balazs tells us of:

> the state's tendency to clamp down immediately on any form of private enterprise . . . or, if it did not succeed in putting a stop to it in time, to take over and nationalize it. Did it not frequently happen during the course of Chinese history that the scholar-officials, although hostile to all inventions, nevertheless gathered in the fruits of other people's ingenuity? I need mention only three examples of inventions that met this fate: paper, invented by a eunuch; printing, used by the Buddhists as a medium for religious propaganda; and the bill of exchange, an expedient of private businessmen. (1964, p. 18)

In addition, Imperial China reserved its most substantial rewards in wealth and prestige to those who climbed the ladder of imperial examina-

6. The following discussion is entirely consistent with that in Landes (forthcoming in 2002), though I had not seen the latter when my discussion was first written.

7. See Balasz (1964, p. 53); Landes (1969, pp. 46–47); Rosenberg and Birdzell (1986, pp. 119–20); and Jones (1987, chapter 5).

tions, which were heavily slanted to "impractical" subjects such as Confucian philosophy and calligraphy. Successful candidates were often awarded high rank in the bureaucracy, a social standing denied to anyone engaged in commerce or industry—even those who gained great wealth in the process (and who often used their resources to prepare their descendants to contend via the examinations for a position in the scholar bureaucracy). In other words, the prevailing "rules of the game" for Imperial Chinese economic activity seem to have been heavily biased against the acquisition of wealth and position through competitive and productive behavior. The avenue to success lay elsewhere.

Because of the difficulty of the examinations, the mandarins (the scholar-officials) rarely succeeded in keeping such positions in their own families for more than two or three generations.[8] The scholar-families devoted enormous effort and considerable resources to preparing their children through years of laborious study for the imperial examinations. During the Sung Dynasty, these were held every three years, and only a few hundred persons in all of China succeeded in passing them each time (Kracke in Liu and Golas, 1969, p. 14). Yet, regularly, some persons not from mandarin families also attained success through this avenue.[9] Wealth was in prospect for those who passed the examination and who were subsequently appointed to government positions. But the sources of their earnings had something in common with those of the Romans.

> Corruption, which is widespread in all impoverished and backward countries (or, more exactly, throughout the pre-industrial world), was endemic in a country where the servants of the state often had nothing to live on but their very meager salaries. The required attitude of obedience to superiors made it impossible for officials to demand higher salaries, and in the absence of any control over their activities from below it was inevitable that they should purloin from society what the state failed to provide. According to the usual pattern, a Chinese official entered upon his duties only after spending long years in study and passing many examinations; he then established relations with protectors, incurred debts to get himself appointed, and then proceeded to extract the amount he had spent on preparing himself for his career from the people he administered—and extracted both principal and interest. The degree of his rapacity would be dictated not only by the length of time he had to wait for his appointment

8. See Marsh (1961, p. 159) and Ping-Ti Ho (1962, chapter 4 and appendix).

9. See, e.g., Marsh (1961) and Ping-Ti Ho (1962) for evidence on social mobility in Imperial China.

and the number of relations he had to support and of kin to satisfy or repay, but also by the precariousness of his position. (Balazs, 1964, p. 10)

Perhaps as a result of recurrent intervention by the state to curtail the liberty of the merchant class and take over any accumulated advantages it had managed to gain for itself through enterprise, "the merchant's ambition turned to becoming a scholar-official and investing his profits in land" (Balazs, 1964, p. 32). Once again, we find no sign in this economy of a vigorous competitive market in which innovation is a primary weapon.[10]

A PUZZLING COUNTEREXAMPLE: AN EARLY INDUSTRIAL REVOLUTION IN THE LATER MIDDLE AGES

There is, however, a historical episode suggesting that innovation can sometimes explode without the presence of competitive market pressures. By the end of the eleventh century in Europe, the Dark Ages had given way to a new set of circumstances. The revival of the towns was well under way. Towns, as entities, had acquired a number of privileges, including some protection from arbitrary taxation and confiscation, and an independent labor force made up of runaway serfs who had been granted their freedom after the requisite one year and a day. The anarchic military activity of the barons—formerly a dominant mode of wealth-accumulating free enterprise—had at least been impeded by the Church's pacification efforts, including the "Peace of God" and the (later) "Truce of God" in France, Spain, and elsewhere. Similar changes were taking place in England (see, for example, Cowdrey, 1970), though free-enterprise military activity by the barons lasted at least through the Wars of

10. The essence of the matter is that in medieval China, as in the Soviet Union, the problem was not just absence of an innovation machine but, worse still, the presence of a mechanism that served to thwart innovation if not to prevent it altogether. Thus, Landes (1998, pp. 341–42) tells us for the Chinese case: "The would-be modernizers were thwarted . . . not only by brittle insecurities but also by the intrigue of a palace milieu where innovations were judged by their consequences for the pecking order. No proposal that did not incite resistance; no novelty that did not frighten vested interests. At all levels, moreover, fear of reprimand (or worse) outweighed the prospect of reward. A good idea brought credit to one's superior; a mistake invariably meant blame for subordinates. It was easier to tell superiors what they wanted to hear. . . . Imperial China is not alone here. The smothering of incentives and the cultivation of mendacity are a characteristic of large bureaucracies, whether public or private [business corporations]." The remark about large corporations is, of course, valid but, unlike despotisms, the market constrains the effects by causing disaster for firms that are paralyzed by bureaucratic resistance to effective change.

the Roses, and Jones (1987, p. 94) suggests that it continued into the reigns of the earlier Tudors in the sixteenth century. Finally, a number of activities that were neither agricultural nor military began to yield handsome returns. For example, the small group of architect-engineers in charge of the building of cathedrals, palaces, bridges, and fortresses were able to live in great luxury in the service of their kings.

A good deal has been written about the successful industrial revolution of the late Middle Ages and the accompanying commercial revolution sparked by inventions such as double-entry bookkeeping and bills of exchange (see De Roover, 1953). It seems to have contributed (as did the considerable changes in agricultural methods) to widespread, though probably modest, increases in living standards. Its two-century duration makes it as long-lived as the more recent Industrial Revolution (see Gimpel, 1976; White, 1962; and Carus-Wilson, 1941).

Perhaps the hallmark and most remarkable technological feature of the earlier industrial revolution was that extraordinary source of productive power, the water mill. These mills covered the countryside in the south of England and crowded the banks of the Seine in Paris (see, for example, Gimpel, 1976, pp. 3–6; and Berman, 1986, pp. 81–89). They were not only simple grain-grinding devices. Rather, they accomplished an astonishing variety of tasks and used an impressive range of mechanical devices and sophisticated gear arrangements. The water mills crushed olives, ground mash for beer production, pressed cloth for paper making, sawed lumber, and hammered metal and woolens (as part of the "fulling" process, which cleaned, scoured, and pressed woven woolen goods to make them stronger and more tightly woven). Water mills also were used to produce coins, polish armor, and operate the bellows of blast furnaces.[11]

Their mechanisms showed many forms of ingenuity. Gears were used to transform the vertical circular motion of the efficient form of the water wheel into the horizontal circular motion of the millstone. The cam (a piece of wood, metal, or some other solid protruding at right angles from a rotating shaft such as the axle of the water wheel) served to lift a heavy hammer. This was pivoted like a seesaw, and the cam let it drop by its own weight, repeatedly and automatically (this mechanism was apparently also known in antiquity, but may not have been used then with water wheels). A crank handle extending from the end of the axle transformed the circular motion of the

11. For a more complete and systematic list of the remarkable variety of applications of the water wheel, see Reynolds (1983, pp. 77, 94).

wheel into the back and forth (reciprocating) motion required for sawing or the operation of bellows. By the beginning of the fourteenth century, according to Gimpel (1976), sixty-eight mills were in operation along less than one mile of the banks of the Seine in Paris, and these were supplemented by floating mills anchored to the Grand Pont. The activity in metallurgy was also considerable—sufficient to denude much of Europe of its forests and to produce a rise in the price of wood that forced recourse to coal.[12]

As White sums up the technological accomplishments of the period, "the four centuries following Leonardo, that is, until electrical energy demanded a supplementary set of devices, were less technically engaged in discovering basic principles than in elaborating and refining those established during the four centuries before Leonardo" (1962, p. 129).[13] The most sophisticated product in this era of mechanical skill and knowledge was the mechanical clock, which appeared toward the end of the thirteenth century. For the first time, humans could tell the time even when cloudy skies prevented use of the sun dial, or when freezing temperatures stopped the water clocks.

In sum, the twelfth–thirteenth-century industrial revolution was a surprisingly robust affair, and it is implausible that improved rewards to industrial activity had little to do with its vigor. Yet there seems to be no reason to ascribe the revolution to competitive-market pressures. Indeed, a prime incentive for such technical advances may have been the monopoly they gave their owners. Such monopoly rights were sought and enforced by private parties (Bloch, 1935, pp. 554–57; Brooke, 1964, p. 84) and by religious organizations. It is a striking fact that the leaders in this industrial revolution were not primarily capitalists struggling to accumulate personal wealth, but the monasteries, notably the Cistercian abbeys.

12. Other historians assert, however, that this did not occur to any substantial degree until the fifteenth or sixteenth centuries, with some question even about those dates; see, e.g., Coleman (1975, pp. 42–43).

13. As already noted, science and scientific method also began to make an appearance with contributions such as those of Bishop Grosseteste and Roger Bacon. Walter of Henley championed controlled experiments and observation over recourse to the opinions of ancient authorities, and made a clear distinction between economic and engineering efficiency in discussing the advisability of substituting horses for oxen. And that obstreperous monk Roger Bacon displayed remarkable foresight when he wrote, circa 1260:

> Machines may be made by which the largest ships, with only one man steering them, will be moved faster than if they were filled with rowers; wagons may be built which will move with incredible speed and without aid of beast; flying machines can be constructed in which a man . . . may beat the air with wings like a bird . . . machines will make it possible to go to the bottom of seas and rivers. (Quoted in White, 1962, p. 130).

Historians tell us that they have no ready explanation for the entrepreneurial propensities of this monastic order.[14] Constance Berman, in a personal communication, suggests that this may all have been part of the twelfth-century monastic drive to reduce or eliminate manual labor in order to maximize the time available for the less onerous religious labors—a conclusion with which Bloch (1935, p. 553) concurs.[15] But the evidence indicates strongly what avid entrepreneurs the monasteries were. They accumulated vast tracts of land; the sizes of their domesticated animal flocks were enormous by the standards of the time; and their investment rates were remarkable. And in all this they were vigorous in their pursuit and exercise of monopoly power—being known, after the erection of a Cistercian water mill, to seek legal intervention to prevent nearby residents from continuing to use their animal-powered facilities (Gimpel, 1976, pp. 15–16). The Cistercians were fierce in their rivalrous behavior and drive for expansion, in the process not sparing other religious bodies—not even other Cistercian houses. There is "a record of pastoral expansionism and monopolies over access established by the wealthiest Cistercian houses . . . at the expense of smaller abbeys and convents . . . effectively pushing out all other religious houses as competitors" (Berman, 1986, p. 112).

Even where private enterprise rather than monastic activity operated the water mills, pursuit of monopoly rather than competition was characteristic. It has just been noted that a very important use of the water wheel was in the laborious process of fulling. In earlier days this had been done by human hand

14. See, e.g., Brooke (1964, p. 69), and also a personal communication from Constance Berman; but see Ovitt (1987, especially pp. 142–47).

15. I have been able to construct some hypotheses to account for the apparently superior entrepreneurship of the Cistercians. The most plausible story is that, by the time in question, attitudes toward labor had changed in other monastic orders. They now held that the labor religious doctrine required the monks to perform could legitimately consist entirely of religious labor, e.g., that of scribes and illustrators of manuscripts. The more onerous tasks in the fields and elsewhere needed to keep the monastery going could then be performed exclusively by hired "lay brothers." According to this account, the Cistercians lagged in acceptance of this view and continued to demand hard physical labor from the members of the order. That provided the incentive for them to seek labor-saving technical improvements, because they were permitted to devote any time saved in this way to more pleasant religious labor. Landes (1998, p. 58) writes: "One might have expected that organized spirituality . . . would have had little interest in technology. Surely the Church, with its view of labor as penalty for original sin, would not seek to ease the judgement. And yet everything worked in the opposite direction: the desire to free clerics from time-consuming earthly tasks led to the introduction and diffusion of power machinery and, beginning with the Cistercians, to the hiring of lay brothers (*conversi*) to do the dirty work." I must admit that this hypothesis is not overwhelmingly convincing and the evidence for it is marginal, though Dr. Berman commented that it was not implausible.

(or foot) and a good deal of the activity had been carried out in London. However, the absence of swift streams in the city put urban fullers at a competitive disadvantage to the mill-using fullers in the countryside. In 1298 (in the reign of Edward I) the London fullers consequently undertook a lawsuit, asking the King for protection, and claiming that if the country mills were permitted to continue their activity there would be "grave damage" to the men employed in the city. The King rejected their request but did offer them some concessions to ease their difficulties (Carus-Wilson, 1941, pp. 55, 58).

The records describe a profusion of monopoly-preserving litigation related to water mills (see, for example, Gimpel, 1976, chapter 1). These included cases in which the mill owner sought to enforce a monopoly by securing a prohibition on the use of human-powered mills by rivals and even by consumers. In other instances, upstream and downstream users fought for the water's power, battling over the dam sites and the height of the dams. One case is reported to have dragged on for more than a century; it was settled, finally, only by the bankruptcy of one of the parties, thereby illustrating one of the strategic approaches still used by litigating rent seekers: by imposing sufficient financial pressure upon the other party (or threatening to do so) one can hope to destroy the opponent or force its surrender, regardless of any decision by the court.

CONCLUDING COMMENT

The historical examples provided in this chapter can easily be supplemented by others. In chapter 5, a few remarks were offered on the Soviet economies, showing how they, too, were characterized by institutions that impeded innovation and growth. All of these cases consistently support two conclusions. First, no earlier or alternative recent form of economy seems to have had as its main driving mechanism free competitive markets, using innovation as a prime weapon. Second, the examples show that the absence of such a free and rivalrous market need not prevent the exercise of ingenuity and the appearance of remarkable inventions. But they indicate, with one noteworthy exception, that its absence does seem to weaken or even undermine the subsequent innovation steps—the steps that lead to widespread use of the inventions to fuel rapid economic growth.

CHAPTER 15

Macroeconomic Models and Relationships That May Limit Growth

although international trade widens the market attainable by a successful innovator and thus raises the incentive to do research, it also raises the cost of research by making labor more productive in manufacturing *[and therefore raising overall wages], with effects that tend to offset each other.*

—Aghion and Howitt, 1998, p. 5, emphasis added

This chapter differs from the materials in parts one and two of this book in two main ways. First, its analysis is macroeconomic rather than microeconomic. Secondly, and more substantially, it examines some of the forces that may conceivably bring the unprecedented growth performance of the capitalist economies to an end, slowing it to the pace of progress of earlier eras.

The question, then, is, how may such an ending come about? Of course, if the end of spectacular growth is sufficiently far in the future it is almost the same, as a practical matter, as never-ending advance. And such a very remote termination period cannot be ruled out, as will be suggested in this chapter and the next. Still, it is a vast understatement to say that all this is uncertain. Therefore, it is less fruitful to speculate about growth rates of the distant future than to examine some of the forces that work toward termination of rapid growth and those that work in the other direction. That is what this chapter and the next will do.

WHY TURN TO MACROECONOMICS?

I have argued here that the nature of the forces that can be credited with the extraordinary record of economic growth of the free-market economies requires us to study the behavior of individual firms and industries. So far, only microeconomic models have been used to investigate several distinctive features of capitalism that stimulate rapid growth. These models have described, for example, how fierce competition puts managements under constant pressure to avoid falling behind in industries where innovations in products and processes are prime weapons of inter-firm rivalry. But this still leaves unexplored how the innovative activities of all these firms add up. In other words, what is the effect on the economy as a whole of the combined innovative efforts of our rivalrous oligopolists? Here, the microanalyst is in danger of committing the fallacy of composition, that is, of arguing, without evidence, that the behavior of an individual enterprise is simply replicated on a larger scale in the behavior of the economy. We know that is not always so, and the main model of this chapter will provide a direct counterexample, in which the growth-promoting activities of the firm automatically generate forces that inhibit growth of the economy.

To deal with such issues, it is clearly useful to turn to macroeconomic analysis. Aggregating the agents of the economy into a small number of broad sectors facilitates analysis and permits clearer implications to be determined. The result will be a macroeconomic model of endogenous innovation, but one very different from many of the valuable constructs—including the work of Arrow (1962), Lucas (1988), Romer (1986, 1990), and others—that have attracted much deserved attention. The model offered here will attempt to deal explicitly and directly, if in a somewhat primitive manner, with the way in which economic forces direct the economy's innovation activities. Moreover, the model here is not ahistoric; that is, it contains elements that, it can be argued, are particularly characteristic of a free-market economy. This contrasts with the other macromodels to which I have just referred. There, decisions affecting innovation occur, so to speak, behind the scenes, so that we can see the results but can only indirectly infer the mechanism and the process that are responsible. Moreover, the production functions that arguably are at the heart of those analyses, like the rest of their structures, contain no particular features representing special characteristics of current historical circumstances. To show more specifically what this means, this chapter begins with a brief review of some pertinent features of those macromodels.

THE RELEVANCE OF MACROECONOMIC MODELS WITH ENDOGENOUS INNOVATION

Recent growth analysis had its beginnings in the 1950s with the work of Robert Solow (1956), who deservedly elicited renewed interest in models of growth and who designed approaches compatible with statistical estimation. For our purposes, it is most pertinent to consider the extent to which these models, notably the more recent ones that have been described as "endogenous innovation models," actually bring out the behavior of the innovation process and its contribution to growth. I will suggest that the endogenous innovation and the growth features of these models are only *implicit,* while my concerns in this book require me to make the innovation process more *explicit,* in order to see just how the historical features of the free-market economy affect the innovation and growth processes. This will require construction of a model in which there are at least two sectors: the innovation sector and the rest of the economy.[1]

The current macromodels, like much of the economic literature, have older roots. Ricardo and other classical economists recognized that innovation does occur.[2] It results in a shifting of the production function and postponement of the stationary state, something that can occur repeatedly and can keep the economy expanding indefinitely. What is missing in the Ricardian story is any endogenous explanation of the innovation process and special historical features that affect it. That is why the innovation process in a formalization of the Ricardian model must be represented simply as $A(t)$, a (stochastic) function of time and nothing else, and with no distinguishing features that differentiate the process in a capitalist economy from that in any other form of economic organization.[3]

The original Solow model—the prototype neoclassical model—contains a representation of innovation not much different from Ricardo's, with invention also autonomous, and undifferentiated as between free-market economies and other economic forms. The model assumes that there are diminishing returns to capital, an attribute that predicts convergence of productivities and per capita incomes in different economies, because wealthier economies have relatively large capital stocks whose productivities, relative to those of poorer countries, are severely reduced by diminishing returns.

Two observations led Romer to argue that this neoclassical model requires some modification. First, he observed that the prediction of universal

1. Though my discussion focuses on endogenous innovation, it is, of course, not meant to imply that exogenous or purely fortuitous developments play no role.

2. And they were far less pessimistic about the future than is sometimes suggested. For the evidence, see Hollander (1998, p. 232) and Ricardo's parliamentary speeches, as reported in Gordon (1976).

3. The following discussion draws heavily on the symposium on New Growth Theory in the *Journal of Economic Perspectives* 8 (Winter 1994), pp. 3–72, and on Paul Romer's contribution in particular (1994b).

convergence—the catch-up of all economies to approximately the same levels of productivity and per capita income—apparently implied by the theory is not confirmed by the facts. The many statistical studies of the convergence hypothesis generally conclude that, although the growth performances of the wealthiest economies have, indeed, been moving closer together, most of the impecunious nations are falling further behind. Secondly, he noted (as students of the subject had long observed) that the innovation process is neither largely autonomous nor largely fortuitous. The amount of activity devoted to innovation, and the output of that activity, are influenced substantially by what else is going on in the economy. This led to a series of constructs referred to as the "endogenous growth models."

There is a common element in the approach to endogenization taken by many of these models. Each focuses on some source of enhanced growth, such as education or innovation. Let the value of this variable, call it innovation activity, contributed by agent j be represented by X_j. For the economy as a whole the corresponding value is, then, $X = \Sigma_j X_j$. If each innovating agent's output of new technology is a function not only of X_j but of X as well, it follows that there are spillovers from this sort of innovative activity. Then all innovators benefit from the activity of all other members of the group, but with the obvious impediment to efficient growth constituted by the resulting difference between private and social benefits of innovation activity. The Lucas model of 1988 is an example of this type of structure. It can be described as taking the production function to be $A(H)$, where H is the investment in human capital of the entire society, as distinguished from H_j, the corresponding investment by agent j. Similarly, the Romer model of 1986 can be taken to use a production function such as $A(R)$, where R is society's investment in the accumulation of knowledge, as distinguished from R_j, the corresponding variable by agent j.

The central point is that each of these models employs a production function that contains a growth component, $A(.)$, but that none of them has any attribute uniquely related to free-enterprise economies rather than some other economic form. That is what makes these models ahistorical. Moreover, where they do take account of innovation, the mechanism of the activity enters only implicitly. There is no equation or other relationship that attempts to describe, for example, the incentive structure that leads to determination of the magnitude of this activity.

Another significant difference between the approach of recent macrotheory and mine is the focus of the former on the role of such influences as learning-by-doing and accumulation of human capital, while I focus on the powerful pressures exerted by the free competitive market. Economic historians—Moses Abramovitz being a notable example—have concluded that economies cannot attain relatively rapid rates of growth without the human and social capability to absorb technology and employ it effectively, and this surely implies that they cannot create improved technology without these either. Thus, the macrotheorists are undoubtedly right in emphasizing the role of human capital and its use in the research process. There is also good reason to concur with Romer's judgment that "[t]his . . . offers one possible way to explain the wide variation in growth rates observed among countries and the fact that in some countries growth in income per capita has been close to zero" (1990, p. S96). On the other hand, it seems hard to explain the poverty in ancient Greece and the apparent absence of rapid growth in per capita incomes in ancient Rome and medieval China as resulting from the absence of human capital. As a matter of fact, in Imperial China human capital *was* sufficient to produce an astonishing stream of inventions, as we saw in chapter fourteen. But, although invention may have been abundant, innovation, defined as the critical step of effective utilization in the production process, was evidently rare in those economies. It is surely plausible that a critical part of the explanation was the absence of an effective incentive mechanism and, in particular, of a drivingly competitive market that rewarded innovation and mercilessly punished failure to take advantage of innovation opportunities.

I have already suggested one further link in this argument. Investment in human capital, like investment in plant and equipment, no doubt is to some degree itself an endogenous variable, and its magnitude is clearly increased by growth in the wealth of a nation. The free-market mechanism, through its stimulation of innovation, has served to create the national wealth that has permitted increased expenditure on education as well as on physical capital. The evidence is clearly consistent with the conclusion that rapid economic growth since the Industrial Revolution has increased real per capita expenditure on education far beyond anything previously experienced. Moreover, before the surge of innovations that launched the Industrial Revolution, the poverty of the economy meant that national savings were far too low to permit any substantial investment in human capital (or in physical capital).

Thus, whereas an upsurge in innovation was arguably a prerequisite for significantly expanded education, marked educational expansion does not seem to have been required for innovation. It took only a few relatively educated individuals in the eighteenth century to launch the "wave of gadgets" that underlay the Industrial Revolution in England. Indeed, neither James Watt nor John Harrison, the creators of probably the era's most economically important technological improvements, seems to have had a very advanced education. It can be argued that it was the free market that transformed such technological improvements into rapid economic growth, and that it was the growth, in turn, that underlay the spread of education. If so, although human capital investment must continue to be considered a necessary requirement for substantial technical progress, it can be argued that the capitalist market mechanism is both necessary and (indirectly) sufficient for the task. This is because the capitalist market mechanism serves not only to provide the incentives required for abundant innovative activity but also to stimulate the indispensable investment in human capital.

Earlier chapters sought to deal with the critical role of competition in innovative activity and growth, but did so at a cost. The microeconomic approach employed for the purpose prevented a formal analysis, even at a rudimentary level, of the implications for the economy as a whole. As a step toward elimination of this gap, this chapter provides a macroeconomic model, but one that is very different from the models that have just been discussed. In doing so, I make no claim of superiority of my model. I claim only that it is tied more closely to the microeconomic structures of earlier chapters, and that it seeks to shed light on aspects of the economy's growth mechanism different from those dealt with in the mainstream macromodels. Specifically, the model focuses on the influence of the cost of the (routine) research and development process, examining how this is affected by the economy's rate of growth of productivity. My arms-race ratchet model of R&D in chapter four will be taken into account, to show how the demand for R&D can be influenced by this cost. This leads directly to a feedback relationship in which R&D affects the future growth of the economy, and that growth, in turn, influences the volume of R&D. The model that describes this feedback will be used to bring together the disparate elements that have just been mentioned, and to tie them into a coherent whole.

DIMINISHING RETURNS TO CAPITAL AND TO INNOVATIVE EFFORT AS LIMITS TO GROWTH

As just noted, a critical feature of the original Solow model is the assumption that the accumulation of capital yields diminishing returns. This premise is necessary to yield the steady state upon which the analysis focuses, along with much of subsequent growth theory that follows its example. Obviously, in a model in which growth is driven by accumulation, diminishing returns to accumulation can be expected to lead to a slowdown.

If, however, innovation is also a primary engine of growth, this premise is not enough to ensure a slowdown. Rather, one must also assume diminishing returns to (accumulated) innovation. The picture must be an intertemporal process, like Ricardo's parable in which the best and most accessible land is utilized first. The story here is that inventors first undertake the projects that are easiest to carry out and that promise the greatest returns. That is, inventions are explored and carried out in the order of their benefit–cost ranking, either because this is the order in which the ideas occur to inventors, or because this is the trajectory adopted by the innovators' rational calculations. Then, as time passes, the net yield of inventive activity must grow ever smaller. New ideas become ever harder to obtain and, in any event, the best ones have generally been exploited previously. This can be expected to make such activity ever less attractive to inventors and investors and, even if no slowdown in the activity follows, the gains from a fixed level of activity must decline. The scenario is straightforward enough to require no further explanation. It is certainly a conceivable course of events. Still, one must beware of casually taking too dim a view of the future of innovation. There is always the warning example of Charles H. Duell, commissioner of the U.S. Office of Patents, who in 1899 said, "Everything that can be invented has been invented," and, in his shortsightedness, recommended that the patent office be shut down (cited in Federal Reserve Bank of Dallas, 1996, p. 5).

I turn next to what seems a less obvious threat to continuation of spectacular innovation and growth in the free-market economies. This involves a mechanism that cumulatively increases the relative cost of the R&D process and consequently threatens to bring a secular decline in the quantity of this activity that is demanded.

COST, DEMAND, AND THE VOLUME OF R&D ACTIVITY

Here, I focus on only two of the endogenous influences that can be expected to affect the volume of innovative activity: the demand for products that use the results of R&D and other innovative activity, and the cost of such innovative effort.

Demand

Schmookler (1966) offers extensive evidence indicating that the amount of innovation is affected by the size of the market for related final products.

That is, the flow of patented inventions in a particular industry appears to parallel closely the volume of sales of a product both over the business cycle and in terms of longer-run trends. It follows that growing population and expanding GDP can both speed up the pace of innovation. In terms of our arms-race ratchet model of innovation, this and other evidence on the role of demand suggest an influence in addition to a technical breakthrough that can lead firms in an industry to exceed the current norm in R&D spending. Rising demand can move the industry to a new and higher norm—an enhanced level of expenditure on innovation that firms in the industry feel it necessary to adopt in order to stay abreast of their rivals.

But, while enhanced demand seems to make a clear contribution to the magnitude of R&D activity in an industry, the role of Keynesian aggregate demand in the economy is not so straightforward. A powerful suggestive example is provided by Ester Fano (1987), the distinguished Italian economic historian. She reports that during the Great Depression in the United States the employment of scientists and technicians *grew* markedly. She tells us, "the evidence shows that industrial research underwent such a sustained boom in the 1930s that it could be expected to produce, in addition to cost-reducing devices, a large number of new products as well" (p. 263). More specifically, she reports:

> Between 1921 and 1938 industrial research personnel rose by 300%. In 1927 approximately 25% of its employees reportedly worked on a part-time basis; by 1938 this proportion had fallen to 3%. Laboratories rose from fewer than 300 in 1920 to over 1600 in 1931 and more than 2,200 in 1938; the personnel employed increased from about 6,000 in 1920 to over 30,000 in 1931 and over 40,000 in 1938. The annual expenditure rose, from about $25,000,000 in 1920 to over $120,000,000 in 1931, to about $175,000,000 in 1938. In 1937, industrial research on an organized basis in the United States ranked among the 45 manufacturing industries which provided the largest number of jobs. (1987, pp. 262–63)

There is probably no more dramatic case than that of the Great Depression to test (and reject) the proposition that weakness of aggregate demand invariably handicaps innovative activity.

Though this fascinating history clearly must entail many influences, a plausible major component of the explanation of Fano's observation, which I believe to be the key to the story, is *cost.* The Great Depression was a period in which the earnings of scientists, engineers, and technicians were extremely low. Since R&D is a labor-intensive activity, the low remuneration meant a major reduction in its relative cost compared with that of activities that are less labor intensive. This brings us to the influence of cost on innovative activity, the central element of the model of this chapter.

The Cost of Innovative Activity

In routinized innovation, as I have emphasized, expenditure on R&D and other innovative activities is just another of the types of investment the firm can use as an input in its production process, that is, as an instrument for the acquisition of revenues and profits. If the relative prices of such inputs change, we can expect substitution to take place, with some degree of replacement of the input whose relative cost has risen by another input whose price has fallen. This at once suggests that the derived demand for investment in innovation has a nonzero cost elasticity that, as Fano's evidence indicates, may well be substantial. In particular, sharp increases in the earnings of technical personnel can lead to a significant cutback in real investment in innovation.

This may appear to conflict with the conclusions of the ratchet model of chapter 4. That model, as we have seen, asserts that innovation expenditure is sticky downward, because in an innovation arms race no firm dares to cut its R&D outlays unilaterally. With no firm willing to take the first step, no such reduction will take place. However, there are two influences that modify this conclusion. First, in a period of extreme economic upheaval, such as a major depression or a serious inflation, clearly the norms guiding business decisions in more settled time are threatened and may well be abandoned.[4] Second, and more directly to the point in the discussion that follows, it is my hypothesis that in the short run the R&D investment norms are calibrated in nominal rather than real terms, at least to a considerable degree. That is, when the costs of R&D rise because technical personnel wages or other costs increase, the R&D norms will not rise immediately or by the fully corresponding amount. It is highly implausible, given what we know of business responses to changing cost and price levels, that expenditures of the firm will be adapted to inflation fully and without any lag. It is even conceivable that, for some interval of time, nominal expenditures will not be adjusted at all, so

4. This is related to an important observation that follows from the valuable work in evolutionary (or out-of-equilibrium) economics of Nelson and Winter (1982) and Amendola and Gaffard (1998). They note that in an intertemporal process analysis, such as the one that follows, it may not be legitimate to assume that the parameter values or the structure of the model itself remain unchanged with the passage of time. Developments that are particularly extreme, including internally generated disturbances, can force the pertinent model to change sharply. Thus, the appropriate model itself can be subject to endogenous modifying forces.

that the price elasticity of demand for innovation investment will be unity. I will discuss this assumption further in chapter sixteen, where some empirical information on the subject is also provided.

It will be argued next that, in the innovation process, such changes in its cost are neither fully exogenous nor exclusively random. On the contrary, the flow of innovation itself has a critical influence on these prices and costs. This follows from the effects of innovation on the rate of productivity growth in the economy as a whole, as well as the persistence of differences in productivity growth rates of different sectors of the economy.

THE COST DISEASE MODEL AND INNOVATION: AN INTUITIVE SUMMARY

A major component of the analysis that follows is based on a model—since called the cost disease model, or the unbalanced growth model—that William Bowen and I introduced some time ago (see, for example, Baumol, 1967) to show how persistent and relatively rapid increases in productivity in some sectors of the economy (the "progressive sectors") must lead to persistent and cumulative increases in the relative costs of the sectors that constantly grow more slowly (the "stagnant sectors"). I will argue that the cost disease of the technologically stagnant personal services can affect research in somewhat the same way that it does education, health care, legal activity, the performing arts, and a number of other services, and can lead to a persistent rise in the real cost of research, in the manner that characterizes other services whose productivity (at least so far) is not easily increased year after year, so that they do not benefit from as much of a productivity offset to rising wages as other economic sectors do. Of course, there are many differences between the cost structure of R&D and, say, health care. My point is only that they do have a common element: the handicraft component of their production processes and the relative difficulty of achievement of reductions in the overall role of that component.

Some years after the cost disease model was introduced, it was extended to include a hybrid sector, the asymptotically stagnant sector, defined to employ in relatively fixed proportions some inputs supplied by the progressive sector and some by the stagnant sector (see, for example, Baumol, Blackman, and Wolff, 1989, chapter 6). The stagnant sector and its behavior play a critical role in the analysis of this chapter. Two industries that seem to fit the description of asymptotic stagnancy rather closely are television broadcasting (whose primary inputs are electronic equipment and live performance) and computer usage (whose main inputs are sophisticated hardware and human labor devoted to software creation,[5] data gathering, and so on). Since the story will be familiar to a number of readers, I will summarize it very briefly and intuitively here, leaving demonstration of its properties to the appendix to this chapter.

The asymptotically stagnant cost is characterized by a distinctive intertemporal cost pattern. Initially, its cost tends to fall rapidly. But after some time this is reversed and the trajectory of the unit cost of the output of the asymptotically stagnant sector approaches closer and closer to that of its stagnant input. The intuitive explanation is simple. The falling cost of the progressive sector input accounts for the initial fall in the real unit cost of the asymptotically stagnant sector. But the very fall in the cost of that input reduces its *share* in the total costs of the asymptotically stagnant sector, leaving the behavior of those costs to be determined largely by the course of the stagnant sector input. Hence, an initial period of decline in the cost of the asymptotically stagnant sector is followed by a future of rising relative cost.[6] It is noteworthy that this sector appears to include some of the economy's most high-tech activities.

R&D AS ASYMPTOTICALLY STAGNANT ACTIVITY

There is reason to presume that the cost trajectory of R&D activity falls somewhere between those of a sector that is purely stagnant and one that is asymptotically stagnant. R&D may, itself, be thought of as using, preponderantly, two types of input—mental labor (that is, human time) and technological equipment such as computers—making it an activity approximating the characteristics of asymptotic stagnancy, though one with some intertemporal variation in input proportions. Innovation is such an activity. The act of thinking is a crucial input for the research process, but have we become more proficient at this handicraft activity than Isaac Newton, Gottfried Leibniz, or Christiaan Huygens? Probably not. The productivity of labor has risen at an annual rate slightly less than 2 percent compounded since roughly

5. However, as has been shown in an unpublished article by François Horn of Université Charles de Gaulle in Lille (2000), productivity in software creation has been rising rapidly, even if not as quickly as in hardware. Thus, it is surely incorrect to characterize all non-hardware inputs into the computation process as stagnant in terms of productivity growth.

6. For some empirical evidence on the cost behavior of the sectors used here as illustrations of asymptotic stagnancy, see Baumol, Blackman, and Wolff (1989, pp. 131–40).

1830, when the Industrial Revolution really took off, so that the real product of an hour of labor has multiplied by a factor of perhaps twenty since that time. This means that the opportunity cost of an hour devoted to the technologically stagnant process of thinking must have risen by about 1,900 percent! If R&D is interpreted as just another input in the production process, such a rise in its relative price must have cut back its derived demand—inducing some substitution away from this input and toward other inputs whose real cost was reduced by technical change. The cost disease of the stagnant component of research, then, may conceivably be a major impediment to acceleration of innovation.

The way in which this works out is best shown with the aid of a model of the feedback relationship between the production and dissemination of information and the rate of growth of productivity in industry. Here R&D is considered to be a sector of the economy that is engaged in the production of information. The magnitude of its information production clearly influences the rate of productivity growth. However, as we will see, that growth rate in turn will affect the output of information, thereby closing the feedback loop, with effects on the trajectory of innovation that may not be obvious without a formal model.

In brief, the analysis has three elements (three sequential steps):

1. Production of new information through R&D activity stimulates productivity growth in industry.
2. As a result, the price (real cost) of information production and dissemination rises. This is because these activities are what my colleagues and I have called "asymptotically stagnant," characterized by productivity growth that is initially high but that, with the passage of time, for reasons to be explained, tends to lag further and further behind that of industry.
3. As information grows relatively more costly, other inputs tend to be substituted for information in the production process. For example, when R&D costs have risen, a firm that wants to increase its output may decide not to invest more in R&D designed to raise the productivity of its machines but, instead, to buy additional machines of the current type. Thus, the rising cost of the innovation process can cut the derived demand for innovative activity. That, in turn, impedes productivity growth, thus reversing the first of the three steps of the intertemporal process in its next iteration.

All of this indicates why R&D activity can be expected to behave very much like an asymptotically stagnant sector. However, this conclusion also suggests others. One of the immediate implications is that, depending upon the price (and income) elasticity of the (derived) demand for R&D, it is possible that its rising relative cost will reduce its use relative to other inputs with the passage of time. Moreover, it can be shown that, with time, in my model (a) output of R&D may decline, (b) total expenditure on R&D may rise, both absolutely and as a share of GDP, and (c) the amount of R&D labor time may fall relative to GDP.

FEEDBACK MODEL: PRODUCTIVITY GROWTH AND ENDOGENOUS INNOVATION

In the basic cost disease model it is assumed that in the progressive sector the productivity of labor grows at a constant percentage rate, *g*. However, this premise ignores a crucial relationship—that between R&D (information production activity) and the technical change in the other sectors that thereby obtain their productivity growth. Thus, instead of *g* being a constant, it must be a function of the quantity of information produced by R&D that is used as an input by other sectors.

To combine all of the resulting relationships and determine their effects, we must modify the formal model further.[7] In the notation here, the subscripts indicating the sector of the economy in question are not needed. Let

g_t = the rate of growth of productivity *outside* R&D (information-producing) industries in period *t;*
y_t = the output (level of activity) of R&D activity;
p_t = the price of the product of R&D;
h = a parameter determining price-insensitive R&D activity.

Here I assume that R&D comes from two sources and will refer, correspondingly, to price-sensitive R&D, y_{pt}, which is generated preponderantly by routine business activity, and price-insensitive R&D, y_{it}, so that

(15.1) $y_t = y_{pt} + y_{it}.$

Then one can formulate the following illustrative relationships:

(15.2) $g_{t+1} = s + by_t$

(R&D contributes to productivity growth),

7. This model is based on earlier writings by Baumol and Wolff (1983).

(15.3) $(p_{t+1} - p_t)/p_t = vg_{t+1}$

(the price of R&D output grows proportionately to g_t);
and, for the case where price-insensitive R&D is zero, so that $y_{pt} = y_t$,

(15.4) $(y_{t+1} - y_t)/y_t = -E(p_{t-1} - p_t)/p_t$

(the R&D demand function),
where $E > 0$ is a bastard intertemporal demand elasticity which, for simplicity of illustration, is assumed to be constant.[8] For simplicity, I will also adopt as the price-insensitive R&D output function

(15.5) $y_{it+1} = hy_t$.

This implies that R&D activity encourages and facilitates independent R&D activity, and that the relationship is proportionate. Later, I will briefly consider some alternative forms of the relationship (15.5).

First, let us assume that there is no price-insensitive R&D, so that $h = 0$ in (15.5). Then, substituting (15.2) and (15.3) into (15.4), we have at once

(15.6) $(y_{t+1} - y_t)/y_t = -k(s + by_t)$, where $k = vE > 0$,

or

(15.7) $y_{t+1} = (1 - ks)y_t - kby_t^2$,

which has the two equilibrium points, at which $y_e = y_t = y_{t+1}$,

(15.8) $y_e = 0$ and $y_e = -s/b$.

We obtain from (15.7)

(15.9) $dy_{t+1}/dy_t = (1 - ks) - 2kby_t$

(15.10) $= (1 - ks)$ at $y_e = 0$ and

(15.11) $= (1 + ks)$ at $y_e = -s/b$.

Next, dealing with the case in which there is price-insensitive R&D, as given by (15.5), I assume that its amount is set using some average or target

8. This negatively sloping demand curve for R&D activity seems an obvious assumption. It is supported by some evidence (see, for example, Schmookler, 1966) and, as described above, in the work of Fano. The assumption is also employed elsewhere in the literature, for example in Grossman and Helpman (1991). It should also be noted that the equation is a generalization of the premise, mentioned earlier in this chapter, that oligopolistic competition forces the firms discussed in chapter 4 to fix their *nominal* R&D expenditure at the level, K, the current industry standard. For then (omitting subscripts) $y = K/p$ so that $y'p = -p'y$, and hence $y'/y = -p'/p$. The subject is discussed further in the next chapter.

share, a, of total R&D as a base, so that the price-sensitive portion of the demand function satisfies, instead of (15.4),

$$(y_{pt+1} - ay_t)/ay_t = -E(p_{t-1} - p_t)/p_t.$$

Consequently,

(15.12) $y_{t+1} = y_{pt+1} + y_{it+1} = (a + h - aks)y_t - akby_t^2,$

which is now our feedback relationship, yielding a trajectory whose properties are studied next.

Setting $y_e = y_{t+1} = y_t$, we now obtain the two equilibrium values

(15.13) $y_e = 0$ and $y_e = (h + a - 1 - aks)/akb.$

To test for their stability we note that by (15.12)

(15.14) $dy_{t+1}/dy_t = h + a - aks - 2akby_t,$

which equals

(15.15) $h + a - aks$ where $y_t = y_e = 0$

and

(15.16) $2 - h - a + aks$ where $y_t = y_e = (h + a - 1 - aks)/akb.$

To determine the implications for the intertemporal trajectory of R&D activity, we must first discuss the parameter values. As in (15.6)–(15.11), I begin with the case $h = 0$, meaning that all innovation is price sensitive. Then we expect $a = 1$ because a is the (target) share of price-sensitive R&D in total R&D. With $h = 0$ and $a = 1$, it is easy to verify that the relationships for the general case (15.12)–(15.16) each reduce to the corresponding relationships (15.6)–(15.11). We can assume that a, h, s, and b are all less than unity except where $h = 0$. This is obvious for h and a, because they can be interpreted, respectively, as the target shares of price-insensitive and price-sensitive R&D as a proportion of total R&D. Parameter s is the rate of growth of productivity in the absence of all R&D activity, and consequently should be very small. Similarly, it is implausible that b, which is dg_{t+1}/dy_t by (15.2), should exceed unity. We have, finally, $k = vE$, where v is the effect on the rate of growth of R&D cost of a change in productivity growth rate in the remainder of the economy, and is presumably small. E, the (absolute value of the) price elasticity of demand for R&D, is likely to be considerably smaller than 2 (indeed, my ratchet model for *nominal* expenditure implies E is near unity). This suggests that k can be assumed not to be far above unity, and presumably below that figure. All of these parameters are presumably nonnegative.

Then (15.10) tells us the equilibrium point $y_e = 0$ will be monotonic and stable when $h = 0$. That is, the slope of the phase graph of (15.9) will be positive but less than unity at the origin, $y_{t+1} = y_t = 0$ (figure 15.1 on page 279). Similarly, by (15.11), equilibrium point $y_e = -s/b$ will be negative and unstable so the time path of R&D will go steadily toward the origin, moving monotonically toward zero R&D and productivity growth rate. That is, we are led in this case to the grim conclusion that successful innovation can handicap and slow further innovation effort, driving it toward a stationary state with zero further outlay on this activity. It can do so by increasingly raising the relative cost of the handicraft portion of research and development activity, leading investment to search for alternatives whose relative cost does not grow so persistently.

As is to be expected, this pattern continues if h becomes positive, though remaining very small, and a declines slightly below unity, as is shown by (15.15) and (15.16). However, when h becomes sufficiently large, that is, if future independent innovation is stimulated sufficiently by the amount of current (and successful) innovation, then, if a does not decline, so that $a + h > 1$ by a sufficient amount, the nonzero equilibrium point will take a positive value and become stable (figure 15.2 on page 280). This is the case that is to be hoped for, with both innovation and output growth expanding "forever," though they both must gradually slow down and approach a fixed upper limit. Then the cost disease will no longer be able to engender stagnation, and outlays on innovative activity, though approaching a positive equilibrium level, which they will have no tendency to surpass, will also have no tendency to decline, with real outlays approaching the equilibrium level for the indefinite future.[9]

---

9. It may be thought, as I once did, that, even in this more fortunate case, there must arise another impediment to growth: the slowing of average productivity growth in the economy as increasing innovative activity leads to a transfer of labor from the (productivity) progressive final-product sector to the asymptotically stagnant innovation sector. For then the average productivity of the two sectors, weighted by the sizes of their labor inputs, must ultimately decline.

However, Nicholas Oulton of the Bank of England (2000) has contributed an important new theorem that entails very different productivity behavior in the economy when, as is true of innovation, this (ultimately) more stagnant activity supplies an intermediate product that is used as an input elsewhere in the economy rather than being used directly by consumers. Oulton shows that, when the allocation of inputs is efficient and entails a shift of primary input from the progressive final-product sector to the stagnant or asymptotically stagnant intermediate-product sector, then the economy's overall productivity can, in rather general circumstances, actually be expected to grow faster. That is, the shift of labor to the stagnant sector can in this case be expected to increase overall productivity growth rather than depressing it. It does so because in this case pro-

With h sufficiently large, so that dy_{t+1}/dy_t becomes negative, the trajectory will grow oscillatory, finally lapsing into explosive oscillation with cycles of increasing amplitude. Ultimately, it may well lead to a limit cycle, to the left of the maximum of the parabola that is the graph of our feedback relationship (15.9). It is even possible that h will reach a value at which a chaotic regime results.

Intuitively, such cycles are generated by the sequence generated by an initial leap in R&D activity. This, thereafter, substantially increases the productivity growth of the economy, causing a sharp rise in the cost of R&D, which in turn slows down productivity growth, and so on and on.

But much more pertinent to our central subject is the implication of the case $h = 0$, $a = 1$, or, more generally, the case $a + h = 1$. Then the only stable equilibrium is $y_e = 0$. As we have just noted, this means that, in an economy that behaves as this model does, rising productivity and the consequently rising cost of R&D will in the long run drive R&D expenditure steadily toward zero. To inquire a bit further into the intuitive reason, roughly, a is the share of past R&D expenditure that the business sector and other price-responsive innovators plan to undertake in the next period. Similarly, h can be viewed, roughly, as the share of past R&D expenditure that other innovators plan to undertake in the following period. Then, $a + h < 1$ implies that the two innovator groups together plan to undertake less innovation in the next period than they did in the past. But this effect is exacerbated by the negative slope of the demand curve for R&D of the first of the two innovator groups. When $a + h = 1$, although the two groups together would have spent the same amount as they did in the previous period if the price of the R&D input had

---

ductivity growth in the two sectors is additive, with growth of labor productivity in innovation, however limited, indirectly adding to the given total factor productivity (TFP) growth in the final-product sector, thereby enhancing productivity growth in the final product of the given labor force of the economy. As Oulton explains the seemingly "very paradoxical" result (assuming, for simplicity, that innovation is produced by labor alone, whereas final product uses both labor and innovation as inputs, as in my model here):

> There are two ways in which the economy can obtain more final product, given that total employment is fixed. One is if TFP rises in final product supply, the other is if TFP rises in innovation. . . . TFP growth in innovation raises the productivity of labor employed there. . . . Hence TFP growth in innovation causes higher final-product output, since the final-product sector buys in the output of the innovation sector. The higher the proportion of the labor force employed in innovation, the bigger the impact on TFP growth in the final-product sector [given the rate of TFP growth in the final-product sector's utilization of its two inputs]. . . . The reason is that such a shift will raise the contribution to the aggregate coming from innovation without reducing the contribution coming from the final-product sector. (2000, pp. 14–15; throughout the quotation, for more direct applicability to the current discussion, I have substituted "final-product output" for "car output" and "innovation" for "business services")

not risen, the previous period's R&D will have increased the economy's productivity and so it will have increased that price. The net result is that, even when the sum of the two parameters is unity, in this model R&D spending will decline steadily. In the next chapter we will see why the scenario of reality is not quite so dismal.

GRAPHIC ANALYSIS OF THE FEEDBACK MODEL

It is perhaps possible to get a clearer picture of the behavior of the model with the aid of the standard pseudo-phase diagram for a difference equation. Figure 15.1 depicts the case in which no price-insensitive R&D is generated, that is, in which $h = 0$ in (15.5). Then, the basic feedback equation (15.7) can be represented in (y_t, y_{t+1}) space as the parabolic locus *LL* in figure 15.1. The equilibrium points are, of course, the points 0 and *E* where *LL* intersects the 45° line, that is, where $y_t = y_{t+1}$. Since, as has been shown, the nonzero equilibrium point in this case is negative, *E* lies to the left of the vertical axis. This equilibrium represents a (nonsensical) negative amount of R&D activity, and is really irrelevant. What is much more to the point is what happens after beginning with an initial position $y_0 > 0$. We see that with the relationships

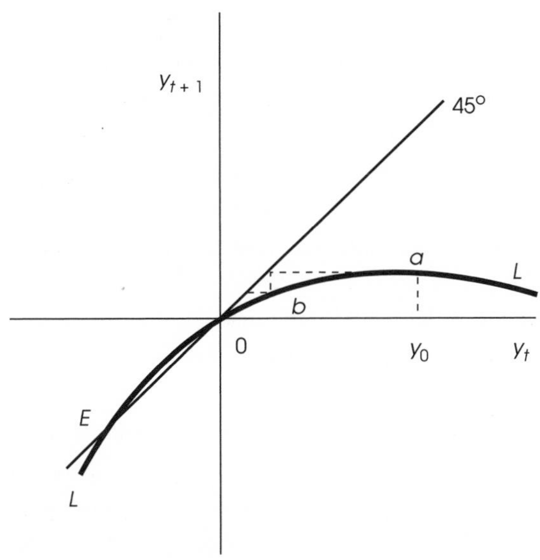

FIGURE 15.1
Determining the Time Path of Innovation Output: Decreasing Output Case

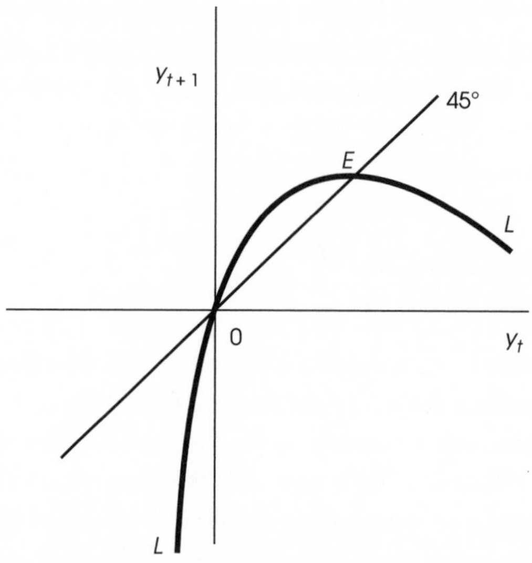

FIGURE 15.2
Determining the Time Path of Innovation Output: Stationary Equilibrium Case

as shown in figure 15.1, with the 45° line above *LL*, there will be a time path y_0ab . . . that leads monotonically (that is, without any deviation), toward $y = 0$, period after period.

Figure 15.2 shows how matters change when the economy also provides some price-insensitive R&D whose quantity follows the expression $y_{it+1} = hy_{it}$, $h > 0$, as assumed in my expanded illustrative model. Since this last relation obviously is represented by a positively sloping straight line through the origin, its addition to (15.7), to obtain (15.12), simply results in a counterclockwise rotation of *LL* in figure 15.1 around the origin, moving it to the position of *LL* in figure 15.2. We see that this tends to move the position of equilibrium point *E* to the right. For *h* sufficiently large, it transfers *E* to the right of the origin, as shown in figure 15.2. The new equilibrium point, with its positive level and growth rate of R&D, can be stable since at that point *LL* can cut the 45° line from above.

The significant role of price-insensitive innovation activity makes it important to emphasize that in our model it can be taken to refer to more than the work of the lone, dedicated inventor who works fanatically in basement or garage. It also can include, for example, the unexpected breakthrough originating in a bureaucratically run corporate R&D facility that induces the firm to undertake a substantial increase in the resources it devotes to innovation. Although this will obviously differ from industry to industry, and can be expected to occur only sporadically, if at all, in any particular firm, in the economy as a whole its expected value may conceivably be fairly predictable.

The discussion of the graphs also indicates how one can analyze cases in which price-insensitive R&D activity is described by possibly more complicated relationships than $y_t + 1 = hy_t$. For example, one may want to explore nonlinear relationships with diminishing returns as enhanced current R&D diminishes the stock of possible innovations that it is easy to explore and develop in the future. Or, alternatively, one can consider the possibility of increasing returns as successful innovation makes further innovation activity less costly and more powerful. Since, in analyzing such relationships, they are added to the part of (15.7) that describes routine business-provided R&D, one need merely see what happens when the graph representing such a relationship is added to *LL* in figure 15.1.

We can readily confirm that the behavior of the model does not depend on the particular functional forms employed in (15.1)–(15.5), and that its qualitative properties remain robust under a considerable broadening of my premises. The analysis indicates that, if there really is a feedback relationship between information activity and productivity growth in industry, this raises the possibility of a non-self-terminating trajectory, with monotonically declining productivity growth and information production. This is certainly a disturbing prospect for productivity policy.

CONCLUDING COMMENTS

A primary purpose of my model has been to show how it is possible to analyze more explicitly the ways in which outlays on R&D and the rate of growth of productivity can be determined endogenously and simultaneously. The model has sought to introduce the role of the price mechanism and significant productivity growth explicitly, taking a first step toward elimination of the ahistorical character of the mainstream macromodels of growth. This at least suggests one of the sources of strength and some of the vulnerability of the market economy as a mechanism that produces innovation and growth.

Specifically, the discussion has taken account of the likelihood that an increase in R&D expenditure will stimulate productivity growth, albeit with some lag. However, it has also recognized that the very rate of productivity growth in other sectors contributed by R&D affects the *relative* cost of R&D and, arguably, tends to increase that relative cost. Thus, the very success of the work of the R&D sector may sow the seeds of a future price impediment to demand for its output.

This rather primitive macroeconomic model appears to paint a rather pessimistic picture for the future. There are, however, built-in offsets that raise the possibility of more promising prospects. This is the subject of the next chapter.

APPENDIX

DERIVATION OF THE PROPOSITIONS ON THE COST DISEASE AND ASYMPTOTIC STAGNANCY

This appendix reviews the relevant derivations of the properties of the cost disease model, which were described earlier in the chapter. In the deliberately oversimplified cost disease model, the economy is taken to be composed of two sectors: a progressive sector, 1, in which productivity grows exponentially, and a stagnant sector, 2, in which productivity remains constant. There is a single input, labor, with quantities L_1 and L_2 used by the respective sectors, and whose outputs are given by

(15.A1) $y_1 = cL_1 e^{rt} \qquad y_2 = bL_2.$

Letting w represent the common wage rate, we have the unit-cost figures

(15.A2) $AC_1 = wL_1/y_1 = w/ce^{rt}, \qquad AC_2 = wL_2/y_2 = w/b.$

This yields for the stagnant sector a relative cost that grows exponentially with time:

(15.A3) $AC_2/AC_1 = ce^{rt}/b.$

Thus we have

> **PROPOSITION 15.A1.** In the cost disease model, the per unit cost of the output of the stagnant sector will rise without limit relative to that of the progressive sector.

Next, I introduce the third prototype sector, the "asymptotically stagnant" sector, a simplified representation of sectors of the economy that include R&D activity. This sector is composed of activities that use in (more or less) fixed proportions two different types of input, one produced by progressive sector 1, and the other of which either is obtained from stagnant sector 2 or is composed of pure labor (or some combination of the two).[10] Assume for simplicity that input–output proportions are absolutely fixed. Let y_3 represent the output of the sector and y_{13} and y_{23} be the inputs of the other two sectors used in the production of y_3. We can then write

$$(15.A4)\quad y_{13}/y_3 = k_1, \qquad y_{23}/y_3 = k_2,$$

where by choice of units we can set $k_2 = 1$. We then obtain for the average cost of sector 3

$$(15.A5)\quad AC_3 = k_1AC_1 + k_2AC_2 = k_1w/ce^{rt} + AC_2.$$

Measured in terms of labor units, that is, holding w constant, the first term of (15.A5) must approach zero asymptotically. Consequently, the behavior of AC_3 over time will approach that of the stagnant sector, 2.

Thus, we have

> **PROPOSITION 15.A2.** The behavior of the average cost of an asymptotically stagnant sector will approach, asymptotically, that of the stagnant sector from which the former obtains some of its inputs.

What is surprising about the phenomenon we are discussing is that the sectors of the economy suffering from the asymptotic stagnation problem in its most extreme form include, in reality, some of those providing the most "high-tech" activities—those in the vanguard of innovation and change. That this is predicted by the theory should be clear from (15.A5), which shows that the more rapid the rate of productivity growth of the sector 1 input—that is, the greater the value of r—the more rapidly will the intertemporal behavior of AC_3 approach that of the nonprogressive sector.

So far, it has been assumed for simplicity that there is a fixed ratio between the input quantities sector 3 derives from the progressive and the stagnant sectors. But this premise was used only for expository convenience. It is easy to show that, over a broad range of patterns of behavior of input proportions, the same sort of cost problems arise for the asymptotically stagnant sector.

10. It makes no difference to the analysis whether sector 3's second input is y_2 or labor itself, since both costs behave similarly. That is, $AC_2 = w/b$, by (15.A2), and the average cost of labor to industry is simply w. Indeed, we can aggregate the supply of y_2 and labor to industry 3 into a single broader sector that offers them both and that is clearly stagnant. If sector 3 uses L_3 hours of labor and y_{23} units of y_2 per unit of y_3 produced, then writing $y_{23} = aL_{23}$ it is clear that a unit of output 3 requires $L_3 + L_{23}$ hours of labor altogether. Thus, we may invent a fictitious output y_2^* satisfying $y_2^*/a = L_3 + L_{23}$ as the product of the aggregated stagnant sector that supplies both labor and y_2 to sector 3.

CHAPTER 16

Feedback: Innovation as a Self-Nourishing Process

Can capitalism survive? No, I do not think it can.

—Schumpeter, 1947, p. 61

The future is like everything else. It isn't what it used to be.

—Attributed to Simone de Beauvoir

Economists can predict everything except the future.

—Recently cited by Alan Blinder

The previous chapter ended on a rather inauspicious note, showing at least one course of events that could end up with the incentives for routine invention activity attenuated, and the rising trajectory of resources devoted to R&D petering out or ceasing altogether. But that scenario was meant primarily to represent a possibility that by no means constitutes an immediate threat or even one for the foreseeable future. Chapter 15 was not meant to draw attention to any imminent crisis but, rather, to call attention to the dangers of the fallacy of composition, which, in this case, involved generalizing from the behavior of individual firms to the behavior of the economy as a whole.

The message of this chapter is that there are good reasons for optimism about the prospects for future innovation. One reason, simply put, is that *innovation breeds innovation.* In addition, I will draw attention to some very powerful countervailing forces that serve at least to mitigate the innovation-depressing process described in chapter 15's macroeconomic model of endogenous innovation. These offsets, related directly to the structure of the model, will be described later in the chapter. But they are not the central focus of the discussion, which is, rather, the innovation feedback process, in which innovation leads to economic developments that, in turn, stimulate and facilitate the innovation process. And, finally, even though long-range economic forecasting is notoriously untrustworthy and perhaps worthless, I will conclude with the sanguine personal view that any slowdown in the pace of innovation is probably still far away, and that there is little evidence that the growth trend in innovative activity is about to lose steam.

THE INNOVATION FEEDBACK PROCESS

Recognized Ways in Which Innovation Induces Further Innovation

The idea that successful innovation leads to further innovation is hardly new. Earlier, I cited Nelson's (1996) cogent observations on this issue. There are various clear ways in which innovation breeds further innovation. Most obviously, one new idea frequently suggests another, particularly when one invention calls for another to make it more effectively workable. The computer gave rise to the need for a mouse, the airship to the need for a parachute. The examples are many.[1] One idea leads to another, as in the invention of transistors and the numerous applications that followed. A new product also invites R&D devoted to improvement of that product (as in the computer) or to the creation of superior substitutes (as in the Salk and the Sabin polio vaccines), or even to improvement of an old product that is threatened with replacement. A standard example is the great improvement in sailing vessels after introduction of the steamboat. Note the role of Schumpeterian competition here: the competitors of an initial innovator are driven to protect themselves by seeking to replicate or, better yet, leapfrog the previous technical improvement.

But that is only the beginning. A newly invented product leads to increased understanding not only of the need for additional and possibly supplementary products, but also of the means by which the new products can be created. That is, innovation also helps to facilitate research and development. And it does so in at least two ways—by teaching us new and more effec-

1. Landes (1998, pp. 191–92) writes, "Innovation was catching because the principles that underlay a given technique could take many forms, find many uses. If one could bore cannon, one could bore the cylinders of steam engines. If one could print fabrics by means of cylinders (as against the much slower block printing) one could . . . print word text faster than by the up-and-down strokes of a press and turn out penny tabloids and cheap novels by the tens of thousands. Similarly, a modified cotton-spinning machine could spin wool and flax. Indeed, contemporaries argued that the mechanization of cotton manufacture forced these other branches to modernize. . . . New, new, new. Money, money, money."

tive ways to carry out research, and by creating new instruments for use in the research process. The electronic computer and the Internet (which so substantially facilitates collaborative research) are but two recent and dramatic examples.

Successful innovation also widens the acceptance of innovative products by business enterprise. This is crucial as an encouragement to innovators and, even more important, as a means to ensure that such products are effectively and rapidly put into use. Earlier, in chapter 14, I pointed out that the problem that beset such activity in ancient Rome and medieval China was not a lack of invention, but the absence of systematization of the rest of the innovation process—the dissemination, adoption, and utilization of the new processes and products. In a market economy, the demonstrated success of innovation in a particular sector is all that is needed to attract the attention and the energies of entrepreneurs. And that, patently, is yet another crucial contribution of successful innovation to further innovation.

Finally, there is the most obvious component of the feedback process—the demonstrated monetary rewards of innovation as a stimulus to further innovation. In its crassest form, the publicized rich rewards of some innovators can be counted upon to attract others into this type of enterprise as surely as the discovery of gold can stimulate a gold rush. The financial success of one innovator makes entry into the activity more attractive to others, and makes it easier to raise the requisite capital. The waves of innovation that have recurred throughout recent economic history probably have been driven at least in part by this influence.

In short, there are many ways in which innovation facilitates innovation and begets further innovation, notably as new technology offers profitable new opportunities for such outlays. But, so far, I have described only the most obvious components of the feedback process. I turn now to elements that are less widely recognized, starting with a brief recapitulation of the critical role of the oligopolistic competition that, this book suggests, is so vital a component of the market economy's innovation machine.

Competition Stimulates Innovation, and Innovation Stimulates Competition

Probably the most powerful force that may well lead to continuation of the remarkable growth in innovative activity is the adoption of innovation as the prime weapon of competition in many of the leading oligopolistic sectors of the economy. As has already been emphasized, the resulting "arms race," in which each firm is forced to keep up with its rivals and to strive to outdo them, is like a Red Queen game, in which all players are forced to keep running as fast as they can in order to stand still. This is an engine of growth of enormous power, and it is a game that participants cannot easily quit. It is also the prime support for optimism about the prospects for continuation of the free-market economy's historically unprecedented innovation explosion and its acceleration during the twentieth century. But recapitulation of this argument, though central to the analysis of this book, is not the point here. What is at issue, rather, is the feedback process, and it arises here because, as I will argue next, innovation facilitates and stimulates the very type of competition that drives the free-market innovation machine. That is, innovation encourages competition, while competition, in turn, is a key driver of the innovation process.

Competition, Innovation, and Foreign Trade as Mutual Stimuli

In the economic literature on antitrust issues, the contribution of innovation to competition is well recognized. For example, it is observed that new products and processes tend to shorten the life of a monopoly and to bring the possession of monopoly power by a dominant enterprise to an earlier end. Entrants that can leapfrog the incumbent monopolist with a better product or a more efficient process will often succeed in sharing the market with the incumbent, or in replacing the incumbent with a new dominant firm whose monopoly power is likely to be equally transitory, as still later innovators enter the market.[2]

But a second way in which innovation has contributed enormously to competition has clearly been its role as the key to the astonishing growth in trade among nations. And that, in turn, has greatly increased the power of competition in many industries. That enhancement of competitive pressures has further stimulated the innovative activities of the affected firms. Transportation's growing speed and reliability and its falling costs have played an important part in the intensification of competition and have internationalized the innovation arms race. Since the Industrial Revolution, world output

2. Yet the literature emphasizes that new technology can also contribute to monopoly power, for example via what are called "network effects." These are cases in which the value of the product is crucially dependent on the number of users and the compatibility of the products they use, as in the case of a computer program that various users employ to communicate with one another. The innovating firm that creates the most popular new program may achieve dominance of the market and the compatibility requirement may make it difficult for rivals to enter.

of goods and services has, as we know, expanded enormously. But the rate of expansion of trade has far outpaced that of production. Maddison (1995, p. 38) estimates that, since 1950, U.S. exports have risen nearly three times as a share of GDP. For the world as a whole, exports as a share of GDP expanded nearly fourteenfold since 1820.

All this was made possible by innovation, which resulted in a revolutionary reduction in the costs, time, and perils of transportation as well as communication. By the end of the eighteenth century, for example, navigators could determine longitude using the chronometer, making it far safer to sail without hugging the shoreline and to enter far nearer harbors that previously were too perilous. Steam propulsion, the end of wooden hulls, the enormous growth in size and speed of vessels, wireless communication, and a host of other profound technical changes were patently the key to the explosion of trade and communication.

The growth of the volume of trade has clearly enhanced competition. In the United States, industry after industry feels the threat of foreign rivalry to a degree never experienced before. Industries such as consumer electronics have to a considerable degree become a preserve of other nations. U.S. leadership in aircraft production is threatened for the first time since the end of World War II. And the automobile market is no longer primarily a domestic affair. The rising competitive pressures from foreign sources are not very different from domestic rivalry in their consequences for the behavior of the firm. Many examples could easily be cited to confirm their effect in intensifying the technological arms race that dictates the innovative activities of the firm.

This chain of relationships indicates yet another way in which the innovation process tends to counteract any tendencies toward diminishing returns and diminishing innovative activity that may affect that process. Innovation acts as a stimulator of the competition that tolerates no letup in innovative activity and that may force its further intensification.

Innovation Extends the Supply of Limited Resources

I turn next to yet another way in which innovation facilitates innovation, one that is also not widely recognized.

Ultimately, one of the prospective impediments to innovation is the finite character of the economy's natural resources that are critical to utilization of the new products and processes that innovation provides. Thus, it may well be suspected that, in a world in which the economy's finite natural resources can only be depleted, this will raise problems for innovation that will grow more serious with the passage of time. After all, most inventions must be embodied at least partly in concrete material objects, requiring metals, fuels, and other scarce resources for their utilization, and this may well become an impediment to innovation—both to its production and to its contribution to the economy's output.

However, it can be argued that, in an important sense, the available quantities of the economy's natural resources can be expanded and, indeed, that this has actually happened. This notion may seem bizarre, yet the fact that, over the decades, the real prices of so many of these resources have *not* been increasing, and that at least some of them have actually declined, must surely suggest that there is something to this notion. And there is a straightforward explanation.

Suppose that inventions constantly decrease the percentage of petroleum that is lost in the process of extraction from a well, and that another stream of inventions constantly increases the number of miles a given quantity of petroleum will enable a vehicle to travel. Suppose both of these developments move far faster than the rate at which the earth's fixed physical stock of oil is used up. Then it should be clear that the inventory of prospective miles of transportation by petroleum-driven vehicles can actually have been expanded. The intellectual input will, in effect, have served to increase the supply of the physical input in the one sense that really counts: the still available capacity of that input to contribute to future output of the economy.[3]

The Acceleration Effect of Innovation on Production

It is important here to note again a relationship between the flow of innovation and the rate of economic growth that is not entirely obvious.

Each successful innovation contributes to the growth of the nation's GDP. Thus, an economy in which R&D produces, for example, an unchanging output of one innovation per month will obtain a GDP that is higher each month than it was in the previous month. The economy's ability to produce output will grow constantly, even though the innovation flow that fuels output growth remains unchanging at one invention per month. In other words, the rate of growth of the value of GDP is an increasing function of the *level* of innovation. This acceleration relationship applies to innovation generally, so that, if the competitive market mechanism leads firms to devote a constant

3. Yet one can expect limits to the extent that innovation can expand what we may call the effective supply of natural resources. On this, see Baumol, Blackman, and Wolff (1989, pp. 357–58).

quantity of resources to R&D, we would expect continued growth of GDP to result.

Of course, the innovation arms race described in chapter 4 tends not only to prevent firms from decreasing their inventive activities, but also encourages them to increase their expenditures on innovation with the passage of time. The acceleration relationship just described tells us about the effects of this, too. It says that, if the level of R&D spending were to increase just once, for example, and then stay at that new higher level forever, the growth rate of GDP would also move upward. GDP would then grow at a faster rate forever. In other words, from a once-and-for-all increase in the level of expenditure on R&D we can expect a permanent increase in the rate of growth of GDP.

THE ROLE OF PRICE INFLATION: REAL VS. NOMINAL TARGETS FOR R&D EXPENDITURE AND THE RISING RELATIVE COST OF R&D

So far, I have discussed a general feedback mechanism that encourages a sanguine view of the prospects for innovation. But I have not yet addressed specifically the possible offsets to the less promising prospects suggested by chapter 15's extended cost disease model.[4] That analysis implied that one of

4. The main issue is whether firms deal with real or nominal costs and that will be discussed below. In addition, we should note that independent R&D pursuits, as related to parameter h (price-insensitive R&D activity), are the nonroutine innovative activities, largely conducted outside the premises of the giant corporations. The magnitude of this parameter, however, is not related to the amount of such nonroutine activity alone. This is because h is a measure of responsiveness of price-insensitive R&D to changes in total R&D. Moreover, independent R&D is surely not entirely price insensitive. Indeed, it is highly plausible that even independent entrepreneurs and researchers are in many cases influenced by the cost of R&D and its implications for the prospect for profit from their activity. It is also very likely that some of their activity will be held back or even terminated if rising costs make it more difficult to raise the funds needed to carry out a successful research and development program.

Still, one suspects that the enthusiasm of at least some independent inventors and entrepreneurs will lead many of them to disregard rising costs and carry on in pursuit of their goals, readily adjusting to the enhanced financial difficulties. The history of invention tells us of many individuals—such as John Harrison, inventor of the first accurate marine chronometer, which enabled navigators to compute their longitude at sea, and Charles Goodyear, who discovered vulcanization, the process that improves the physical properties of rubber—who devoted lifetimes to the monomaniac pursuit of their targets. Their stories include episodes of financial stringency that nonetheless did not stop their activities. In short, there is inventive activity that, for all practical purposes, is not deterred by rising costs—at least if those cost increases are not enormous or unforeseeable.

the probable consequences of the innovation arms race and the growth of innovation stimulated by the feedback process is an ever-rising cost of R&D that can ultimately choke this activity off. The cost disease model raised the prospect of steady long-term decline in the real resources devoted to R&D, under the pressures of constantly rising relative costs of this activity—a result of its own success in raising productivity growth in other sectors of the economy. This story rests on two premises: first, money illusion, which leads firms to sustain only their nominal outlays on R&D (with no adjustment for the effects of price inflation), thereby allowing the real outlays to decline as price inflation grows; and, second, a paucity of price-insensitive innovation activity.

The role of money illusion here is the possibility that the rising dollar spending on innovation that is induced by the arms-race process will be insufficient to prevent reductions in the amount of purchasing power used for this purpose, as rising price inflation in the economy erodes the value of the dollar. For example, if private industry raises its dollar R&D spending by 20 percent but, at the same time, inflation cuts the purchasing power of the dollar by, say, 45 percent, then evidently the net result will be a decline, not an increase, in innovative activity.

This issue came up early in the book. The basic microeconomic model of chapter 4 yielded the conclusion that oligopolistic competition can be expected to enforce standards for R&D spending by firms in high-tech industries. Each firm is driven to live up to industry spending norms by the fear that, if it fails to do so, its rivals will come up with superior products and processes and thereby cut into its sales or drive it from the market altogether. Now the behavior of chapter 15's model rests on the premise that these industry norms for R&D expenditures are set in terms that are nominal (not adjusted for inflation) rather than real (that is, inflation adjusted). The reason this assumption plays such a role in the model is easy to see. If firms raise their nominal expenditures sufficiently every time that relative productivity growth in other sectors increases the cost of innovative activities—that is, if they automatically prevent any fall in real expenditure—then the cost disease, by definition, will have no effect on the flow of innovation. But if the

---

This implies that parameter h is not zero and may conceivably be well above it, meaning that a rise in successful R&D in the economy can lead to a proportionately significant increase in price-insensitive innovative activity. Basically, if success in innovation is sufficiently effective in breeding further pursuit of innovative success, this can overcome the depressing effects of the systematically rising cost of the process.

firms think in terms only of the number of dollars they devote to innovation activities, regardless of the purchasing power of those dollars, then rising prices and, in particular, any rising cost of R&D resulting from the cost disease will tend to offset and even undermine altogether the arms-race growth mechanism.

The question, then, is whether the expenditure norms in my analysis are fixed in real or in nominal terms, or something in between. Observation of business behavior suggests that business persons do adjust their expenditure to inflation, but that there is often a lag and often failure to recognize the full amount by which a rising price level has reduced the purchasing power of the amounts they budget. The available statistical evidence, as we will see, also indicates that the answer is somewhere in between the two extremes. Money illusion does appear to play a role in R&D funding, sufficient to preserve the relevance of the chapter 15 story. But there also appear to be competitive pressures that are strong enough to offset much of this price-inflation effect and thus to sustain the growth in the resources devoted to innovation. The relevant data for the United States seem not to be broadly consistent either with business behavior that is governed entirely by money illusion, at the one extreme, or with total absence of that influence, at the other.

Data provided by the National Science Board (2000) indicate that, since World War II, total U.S. *nominal* expenditure on R&D has risen in a near-exponential pattern. But the evidence indicating that the innovation arms race is not undermined by money illusion is that *real* U.S. R&D expenditure (deflated by the consumer price index for all items [CPI-All Items]) also rose at an average annual growth rate of more than 4 percent (from some $19 billion 1982–84 dollars in 1953 to nearly $140 billion in 1998). The pattern of R&D spending by private industry alone is very similar (figure 16.1). Nominal industry spending increased almost fortyfold (the curve labeled "nominal expenditures" in the graph) and real industry spending, calculated as before, rose more than sevenfold (the broken curve) over the forty-five year period (a remarkable average rate of growth of more than 5 percent per year).

Yet there were exceptions that seem consistent with some role of money illusion. Total U.S. real expenditures on research and development actually fell in eight of the forty-five years for which data are reported. The first significant instance was the era of the 1970s, when the economy experienced inflation extraordinary for peacetime in the United States. The National Science Board writes, "Starting in 1969 . . . and for nearly a decade thereafter, R&D growth failed to keep up with either inflation or general increases in

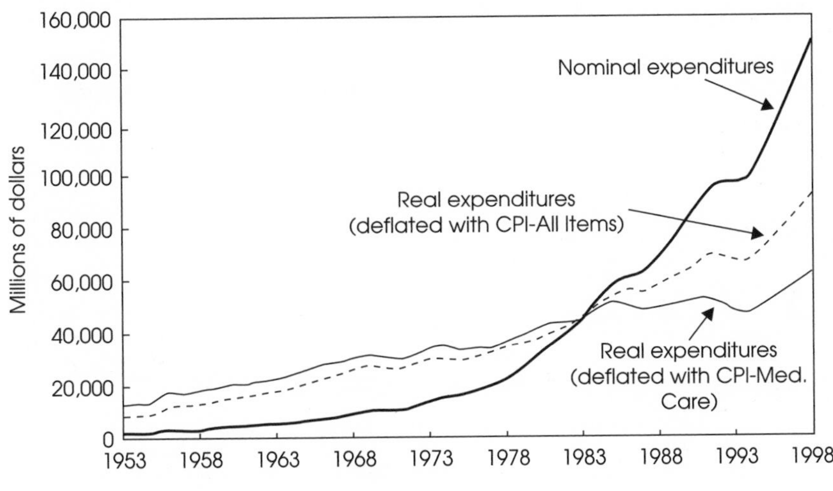

FIGURE 16.1

U.S. private industry R&D expenditures, 1953–98: nominal vs. real (1982–84) dollars. Sources: National Science Board (2000) and Bureau of Labor Statistics (www.bls.gov).

economic output" (2000, p. 2–7). Real R&D spending declined in the years 1969, 1970, 1971, 1974, and 1975. In these years, then, firms corrected very imperfectly for inflation in their R&D outlays. The second period with very slow or even declining real R&D outlays included the end of the 1980s and the beginning of the 1990s, with actual declines in 1992, 1993, and 1994. But here the story does not fit in directly with a simple cost-inflation scenario, since the compensation of scientists and engineers slowed markedly between 1989 and 1993, and began to rise rapidly only after that (see figure 16.2).[5]

The generally upward trend in R&D spending is clearly consistent with the ratchet model of chapter 4, while the cut in real spending in the 1970s is consistent with the assumptions underlying the model of chapter 15. The implications of the second period of slow growth and real decline, also nearly a decade in duration, are less clear. Taken as a whole, the evidence indicates

5. The declines in figure 16.1 are enhanced by the possibility that the cost of R&D rose substantially more quickly than the overall rate of inflation as a result of the cost disease. This is illustrated by deflating the graph using the assumption that R&D costs rose as quickly as those of health care. Using the CPI-Medical Care price index for this purpose, we obtain the flattest of the curves in figure 16.1. The qualitative properties of the time path still remain the same—a general rise over the forty-five-year period as a whole, more than trebling real expenditures. But, calculated using the medical care index, there are sixteen years of decline in real R&D expenditures (about one-third of the period).

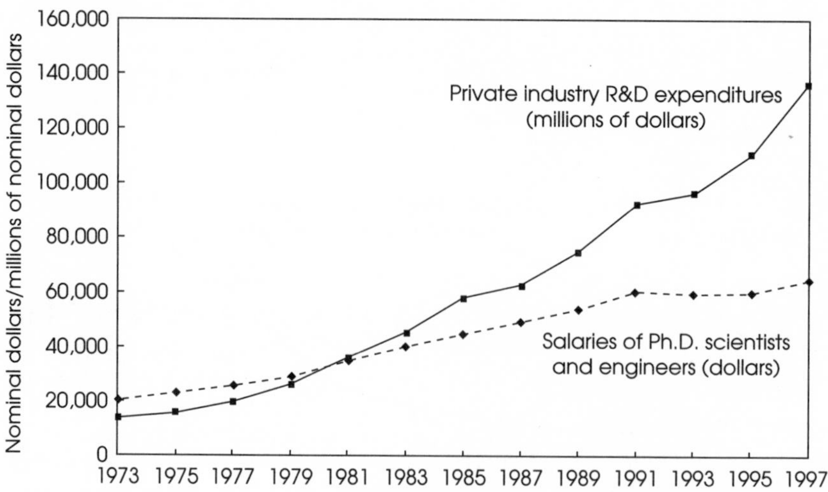

FIGURE 16.2

Median annual salaries for U.S. Ph.D. scientists and engineers (in nominal dollars) and U.S. private industry R&D expenditures (in millions of nominal dollars), 1973–97. Sources: National Science Board (2000) and personal correspondence, October 23, 2000, from Rolf Lehming, Director, Integrated Studies, Science and Engineering Indicators, National Science Foundation.

that R&D outlays by industry do not respond reliably to inflation by an offsetting rise in nominal spending.[6]

The point for the discussion of this chapter is that, although money illusion and related influences can indeed plausibly be assumed to result in some cut in real R&D spending when its cost increases, one must not take this observation to extremes. People in business do recognize inflation and they also, at least eventually, recognize when it has eaten substantially into real outlays. In the longer run, we can expect that the oligopolistic competition discussed in chapter 4 will lead to some adjustment in nominal outlays on innovative activities by business firms that may well continue to make up for the periods of erosion by rising inflationary costs and more. Accordingly, the trajectory of R&D spending reported by the data just cited does show an overall and persistent trend in the real resources devoted to R&D. The cost disease

6. The conclusion is supported by a regression using the preceding data for 1953–98, with the growth in nominal U.S. R&D outlays by private industry as the dependent variable, and time and the rate of growth of inflation as the two independent variables. This yielded a very small and statistically insignificant coefficient for the latter.

may indeed pose some threat to growth in real outlays on R&D, but not nearly as severely or as persistently as the simplest form of the model may suggest.[7]

THE PROSPECTS: WHAT CAN WE EXPECT?

After this description of some of the forces that may conceivably terminate the extraordinary growth achievements of capitalism, as well as the powerful forces that work in the other direction, the reader is entitled to ask: Where does the balance lie? My answer is that there is certainly no evidence of any imminent weakening, much less termination, of human ingenuity, or of the flow of products it creates, or, perhaps more to the point, of the competitive mechanism that drives it on.[8] This book has described a powerful mechanism that is built into the capitalist economy and that spurs it relentlessly to innovation and growth. The fierce oligopolistic competition in innovations, the serendipity between investment in the innovation process and the markets in licenses that ensure rapid dissemination of new technology, along with financial rewards to its proprietors, and the incentives that entice entrepreneurs into productive rather than rent-seeking activities—these are all powerful and continuing forces. These forces are supplemented strongly by the feedback process described in this chapter: the stimulus that innovation provides to further innovation. I see no evidence that any of these mechanisms is about to weaken.

7. For an excellent characterization of the literature on money illusion, and further empirical evidence that behavior in reality falls somewhere well in between the two extremes of exclusive reliance on either real monetary quantities or nominal quantities, see Shafir, Diamond, and Tversky (1997).

8. We must be careful to avoid prediction based only on extrapolation of temporary slowdowns or leaps of progress and the assumption that they will persist indefinitely. When growth in the United States slowed markedly between about 1972 and 1990, many were prepared to conclude that the end was near for American economic leadership. I cannot resist claiming that my colleagues Sue Anne Batey Blackman and Edward Wolff and I were among the first to gather evidence indicating that there was no basis for this gloomy forecast, though we, too, were initially inclined to accept it. Another noteworthy example is the long period during which the adoption of computers displayed little or no effect on productivity. Paul David (1989) was able to show, in his usual perceptive way, that it had taken a correspondingly long period for electrification to make its mark on output and productivity, warning us that we should not expect major instantaneous economic effects from technical breakthroughs.

The facts seem to support this inference from the theory. Recent decades have introduced a flood of extraordinary new products. After a period of slowdown during the 1970s and 1980s, which less sanguine observers described as the "end of the golden age," productivity growth once more went on the march. There are even signs that the computer revolution is at last beginning to make a discernible contribution to economic welfare. U.S. economic growth in the last several years attained a pace that astonished everyone who has studied the general subject, though, predictably, it has since been slowed once again by recession. Of course, future progress can also be expected to continue to have its declines and recoveries. But I have yet to see any portents for the longer run suggesting that the economic accomplishments of the free market are about to undergo permanent decline.

However, it is not the purpose of the book to provide forecasts about prospective innovation and growth. My goal has been to suggest useful explanations of the incredible growth in output and innovation that has already occurred. I have offered a set of explanatory hypotheses along with some evidence and some analysis pertinent to each of them. Yet it must be recognized that the very nature of the subject condemns the evidence to be spotty and unsystematic, for how can one really hope to prove what has stimulated such things as invention and entrepreneurship, when neither of these can even be measured? Moreover, the set of explanations offered here is surely far from complete, though one can hardly aspire to completeness in such an arena.

None of this is meant to be apologetic; it is intended only to suggest the limitations inherent in my undertaking with some degree of frankness. On the contrary, I believe that, when the set of candidate explanations I have proposed is considered carefully, the importance of their role will appear self-evident.

- Surely, competition with innovation as a weapon must be a powerful stimulus for invention and its utilization in the economy.
- Surely, the profits offered by dissemination via the market mechanism must materially speed the replacement of obsolete products and production processes.
- Surely, routinization must help to reduce the fortuitous component in the stream of innovation.
- Surely, success in innovation has led to further innovation.
- And, surely, such developments as the rule of law must have vastly enhanced the incentive for independent innovative activity.

That this cannot be the entire story I am readily prepared to acknowledge. It nevertheless seems evident that the forces to which I have drawn attention have played a crucial role and, by themselves, could have contributed a substantial explosion in innovation and growth. I claim no more, but with this claim my tale must end.

BIBLIOGRAPHY

Abreu, Dilip, Paul Milgrom, and David Pearce. 1991. Information and Timing in Repeated Partnerships. *Econometrica* 59(6): 1713–33.

Agarwal, Rajshree, and Michael Gort. 2001. First Mover Advantage and the Speed of Competitive Entry, 1887–1986. *Journal of Law and Economics* 44(April): 161–77.

Aghion, Philippe, and Peter Howitt. 1998. *Endogenous Growth Theory,* Cambridge, Mass.: MIT Press.

Akerlof, George. 2000. Comment, on William J. Baumol, Rapid Economic Growth, Equitable Income Distribution, and the Optimal Range of Innovation Spillovers. In George L. Perry and James Tobin, eds., *Economic Events, Ideas, and Policies,* 3–42 (comment on 31–35). Washington, D.C.: Brookings Institution Press.

Allen, Thomas J., Diane B. Hyman, and David L. Pinckney. 1983. Transferring Technology to the Small Manufacturing Firm: A Study of Technology Transfer in Three Countries. *Research Policy* 12(August): 199–211.

Amendola, Mario, and J. L. Gaffard. 1998. *Out of Equilibrium.* Oxford: Clarendon Press.

Andronow, A. A., and C. E. Chaikin. 1949. *Theory of Oscillations.* Princeton, N.J.: Princeton University Press.

Arrow, Kenneth J. 1962. The Economic Implications of Learning by Doing. *Review of Economic Studies* 28(June): 155–73.

———. 1964. Optimal Capital Policy, the Cost of Capital and Myopic Decision Rules. *Annals of the Institute of Statistical Mathematics* 41(1–2): 21–30.

Ashton, T. S. 1948. *The Industrial Revolution, 1760–1830.* London: Oxford University Press.

Balaszs, Etienne. 1964. *Chinese Civilization and Bureaucracy.* New Haven, Conn.: Yale University Press.

Baumol, William J. 1951. *Economic Dynamics.* New York: Macmillan.

———. 1952. *Welfare Economics and the Theory of the State.* London: Longmans Greene. [Revised and reprinted, Hampshire: Gregg Revivals, 1993.]

———.1967. Macroeconomics of Unbalanced Growth: The Anatomy of Urban Crisis. *American Economic Review* 57(3): 415–26.

———. 1971. Optimal Depreciation Policy: Pricing the Products of Durable Assets. *Bell Journal of Economics and Management Science* 2(Autumn): 638–56.

———. 1993. *Entrepreneurship, Management and the Structure of Payoffs.* Cambridge, Mass.: MIT Press.

Baumol, William J., and Dietrich Fischer. 1978. Cost-Minimizing Number of Firms and Determination of Industry Structure. *Quarterly Journal of Economics* 92(August): 439–67.

Baumol, William J., and D. G. Swanson. Forthcoming. What Really *Is* Monopoly Power?: Economically Defensible and Indefensible Tests in the Presence of Sunk, Fixed and Common Costs. Manuscript.

Baumol, William J., and Edward N. Wolff. 1983. Feedback from Productivity Growth to R&D. *Scandinavian Journal of Economics* 85(2): 147–57.

Baumol, William J., Elizabeth E. Bailey, and Robert D. Willig. 1977. Weak Invisible Hand Theorems on the Sustainability of Multiproduct Natural Monopoly. *American Economic Review* 67(3): 350–65.

Baumol, William J., John C. Panzar, and Robert D. Willig. 1988. *Contestable Markets and the Theory of Industry Structure,* revised ed. San Diego: Harcourt, Brace, Jovanovich.

Baumol, William J., Sue Anne Batey Blackman, and Edward N. Wolff. 1989. *Productivity and American Leadership: The Long View.* Cambridge, Mass.: MIT Press.

Berman, Constance H. 1986. *Medieval Agriculture, the Southern French Countryside, and the Early Cistercians.* Philadelphia: American Philosophical Society.

Bernheim, D., and D. Ray. 1989. Collective Dynamic Consistency in Repeated Games. *Games and Economic Behavior* 1: 295–326.

Berry, Steven. 2000. *Preliminary Expert Report.* In the Matter of the United States Department of Justice v. AMR Corporation (DOJ vs. AMR).

Blaug, Mark. 1999. The Concept of Entrepreneurship in the History of Economics. In *Not Only an Economist: Recent Essays.* Cheltenham, U.K., and Northampton, Mass.: Edward Elgar.

Bloch, Marc. 1935. Avènement et conquêstes du moulin à eau. *Annales d'Histoire Economique et Sociales* 7: 538–63.

Blum, Jerome. 1978. *The End of the Old Order in Rural Europe.* Princeton, N.J.: Princeton University Press.

Brands, H. W. 1997. *T.R.: The Last Romantic.* New York: Basic Books.

Braudel, Fernand. 1979. *Civilization and Capitalism, 15th to 18th Century,* vol. 1. New York: Harper & Row.

Brooke, Christopher. 1964. *Europe in the Central Middle Ages, 962–1154.* London: Longman.

Carus-Wilson, Eleanor M. 1941. An Industrial Revolution of the Thirteenth Century. *Economic History Review* 11(1): 39–60.

Chung Yi Tse. 1996. Productivity and Research Portfolio. Ph.D. thesis, New York University, May.

Cloulas, Ivan. 1989. *The Borgias.* New York: Barnes & Noble.

Coleman, D. C. 1975. *Industry in Tudor and Stuart England.* London: Macmillan.

Cournot, A. A. 1897 [1838]. *Researches into the Mathematical Principle of the Theory of Wealth.* New York: Macmillan.

Cowdrey, H. E. J. 1970. The Peace and the Truce of God of the Eleventh Century. *Past and Present,* No. 46 (February): 42–67.

Dana, James D., Jr. 1998. Advance-Purchase Discounts and Price Discrimination in Competitive Markets. *Journal of Political Economy,* 106(April): 395–422.

Dasgupta, Partha. 1988. Patents, Priority and Imitation or, the Economics of Races and Waiting Games. *Economic Journal* 98(March): 66–80.

Dasgupta, Partha, and Joseph Stiglitz. 1980. Industrial Structure and the Nature of Innovative Activity. *Economic Journal* 90: 266–93.

D'Aspremont, Claude, and Alexis Jaquemin. 1988. Cooperative and Noncooperative R&D in Duopoly with Spillovers. *American Economic Review* 78(December): 1133–37.

David, Paul A. 1990. The Dynamo and the Computer: An Historical Perspective on the Modern Productivity Paradox. *American Economic Review, Papers and Proceedings* 80(May): 355–61.

DeLong, J. Bradford. 2001. The Economic History of the Twentieth Century: Slouching Toward Utopia? http://www.j-bradford-delong.net, accessed September 2001.

De Meeüs, Adrien. 1962. *History of the Belgians.* New York: Frederick A. Praeger.

De Roover, Raymond. 1953. The Commercial Revolution of the 13th Century. In F. Lane and S. Riemersa, eds., *Enterprise and Secular Change.* London: Allen & Unwin.

De Soto, Hernando. 2001. *The Mystery of Capital: Why Capitalism Triumphs in the West and Fails Everywhere Else.* New York: Basic Books.

Dickinson, H. W. 1937. *Matthew Boulton.* Cambridge: Cambridge University Press.

Dupuit, Jules. 1853. De l'utilité et de sa mesure: De l'utilité publique. *Journal des Economistes* 36: 1–27.

Edgeworth, F. Y. 1925. Differential Pricing in a Regime of Competition, vol. 1, 100–107, and Discrimination of Prices, vol. 2, 404–28. In *Papers Relating to Political Economy.* London: Macmillan.

Fano, Ester. 1987. Technical Progress as a Destabilizing Factor and as an Agent of Recovery in the United States between the Two World Wars. *History and Technology* 3: 249–74.

Farrel, J., and E. Maskin. 1989. Renegotiation in Repeated Games. *Games and Economic Behavior* 1: 327–60.

Federal Reserve Bank of Boston. 1996. The Rewards of Investing in High Tech. *Regional Review* 6(Fall).

Finley, M. I. 1985. *The Ancient Economy,* 2d ed. London: Hogarth Press.

Forbes, R. J. 1955. *Studies in Ancient Technology.* Leiden, The Netherlands: E. J. Brill.

George, Kenneth, and Caroline Joll. 1981. *Industrial Organization,* 3d ed. London: Allen & Unwin.

Gifford, Sharon. 1998. *The Allocation of Limited Entrepreneurial Attention.* Boston: Kluwer Academic Publishers.

Gimpel, Jean. 1976. *The Medieval Machine: The Economic Revolution of the Middle Ages.* New York: Holt, Reinhart and Winston.

Gomory, Ralph E., and William J. Baumol. 2000. *Global Trade and Conflicting National Interests.* Cambridge, Mass., and London: MIT Press.

Gordon, Barry. 1976. *Political Economy in Parliament 1819–1823.* London: Macmillan.

Graham, M. B. W. 1986. *The Business of Research: RCA and the VideoDisc.* Cambridge: Cambridge University Press.

Griliches, Zvi. 1979. Issues in Assessing the Contribution of Research and Development to Productivity Growth. *Bell Journal of Economics* 10: 92–116.

———. 1989. Recent Patent Trends and Puzzles. In *Brookings Papers on Economic Activity.* Washington, D.C.: Brookings Institution.

———. 1992. The Search for R&D Spillovers. *Scandinavian Journal of Economics* 94(Supplement): 29–47.

Grossman, Gene M., and Elhanan Helpman. 1991a. Trade, Knowledge Spillovers and Growth, *European Economic Review* 35(May): 517–26.

———. 1991b. *Innovation and Growth in the Global Economy,* Cambridge, Mass.: MIT Press.

———. 1994. Endogenous Innovation in the Theory of Growth. *Journal of Economic Perspectives* 8(Winter): 23–44.

Hall, Bronwyn. 1993. Industrial Research during the 1980s: Did the Rate of Return Fall? In *Brookings Papers: Microeconomics.* Washington, D.C.: Brookings Institution, 289–342.

Hausman, J. A., and J. K. Mackie-Mason. 1988. Price Discrimination and Patent Policy. *RAND Journal of Economics* 19: 253–56.

Hollander, Samuel. 1998. *The Literature of Classical Political Economy,* 2d ed. London and New York: Routledge.

Horn, François. 2000. Note sur la "productivité" dans la production des logiciels. Université Charles de Gaulle, forthcoming.

Horrox, Rosemary. 1989. *Richard III, A Study of Service.* Cambridge: Cambridge University Press.

Jones, C. I. 1995. R&D-Based Models of Economic Growth. *Journal of Political Economy* 103(August): 759–84.

Jones, Eric. 1987. *The European Miracle.* Cambridge: Cambridge University Press.

Jorgenson, Dale W., and Zvi Griliches. 1967. The Explanation of Productivity Changes. *Review of Economic Studies* July: 249–83.

Jorgenson, Frank, and Barbara Fraumeni. 1987. *Productvity and U.S. Economic Growth.* Cambridge, Mass.: Harvard University Press.

Kalt, J. P. 2000. *Initial Expert Report.* DOJ vs. AMR, 11 October.

Katz, Michael L., and Janusz A. Ordover. 1990. R&D Cooperation and Competition. In *Brookings Papers on Microeconomics,* 137–203. Washington, D.C.: Brookings Institution.

Keynes, John Maynard. 1932. *Essays in Persuasion.* New York: Harcourt, Brace and Co.

Khalil, Elias L. 1997. The Red Queen Paradox: A Proper Name for a Popular Game. *Journal of Institutional and Theoretical Economics* 153(2): 411–15.

Knight, Frank H. 1921. *Risk, Uncertainty and Profit.* Boston: Houghton Mifflin.

Krugman, Paul R. 1979. Increasing Returns, Monopolistic Competition and International Trade. *Journal of International Economics* 9:469–79.

Laffont, Jean-Jacques, and Jean Tirole. 2000. *Competition in Telecommunications.* Cambridge, Mass.: MIT Press.

Landes, David. 1969. *The Unbound Prometheus.* New York: Cambridge University Press.

———. 1998. *The Wealth and Poverty of Nations: Why Some Are So Rich and Some So Poor.* New York: W. W. Norton.

———. 2001. East Is East and West Is West. Paper presented at the FEEM (Fondazione Eni Enrico Mattei) Conference on the Economics of Knowledge, Palermo, April, forthcoming.

Leijonhufvud, Axel. 1983. Inflation and Economic Performance. *Kieler Vortrage,* No. 101. Also in Barry N. Siegel, ed., *Money in Crisis: The Federal Reserve, the Economy, and Monetary Reform.* Cambridge, Mass.: Ballinger Press, 1984.

Levin, Richard C. 1988. Appropriability, R&D Spending, and Technological Performance. *American Economic Review* 78(May): 424–28.

Levin, Richard C., A. K. Klevorick, R. R. Nelson, and S. G. Winter. 1987. Appropriating the Returns from Industrial Research and Development. In *Brookings Papers on Economic Activity* 3, 783–820. Washington, D.C.: Brookings Institution.

Levine, Michael E. 2000. Price Discrimination without Market Power. Discussion Paper No. 276, Harvard Law School, February.

Lichtenberg, Frank R. 1998. Pharmaceutical Innovation as a Process of Creative Destruction, February (NBER paper). Similar paper (Pharmaceutical Innovation, Mortality Reduction, and Economic Growth) in Kevin Murphy and Robert Topel, eds., *The Value of Medical Research.* Chicago: University of Chicago Press, forthcoming.

Littlechild, S. C. 1970. Marginal Cost Pricing with Joint Costs. *Economic Journal* 80(June): 223–35.

Liu, J.T.C., and Peter Golas. 1969. *Change in Sung China.* Lexington, Mass.: D. C. Heath.

Lucas, Robert E., Jr. 1988. On the Mechanics of Economic Development. *Journal of Monetary Economics* 22(July): 3–42.

McCullough, David. 1977. *The Path between the Seas.* New York: Simon and Schuster.

McGrattam, Ellen R. 1998. A Defense of AK Growth Models. *Federal Reserve Bank of Minneapolis Quarterly Review* 22(Fall): 13–27.

Maddison, Angus. 1995. *Monitoring the World Economy,* 1820–1992. Paris: Organisation for Economic Co-operation and Development, Development Center.

———. 2001. *The World Economy: A Millennial Perspective.* Paris: Organisation for Economic Co-operation and Development, Development Center Seminars.

Mankiw, N. G., David Romer, and D. N. Weil. 1992. A Contribution to the Empirics of Economic Growth. *Quarterly Journal of Economics* 107(May): 407–37.

Mansfield, Edwin. 1985. How Rapidly Does New Industrial Technology Leak Out? *Journal of Industrial Economics* 34(December): 217–23.

Mansfield, Edwin, Mark Schwartz, and Samuel Wagner. 1981. Imitation Costs and Patents: An Empirical Study. *Economic Journal* 91(December): 907–18.

Marsh, Robert M. 1961. *The Mandarins.* Glencoe, Ill: Free Press.

Marshall, Alfred. 1920. *Principles of Economics,* 8th (and final) ed. London: Macmillan; 1st ed. 1890, 4th ed. 1898, 9th (Variorum) ed., edited, with a volume of notes, by C. W. Guillebaud, 1961.

Marx, Karl. 1906 [1867]. *Capital,* vol. 1. Chicago: Charles H. Kerr.

Marx, Karl, and Friedrich Engels. 1847. *Manifesto of the Communist Party.* London.

Merges, Robert P., and Richard R. Nelson. 1994. On Limiting or Encouraging Rivalry in Technical Progress: The Effect of Patent Scope Decisions. *Journal of Economic Behavior and Organization* 25(1): 1–24.

Mitchell, Thomas N. 2001. Roman Republicanism: The Underrated Legacy. *Proceedings of the American Philosophical Society* 145(2): 127–37.

Mohnen, Pierre. 1992. *The Relationship between R&D and Productivity Growth in Canada and Other Industrial Countries.* Ottawa: Canada Communications Group.

Mokyr, Joel. 1990a. *Twenty Five Centuries of Technological Change: An Historical Survey.* Chur, Switzerland: Harwood Academic Publishers.

———. 1990b. *The Lever of Riches.* New York: Oxford University Press.

Murphy, Kevin J., Andrei Shleifer, and Robert Vishny. 1991. The Allocation of Talent: Implications for Growth. *Quarterly Journal of Economics* 106(2): 503–30.

Nadiri, M. Ishaq. 1993. Innovations and Technological Spillovers. NBER Working Paper No. 4423, Cambridge, Mass.: National Bureau of Economic Research, August.

'ational Science Board. 1996. *Science and Engineering Indicators, 1996,* NSB 96–21. Washington, D.C.: U.S. Government Printing Office.

——. 2000. *Science and Engineering Indicators–2000.* Arlington, Va.: National Science Foundation.

Navaretti, G. Barba, P. Dasgupta, K.-G. Mäler, and D. Siniscalco, eds. 1998. *Creation and Transfer of Knowledge.* Berlin: Springer.

Needham, Joseph. 1956. Mathematics and Science in China and the West. *Science and Society* 20: 320–43.

———. 1964a. *The Development of Iron and Steel Technology in China.* Cambridge: W. Heffer.

———. 1964b. *Science and Civilization in China.* Cambridge: Cambridge University Press.

———. 1981. *Science in Traditional China.* Cambridge, Mass.: Harvard University Press.

Nelson, Richard R. 1990. Capitalism as an Engine of Progress. *Research Policy* 19(June): 193–214.

———. 1996. *The Sources of Economic Growth.* Cambridge, Mass.: Harvard University Press.

Nelson, Richard R., and Sidney Winter. 1982. *An Evolutionary Theory of Economic Change.* Cambridge, Mass.: Harvard University Press.

Nordhaus, William D. 1969. *Invention, Growth and Welfare.* Cambridge, Mass.: MIT Press.

———. 1997. Do Real-Output and Real-Wage Measures Capture Reality? The History of Lighting Suggests Not. In Timothy F. Bresnahan and Robert J. Gordon, *The Economics of New Goods,* 29–66. Chicago: University of Chicago Press.

North, Douglass C., and Robert Paul Thomas. 1973. *The Rise of the Western World: A New Economic History.* Cambridge: Cambridge University Press.

Okun, Arthur. 1975. *Equality and Efficiency: The Big Tradeoff.* Washington, D.C.: Brookings Institution, 46–47.

Ordover, J. A. 2000. *Initial Expert Report.* DOJ vs. AMR, 11 October.

Oulton, Nicholas. 2000. Must the Growth Rate Decline? Baumol's Unbalanced Growth Revisited. Bank of England Working Paper Series 107, January.

Ovitt, George, Jr. 1987. *The Restoration of Perfection: Labor and Technology in Medieval Culture.* New Brunswick, N.J.: Rutgers University Press.

Palmer, Robert. 1964. *The Age of Democratic Revolution,* vol. 2. Princeton, N.J.: Princeton University Press.

Pearce, D. 1987, 1990. Renegotiation-Proof Equilibria: Collective Rationality and Intertemporal Cooperation. Cowles Foundation Discussion Paper No. 855. New Haven, Conn: Yale University.

Petit, Maria-Luisa, and Boleslaw Tolwinski. 1993. Learning by Doing and Technology Sharing in Asymmetric Duopolies. *Annals of Dynamic Games* 1.

Petroski, Henry. 1996. *Invention by Design.* Cambridge, Mass.: Harvard University Press.

Pigou, A. C. 1938. Discriminating Monopoly. In *The Economics of Welfare,* 4th ed., part II, chapter XVII, 275–89. London: Macmillan.

Ping-Ti Ho. 1962. *The Ladder of Success in Imperial China, 1368–1911.* New York: Columbia University Press.

Reynolds, Terry S. 1983. *Stronger Than a Hundred Men: A History of the Vertical Water Wheel.* Baltimore: Johns Hopkins University Press.

Ricardo, David. 1817. *Principles of Political Economy.* London.

Robinson, Joan. 1960. *The Economics of Imperfect Competition,* 2d ed. London: Macmillan

Romer, Paul M. 1986. Increasing Returns and Long-Run Growth. *Journal of Politica Economy* 94(October): 1002–37.

———. 1990. Endogenous Technical Change. *Journal of Political Economy* 98(Octobe S71–102.

———. 1994a. New Goods, Old Theory and the Welfare Costs of Trade Restrictions. *Journal of Development Economics* 43: 5–38.

———. 1994b. The Origins of Endogenous Growth. *Journal of Economic Perspectives* 8(Winter): 8–22.

Rosenberg, Nathan. 1976. *Perspectives on Technology.* Cambridge: Cambridge University Press.

———. 1982. *Inside the Black Box: Technology and Economics.* Cambridge: Cambridge University Press.

Rosenberg, Nathan, and L. E. Birdzell, Jr. 1986. *How the West Grew Rich: The Economic Transformation of the Industrial World.* New York: Basic Books.

Ross, Charles. 1974. *Edward IV.* Berkeley: University of California Press.

Ruffin, Roy J. Forthcoming. A Simple Vertical Competition Model: Structure and Performance. University of Houston [November 2001 draft].

Samuelson, Paul A. 1954. The Pure Theory of Public Expenditure. *Review of Economics and Statistics* 36(November): 387–89.

Say, J. B. 1819, 1834. *A Treatise on Political Economy.* Philadelphia: Claxton, Remsen and Haffelfinger.

Scherer, Frederic M. 1965. Firm Size, Market Structure, Opportunity and the Output of Patented Inventions. *American Economic Review* 59: 1097–1125.

———. 1980. *Industrial Market Structure and Economic Performance,* 2d ed. Chicago: Rand McNally.

———. 1999. *New Perspectives on Economic Growth and Technological Innovation.* Washington, D.C.: Brookings Institution.

Scherer, Frederic M., and David Ross. 1990. *Industrial Market Structure and Economic Performance,* 3d ed. Boston: Houghton Mifflin.

Schmookler, Jacob. 1957. Inventors Past and Present. *Review of Economics and Statistics* August: 321–33.

———. 1966. *Invention and Economic Growth.* Cambridge, Mass.: Harvard University Press.

Schumpeter, Joseph A. 1911. *The Theory of Economic Development.* Cambridge, Mass.: Harvard University Press. [English translation 1936.]

———. 1947 [1942]. *Capitalism, Socialism, and Democracy,* 2d ed. New York: Harper & Brothers.

Shafir, Eldar, Peter Diamond, and Amos Tversky. 1997. Money Illusion. *Quarterly Journal of Economics* 112(May): 341–74.

Shapiro, Carl. 2000. Competition Policy in the Information Economy. In *Foundations of Competition Policy Analysis.* London: Routledge.

———. 2001. Navigating the Patent Thicket: Cross Licenses, Patent Pools, and Standard-Setting. In Adam Jaffe, Joshua Lerner, and Scott Stern, eds., *Innovation Policy and the Economy.* Cambridge, Mass.: MIT Press.

Sidgwick, Henry. 1887. *Principles of Political Economy,* 2d ed. London: Macmillan.

Smith, Adam. 1904 [1776]. *The Wealth of Nations.* Edited by Edwin Cannan. London: Methuen.

Solow, Robert M. 1956. A Contribution to the Theory of Economic Growth. *Quarterly Journal of Economics* 70(February): 65–94.

———. 1957. Technical Change and the Aggregate Production Function. *Review of Economics and Statistics* 39(August):312–20.

Spengler, Joseph J. 1950. Vertical Integration and Antitrust Policy. *Journal of Political Economy* 58(August): 347–52.

Stiglitz, Joseph. 2000. *Preliminary Expert Report.* DOJ vs. AMR.

Strayer, Joseph. 1980. *Philip the Fair.* Princeton, N.J.: Princeton University Press.

Taylor, Christopher T., and Aubrey Silberston. 1973. *The Economic Impact of the Patent System: A Study of British Experience.* Cambridge: Cambridge University Press.

Teece, David J. 1977. Technology Transfer by Multinational Firms: The Resources Cost of Transferring Technological Know-How. *Economic Journal* 87(June): 242–61.

Ten Raa, Thijs. 1984. Resolution of Conjectures on Sustainability of Natural Monopoly. *RAND Journal of Economics* 15(Spring): 135–41.

Turvey, Ralph. 1969. Marginal Cost. *Economic Journal* 79(June): 282–99.

U.S. Census Bureau. 2000. *Statistical Abstract of the United States: 2000.* Washington, D.C.: U.S.Government Printing Office.

U.S. Federal Reserve Bank of Dallas. 1996. *The Economy at Light Speed: Technology and Growth in the Information Age—and Beyond.* Annual Report.

Varian, Hal R. 2000. Differential Pricing and Efficiency. *First Monday* June: 1–16.

Veblen, Thorstein B. 1904. *The Theory of Businesss Enterprise.* New York: Charles Scribner's Sons.

Von Hippel, Eric. 1988. *The Sources of Innovation.* New York: Oxford University Press.

White, Lynn, Jr. 1962. *Medieval Technology and Social Change.* Oxford: Clarendon Press.

Willig, Robert D. 1979. The Theory of Network Access Pricing. *Issues in Public Utility Regulation* 109: 109–52.

Wolff, Edward N. 1997. Spillovers, Linkages and Technical Change. *Economic Systems Research* 9: 9–2.

World Intellectual Property Organization. *Industrial Property Statistics, Part 1: Patents.* www.wipo.org.

Young, Alwyn. 1992. Substitution and Complementarity in Endogenous Innovation. March. Cambridge, Mass.: Sloan School of Management, Massachusetts Institute of Technology.

INDEX